# *Professionals and Urban Form*

# *Professionals*

STATE UNIVERSITY OF NEW YORK PRESS

# *and Urban Form*

edited by

JUDITH R. BLAU   Department of Sociology
State University of New York at Albany

MARK LA GORY   Department of Sociology
University of Alabama in Birmingham

JOHN S. PIPKIN   Department of Geography
State University of New York at Albany

ALBANY

Published by State University of New York Press, Albany

© 1983 State University of New York

For information, address State University of New York Press, State University Plaza, Albany, N.Y., 12246

**Library of Congress Cataloging in Publication Data**
Main entry under title:

Professionals and urban form.

Includes index.
1. City planning—Addresses, essays, lectures.
2. Architecture—Human factors—Addresses, essays,
lectures. 3. Architects and community—Addresses,
essays, lectures. I. Blau, Judith R., 1942-
II. La Gory, Mark. III. Pipkin, John.
NA9040.P74    1983       711'4       82-10422
ISBN 0-87395-675-3
ISBN 0-87395-676-1 (pbk.)

# Contents

# Contents

# Preface

When we weigh the odds for aesthetic excellence in the design and reconstruction of the city, we must consider those professionals most concerned with the intrinsic qualities of buildings and spaces, notably architects. When we weigh the odds for equitable solutions in the design and reconstruction of the city, it is the planner we must consider. Yet on both counts there are questions. The architect, whose chief commitment is to a particular building—how it looks and how it functions—often fails to take into account the aesthetic integration of the block, the neighborhood, and the city, or the building's impact on the quality of people's work and daily lives. And the planner is often constrained to place technical considerations above social concerns, the interests of special groups above the public welfare, and the demands of the suburban middle class above those of the urban poor.

But two significant changes have recently occurred, and both are evident in various papers in this collection. First, planners, increasingly disillusioned with a planning theory in which their technical expertise serves to perpetuate the inequalities of a capitalist society, are reassessing their roles in the political and economic spheres, and they are also raising the question of how equity can be incorporated into models of practice. At the same time, architects are beginning to consider specific social issues, such as energy conservation and revitalization of the inner city, and they have started to worry about how to bring into balance the needs of the larger public with those of the private clients they typically serve. Second, there is a growing belief within both planning and architecture that the meanings (codes) of design ought to reflect democratic rather than elite values. Although the rhetoric is often radical, it is unlikely that there will be, at least in the foreseeable future, revolutionary changes that profoundly affect the day-to-day practice of planners and architects. Yet

*vii*

at the same time, it is clear that there will be perceptible movement in new directions, if for no other reason than the glaring contradictions that presently exist within the institutional structure of practice, a point more fully explored in the introduction to this volume. An important implication of these changes within the fields of planning and architecture is that many of the traditional gaps between them are likely to be bridged in the process. For that reason there is a compelling need to treat the two fields together in order to evaluate the possibilities of an integrated design theory and of structural complementarity—if not convergence—in design practice.

There have always been three basic similarities between architecture and planning. First, both professions are primarily concerned with shaping spaces and transforming the environment. Indeed, the specialty of urban design, as an amalgam of architecture and planning, developed from an awareness of these overlapping concerns. Second, social responsibility, good taste, and usefulness—however ordered—are criteria employed by both architects and planners. This combination of objectives is shared by no other occupational group. Third, to a greater extent than for other professions, practice is carried out in offices that are more or less bureaucratized and more or less under managerial control. For planners, the office is part of a larger bureaucracy, which in turn is part of a political system. Special-interest groups play a significant role here, sometimes consistent with the public welfare, but often not. For architects, clients and the market play a large role in shaping practice. Thus, while external constraints affect both planners and architects, the extent to which these constraints originate from political or economic sources is somewhat different for the two professions.

Yet a broader view of state capitalism raises questions about the usefulness of distinguishing between private and political domains because the political system tends to serve the interests of private enterprise, and corporate needs tend to shape public policy. Architects, having lost a dominant position in large-scale planning, often ignore the political origins and consequences of their entrepreneurial activities. And planners who believe that they serve the public in fact work at the whim of congeries of politicians, pressure groups, developers, and large corporations. Although planners are aware of the essentially political context of practice, they often fail to see the bearing of that context on their ideological commitment to the advancement of equity. As is evident from the papers in this volume, there is growing sensitivity in both professions to the politico-economic significance and context of practice. This entails questions about the relations between the power holders and economic structures, about the relations between the providers of service and the recipients of service, about the coalitions of political and economic elites, and also about the procedures and rationality underlying the allocation of resources. Social scientists can help clarify these problems by theoretical and empirical analyses that have bearing on these questions. In any case, this recent focus on the political economy of professional practice suggests to many a need for a new orientation and a restructuring of the relationship of practice to the state and the private sector.

Another basis for conceptual convergence between architecture and planning has its source in the re-evaluation of the social implications of aesthetic values. Architects historically (with occasional lapses) have valued diversity of spatial arrangements and complexity of form. Until quite recently, planners have emphasized large-scale planning projects and promulgated zoning laws that resulted in the low mix of land use, segregation of activities, and thus neighborhood homogeneity. Following Jane Jacobs, such architects as Christopher Alexander were among the first to recognize the full negative effects that such an approach had on the aesthetics of urban space and the vitality of cities. More recently, social scientists, including Herbert Gans and Richard Sennet, have centered attention on the full range of negative results wrought by "rational planning theory," including impaired intergroup relations, unequal services for the poor and the middle classes, and intolerance of social and cultural differences. It now appears that the concept of urban diversity is increasingly being supported on aesthetic grounds by architects and on technical and social grounds by planners.

Such observations as these are the basis for considering architects and planners together. A main theme of this volume is that the structural and intellectual developments in these two forms of practice have brought them together in a symbiotic relationship. At the same time, social science theory and research have been increasingly incorporated into the developments in these fields. One focus of this collection is the nature of professionalization of planning and architecture and the problems of legitimation it entails. The introduction highlights the central questions of professionalization, suggesting that the complex issues at the core of legitimacy have contradictory implications for the institutional and ideological integrity of the design field.

The institutional or structural context of practice and the way in which that context relates to the intellectual and ideological aspects of professional work provide another focus. The historical conditions that have shaped professional practice—including the tensions between art and technique, dependence and autonomy, and patronage and public accountability—are analyzed in Part 1, *Historical Origins of Practice*. Questions concerning the relationships between theories *of* practice and theories *in* practice build on some assumptions about the institutional matrix of practice, but the greater concerns raised by those questions are dilemmas involving utility and justice, dilemmas of choice and constraint, problems of ethics and truthful communication. These issues are taken up in Part 2, *Epistemology and Urban Design*. Part 3, *Professions and Practice*, emphasizes the way in which professional work is currently carried out, which raises issues about potential conflict between bureaucratic objectives and individual goals and between profitability and the quality of design. Considered here, too, is the extent to which architects and planners can be considered members of elite professions or hardly distinguishable from workers, who lack control over production and the political process. The final section, *Controversies in Practice*, centers on debates dealing with social justice, the extent to which architecture and planning are political enterprises, and the prospects for democratization in practice.

It is worthwhile to reiterate these themes in terms of the assumptions that have guided the compilation of these papers. We maintain that, despite signs of disenchantment with the growing rapprochement between the design professions and social scientists, these newly forged bonds should be strengthened, not severed. Strengthening them would help serve the important need to integrate the theory and practice of design. Although the implementation of such an integration is the task of the practitioners, social scientists can help assess the fit and its likely consequences. Research by social scientists—on such questions as, for example, the effects of housing policies on low-income residents, the relationship between propinquity and friendship, or the consequences of high density—can inform and improve the decisions of practitioners. Whereas the tradition is unabashedly positivist, there are clear implications for ethical judgments. Finally, although planning and architecture have unique histories, we consider it important that their underlying similarities be recognized in light of the evidence of new convergences. These assumptions underlie the themes for this collection of papers on the professionals of urban form, and they are also evident in the companion volume, *Remaking the City: Social Science Perspectives on Urban Design*, which deals with the forces that shape the city—forces with which planners and architects must contend if they hope to affect urban form and the quality of urban life.

In soliciting and selecting papers for this book, we cast our net broadly to encompass diverse aspects of the design professions and their relation to society. Thus, we include papers that deal with historical issues, the bases of professional knowledge and the use to which that knowledge is put, the nature of professional practice and organization, and various prognoses for the future of the design professions and the possibilities for change. Many papers deal explicitly with both architects and planners, and those that deal with only one profession have clear implications for the other. We believe this to be a distinctive synthesis of theoretical and practical issues concerning professions of urban form.

We wish to thank William Eastman and Suellen Wenz of the SUNY Press for their support, guidance, and diligent work throughout the preparation of the manuscript. For assistance with typing, we are grateful to Eileen Crary, and we also appreciate the help of Reva T. Blau with the index.

Finally, our families, who provided a supportive and encouraging environment, as well a questioning and critical one, deserve our wholehearted thanks.

Judith R. Blau
Mark La Gory
John S. Pipkin

# Introduction

*Professions also, perhaps more than other kinds of occupations, claim a legal, moral and intellectual mandate. Not merely do the practitioners, by virtue of gaining admission to the charmed circle of colleagues, individually exercise the license to do things others do not do, but collectively they presume to tell society what is good and right for the individual and for society at large in some aspect of life.*
———Everett C. Hughes, *Men and Their Work*

## PROFESSIONALIZATION

Both the reform and the rationalist traditions portray planners as agents of change. In the reform tradition the goals of change have been presumed to be self-evident in the ills of industrial urbanism, while in the rationalist tradition goals of change have been extended from planning proper into the political process. In architecture, too, change in the urban fabric is seen as a self-evident need, although needs in architecture have been more often defined by clients than by the public good. In point of fact, the most radical calls for change in the urban fabric, and the most detailed specification of goals, have come from such architects as Frank Lloyd Wright and Le Corbusier, rather than from professional planners.

The aspirations for fundamental change that pervade the literature of planning and architecture are severely constrained by bounds imposed on their practice in all contemporary political systems. The possibilities envisioned in idealistic and visionary prescriptions are categorically precluded in all but the most unusual cases, such as Brasilia, or Welwyn Garden City. Yet the residue of autonomy and scope for action in design professions is still substantial. Because the kinds of action accessible to practice are partly or largely in the public domain, action requires sanction. Sanction requires perceived legitimacy, and in the struggle for legitimacy, architects have fared somewhat better than planners.

Authority to act derives from the perceived legitimacy of the role performed and of the individual performing the role. As Lukes (1978: 639)

*1*

suggests, "to exercise authority is precisely not to have to offer reasons, but to be obeyed or believed because one has a recognized claim to be." To accept authority, then, is to acknowledge an individual's legitimate right to action. Legitimate authority can, according to Weber (1964), derive from several sources. Authority can be validated by tradition (an assumption that what has occurred previously is valid), by emotional attachment (in which validity is derived from certain charismatic qualities of the individual exercising control), by rational belief in the absolute value of the role, or by acceptance of the legality of the act. Weber combines these to talk of three historical forms of authority: traditional, charismatic, and rational-legal.

A significant portion of the professional literature from the last several decades documents the quest for authority in planning and architecture. The reasons for this overarching concern for establishing legitimacy are not hard to discern. The historic dialectic between public and private goods has been one clear source of tension in this process. Polanyi (1957) describes modern society as involving two distinct movements: the private market expands continuously, but this expansion is met by a countervailing movement which checks its development in certain directions. This countermovement protects the public good, but is incompatible with a self-regulating marketplace. Larson (1977) suggests that the growth of the professions is a distinct feature of this countermovement in industrial capitalism. In particular, the countermovement involves the professionalization of public sector roles.

For professionals in the public sector, legitimacy is more tenuous, more likely to be questioned. As Moore (1978) suggests, professionals in the political arena, making decisions about public welfare, are more likely to encounter opposition than those in the private sector. The role of the planner is to oversee the rational use of public goods by reducing the costs and the benefits accruing to individuals from the externalities of various publicly produced structures. Such actions necessarily pit the planner against certain factions of the community who will quite naturally challenge the legitimacy of their actions. In a pluralistic society such as that of the city these structural tensions are to be expected when the public good is invoked. This fact alone requires a certain degree of structural autonomy and legitimation if the professional's activity is to gain the desired effect. It is worth remarking that a price paid for legitimacy is a further compromise in aspiration for radical change. This is evident in the frankly conservative role cast for the local planner in the United States, where a substantial part of daily effort involves zoning or use-permit decisions that are unambiguously used to support existing values and interests.

The concern for public recognition of the validity of their actions is, however, not the only legitimation issue planners face. While planners derive some authority from their position in agencies of government, positional legitimacy is insufficient to validate or sanction planning activities. Positional legitimacy does not extend to decision making itself (Burke, 1979). Planners serve as advisors to some governmental body, not as autonomous decision makers. Cognitive and interactional skills are thus necessary to legitimize the planner's status in the eyes of decision makers. Such acceptance is necessary if the planner is to be an effective agent of change. Since many planning activities and goals are directed toward the complex urban or regional system, their actions will cut across a variety of decision makers' separate turfs. Generally, then, these efforts at legitimation will be extensive and complex.

The quest for legitimacy by planners and architects is one aspect of a natural tendency on the part of select occupational groups to control private market forces in order to gain status benefits. This process is generally termed professionalization. Professionalization is an especially critical process for the occupational groups involved in modifying the private market to distribute public goods efficiently. All planners, and a good many architects, derive their sanction for action from the polity. This sanction is limited in scope to advisement rather than decision making. Despite this severe limitation, the planner's role is to devise strategies to maximize the public good at minimal cost. It is obvious that such a broad role conflicts directly with the limited positional, or status, autonomy of planners. Such structural conflict frustrates the planning process and motivates a search for autonomy.

How can autonomy be increased? The answer to such a question can only be provided by analysis of the general sociological literature on professionalization.

The autonomy of a profession is a derivative function of its ability to enhance the degree and range of its legitimacy as well as to capture and control an expanded market for its services. In short, autonomy is a function of evaluative and structural factors. The evaluative aspect of autonomy has been discussed at great length by Weber under the rubric of authority. Authority derives from one of the three sources—traditional, rational-legal, or charismatic—already discussed. While Weber sees authority as generally determined by a simple source, he recognizes that under certain circumstances legitimacy can derive from multiple sources. Ritchey (1981) points out that multiple based authority actually enhances autonomy. He cites the case of the medical profession. Medicine has been able to control the rationalization of health service delivery to its advantage, because of its ability to call upon charismatic and traditional sources of validation. Although architects, to a degree, can rely on charismatic and traditional authority, planners cannot. Their sanction to act derives from a rational-legal base created by the state. As already noted, this base is highly constrained by the position of the occupation within a larger organizational matrix. While planners cannot hope to extend their authority into other spheres (charismatic and traditional), they can extend their autonomy in the rational-legal dimension. By clearly defining their roles, as well as establishing their capabilities, they can develop a clearer sanction to act on the urban environment. In essence, this requires establishing a cognitive base for the drive to professionalism. The academy, with its emphasis on the liberal arts as well as professional training, is the source for this base. It is no wonder, then, that a goodly number of articles in the *Journal of the American Institute of Planners* and in readers (e.g., Faludi, 1973) emphasize the need for changes in the training process itself. Education is one mechanism for controlling the market for one's services; this control enhances both professional status and power (Collins, 1971).

The search for professionalism, in short, involves more than a simple attempt to enhance the sanction of action. It involves as well a structural attempt to manipulate the market for services. This is achieved by several overt interlocking activities (Larson, 1977):

1. A market for the product must be identified and nurtured.
2. A distinctive product has to be produced.
3. A "monopoly of competence" must be established.
4. This monopoly of competence should serve to create a seller's market in which the number of competent suppliers is considerably smaller than the number of those demanding the service.

Architects and planners have both experienced difficulty in achieving these professional market goals. By attempting to establish a monopoly of competence they have met with resistance in the academy itself, where the already established social sciences lay claim to some of the competencies required. Additionally, establishment of a market is itself dependent on the state, for the state controls public goods. In short, the drive to structural autonomy by the form-giving professions has not been completely successful.

The incomplete professionalization of planning is evident on several levels. Unlike certified surveyors, accountants, and electricians, planners are not held legally liable for defects in their products (although some planning commissioners do take out liability insurance). Control of the educational process is incomplete. Several prestigious planning schools lack A.P.A. certification and feel no need to seek it. And there is no effective control of entry. It is far easier to become a planner than, say, to join a plumbers' or carpenters' union local. It is difficult to imagine that planning can ever establish even a small portion of the autonomy of other professional occupational groups. Forces at large in the academy compete with planning for a singular, distinctive cognitive base of legitimacy. At the same time, forces within the state strive to limit planning's legal authority.

There is a natural dialectic, which Larson (1977) notes, in each of the professions between its "civilizing function" (its attempt to modify the inefficiencies of services provided by the private sector) and its "market orientation" (its attempt to accumulate status and power in the market). In the planning and architectural professions this dialectic is particularly worthy of note. This natural rift between public and private interests is apparent in the literature on planning, though it is often disguised in academic language. The dialectic is not easily discerned in the evolution of the architectural profession because the market is state-determined, and thus the professional drive to limit the market is less overt.

One particularly important task of this book, then, is to place planners and architects in a comparative perspective. The literature accumulating on planning and architecture can be used as a record of the professionalization process. Although these two professions hold unique positions in relation to other professions, the questions of legitimation and market control are of overriding importance. By understanding the organizational and valuational structure of these two professions we can shed new light on their present capacities and future possibilities.

## PROFESSIONAL KNOWLEDGE AND INSTITUTIONAL CONTEXT OF PRACTICE

The urban designer plays three distinct roles: as a broker of information from the social and technical sciences, as a professional practitioner, and as a decision maker operating within a larger organizational and political context. Clearly, both structural (institutional) and intellectual (conceptual) factors affect the ways in which these roles are enacted. Yet structural and intellectual developments seldom proceed at the same pace, a fact well illustrated by the past two decades in the professions of planning and architecture in the United States.

Until the 1930s, the notion of large-scale intervention in urban processes was still an anathema for fundamental ideological reasons; in the absence of guidelines for meeting social responsibility, architects designed for other architects, with the support of wealthy elites. Since that time diagnoses of urban problems from all political viewpoints concede at least some formal role to institutional regulation. Partly because of this change in political climate, and partly because of the general expansion of higher education, both planning and architecture have gained a foothold as professional activities and as distinct fields in college curriculums.

As we have indicated, the alleged professionalization of planning and architecture does not fully meet the criteria usually applied, say, to the medical professional. But institutionally, professionally, educationally, and in public perception the design professions have arrived. The institutionalization is somewhat different for each, but both planning and architecture are fragmented. Whereas the context of planning includes academia, city government, and private consulting agencies, that of architecture includes academia, the private professional office, and large, public and private organizations. This fragmentation has clear implications for both communication and the formation of consensus within these respective establishments.

The most marked line of cleavage is between practitioners and academic theorists. Planning practitioners, in particular, are apt to find little difference between planning theory and social science theory, and little of value in either field. Accounts of day-by-day practice of planning bring home the irrelevance of theoretical prescriptions in the essentially political dynamics of getting things done (Jacobs, 1978). Both academic planners and architects, however, have been at pains to distance their work from social science. This position has merit on a conceptual level, as suggested below, but it must surely also be understood as an institutional-structural pressure to define and demarcate distinctive academic fields.

The perspective that traces divergence and communication problems to institutional-structural cleavage is particularly useful in identifying the global and ideological presuppositions underlying specific research and decision making. For example, radical urbanists emphasize the structural relationship of designers to the ownership and control of production, and have suggested that design work serves the existing order ideologically (symbolically) and substantively (in the reproduction of existing sociospatial forms). (See, for example, Lefebvre, 1974; Castells, 1977; Harvey, 1973; Tafuri, 1976; Collins, 1975.) The tenor of structural criticisms of this kind has been predominately negative. It has produced relatively few prescriptions that can be realized soon. For example, an eloquent call for a radical reconstitution of urban planning (Grabow and Heskin, 1973) identified several specific needs, including societal, ecological, ethical, and systematic requirements of a radical planning that seem far less attainable in 1983 than they did ten years before.

Beauregard (1978), however, has shown how structural considerations can point to areas of convergence between planning practice and social science theory. He suggests that conceptual ("idealistic") definitions of intellectual domains, rife with distinctive terminologies, tend to obscure fundamental similarities in the structure and practice of research (for example, the common source of government-controlled funding, commonalities in the posing and answering of questions in the research process itself, and similarities in the internal organization of academic and agency departments). Comparable areas of convergence between architectural practice and social science theory include research on environment and behavior (Brolin, 1976) and studies of stylistic preferences (Blau, 1980).

At any rate, in recent decades, the institutional structure and allegiances of American design professionals have become increasingly standardized and clear. It is hard to envision really major changes in this institutional structure in the near future, aside from continuing attrition of offices, agencies, and academic departments, stemming from economic and demographic changes.

Matters are less clear concerning the conceptual or intellectual foundations of the design fields. Academic planning and architecture are in a state of intellectual ferment. For both architecture and planning, this may be traced to a disillusionment with the ability of social science to inform the design process. In academic planning there is a growing consensus that planning should develop theory of its own; in academic architecture there is considerable uncertainty about the relative merits of aesthetic, social, or technically based theory.

Dissatisfaction with the products of social science theory is, in part, a consequence of the genuinely fragmented and heterodox state of American social science. Standard positivist-nomological modes of explanation can be said to be in retreat before newer philosophies ranging from European Marxism, French structuralism, and phenomenology, to existentialism and to earlier positions in humanism, idealism, verstehen, and exceptionalism, which were apparently down but not out. This diversity may be entirely necessary and desirable in pursuing the intrinsic goals of social science (e.g., Merton, 1981). But for a planner or an architect seeking reasonably explicit statements on relationships within a set of variables, it is apt to appear as Babel.

The standard positivist model bore the promise, inherent in its nomological focus on functional relationships, of "showing how variables covary" and of identifying "causal relationships." Although formidable problems of operational definition and verification remained, this account could easily be articulated with rationalistically conceived design, bent on manipulating spatial variables. The epistemologies of other contemporary positions in social science are less easily grasped; or at least they cohere less clearly with manipulative design. For example, the 'interpretive understanding' central to humanist methodology, and the 'operational structuralism' of radical urbanism both imply a profound break with standard modes of data description and analysis. Ironically, the successful import of statistical, questionnaire, and other techniques into architecture and planning militates against subsequent introduction of alternative methodologies.

But dissatisfaction with social science runs far deeper than perplexity in the face of internecine debate. Several lines of argument suggest that planning can and should devise indigenous theory. In planning this often involves the assertion that planning methodology is distinct from the positive, descriptive methodology of social science because of the centrality of values and ethics in planning. However, Klosterman (chapter 4) suggests that by appealing to recent developments in the theory of ethics, ethical reasoning can be fused with a logic of inference. This position has much in common with recent, parallel arguments for a humanistic social science. Allen (1975) indicates plausible means by which a strictly individual or subjectivist constitution of value can be avoided. Normative and factual statements have usually been conceived of as independent, in the sense that no normative statement can figure as a theorem, deduced from factual statements. Allen shows one way to carry out this synthesis, by tying objects of evaluation to "one or some of the general logical conditions of the satisfaction of human interests." Thus, although the ethical argument suggests an intrinsic difference between a "logic of intervention" and a simply conceived positivist logic of explanation, this distinction does not differentiate planning from social science, because the social sciences themselves have moved toward ethical inferences, calculi of social justice (e.g., Rawls 1971), and values generally.

Another type of differentiation between planning and social science has been extensively developed (e.g., Faludi, 1973), based on a distinction between theory 'in' and 'of' practice. Although Faludi is concerned exclusively with planning, the same distinction can be made for architecture, and for that matter, any other type of professional practice. Theory in design, according to Faludi, is taken to be theory on the workings of the city, but any substantive theory relevant in practice must also include theory on spatial perception, effects of environment on behavior and attitudes, and engineering and other technical knowledge.

Theory of design practice pertains to knowledge of the decision-making process, of the institutional context, and of professional practitioners. Although extensive theory on choice, decision making, and practice exists in management and operations research, proponents of the "theory of design practice" feel that the institutional process surrounding, in one instance the disposition of urban land, and in the other instance, physical alteration of space, is sufficiently distinctive and problematic to constitute a core for the respective fields of planning and architecture.

To draw a distinction between theory 'in' and 'of' design practice has the effect of shifting attention from substantive questions of urban structure and built environment to the processes by which decisions are made. This is a crucial concern, and this shift of emphasis is a predictable consequence of professialization. Of itself, though, the dichotomy throws no light on the substantive relevance of social science to urban design. Nor does it have the effect of distancing theory 'of' design from social science (though its proponents seem to feel that it does). For the institutional, organizational, interpersonal, and cognitive aspects of consensus formation, evaluation and decision making are themselves subjects of critical social science scrutiny in both planning (e.g., Downs, 1967), and architecture (Salaman, 1974). Recently, social scientists have shown a concern for prescribing decision-making tools for planners (e.g., Calkins's [1979] concept of planning monitor), and for studying attitudes and images of planners qua decision makers (Knox and Cullen, 1981). Research by Lipman (1970) and MacKinnon (1963) on the characteristics of architects and their professional priorities provides other examples.

In architecture, dissatisfaction with social science stems from two main sources, which are themselves quite distinct. The first is that architecture has potentialities beyond the banalities of existing forms, and these potentialities can be realized through visionary means, never by means of empirical social science research on existing forms and people's preferences (Goodman and Goodman, 1960). Although the Goodman's argument is based on ethical as well as aesthetic considerations, a second source of dissatisfaction deals with the failure of social science to deal with the issue of the uniqueness of place that characterizes every design problem; this issue must be handled in a creative and intuitive manner. This source of dissatisfaction is chiefly aesthetic.

On a conceptual level, the present relationship between social science theory and design practice is very complicated, far more complicated than that envisioned in the rational-instrumental model. Recently, planning theorists have attempted to distinguish planning theory from social science by its normative-ethical content, and by a focus on the planners' decision-making process. Academic and practicing architects have always been more critical of empirical social science models, but articles in this volume written by architects (Freidman) and by social scientists

(Gans, Larson) suggest that new links are being forged between architecture and social science theory in terms of the normative-ethical concerns of practitioners. Within social science the cluster of commitments loosely referred to as positivism has been under attack for many years. Specifically, many social science parallels can be found to Klosterman's argument for an ethically based specification of goals. Moreover, many radical social scientists are inclined to cast practitioners as part of the problem: for example, the allegation that architecture and planning serve unacknowledged ideological ends in reproducing a structure of sociopolitical organization that itself lies at the root of urban problems (Castells, 1977).

Attempts to differentiate a theory of practice from a substantive theory may be understood as a response to the institutionalization of the design professions. This polarization has had several useful effects, above all a careful, critical analysis of the inadequacies of social science theory by theoretically oriented planners (Bolan, Faludi, Forester, Grabow, Klosterman) and by theoretically oriented architects (Tafuri, Allsop).

The foregoing remarks suggest that recent attempts to define separate spheres of operation for social sciences and planning are fundamentally flawed. Such attempts may be understood primarily as consequences of structural and institutional segregation and self-definition in various academic fields. They represent, in the last analysis, distractions from the task of fusing theory and practice. It is not accidental that some of the most penetrating criticisms of practice, including modern radical critiques, trace theory and action to identical roots in our conceptualization of a social reality. A currently fashionable attempt to criticize and synthesize social science theory and political practice is Habermas's universal pragmatics, which unifies substantive theorizing and political action by viewing them as communicative processes, bound by preconditions (enabling rules) on several levels, including objective truth, truthfulness ('sincerity'), normative (legal) acceptability, and comprehensibility. Some implications of this program for urban planning are indicated by Forester (chapter 3) and Hemmens (1980). Whatever the specific merits of Habermas's ideas, they indicate a fruitful strategy for understanding potential relationships between social science and planning, treating them as complementary endeavors growing from identical material problems and contradictions in urban life, and in our conceptualization of the world.

# REFERENCES

Allen, R.
1975    "The idea of a value free social science." Journal of Value Inquiry 9: 95–117.

Beauregard, R.
1978    "Urban theory, urban practice and the state." Pp. 68–89 in Conference Proceedings, J. Pipkin and M. LaGory, Theory and Practice, State University of New York at Albany.

Blau, J. R.
1980    "A framework of meaning in architecture." In G. Broadbent, R. Bunt, and C. Jencks (eds.), Signs, Symbols and Architecture. New York: John Wiley.

Brolin, B. C.
1976    The Failure of Modern Architecture. New York: Van Nostrand Reinhold.

Burke, E.
1979    A Participatory Approach to Urban Planning. New York: Human Sciences Press.

Calkins, H. W.
1979    "The planning monitor: an accountability theory of plan evaluation." Environment and Planning, 11: 745–58.

Castells, M.
1977    The Urban Question. Cambridge, Mass.: M.I.T. Press.

Collins, P.
1971    Architectural Judgment. London: Faber and Faber.

Downs, A.
1967    Inside Bureaucracy. Boston: Little, Brown.

Faludi, A.
1973    Introduction. In A. Faludi (ed.), A Reader in Planning Theory. New York: Pergamon.

Goodman, P. and P. Goodman
1960    Communitas. New York: Vintage.

Grabow, A. and D. Heskin
1973    "Foundations for a radical concept of planning." Journal of the American Planning Association 39: 106–114.

Harvey, D.
1973    Social Justice and the City. London: Arnold.

Hemmens, G. C.
1980    "New directions in planning theory." American Planners Association Journal 46: 259–60.

Jacobs, A.
1978    Making City Planning Work. Chicago: American Society of Planning Officials.

*11*

Knox, P. and J. Cullen
1981 "Planners as urban managers: an exploration of the attitudes and self-image of senior British planners." Environment and Planning 13: 885–98.

Larson, M. S.
1977 The Rise of Professionalism: A Sociological Analysis. Berkeley: University of California Press.

Lefebvre, H.
1974 La Production de L'Espace. Paris: Anthropos.

Lipman, A.
1970 "Architectural education and the social commitment of contemporary British architects." Sociological Review 18: 5–27.

Lukes, S.
1978 "Power and authority." Pp. 633–76 in T. Bottomore and R. Nisbet (eds.), A History of Sociological Analysis. New York: Basic Books.

MacKinnon, D. W.
1963 "Creativity and images of self." In R. W. White (ed.), The Study of Lives. New York: Atherton Press.

Merton, R. K.
1981 "Remarks on theoretical pluralism." Pp. i–vii in P. M. Blau and R. K. Merton (eds.), Continuities in Structural Inquiry. Beverly Hills, Cal.: Sage Publications.

Moore, T.
1978 "Why allow planners to do what they do? A justification from economic theory." American Institute of Planners Journal 44: 387–98.

Polanyi, K.
1957 The Great Transformation. Boston: Beacon Press.

Rawls, J.
1971 A Theory of Justice. Cambridge, Mass.: Belknap Press of Harvard University.

Ritchey, F.
1981 "Medical rationalization, cultural lag, and the malpractice crisis." Human Organization 40: 97–112.

Salaman, G.
1974 Community and Occupation. Cambridge: University Press.

Tafuri, M.
1976 Theories and History of Architecture. New York: Harper and Row.

Weber, M.
1964 Basic Concepts in Sociology. H. P. Secher (trans.). New York: Citadel Press.

# PART I

# *Historical Origins of Practice*

## INTRODUCTION

*It was so wonderfully thrilling! It didn't seem possible to me that any Master Builder in the whole world could build such a tremendously high tower. And then to see you up there yourself—right at the very top—as large as life!*

—Henrik Ibsen, *The Master Builder*

*In the construction of a county it is not the practical workers but the idealists and planners that are difficult to find.*

—Sun Yat Sen, *Chung-shan Ch'uan-shu*

The designer, historically, has been the epitome of art, civil order, and auspicious power. Yet it is difficult to escape the patent evidence that the designer has had to struggle for autonomy and influence. The following two chapters, by Meadows and Larson, examine the factors that help to explain this paradox historically, and they provide the theoretical background for the more specifically focused papers in other sections of this volume.

Moreover, they supply a main conceptual link between two themes running through the book: the knowledge *used* by architects and planners, and knowledge *of* professional theory and practice. Meadows traces how morpohological and conceptual theories of physical form have influenced the variable definitions of form givers (both architects and planners), and in turn, how form givers have in different ways intervened to influence physical form. To posit, thus, a reciprocal dynamic between form and form givers, while considering planners and architects

*13*

from a unified perspective, Meadows provides a uniquely comprehensive model that helps to transcend divergent perspectives in the study of architecture and planning.

One theme of Meadows' paper is that the very historical conditions which bestow on form givers their special identity at the same time cast them in roles that entail complex and at times contradictory relations with the public, the state, and clients. Meadows' comprehensive and rich account of the historical processes that govern the ideas about form and the nature of the form giving professions will provide the reader with a new perspective on the relation between architects and planners and on the relation between form and space. History for Meadows is not a simple sequence of events but rather a series of transformations that involves emergent structures. And the structures that emerge themselves reveal new contradictions and new possibilities.

Also employing the tools of social science theory and the materials of history, Larson focuses on the structural conditions of architecture, and more specifically, the paradoxical consequences that these conditions tend to create. One such paradox arises from the fact that architecture is simultaneously defined as the relationship between *telos* (symbolic intention) and *techne* (materialization), another from the fact of patronage. The significance of this for the professional role, the conception of design, and the ideologies of architects is deeply rooted in the dialectics of history; but architects' direction over *techne* and *telos* depends on the nature of patronage as well.

Larson thus views architecture as both social relationship and a dynamic tension between art and technique. She then develops a theoretical model that accounts for those conditions under which architects can, through the appropriation of telos, acquire charisma, and those under which patrons dominate. With the increasing complexity of building functions and technology, rival professions acquire significance, and the patron-architect relationship is transformed.

# 1 Cities and Professionals

## PAUL MEADOWS

*I have stored up in my mind a vision of a heavenly city; whether it shall come to be I do not know; but for this I shall work and for no other.*
———Plato

*With the remnants thereof he maketh a god.*
———The Bible

*Man is no Aristotelian god contemplating all existence at one glance.*
———Walter Lippmann

## INTRODUCTION

### Form and Form Giving

This chapter explores some of the implications for professional men and women of the fact that the city, in all places and at all times, has been characterized by form. In this discussion form is regarded as a primitive and universal category. The significance of this premise will be described in terms of the reciprocal implications of urban form for professionals and of professionals for urban form.

That the city is characterized by form is an abundant empirical fact, one of global historicity and impressive variety, of manifold physical and social expression. Viewed as physical shape, urban form exhibits huge variation: star-shaped cities, radial/lineal cities, circular cities, triangular cities, plaza cities (surrounded by gridirons of streets), axial cities (extending along an axis of growth from a dominant economic base), concentric cities (with identifiable zones of dominant functions/populations), sector cities (with identifiable gradients of dominant functions/populations), and so on.

But urban form is not simply a matter of descriptive geometry. A similar though sometimes less immediate imagery emerges when one turns from total to component urban form and examines the arrangements of parts within the whole. Urban form is thus presented as a vast theater in which a polyglot variety of human encounters, paths, and locations occurs: as a mosaic of "adapted spaces"; as a system for access and transaction; as a time-binding system of arrangements of parts in which the manifold structures serve as points of intersection between past, present, and future; and as a pattern of spatial clustering of such functions and populations as those identified as natural areas, neighborhoods, enclaves, zones, sectors, and nuclei.

The perception of urban form that reports the urban scene as a set of *stocks* at a given time also reports it as the structuralization of *flows* over time. One way of depicting this perception is to visualize urban forms as expressions of human objectification (Weingartner, 1962). Physically, form is seen in terms of the fruitful marriage of technology and aesthetics under the sponsorship of highly variable coalitions of enclaves of special interest. Socially, urban form is seen as the product of a variety of unions of methods and ideologies sponsored by numerous configurations of functions and populations. In either case, form is conceptualized as a product of processes: some create form, some articulate it, and some mangage and maintain it. We will return to this theme of objectification further on in this discussion.

The relationships of form-oriented professionals to the city must, by definition, be considered in terms of the city as form. Fully to appreciate these relationships in all of their significance, one must begin with the idea of form itself, with form as a "basic unit-idea" (Lovejoy, 1936), which, like all other such ideas, has a history, has variability, and has utility. Historically, the theory of the idea of form has developed a distinction between its morphological and its conceptual aspects (Tararkiewicz, 1973). Morphologically (stemming from *morphe*) the idea of form has referred to its visible aspects. Conceptually (stemming from *eidos*), the idea of form has referred to its componential and inferential aspects. In the first case, the theory of form has portrayed it in terms of appearance, of imputation, and of differentiation of parts. In the second case, the theory of form has portrayed it in terms of appearance, of imputation, of differentiation of parts. The significance of these intellectual traditions for the conceptualization of urban form is suggested in table 1.1.

Historically, the idea of form has had a prodigious variability, as might be expected. Much of this variability has been generated by regarding form, either morphologically or conceptually, as a matter of relationships between form and context. Variation in form tends to be

TABLE 1.1

*Themes in the Historic Idea of Form*

| TYPES | PHILOSOPHICAL CONCEPTUALIZATIONS OF FORM: AS | COUNTERPART CONCEPTUALIZATIONS OF URBAN FORM: AS |
|---|---|---|
| Morphological | Arrangement of parts | Naturalistic order |
| | Boundaried entity | Operational system |
| | Realization of essence | Structuralization of purposes, goals, needs, interests, functions |
| Conceptual | Appearance | Directly visible and less visible, inferred structures; physical/social/cultural |
| | Imputation | Symbolic pattern, physical, social |
| | Differentiation | Heuristic pattern |

minimal in situations of little cultural change, great social homogeneity, and cultural unself-consciousness (Alexander, 1966). Variation in form tends to be maximal in situations of intense cultural change, great social heterogeneity, and cultural self-consciousness. The latter illustrates very well D'Arcy Thompson's description of form in nature as the diagram of forces for irregularities (1959). In either case, whether of change or stability, form is seen as the product of variability of contexts, as suggested in table 1.2, which relates historical theories of form to types of determinants of form.

The variety of form may be considered in terms of the contextual variations of functions and intentions. Thus, the idea of form may be formulated in terms of the varying relationships between form and function. Thus, form follows function. It is fitted to function. Function is fitted to form. And form follows form, as in traditional architectural styles.

Variation of form may, as in the case of the city, be seen as adjustment to the level of function: as an adjustment to the requirements of first-order functions (those of defense, security, worship, therapy); as an adjustment to the requirements of second-order functions (those of transportation, business, industry); as an adjustment to the requirements of third-order functions (those of major institutional systems, e.g., the polity, the economy); and as an adjustment to the requirements of fourth-order functions (those of individual life styles, access to the social structure, choice, mobility).

The contextual perspective on variation of form yields another set of conceptualizations of form: in the case of the city, form *of* and *in* the city. This distinction is developed in table 1.3.

TABLE 1.2

*Urban Form as Process*

| Theories of Form | Determinants of Form | |
| --- | --- | --- |
| | Pregiven | Constructed |
| Morphological | Physical, ecological, market determination or urban form | System determination of city functions, location, articulation, pattern |
| | Interests, needs, goals, values as pregiven and as determinant | Planned and designed unit and collective forms as determined by interests, needs, goals, values as pregiven and as determinant |
| Conceptual | Physical structures of cities regarded as determinant of social structure/organization | Urban social structure seen as determinant of physical structures of cities |
| | Traditional/dominant cosmo-logical/other symbol systems held to be determinant of urban form | Technological and architectural canons, styles, resources, logic, end-states considered to be deter-minant of urban form |

TABLE 1.3

*Form of and in Cities: Conceptual Approaches*

| Conceptual Emphasis | Focus | Ideal-type | Proponents |
| --- | --- | --- | --- |
| Form Of Cities | *Total* urban form in terms of composi-tional pattern/ Gestalt | *Unitary* gover-nance and cul-tural situation | *Comprehensive* urban planners and management/ development personnel |
| Form In Cities | *Component* urban form in terms of building types, design styles, land-use patterns and projections, etc. | *Pluralistic* gover-nance and cul-tural situation | Architectural, engineering, planning professionals; Sponsors, developers, contractors, corporate/ civic enterprises, fiscal organizations, urban administrative personnal |

The contextual perspective on variation of form may reflect the role of intentionality in the determination of form. Thus, urban form has been interpreted as a microversion of the cosmos: total urban form as a symbolic componential pattern, as in the case of the shrine cities of archaic urbanisms (Wheatley, 1969). Urban form has been depicted as a matter of power: total urban form as a vehicle of impression management and life control, as in the case of the monumental city of Roman urbanism or the baroque city of Renaissance Europe (Mumford, 1961). Urban form has been regarded as an agency of input-output processes: component urban form as an instrument or system of commerce and industry (Weber, 1958). It has been conceptualized as a complex pattern of paths and locations for urbanities: component urban form as social space (La Gory and Pipkin, 1981).

In all these instances of the idea of form there is an unmistakable linkage between form as product and form as process, that is, between form and form giving. Some aspects of this linkage are suggested in table 1.4.

## Urban Form Giving and Form Givers

The temporal view of urban form is an attempt to account for it as the product of a process summarized in the concept of form giving. The general theory of urban form giving has wrestled with two versions of the process, each anchored in its own set of data and interpretations. A naturalistic version, prompted by an evolutionary perspective, locates the discussion of urban form giving in the data of market determinations and ecological processes which together are regarded as determinants of the additive and accumulative pattern held to be characteristic of urban form giving. A construction view, prompted by voluntaristic and intentionalistic philosophy of action, locates the discussion of urban form giving in the data of human interests, needs, goals, and decisions, which together are regarded as determinants of the purposive, enacted, and designed pattern held to characterize historic urban form giving. In both cases form giving is depicted as a landscape of change and variation (Blumenfeld, 1949). By definition, the scene is interpreted dynamically (Passoneau, 1965).

We have seen how variation in the idea of form has been a function of the conceptualization of context: form $= f($context$)$. So here also the role of context becomes critical. The crucial role of context in generating variability in urban form giving may be seen from a number of perspectives. Different interests are involved in any conceptualization of urban form giving. We must differentiate between the construction of urban forms, whether unit or collective in character—that is, whether a park or a master plan, an expressway or total urban pattern. Similarly, we must differentiate between the adaptation of urban forms and their maintenance, between their displacement and their replacement, between recovering or rehabilitating them and evaluating or appreciating them,

*19*

TABLE 1.4

*The Idea of Form and Urban Form Giving*

| | CONCEPTUALIZATIONS OF URBAN FORM GIVING |
|---|---|
| Morphological | |
| *Arrangement of parts* | Market determination of land use patterns and building types; |
| | Topographical/geographic determination of land use patterns and building types; |
| | Ecological distribution patterns and processes; |
| *Boundaried entity* | System determination of urban functions, location, articulation, pattern; |
| | System models in planning and management development of cities; |
| *Realization of essence* | Urban physical/social structures as developmental functions of interests, needs, goals of the human community; |
| | Utopian, ideal, designed cities as realization of human values inherent in the human community; |
| Conceptual | |
| *Appearance* | Physical structures of city = f (urban social structures); |
| | Social structures of city = f (urban physical structures); |
| *Imputation* | The symbolic shrine/palace city of archaic/classical urbanisms; |
| | Urban forms as social/perceptual spaces; |
| | Urban social form as social constructions; |
| *Differentiation* | Types of city in terms of dominant functions; |
| | Types of cities in terms of dominant culture/economy/polity; |
| | Types and functions of urban social structures. |

between developing and managing them. Each interest contributes to the total process of urban form giving, but obviously in different ways. Clearly, any single action of form giving—whether designing and building high-rise structures or master planning the long-range growth pattern of a city—cannot possibly be the whole story of urban form giving.

The whole story can be summarized in Simmel's valuable conception of human creativity, and indeed of human action in general, as objectification, seen as the external embodiment or manifestation of human beings and human society (Weingartner, 1962). Man expresses himself in and by and with the cultural object, whether in the form of language or institutions or art or technology or whatever. This theme has been the premise of three different traditions. First, there is the traditional concern for the object in itself (as in design: the city as an art form, as symbol, as "machine for living," and so on). Second, there is the traditional concern for the object in terms of the actor (as in art or invention: the city as social or physical creation, as theater for human actions, as vehicle or instrument for human expression: the city is the people). Third, there is the traditional concern with the object in terms of the range of social uses and functions that can conceivably be served by the object: the city as a social utility, as human habitat, as social space, as a containing community.

Inevitably, the conceptual perspective on urban form giving turns to the variable settings in which form giving occurs. Social and physical settings may be seen as responsible for the variability in form-giving processes: one thinks of the differences in water-front or hill country settings, of rivers, highways and airways, of crossroads and outposts, and so on. But one must include in the variety of city settings the historical cultural contexts—archaic urbanisms, classical urbanisms, imperial urbanisms, commercial and industrial urbanisms: preindustrial, industrial, and postindustrial urbanisms (Sjoberg, 1960; Bell, 1973). There is also the critical distinction between unitary and pluralistic settings: between situations where decisions, goals, values, and methods are shaped by a single source of power and authority and situations where they are subject to a variety of active levels of authority, jurisdictions, interests, even problem situations. This is not merely the distinction between archaic or imperial or authoritarian urbanisms and democratic-industrial urbanisms, for urban form giving can be unitary within a highly pluralistic society, as it is in instances of corporate determination or machine government (Mumford, 1961).

The point is that the historic social-cultural-physical settings enter into the urban form-giving processes as sets of options and constraints (Artle, 1963; Friedmann, 1972; Gutnov, 1965). The urban form giver is free—within the context. Some of the ways in which settings enter into urban form giving as options and constraints are suggested in table 1.5.

Finally, the contextual perspective on urban form giving focuses on the form giver themselves. Historically, the company of urban form givers, it seems, has been a very diverse group. The diversity is a function of the history of the city and its society (Mumford, 1961; Weber, 1958).

TABLE 1.5

*Options and Constraints Governing Urban Form Giving*

| KINDS OF OPTIONS: ACCORDING TO SOURCES | KINDS OF OPTION CONDITIONS | | |
|---|---|---|---|
| | *Idealistic: Those of:* | | *Realistic: Deriving from:* |
| Whose? | Professionals' reference groups and reference fields | | Compromises and trade-offs and pressures of local *political* situations and processes |
| | Traditions/culture of the local city | | Constraints and possibilities of local *built* and *physical* environment |
| | Power/interest enclaves of local city | | Constraints and possibilities of local *economic* situations and processes |
| | Public/private persons and groups of local city (e.g., residents, business firms, developers, contractors, civic associations, public agencies | | Local/regional/national *resources* and *policies* for action |
| For What? | Types of Urban Form | Types of Form Determinants | Types of Planning Goals |
| | Unit form | Pre-given | Short-term/long-range planning |
| | Collective form | Constructed | Limited/comprehensive planning |
| | | | Physical/social planning |
| | | | Development management planning |

The genealogy of urban form givers starts with the princes of the sword; then come the princes of the robe; next are the patrons, that historically varied stratum of people of wealth and wisdom; they are followed by the urban commissioners—the governing bodies of the city; there are the contemporary patrons—the entrepreneurial organizations, corporate or civic; and finally a truly diversified crew consisting of artists and architects, technologists and engineers, humanists and scientists, and professional planners. Retrospectively it has been an evolution not only of power but also of authority, in more recent times the authority of expertise and sensibility (Larson, 1977; Noble, 1977).

## CITIES, PROFESSIONALS, AND FORM

### *Professional Urban Form Givers:*
### *Structural Variables and Themes*

Historically, what has indeed happened has been the professionalization of urban form giving. In the long and global view of the city in history, form giving has been a function of continuing differentiation and specialization. Over time, each area of social differentiation and specialization has itself participated in and contributed to urban form giving: the throne, the altar, the guild, the council, the corporation, the council and assembly, the civic enterprise, the citizen home builder. Historically the patronage essential to the varying arts of form giving has shifted from the throne, the church, the barracks to ascendant social classes, public assemblies, and administrative agencies. Form-oriented professionals—architects, engineers, planners, for example—belong in a very special sense to the later phases of the historic processes of social differentiation and specialization that underlie all urban form giving.

In earlier urbanisms, urban form giving was a function of direct impact by unitary governing and cultural systems, as in the case of archaic and classical urbanisms. In later urbanisms, urban form giving has been a function of the emergence of dispersed, pluralistic governing and cultural systems, creating the complex relationships of urbanists and urbanites: that is, the relationships of those whose business *is* the city and of those whose business is *in* the city. In the earlier urbanisms, the impact of form-giving professionals (such as they, indeed, were) was a matter of immediate proximity to and participation in the unitary governing and cultural system. In later urbanisms, form-oriented professionals have, basically, had only an instrumental, typically residual impact. They are in fact only part of the large, variegated company of urbanists with a primary concern for the city—administrators, academicians, intellectuals—all of whom have differential and restricted access to the decision-making and form-giving processes of the modern city (Bolan and Nuttall, 1975; Goode, 1959).

It is this historically shifting context of social structure that prompts the formulation of a number of interpretative themes seen as integral to

*23*

an appreciation of the status and roles, and of the options and constraints, of professionals in the modern city. These themes can be summarized as follows:

Theme I
> *General.* As do all other groups in the city, professionals have a distinctive pattern of interaction and interdependence with the city.
>
> *Specific.* The contributions of professionals to the process of urban form giving occur within the contexts of this distinctive pattern.

Theme II
> *General.* Professionals have relationships with urban form giving that are characterized by certain *differential* patterns.
>
> *Specific.* 1. Some aspects of urban form giving are independent of professionals.
> 2. In some other aspects of urban form giving, professionals have a limited or perhaps residual relationship.
> 3. In still other aspects of urban form giving, professionals have a major relationship.
> 4. However, even in these particular aspects, some professionals have no direct relationship whatsoever with urban form giving.

Theme III
> *General.* The relationships of professionals to urban form giving are characterized by certain *structural variables.*
>
> *Specific.* 1. In those situations where some professionals have major relationships to urban form giving, it is necessary to distinguish between variables that are associated dominantly *with the city itself* and those that are a function of the *professionals themselves.*
> 2. It is also important to distinguish situations in which professionals' *contributions* to urban form giving are a function of certain *contexts of action* in the city and those unique and significant contributions which they bring as professionals *to* the contexts of action in the city.
> 3. It is important to identify those situations and circumstances in which *contributions* by professionals to urban form giving have been and/or can be *maximal* or *optimal.*
> 4. Knowledge of the situations and contexts in which professionals do have significant relationships to urban form giving enriches our understanding not only of urban form giving itself but also of the structure and dynamics of the city.

## Professional Form Givers
### and the Freedom of the City

The urban form giver, we have said, is free—within the context. He does not and cannot have unconditioned freedom. In what sense, then, is he free?

We may define freedom as the capacity to act (Fosdick, 1939). It is not merely the absence of restraints, which is liberty, but the power to act (Meadows, 1948). In the context of the concerns of this volume, the urban form giver's capacity to act may be seen, first, as a function of the urban situation and, second, as a function of the professional situation. These two functions are discussed in turn, below.

The city, which is ancient as well as modern, preindustrial as well as industrial, Western as well as Asian, small as well as megalopolitan, can hardly be contained in a single contextual perspective. To simplify our discussion, we will center on the Western modern industrial city of Europe and of North and South America. And to simplify further, we will enlarge on a familiar technique of interpretation, that of epitomization, which collapses a range of diverse elements into a single summary, a trope, so to speak, which represents the whole. The city may be epitomized as a built environment, as a complex of multiplying functions that require structures. And it may be epitomized as an environment of ethologically and politically significant space. These epitomes, it must be acknowledged quickly, can provide only an incomplete account of the urban scene, but a very useful part of it (Banz, 1970; Beshers, 1962; Foley, 1964; La Gory and Pipkin, 1981).

As a built environment, the city is an objectification of many functions requiring structures, physical structures that:

Have to be designed, funded, constructed, operated, maintained, and in due course of time rehabilitated or replaced

Have to be coordinated, articulated, managed, limited, regulated, prohibited, encouraged, guided

Are responses to a spectrum of human needs and values, both public and private

Have a spatial pattern significant in terms of different dimensions of human objectification

As an environment of power and political process, the city in both its spatial and a-spatial dimensions is characterized by social structures that:

Organize, order, and control the city's spatial pattern

Organize, order, and control the city's a-spatial pattern

Are responses to both ethological and political human needs and values, public and private

Have a liberating and limiting impact on human objectification in the city

These epitomes set the stage for an understanding of the sense in which and the extent to which the city offers professional form givers the capacity to act.

The first and most vivid view of the city is the optical impact of its physical structures (Rapoport, 1977). These are, of course, the primary domain of concern of the professional form giver. It is a twofold concern. On the one hand, the city, even the new Western industrial city, is a complex of old structures in need of redesigning and rehabilitation or replacement. This obsolescence has many sources: environmental pollution, intensive use and overuse, technological and functional inadequacy, failures of maintenance, hazards of fire and other damages, and so on. Obsolescence likewise varies by unit and by area, so much so that in time abandonment increasingly prepares the way for new structures and new uses.

On the other hand, the city is a complex of new structures, generally representing a response to an emerging pattern of relocation of old functions or new locations of new functions: the city as the center of mass industrial production versus the city as an office park, if not also a sandbox or reservation (Sternlieb, 1971; Long, 1971; James, 1974; Ganz and O'Brien, 1973). The modern city is a landscape of change, extending from its center in waves of expansion and along tentacular outreaches into its hinterland, converting open spaces along its periphery as well as filling in open spaces in its areas of containment. Additions and subdivisions, aided and abetted by the rapid transit of earlier—and the expressways of later—decades, create a large inventory of needs for new structures, both commercial/industrial and residential. The familiar demand-supply curves of economists appropriately diagram and project these patterns. The city as a complex of old and new structures not only gives graphic meaning to the concept of the built environment but also to the concept of the city as a property machine, a multiproduct organization of production responsible for both the infrastructures and the functional structuralization of all the other abundant urban needs (Pahl, 1970; Salisbury, 1964; Thompson, 1974).

To this consideration of the city as built environment must be added the no less important consideration of the human dimensions of urban physical structure. Itself a product of the new environmentalism which insists on the totality of meaning of the physical city (Pahl, 1970; Passoneau, 1965), the conception of human dimensions adds a number of contextual perspectives to the physical structure of the city. A populist version of this conception stresses the thesis that the city is, after all, *of* and *for* its people, if not always *by* them. A more conventional version stresses the theme that the city is also an organization of social time, human interests and values and communication processes. It envisions the city not only in terms of its many unit functions but also in terms of the numerous subcommunities of its people (Suttles, 1973). The city is described—and evaluated—in terms not only of the megascale of urban concentration and expansion but also of the various microscales of human perception, identity, interaction, and mobility (Banz, 1970). The megaform of the *total* city, in which divergent elements are integrated and articulated in various human contexts, and the miniforms of the *component* city, in which separate elements of urban society pursue their own "community of limited liability"—their interests, which are not identical with the communal system—both visualize the city as a manifold theater of human encounters. The increasing research literature on the image of the city is reporting an impressive spread of cognitive, perceptual, and symbolic meanings of the city (Lynch, 1960). What is indeed emerging is a social mapping of the city, not only in terms of its more obvious demographic and functional attributes, but also in terms of its rich range of human meaningfulness (La Gory and Pipkin, 1981; Crane, 1960; Wheatley, 1969).

When one turns from the optical approach to urban physical structure to the conceptual interpretations of urban space, the language of observation becomes inherently and revealingly political. From the days of archaic urbanism to modern industrial urbanism, the city has always been the scene of a highly varied social politics. The city is not only a land and building market but a political arena and forum. In unitary governing and cultural systems, as we have seen, the politics of space was not only traditional but also explicit: functions and people had a fairly stable pattern of location (Kuper, 1972). The pattern was a function of central power and authority, typically sacerdotal in mythology or rationale, but reinforced by the central institutions of power (Gutnov, 1965). Territoriality, locality, propinquity, and contiguity were properties of custom-supported and power-sanctioned arrangements.

The rise of pluralistic governing and cultural systems has generated another view of the politics of space, a mechanistic and individualistic one. In this view, whether seen as a system or a process (Rogers, 1967), the locational pattern of functions and people is perhaps best interpreted in terms of a probabilistic calculus of a universe of individual decisions (Smith, 1976). Characterized by discretionary social behavior, the modern urban community is dominated by decision-making processes in which individual values and choices and goals, mediated by differential and stratified access to income and to power, account for both the collective and the unit forms of the city (Hunter, 1953; Beshers, 1962; Salisbury, 1964; Burrows, 1979). The imagery which emerges with this conception of the social politics of the modern city is that of a spatial pattern, not only of "ordered segmentation" (Suttles, 1973) and horizontal as well as vertical stratification, but also of an ordering organization in which congeries or groupings or coalitions of wealth and power have a major if not always total impact on the composition and direction, the speed and intensity of urban change, including growth (Form, 1954; Artle, 1963; Foley, 1964; Laumann and Pappi, 1973). The dynamics as well as the structures of this ordering organization is discussed more fully later in this chapter. Here it is presented simply as part of the urban form givers' capacity to act, their freedom as form givers.

## Professional Form Givers
### and the Freedom of the Professions

The freedom of the professional, we have said, lives in the capacity — the power—to act. Part of that freedom lies in the nature of professional work itself. The attributes that describe the source of the professional worker's freedom are suggested by two sets of indicators: (1) the fact that professional work is a function of a high and special level of knowledge and skill, and (2) the fact that it has a close affinity with modern industrialism as a knowledge-based society. Much of the professional person's capacity to contribute to urban form giving is generated by those particular aspects of the professions and of contemporary society.

The professional person has historically been regarded as the possessor of information and skills of extraordinary consequence for his community. This view, which dates back to the stonemasons and craftsmen of archaic urbanism, who shared in the numinous legitimacy of the throne and altar (Frankl, 1968; Znaniecki, 1965), has found increasing corroboration in the spreading specialization of industrial urbanism. Both historical commercialization and industrialization have sponsored a widening range of knowledge-based technologies, not merely those of physics and chemistry but of all the applied sciences that have been responsible for the enlarging company of mechanical and electronic, organizational and psychosocial, and institutional, technological extensions. Ours is indeed a "multitechnological" society, and the men and women of knowledge are to be found in a multitude of multicontextual roles, all funded by a growing stock of special knowledge and skills (Bell, 1973; Etzioni, 1969).

In the context of the industrial city especially, it is necessary to stress the occupational frame of reference, which tends to be passed over by the traditional gentrified rhetoric of "service" and other supposedly unique traits of the professions. Professional work is, after all, work, and in an industrial culture this entails a number of things. All occupations in industrialism are, to some extent and in different ways, knowledge-based, the professions quantitatively and qualitatively more so, requiring as they do a span and degree of education and training well beyond that of most other occupations. This fact signals not only the societal expectation of significant benefits for which the society is willing to pay but also significant rewards for the professionals themselves (Goode, 1959, 1969; Moore, 1970).

Nonetheless, the professions have their own market orientation and dependency, which they protect and promote, often with guildlike closure and conceit. The professions have their own pattern of organizational linkage to the market of services, paying full attention to the necessities and nuances of recruitment, selection, support, training, credentialing, and licensing (Larson, 1977). The professional associations provide a covering bond not only to the market of industrialism but also to the state, with the latter fully and actively participating in the preparation and conduct of professional work. They likewise provide a covering bond with their own histories, thus maintaining—with appropriate selectivity—their traditions and their own sense of unique "community within the community" (Goode, 1969).

The professions, in other words, have unusual and important ties to the social structure (Znaniecki, 1965). These relationships must be variously described, for they differ with the given profession as well as the given national culture. Their historic rooting in the intellectual disciplines of *academe* and the scientific basis of their technological knowledge and skills have, on the one hand, encouraged a universalism of service. But, on the other hand, their location in the industrial occupational system has committed them to an instrumental view of their work, one that while protecting the society, also protects and rewards the professional (Fuchs, 1968; Galbraith, 1967; Johnson, 1972). The insistent demands of the industrial culture for the rationalization and science-based character of work have had an impact on the professions no less than on all other occupations. This impact may be described in terms of a spread of the professional role, one that has created a range of recognizable types—subprofessions (Gross, 1971)—as well as extending the boundaries of professionalism, but perhaps blurring them at the same time (Etzioni, 1969).

The ubiquitous market orientation of professional services describes another phase of the relationships of the professions to the social structure (Larson, 1977). Professional work may be characterized dichotomously as "solo" and as employed (Hall, 1968). It may also be characterized dichotomously as person-centered and as product-centered. The implications of this latter polarity are suggested in table 1.6.

*29*

*Paul Meadows*

## TABLE 1.6

*Market Orientations of Professional Services*

| PERSON-CENTERED | PRODUCT-CENTERED |
|---|---|
| Client | Customers/constituents |
| Professional work<br>= $f$(clientage) | Professional work<br>= f(patronage) |
| Interpersonal, fee-for-<br>service contractualism | Organizational, corporate,<br>agency-salaried contractualism |
| Client as beneficiary | Organization as beneficiary |
| | Customers, constituencies as<br>beneficiaries |
| Technopersonal<br>professionalism | Technobureaucratic<br>professionalism |

Whether solo or employed, whether person-centered or product-centered, the actual professional work situation obviously has a sizable impact not only on the clientage aspects of professionalism but also on the supposed universalism of the professional work ethic and on the supposedly effective neutrality of professional scientific dedication. Nevertheless, such a role spread, while it undoubtedly generates varying degrees of role strain and varying types of role-strain resolution, also generates, from the standpoint of the professional's creative capacity to act, an almost limitless frontier for responsive and responsible innovativeness.

The first indicator of professionalism is its base in scientific-technological knowledge and skills (Znaniecki, 1965). This background suggests the second indicator, really an extension of the first: the very special affinity of the professions with "the knowledge society" (Bell, 1973). We have already noted some aspects of this affinity: the mandatory and extensive preparation in education and training, the credentialing and licensing by the state, the rationalization impacts of the industrial culture. To these must be added other close ties. The knowledge-based society of industrialism has been one of increasing abstractness and complexity, of such magnitude and intricacy that only a background-ing in the historic intellectual disciplines of *academe* can provide a comfortable competence (Bell, 1973). Not unexpectedly, such a social organization has come to be epitomized by one of its key component processes—information processing. This and similar epitomes—the cybernetic society, the electronic society, the postindustrial society, and other McLuhanesque tropes—all point to its dominantly pluralistic as well as symbolic character. The pattern of information collection, organization, storage, retrieval, transmission and utilization is competitively multicentered, but with some of the very familiar hazards that accompany vigorous competition—differential access to information, plus the unmistakable evidence of oligopoly, if not monopoly, of the information processes (Chapin, 1973; Dahinden, 1972). Such evidence, it must be emphasized, is not confined to Western capitalism (Smith, 1979; Webber, 1965).

One remarkable aspect of the affinity of the professions with the structure and functions of the knowledge-based society is the tendency toward, if not downright fascination with, elitism, which appears pervasively in the literature by and about the professions. It is not the elitism of their aristocratic ancestors with their *noblesse oblige*, which is after all a class trait. Professional elitism is fundamentally a role concept, one that highlights the peculiar importance of the men and women of knowledge to the men and women of power. Anticipated and praised by Saint-Simon and his erstwhile secretary, Comte, the elite position of professionals and intellectuals has been reinforced by the university system of the modern state and the myriad ventures of corporate enterprise. The historical patronage of the professions has shifted from the aristocracies of sword and robe to the patronage of the state and business. It is a patronage that has been responsible, as we have noted, not only for an extended professionalism but also for an indentured professionalism, to use Ralph Nader's phrase. The decade-by-decade occupational disclosures of the Census Bureau only underscore with increasing numbers something that the logic of industrial production has long since spelled out—the strategic position of the person of knowledge and skill in the industrial society. Galbraith's now familiar phrase, "technostructure," has itself become part of the "conventional wisdom" (Galbraith, 1967).

The incessant and mounting demand for the work of the professionals has its source not only in the functional specifications of industrialism but also in the normative specifications of urbanism, that is, in the rising and expanding requirements for services by industrial society, and especially by the industrial city. Such requirements refer not merely to those of functions calling for structures, but also to those of problems calling for solution. Industrial society and the industrial city have an insatiable appetite for both. In both cases knowledge and skill are the heart of the matter (Barr, 1972). In both cases the professional worker is riding a wave of demand that has not even begun to crest (Spilhaus, 1961).

# URBAN FORM GIVING IN THE CONTEXT OF COMMUNITY INTERVENTION

## *Urban Form Giving as Community Intervention*

One phase of urban form giving involves physical and spatial construction and reconstruction; another phase involves social construction and reconstruction (Haar, 1967). Each requires the other, and both represent actions of intervention in the space and life of the city (Gross, 1971; Harris, 1965). Urban form giving assumes both the need and the possibility for changing a given situation or trend in the city in some way, in some direction, for some desired end product or goal (Burrows, 1979).

Planned urban intervention may be limited or comprehensive. In either case there are certain characteristic elements, as table 1.7 seeks to point out (Altschuler, 1965; Bolan, 1967; Friedmann, 1972; Mayer, 1972; Petersen, 1966; Peattie, 1968).

Community intervention may be described as occurring within two broad patterns of change. One is the more familiar, certainly more conventional, pattern of social planning; it is the pattern to which professionals in the city probably more easily relate and with which they more commonly work. The other is the intervention pattern of the social movement, which is less structured, less bureaucratic, usually more emotional, and often far more urgently expressed (Rein, 1969). The contrasts between the two patterns are brought out in table 1.8.

Whether it occurs as the form-giving intervention of a single unit or of total form, whether the scope is comprehensive or limited, whether the style is social planning or action, whether adversarial or advocacy planning, the work of the urban form givers is that of intervention. It is important to examine some of the implications of this fact.

## *The Client Setting of Community Intervention*

Professionals become involved in the problem-solving activities of community intervention ordinarily through employment in some capacity by a client who wishes to use their expertise. As persons of knowledge and skills that identify and determine their status, professionals enter into situations of community intervention in a variety of roles. Their professional status is an important determinant of these roles. Their status

TABLE 1.7

*Planned Urban Intervention: Types and Elements*

| Elements | Types | |
|---|---|---|
| Scope | Limited | Comprehensive |
| Major instrument of action | Project proposal and completion | Master Plan |
| Responsibility for initiating action | Entrepreneurial organizations and civic associations | Planning Commission/ Board |
| Rationale | Correction/enhancement of selected local situations | System impact and development |
| Calculus | Costs/benefits | Impact assessment |
| Action pattern | Tactical | Developmental |
| Rhetoric of appeal | Present and immediate future "needs" | Future-oriented impact theory |
| Sector involvement | Private and public mix | Dominantly public |
| Dominant emphasis | Physical/economic requirements | Balanced and consensual assessment of total physical/ social environment |

derives from a number of different sources, depending on the one hand upon the professionals themselves and on the other hand upon the community situation. Typical sources of their status include:

Credentialed expertise

Control over information

Political access and sensitivity

Political and other "connections" of the agency or firm to which they may belong

Professional reputation and prestige

The "loftiness" of the professional as expert: the fact that professionals may be seen as above and in some ways perhaps beyond and purer than the community itself, possibly as unconstrained by it

The disinterestedness of the professional

Group or organizational support or affiliation which they may bring to the job

*33*

TABLE 1.8

*Community Intervention: Situations and Aspects*

| ASPECTS | SITUATIONS | |
| --- | --- | --- |
| | Social Planning | Social Action |
| Goals | Immediate/long-range problem solving | Alteration in direction of decision making, in institutional leadership procedures/policies, in power structure |
| Change Strategy | Collection/dissemination/judgment about facts; acceptance of propoasl | Identification of targets, resources, procedures, phases of action |
| Assumptions | Existence of physical/social problem situations present/future requiring solution | Presence of social inequities, imbalances, needs but also of possible benefits/values justifying intervention |
| Typical Procedures | Consensus as goal; methods for reconciling differences; debate/persuasion | Contest/confrontation/conflict but also accommodative efforts seeking widening support |
| Agencies of Intervention | Public/private planning boards, commissions, councils, citizen groups as clients | Social movements; coalitions of interest groups; rights councils; public forums; client constituencies and organizations |
| Personnel | Representatives of public/private agencies, firms, consulting groups, concerned professionals | Organizers local, regional, national public/private organizations; local volunteers; representatives of concerned civic groups |
| Experts | Social scientists; public administrators; planning specialists; engineers, architects and other professional groups | Private social action consultants; national special-interest association personnel; minority group organizers; militant rights workers; community organization specialists |

Urban form giving as community intervention requires the application of relevant and useful knowledge and skills. In a situation of intervention, professionals join a large company of men and women who participate in this process of planned change; they are a changing corps of agents of change, each of whom has in addition to some personal stake in the action a stock of knowledge and skills (Grabow and Grabow, 1973). The engagement of professionals in community intervention usually occurs in a setting of client relationships. Urban form giving is, from the standpoint of the professionals, therefore, a clienting process.

Certain elements of the clienting process bear directly on the functions and roles of professionals in the intervention that urban form giving requires (Bolan, 1971; Howe and Kaufman, 1979). These elements may be summarized as follows:

> Professionals are engaged in community intervention because of certain status values they bring to the roles integral to the intervention process.
>
> Their engagement occurs through the client-professional relationships: community client groups employ them to do certain things; in addition to the central tasks ordinarily specified in the employment contract there are many other functions they may be called upon to perform as part of the total process.
>
> Consideration of the central tasks of professionals as intervenors must include various dimensions of the client-professional relationships, which form the nucleus of the clienting process.
>
> This process takes place in a community setting and may thus be variously described in terms of the variables in community problem-solving actions; these variables create a large number of activity options—and risks.

Professionals bring to the highly assorted tasks of community intervention not only their knowledge and skills but also definable functions and roles that put their knowledge and skills to work. In schematic form these interrelationships are depicted in table 1.9.

The clienting process that makes possible the active participation of professionals in the work of community intervention centers on the relationship between the client or user, on the one hand, and professionals' functions and roles, on the other (Moore, 1970). There are in this complicated set of relationships at least four dimensions of consideration, as depicted in figure 1.1 (Form, 1954; Hunter, 1953; Laumann and Pappi, 1973; Rogers, 1962).

The contributions of professionals to the involvements of this network of relationships stem from the resources that professionals bring to the tasks of intervention. These resources consist, as we have said, in the functions and roles for which professionals have been prepared (Yarmolinsky, 1978; Argyris and Schon, 1974). This preparation is based on the interplay between the knowledge and skills they have learned, a learning process that comes through the informed formulation of relevances, of inferences, and of decisions, as portrayed in figure 1.2.

TABLE 1.9

*The Professional Worker in Community Intervention*

| | FUNCTIONS | ROLES |
|---|---|---|
| Substantive Knowledge | Institutional sciences/arts essential to skill-set | Field experiences contributing to role performance |
| | Experientially acquired information contributing to skill-set | Community culture/economy/politics as role contexts |
| | Legal mandates/constraints in exercise of skills | Professional normative requirements concerning role performance |
| | History/culture of the profession | |
| Professional Processes | Acquisition and competence in primary and ancillary skills | Client-related/contractual expectations and committments |
| | Credentialing/licensing memberships | Professional association |
| | Client negotiations/contract | Civic association memberships |
| | Work assignments/tasks; schedules | Work organization membership |
| | Work evaluation and assessment | |

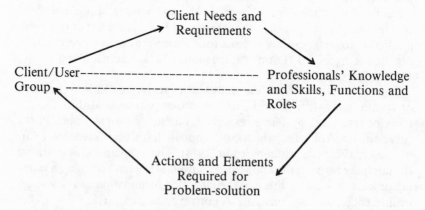

Fig. 1.1 Dimensions of the client relationship

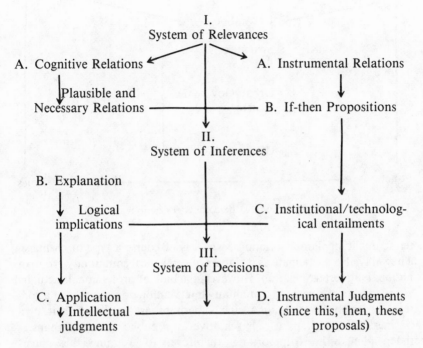

KNOWLEDGE                    SKILL

I.
System of Relevances

A. Cognitive Relations          A. Instrumental Relations

Plausible and
Necessary Relations ——————— B. If-then Propositions

II.
System of Inferences

B. Explanation

Logical                 C. Institutional/technolog-
implications ——————————— ical entailments

III.
System of Decisions

C. Application              D. Instrumental Judgments
Intellectual ——————————— (since this, then, these
judgments                    proposals)

**Fig. 1.2.** Interrelationship between professional knowledge and skill

Although we have emphasized the client setting of the work of intervention, we must also underline as equally important the community setting. The city as setting is such a maze of involvements and requirements, of claims and counterclaims, of interests and disinterest, that some form of condensation of its manifold reality is essential (Bolan, 1980; Eisinger, 1971). The schematic in figure 1.3 is intended to be merely a short-hand device, a highly selective (and therefore inherently unsatisfactory) map in terms of which the intervention process from initiation to completion takes place. It exhibits both the limitations and possibilities by which both clients and professionals go about the management of intervention (Robinson, 1965).

### Clientage: Social Structure

Not all urban form givers are professionals employed by a client (Hall, 1968). Some are academic specialists whose interest is a function of their research specialization, shared in a variety of forums—legislative/administrative hearings, classroom or public lectures, books and articles. They may also serve as unpaid advisors and consultants to special in-

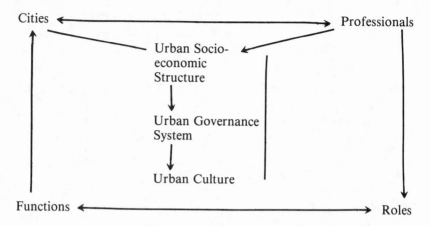

**Fig. 1.3.** Cities and professionals: the contexts of action

terest/public opinion associations, which is of course a type of clientage. They may also participate as members of some local community group or national interest association. However, the bulk of professionals actually engaged as participants in community intervention do so as part of a contractual arrangement with a client—perhaps as agents of their own business firm, perhaps as representatives of a public agency, perhaps as independents. It is important, therefore, to examine this client-professional relationship, called here simply clientage, which is defined by the Oxford Dictionary as "the relation of a client to his patron."

The word "patron" suggests something about the history and the sociology of clientage. In earlier periods the client worked for the patron, who was "bound," as the Oxford Dictionary says, "in return for certain services, to protect his client's life and interests." Later usages indicate a status and role shift, as in other Oxford entries: "One who employs the services of a legal advisor in matters of law"; and still later, the client as one "who employs the services of a professional or businessman in any branch of business, or for whom the latter acts in his professional capacity."

The history of the role of clientage, thus, shows a major shift: the professional is—theoretically, it must be pointed out—the agent of the client, thus a subordinate. However, reflecting the huge dependence the client may have, or feel, about the professional as a result of his attributed knowledge and skill (by which he protects and furthers the interests of the client), the professional may actually have some of the status values inherent in the old patrons.

Clientage is clearly, thus, an exchange relationship, one whose constituents historically have included Italian *condottieri* and merchants, kings and artists, lawyers and citizens. Contemporary professionals are relative newcomers to this ancient company of clientage. They enter clientage as professionals offering the client trained capacities (or, unhappily sometimes, trained incapacities) deriving from credentials of training and experience. It is nonetheless an exchange relationship: in social terms, it is a relationship of reciprocity in which knowledge-based services are exchanged for income.

The client and the professional bring to clientage different sets of relationships, commitments, backgrounds, and influences as significant components of the clienting process. These components of clienting are suggested in figure 1.4.

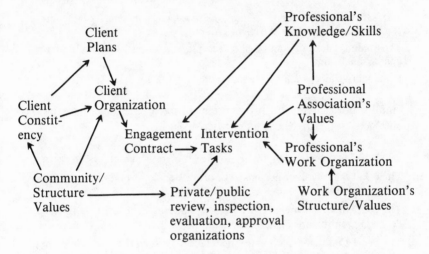

**Fig. 1.4.** Components of client-professional relationships

The actual establishment of clientage is a function of the client group's having a problem, present or future, for which it needs knowledge-based assistance of some sort. The kind of clientage that follows upon the client's recognition and statement of his problem and/or perceived opportunities is a function of:

The client group's status in the local community and in a professional community

Its economic and organizational resources

The complexity, size, clarity, definiteness (etc.) of its problem situation

Its previous experiences with clientage

The group and extra-group support for clientage

Its capacity to utilize the services of the professional

Its freedom from or its involvement in politicalization processes, both within and without client group, which affect the operation, direction, and utilization of clientage

The establishment of clientage is also affected by factors directly influencing the professional including:

His or her route to a given client relationship: his or her personal reputation for never having been wrong in the past (and therefore a good conservative bet); being "a good old boy"—or a known independent; possession of an armament-arium of shiny tools (e.g., computers); a network of established influentials that may be called upon as part of the politics of obligation, etc.

The satisfactoriness—completeness, clarity, precision, etc.—of the professional's contract with the client group

The ubiquity, dexterity, and general acceptability of his social/political/organizational skills

Personality traits as a professional and as a person

Finally, both client and professional bring to clientage a mythology about facts, some of whose elements consist in:

The belief that there is an answer to the problem which hinges on facts

The belief that there are persons—the professionals—who know or can get the facts

The belief that facts are all right; in fact, they may of course be all wrong, depending on the prevailing interpretation

The belief that there is a one-to-one relation between talent and integrity; time may show that this is not necessarily true

The belief that, in situations of contest, "facts" will make the difference, will indeed prevail

The belief that facts are strong enough to stand on their own feet (despite very well-known accounts in which "infirm" facts have indeed been "doctored")

The belief that the client's own sense of his problem situation is sufficient as well as necessary, or that it ought to be (but indeed often is not), and that in any case he is entitled by virtue of clientage to know "all the facts"

The list can be extended. But even a lengthier list could hardly add significantly to this statement of clientage: that clientage is an "interface" situation, fraught with complexities and perplexities, expectations and risks, rights and obligations. Like any interface, it is not always well known, or well managed (Rein, 1969).

### *Clientage: The Dual Agendas*

Professionals engaged in some kind of community intervention serving the purposes of urban form giving are, by virtue of clientage, agents of the client group. The dual nature of the professional role—obligations to the client as well as to the public organization and to public law—creates a complicated knot of relationships far from being easily unravelled (Aleshire; 1972; Damer and Hague, 1971; Rogers, 1967; Van Til and Van Til, 1970).

Perhaps the most succint way of getting at the agency character of clientage is to observe that the clienting process itself generates several kinds of agendas, all of them polarities (hence the term "dual agendas"), not all of which are spelled out, one may be sure, in the employment contract. Some of them are official, overt, precise, clear; others often remain murkily ambiguous, even unstated; sometimes they are untested and therefore become contested, with disturbing consequences.

Some of the dual agendas predate the actual employment of professionals in a given situation of community intervention: they represent polarities of attitudes and actions that professionals, by virtue of their training and experience, bring to the job. Other dual agendas of agency are specific and particular to the intervention action itself, and are in fact dimensions of the social interactions that inevitably go on between clients and professionals. The first group of dual agendas we may call "precontractual," the second, "contractual."

1. *Precontractual* dual agendas of agency represent the expectations, preferences, commitments and obligations that professionals acquire through the processes of their socialization as professionals. These agendas of agency in situations of community intervention include considerations of:

The distinction between the *sciences* and the *professions* as to the nature, uses, limitations, advancement of knowledge

The distinction between matters of *fact* and matters of *value*

The distinction between the *ethos of science* and the *ethos of action*—i.e., between the universalism, disinterestedness, and skepticism of science and the particularism, commitments, and fideism of action

The distinction between *professional* ethics, which tend to be abstract, general, and universal, and *situational* ethics, which require empirical, specific, particular, and flexible judgments, often without sufficient guidelines from professional ethics

The distinction between *academic* research, which may be pure, basic, objective, and abstract, and *practical* research, which may be selective, subjective, value-oriented and limited

The distinction between the *status* expectations of professionals, on the one hand, their *role* expectations in the management of a given task situation, on the other

TABLE 1.10

*Components of Professional Responsibility*

| SOURCES | NORMATIVE BEHAVIORS | SANCTIONS |
|---|---|---|
| *Professional* | Client allegiance; professional autonomy, knowledge/competence; guild loyalty | Ethical codes; traditions of the profession; contractual agreements; association structure controls |
| *Public* | Concern for the public welfare/interest; right of dissent; judicial appeal | Public administrative stipulations, regulations, safeguards, penalties; public opinion/sentiment |
| *Legislative* | Statutory mandates and constraints; mandatory impact assessment | Legislative/administrative sanctions; judicial sanctions |
| *Academic* | Integrity/advancement of science | Ethos of science; scientific/professional review, criticism, evaluation |

2. The *contractual* dual agendas of agency represent the expectations, preferences, commitments, and obligations that the professionals assume as part of their engagement in a given situation of community intervention. These agendas of agency include considerations of:

The distinction between the *client group's* perceptions of their needs and the *professionals'* perceptions

The distinction between the requirements and procedures of *service-oriented* intervention and *product-oriented* intervention

The distinction between *task-oriented* and *extratask* expectations and stipulations

The distinction between the limited and specified *methodology of action* and "the politics of civility," which one writer has called the activities of persuasion, bargaining, compromising, negotiating, influencing

The distinction between *advocacy* action in behalf of the client and *adversary* action directed at a client group's target or targets

The distinction between the directly *utilitarian* ethics of an intervention action and the related and *consequential* (often unanticipated) ethics of that action

It may be argued that the considerations of these dual agendas of agency are unfairly disproportionate and unbalanced in clientage. Correction of this imbalance is, many observers feel, one of the responsibilities of the professional associations, certainly of the intervening professionals, who must, as an aspect of their contractual arrangements, identify the distinctions listed above: in other words, literally educate the client. It is, unfortunately, not an option available to professionals in all intervention situations. The failure to educate clients and the frequent abuses of clientage have prompted increasing recourse to legislative mandates and administrative guidelines affecting both client and professional—in other words, the increasing public control of clientage through regulations, credentialing, licensing, review, and impact assessment. The pattern of professional responsibility in urban form giving has come to embrace a fairly wide range of components, as table 1.10 shows.

# REFERENCES

Aleshire, R. A.
  1972  "Power to the people: an assessment of the community action and model cities experience." Public Administration Review 32: 428–42.

Alexander, C.
  1966  Notes on the Synthesis of Form. Cambridge: Harvard University Press.

Alonso, W.
  1967  "The historic and the structural theories of urban form: their implications for urban renewal." Land Economics 40: 227–31.

Altschuler, A.
  1965  "The goals of comprehensive planning." Journal American Institute of Planners 31: 186–97.

Appleyard, D.
  1979  "The environment as social symbol." Journal American Institute of Planners 45: 143–57.

Argyris, C. and D. R. Schon
  1974  Theory in Practice. San Francisco: Jossey-Bass.

Artle, R.
  1963  "Public Policy and the Space-Economy of the City." Pp. 155–62 in L. Wingo, Jr. (ed.), Cities and Space. Baltimore: Johns Hopkins Press.

Banz, G.
  1970  Elements of Urban Form. New York: McGraw-Hill.

Barr, D. A.
  1972  "The professional urban planner." Journal American Institute of Planners 38: 155–59.

Bell, D.
  1973  The Coming of Post-Industrial Society. New York: Basic Books.

Paul Meadows

Beshers, J. M.
1962    Urban Social Structure. New York: Free Press.

Blumenfeld, H.
1949    "The theory of city form, past and present." Journal Society Architectural Historians 8: 7-16.

Bolan, R. S.
1967    "Emerging views of planning." Journal American Institute of Planners 33: 233-45.

1971    "The social relations of the planner." Journal American Institute of Planners 37: 386-96.

1980    "The practitioner as theorist: the phenomenology of the professional episode." Journal American Institute of Planners 46: 261-74.

Bolan, R. S. and R. L. Nuttall
1975    Urban Planning and Politics. Boston: D. C. Heath.

Burrows, L. G.
1979    Growth Management. Rutgers: Center for Urban Policy Research.

Catanese, A. J.
1974    Planners and Local Politics. Beverly Hills, Cal.: Sage.

Chapin, Jr., F. S.
1973    "Techniques for shaping urban growth." Journal American Institute of Planners 31: 76-87.

Crane, D.
1960    "The city symbolic." Journal American Institute of Planners 26: 280-301.

Dahinden, J.
1972    Urban Structures for the Future. New York: Praeger.

Damer, S. and C. Hague
1971    "Public participation in planning: a review." Town Planning Review 42: 217-32.

Davidoff, J.
1963    "Advocacy and pluralism in planning." Journal American Institute of Plans 31: 331-337.

Dyckman, J. W.
1969    "The practical uses of planning theory." Journal American Institute of Planners 35: 298-300.

Eisinger, P. K.
1971    "Control-sharing in the city." American Behavioral Scientist 15: 36-51.

Etzioni, A., ed.
1969    The Semi-Professions and Their Organization, New York: Free Press.

Foley, D. L.
1964    "An approach to metropolitan spatial structures." Pp. 21-78 in M. M. Webber (ed.), Explorations into Urban Structure. Philadelphia: University of Pennsylvania Press.

Form, W. H.
    1954    "The place of social structure in the determination of land use."
            Social Forces 32: 317–23.

Fosdick, D. E.
    1939    What is Liberty? A Study in Political Theory. New York: Harper.

Frankl, P.
    1968    Principles of Architectural History. Cambridge: M.I.T. Press.

Friedmann, J.
    1965    "The urban field as human habitat." Journal American Institute of
            Planners 31: 312–20.

    1972    "The spatial organization of power in the development of urban
            systems." Comparative Urban Research 1:2.

Fuchs, V. R.
    1968    The Service Economy. New York: Columbia University Press.

Galbraith, J. K.
    1967    The New Industrial State. Boston: Houghton Mifflin.

Ganz, A and T. O'Brien
    1973    "The city: sandbox, reservation or dynamo?" Public Policy 21:
            107–23.

Goode, W. J.
    1959    "Community within a community: the professions." American
            Sociological Review 22: 194–200.

    1969    "The theoretical limits of professionalization." In A. Etzioni, op.
            cit. chap. 6.

Grabow, S. and A. Grabow
    1973    "Foundations for a radical concept of planning." Journal American
            Institute of Planners 39: 106–14.

Gross, B. M.
    1971    "Planning in an era of revolution." Public Administration Review
            31: 259–97.

Gutnov, A. et al.
    1965    The Ideal Communist City. New York: G. Braziller.

Guttenberg, A. Z.
    1960    "Urban structure and urban growth." Journal American Institute of
            Planners 26: 104–110.

Hall, R. H.
    1968    "Professionalization and bureaucratization." American Sociolog-
            ical Review 33: 92–104.

Haar, C. M.
    1967    "The social control of urban space." Pp. 175–229 in L. Wingo, Jr.
            (ed.), Cities and Space. Baltimore: Johns Hopkins Press.

Harris, R.
    1965    "Urban development models: new tools for planners." Journal
            American Institute of Planners 31: 90–95.

Howe, E. and J. Kaufman
1979    "The ethics of contemporary american planners." Journal American Institute of Planners 45: 243–55.

Hunter, F.
1953    Community Power Structure. Chapel Hill: University of North Carolina Press.

James, Jr., F. J.
1974    "The city: sandbox, reservation or dynamo?" Public Policy 22: 39–51.

Johnson, T. J.
1972    Professions and Power. New York: Macmillan.

Kuper, H.
1972    "The language of sites in the politics of space." American Anthropologist 74: 411–25.

Kelman, S. et al.
1981    "Planning the planners." Social Policy 11: 46–50.

La Gory, M. and J. Pipkin
1981    Urban Social Space. Belmont, Calif.: Wadsworth.

Larson, M. S.
1977    The Rise of Professionalism: A Sociological Analysis. Berkeley: University of California Press.

Laumann, E. O. and F. U. Pappi
1973    "New directions in the study of community elites." American Sociological Review 38: 712–30.

Long, N.
1971    "The city as reservation." The Public Interest 25: 22–38.

Lovejoy, A. O.
1936    The Great Chain of Being. Cambridge: Harvard University Press.

Lynch, K.
1960    Image of the City. Cambridge: M.I.T. Press.

Mayer, R. R.
1972    "Social system models for planners." Journal American Institute of Planners 38: 130–39.

Meadows, P.
1948    The Culture of Industrial Man. Lincoln: University of Nebraska Press.

Moore, W. E.
1970    The Professions: Rules and Roles. New York: Russell Sage.

Mumford, L.
1961    The City in History. New York: Harcourt, Brace.

Noble, D. F.
1977    America by Design. New York: A. A. Knopf.

Pahl, R. E.
1970    "Whose City?" New Society 379.

Peattie, L. P.
 1968   "Reflections on advocacy planning." Journal American Institute of
        Planners 34: 80–88.

Passoneau, J. R.
 1965   "The emergence of city form." Pp. 9–27 in W. J. Hirsch (ed.), Ur-
        ban Life and Form. New York: Holt, Rinehart and Winston.

Petersen, W.
 1966   "On some meanings of 'Planning.' " Journal American Institute of
        Planners 32: 130–43.

Rapoport, A.
 1977   Human Aspects of Urban Form. New York: Pergamon.

Rein, M.
 1969   "Social planning: the search for legitimacy." Journal American In-
        stitute of Planners 35: 233–43.

Robinson, I. M.
 1965   "Beyond the middle-range planning bridge." Journal American In-
        stitute of Planners 31: 304–12.

Rogers, A.
 1967   "Theories of inter-urban spatial structure: a dissenting view." Land
        Economics 47: 108–11.

Rogers, D.
 1962   "Community political systems." Pp. 31–48 in B. E. Swanson (ed.),
        Current Trends in Comparative Community Studies. Kansas City,
        Mo.: Community Studies, Inc.

Salisbury, W.
 1964   "Urban politics: the new convergence of power." Journal of Politics
        26: 775–97.

Sjoberg, G.
 1960   The Pre-Industrial City. New York: Free Press.

Smith, M. P.
 1979   The City and Social Policy. New York: St. Martin's Press.

Smith, R. A.
 1976   "Community power and decision-making: a replication of Hawley."
        American Sociological Review 41: 691–703.

Solesbury, W.
 1974   Policy in Urban Planning. New York: Pergamon.

Spilhaus, A.
 1961   "The experimental city." Science 159: 710–15.

Sternlieb, G.
 1971   "The city as sandbox." The Public Interest 25: 14–21.

Suttles, G.
 1973   The Social Order of the Slum. Chicago: University of Chicago Press.

Tararkiewicz, W.
 1973   "Form in the history of esthetics." Dictionary of the History of
        Ideas, vol. 2: 216–25.

*Paul Meadows*

Thompson, D'Arcy
  1959  On Growth and Form, 2nd. ed.. Cambridge: Cambridge University Press.
Thompson, W.
  1974  "The city as a distorted price system." Pp. 74–86 in H. M. Hochman (ed.), The Urban Economy. New York: W. W. Norton.
Van Til, J. and S. B. Van Til
  1970  "Citizen participation in social policy: the end of the cycle?" Social Problems 17: 313–23.
Webber, M. M.
  1965  "The role of intelligence systems in urban-systems planning." Journal American Institute of Planners 31: 289–96.
Weber, M.
  1958  The City. Glencoe: Free Press.
Wheatley, C.
  1969  City as Symbol. London: Lewis.
Weingartner, R. H.
  1962  Experience and Culture: The Philosophy of Georg Simmel. Middletown, Conn.: Wesleyan University Press.
Yarmolinsky, A.
  1978  "What future for the professional in American society?" Daedalus 107: 159–75.
Znaniecki, F.
  (1940)  The Social Role of the Man of Knowledge. Chicago: Octagon
  1965   Books.

# 2 Emblem and Exception: The Historical Definition of the Architect's Professional Role

## MAGALI SARFATTI LARSON

*Fancy a painter unable to make pictures except when someone says to him: Paint now, paint this or that, and paint it thus and so. . . . Imagine this, and you will realize the architect's actual position and the contrast between his life and that of other artists. Of course, the difference . . . is the natural result of the fact that architecture is not an art pure and simple. . . . Its products . . . are useful objects made beautiful, and they cannot be spun out of the artist's brain, but must cost a great deal of money.*

Thus spoke Mariana Van Rensselaer in 1890 from the pages of the *North American Review*, in an exhortation addressed more to the "public" than to the "profession" for, indeed, she thought that "the public must learn to bear itself as intelligently and honorably as the profession does" (Van Rensselaer, 1972: 260, 268).

After decades of public derision of "architects' follies" and suspicion of both their probity and their competence, Mrs. Van Rensselaer's conviction may have surprised many of her readers. The 1890s, however, were times of general striving for status and economic position. In the multiethnic American scene, strategies of cultural defense or cultural dominance crisscrossed the broader lines of cleavage opened by class conflict.[1] Merging with Anglo-Protestant exclusiveness, self-declared professional elites aimed their exclusive strategies at effecting a linkage between the emergent educational system and the occupational structure.[2] Since 1857, the American Institute of Architects, a self-coopted group of "enlightened gentlemen" like most other early professional societies,

The author is grateful to the Design Arts Program of the National Endowment of the Arts for a fellowship (Grant No. 11–4213–093), and to Temple University for a study leave which together allowed her to do the research and to write this paper. Without the intellectual encouragement and practical support of Charles Larson, it could not have been written.

had joined the fray for professional reform, and its efforts seemed to be paying off in the 1890s. The numbers seeking formal education in the nine existing schools of architecture were still too few to provide a credential base for exclusive legislation; it was thus on the basis of jurisdiction—that is, on the scale and cost of the buildings reserved for "real" architects—that Illinois architects sought to establish their claims against "mere builders."[3] Theirs, indeed, was the first registration law for the practice of architecture in the United States; it passed in 1897, undoubtedly helped by the tremendous public impact of the Chicago World Exposition of 1893.[4] As a critic writing on architecture for an educated public, Mrs. Van Rensselaer was thus aligning herself on the side of these reformist efforts.

In this essay, I do not intend to follow the story of architectural professionalization in the United States. Using historical materials broadly, I will attempt to develop an argument that can be read as implicit in Mrs. Van Rensselaer's statement: the specificity of its products ties architecture to sponsorship, barring them from circulation in the special channels of the art and luxury markets. At the same time, this product specificity and the artistic component of its historical identity assign to architecture a special place in the credentialed labor markets characteristic of modern professionalism.

It is impossible to consider the specificity of architectural products in any but the most partial and simplistic way. Since the Greeks, architecture has inspired a ceaseless flow of writings, not only technical or critical, but philosophical, elegiac, and propagandist as well. I will therefore allude only to the components of architecture that are most relevant for understanding the changing social position of architects. After examining the constitution of their "classic" historical identity, I will argue that the great transformation, leading to the political and industrial revolutions of the late eighteenth century, "de-structured" this identity by the radical changes it brought to bear on the nature of its social supports.

My general interpretation is that the contradictions of the architectural function were impossible to reconcile in the historical forms and contexts in which they were given; attempts at resolution acquired therefore a principally ideological cast, as I will suggest by a brief reference to the modern movement of the 1920s and 1930s. In conclusion, I will review the special position of architecture among other professions and try to discern what in this historical situation appears to be, not exceptional, but emblematic of modern professionalism.

# PATRONS, ARCHITECTS, AND ARCHITECTURE:
# ELEMENTS OF THE HISTORICAL REPERTORY

Underlying conventional definitions of social roles are the material conditions of their practice. The first condition for the appearance of specialized economic roles is the existence of economic surplus, which must attain relatively high levels to allow the diversion of resources from subsistence to large-scale construction. The symbolic or monumental buildings that we traditionally regard as architecture imply, furthermore, that specialized occupations have developed to procure special materials from sometimes distant lands and to make special ornaments and features of the buildings. Monumental architecture presupposes the development of a productive agriculture that is associated with the beginnings of urban life: in Mesopotamia, large and elaborate temples date from the fifth millenium B.C., some two thousand years before the age of Egyptian pyramid building and some three thousand before Stonehenge.[5] The origins of architecture are sacred—religious or funerary; only much later, in the third millenium, did the royal palace appear beside the temple in the Sumerian city-states. The diversification of architectural types thus appears to depend on the relationship that exists between the divine power of the priests and the military-political power of the kings.

Because monumental construction was a function of power, a few Egyptian architects attained the highest ranks in the Pharaoh's service; but, as in earlier civilizations, architectural forms were part of the ritual and theological knowledge monopolized by the priesthood. The conception of the most important buildings was thus directly governed by what Weber calls the priests' "effective manipulation of charisma," in the service of the king's glory or of their own social power.[6] For the architect to gain a measure of the divine charisma, the *telos* and the *techne* of building had to merge; but it was, at best, a restricted and ambiguous path to immortality, for patrons dispersed charisma only to the smallest minority, who were thereby separated from the ranks of other builders. It was the patrons, as well, who defined the *telos*, the form and the function, of architecture.

In Greek cities, there were no kings. The differentiated functions of the *polis* admitted other buildings than the sanctuary to comparable dignity in the civic constellation. Through Rome and the Renaissance, Greece gives to Western architecture not only a classic past, but a parameter of perfection, the language of all but the Gothic transformations and revivals. There is more, perhaps: writing at the end of the first century B.C., Vitruvius discovers in the secular position attained by the

*51*

elite of Greek architects a means for the ennoblement of his calling. This means is a broad education in the liberal arts; it not only gives the architect membership in the cultivated intellectual circles of the *polis*, but gives an autonomy of sorts to the architectural function. The architect's knowledge, says Vitruvius, is expressed not only in design and construction, but also in theoretical writing. Here is what he recommends for the aspiring architect:

> Let him be educated, skillful with the pencil, instructed in geometry, know much history, have followed the philosophers with attention, understand music, have some knowledge of medicine, know the opinions of the jurists, and be acquainted with astronomy and the theory of the heavens. (Quoted by MacDonald [1977: 38-39]).

If the roots of Western architecture are formally and, one could say, ideologically Greek, then typologically, conceptually, and technically, they are Roman. For Siegfried Giedion, Roman achievements constitute the second space conception of architecture, centered on the majestic development of interior space. In Rome, we may venture to say, the relations between *telos* and *techne* are *decisively* reversed: from the barrel vaults of the sewers and the arches of the huge granaries before our era, to the supreme achievement of the Pantheon dome in the second century, Roman architecture develops by endowing "with symbolic meaning . . . forms previously employed only for utilitarian purposes. . . . Entirely practical structural forms are suddenly exalted. This even includes building materials. Roman concrete . . . was a prerequisite of all large scale architecture" (Giedion, 1971: 78).[7] Finally, the expansion and development of Roman architectural types express the unprecedented problems of administration faced by the Roman state and the functions it assumed on behalf of the urban masses: amphitheaters and public baths, diversified market complexes, water and transportation systems attest to a much more direct sociological kinship between Roman architecture and that of our own time than between the former and medieval Europe (Giedion, 1971: 179).

In the concern it reveals for the needs of the owners, Roman domestic architecture shows that a new role has emerged for the architect as the interpreter of individual needs. And next to the architect appears another new figure, destined to play an important part in Renaissance architecture and after, notably in seventeenth century England and in America (Wilton-Ely, 1977: 181-183; Ettlinger, 1977: 115-120): this is the figure of the private patron as amateur architect, a role that Hadrian, the architect of his own villa, developed to the fullest. The relationship between architects and emperors, in contrast to that between architects and private patrons, symbolizes the dual function that patronage provided Roman architects: the first is the spatial articulation of a private sphere of life; the second is the service of the state, as conceivers and administrators of civil and military works. The post-Renaissance development of the architectural profession moves between these two poles, private and public, which merge, of course, in the grandiose private programs of the absolute monarchs.

The Renaissance conferred upon architects a new social status. It may appear as a consecration of the process of social ascension by which master masons, from the thirteenth century onwards, had separated themselves from other craftsmen, overcoming the low social status that had befallen builders after the fall of Rome (Kostof, 1977: 59–60). The Italian Renaissance signaled a change in the repertory of practices and ideas from which architects could draw to influence the social definition of their role. It was more than just a change of emphasis. To understand its import, we must clarify the elements of analysis that have been implied until now: the kind of building we call architecture is not only defined in its essence by the relationship of *telos* and *techne*—conception and execution, symbolic intention and materialization—but also by the fact of patronage.[8] In certain historical situations, a special group of builders or exceptional individuals appear to mediate the "affinity" between elites and stylistic conventions.[9] For the sake of clarity, we call these builders "architects"; but, like all other builders, they were first of all *in control of the technique of building*. In the most ancient civilization that produced a monumental architecture, the special builders left us with no historical trace.[10] What features of the triangular relation of patronage appear, then, to have been favorable to the architect, allowing him, as it were, to insert himself between the *telos* and *techne* of building? Among the hypothetical answers, technology should come first. When it was novel or complex, the architect appears to have been better able to enter his name in the historical record, to claim a measure of authorship from the patron. The scale of a project, which commands the complexity of the division of labor, is the organizational dimension of the technological base.[11]

The second tentative answer lies in the nature of power and in the differentiation of its functions. Obviously, the preconditions for architectural development and the multiplication of types are relative prosperity and relative peace; the *nature* of political power, however, is significantly related to the social definition of the architect's role. When kings are gods, architecture is sacred and only building for the king *is* architecture; no one, indeed, however noble or powerful, can imitate a god. When power requires confirmation, architecture is less a manifestation of sacred power than its symbolic legitimation; moreover, when it is possible to contest political power or gain access to it, architecture becomes a field of rivalry and emulation and an *expression of social stratification*. This does not give autonomy to the architect in his relation to patrons, but it greatly expands the possibilities and the definition of his role.

Third, related to the complexity of social stratification and therefore to the political and economic base, are the emergence of intellectual specialists and the development of theory for theory's sake. C. S. Smith (1971) has persuasively argued that technological inventions have been tied to aesthetic intentions in the decorative arts since the remotest antiquity. With oversimplification, it may be said, however, that *theorizing* about technology and about aesthetics was a Greek invention. To circles of artists and intellectuals, architects could address *their own theoretical writings*; thus, in a manner that Vitruvius nostalgically tried to imitate, architects had found a direct, though utterly symbolic, way of appropriating the *telos* of building. Conversely, it could be argued that in the fourteenth century crisis of the feudal order, the social distance between master masons and intellectuals was a factor that still kept late medieval architects among the crafts.

Thus, three avenues of collective social upgrading may theoretically be distinguished in the historical repertory of architecture: one is preeminently based on the development and mastery of technology; the other passes through the service of the state; finally, the "intellectual" avenue aims directly at the symbolic and aesthetic dimensions of architecture. These three ways overlap and coexist, and in each historical situation some alternatives are either actually closed or ideologically rejected, or both. From this point of view, the significance of the Italian Renaissance lies in the architect's resolute effort to appropriate the *telos* of architecture by intellectual and almost *purely stylistic* means. The Renaissance, as Ackerman (1970: 151–52) says, "is one of the few eras in which a new style emerges without the assistance of any remarkable structural innovation."

Indeed, the development of the Gothic provided the fifteenth and sixteenth centuries not only with remarkable constructional means but also with a labor force whose technical competence has not since been equaled. Like patrons in the early Middle Ages, Renaissance architects only needed to know "what was technically possible in order to command to the executants" (Du Colombier, 1973: 68, my trans.). All the important architects of the Italian Renaissance came to architecture, often late in life, from apprenticeships in sculpture, painting, or another decorative art, and the only ones who rose from the building trades were Antonio da Sangallo the Younger (whose uncles were celebrated architects and military engineers, and, one generation later, Andrea Palladio (Ackerman, 1970; Ettlinger, 1977: 016; Zerner, 1977: 138). Due, in part, to the weakness of the building trades, Italian and in particular Tuscan designers were able to seize the new chances offered by patronage. The distance they established between themselves and their technical base was never to be closed in the subsequent evolution of the architect's role. Only the barest outline of this process can be sketched here.

The Renaissance is the transitional time "between the relaxation of the medieval social hierarchy and the consolidation of a modern one." The emergence of relatively emancipated artists and intellectuals belongs, thus, to the brief historical phase "in which the decadence of the old chivalric nobility is achieved and the installation of the new absolutist strata of courtiers" is only beginning (Elias, 1973: 105, my trans.). In the Italian city-states, the ascension of new ruling groups during the four-teenth and fifteenth centuries produced, at the top of the social hierar-chy, a social and cultural space into which "free intellectual workers" could move (Hauser, II, 1960: 52 ff.). This "space" was artificially maintained by the plurality of competing and warring political centers, even as plutocracy and despotism sank deep roots. In the larger historical context, the two major, interdependent lines of force are clearly discerni-ble: the world economy, within which begins the "great transformation," the release of the economy from its social and moral shell; and the absolutist state, with growing powers of domination and coordination. In terms of these forces, sixteenth-century Italy was already peripheral; it was, one could say, the new Greece, to be culturally imitated and plundered by many new Romes.

In itself, the stylistic revolution was not sufficient to redefine the ar-chitect's role. Even as the new style of individual patronage innovated by Cosimo de Medici was spreading, and even after the mature works of Brunelleschi, Alberti, and Michelozzo, the architect was ignored in historical records: "the convention of considering the patron as the author of a building" was tenacious (Jenkins, 1970: 168, 169). The social ascension of artists and architects was made possible by the political economy of patronage, but it was directly prompted *by an ideology* that reflected the conscious elitism of an emancipated minority of educated men. Out of neo-Platonist and Pythagorean ideas, permeated by elements of the ancient Hermetic tradition, the humanists fashioned a ra-tionalist vision of man and nature, from which modern science was to emerge in the seventeenth century (Rattansi, 1972; Santillana, 1969).[12]

The interpretation of Vitruvius and the analysis of Roman antiquities nourished the rediscovery of the Orders. Since Alberti, the latter were in-tegrated with a theory of harmonic proportions that made of architecture the spatial materialization of mathematical "truths" (Wittkower, 1971: 67–69 and pts. 3 and 4; Argan, 1970). Once it had been thus endowed with theoretical foundations, *architecture had to be studied*. The

Renaissance architect, precisely because he was "less trained in the technique and less organized in the practice of his calling than any of his contemporaries in the arts," was the first to break the bonds of the medieval shop system and to claim for architecture the liberal status of a profession (Ackerman, 1970: 171). By the late sixteenth century, with the first academies, architects began once again to write about practice for other architects.[13]

Though architects consolidated their new rights over the conception of design, their new autonomy was nevertheless—and inevitably—bound by different patronage situations; it resulted, therefore, in different elaborations of the classic code, in which the problem of giving adequate aesthetic expression to different *types* of building was to become increasingly and overwhelmingly important for theorists and practitioners (Vidler, 1977).[14] The context and structure of patronage relationships, as they determine the architects' practice, influence the solutions the latter bring to constructional and aesthetic problems. Thus, the Baroque "contradiction" between dynamic, "open" forms and rigid formalism is partly one between individual buildings and the relentless axiality of large-scale projects. The architects' consolidation of their role as artists-conceivers depends, thus, on much more than just the stylistic complexity of individual buildings in the age of Baroque: their gains come in the wake of the increasing concentration of power and conspicuous consumption in the court and the capital city. The principles of political concentration and centralization are interrelated: they are taxation, the standing army, and the state's bureaucracy.

Not surprisingly, the passage of the aspiring profession into an increasingly academic and official phase began in France, where the monarchy's control over its administration of buildings had been developed through three centuries (Moulin, 1973: 13–36; Rosenfeld, 1977). As Louis XIV's phenomenal building programs (Versailles, in particular) set new standards of magnifiscence for other courts to emulate, so did the Royal Academy of Architecture, founded by Colbert in 1671, serve as model for the organization and control of the architectural-urbanist function by other "enlightened" monarchs. While the Royal Administration of Buildings was reorganized along clearly bureaucratic lines by Colbert, the Royal Academy integrated the Renaissance "charismatic" conception of the architect-as-artist with an *ancien regime* variant of the civil servant's role. First-class academicians were barred, in principle, from profitable entrepreneurship, even on the king's own projects; so were, after 1690, the "sworn experts" who, unlike the academicians, could buy their office (Moulin, 1973: 21).

Under royal patronage, in France, a minority of "magistrates of the beautiful" (Moulin, 1973: 21) could thus affirm its autonomous control over the symbolic and aesthetic dimension of architecture, and routinize it in the academy. Its entrenchment in the esoteric allowed the Academy to survive the Revolution: dissolved in 1793, it reappeared shortly thereafter as the Fine Arts section of the new Institute of France, endowed with a teaching function. With the creation of the *Ecole des Beaux Arts* in 1819, the *ancien régime* conception of the architect's role as a specialist in the elaboration of stylistic codes was carried into the modern period. The lasting institutionalization of architectural "charisma" defined the architect's modern function; even in the age of absolutism, however, it had not made him immune to the challenges of other builders.

In his masterful synthesis of urban history, Lewis Mumford emphasizes the fundamental part played by the evolution of warfare in shaping the postmedieval city (Mumford, 1961: 356–71). Indirectly, it was also to shape the social definition of the architect's role. In changing the fundamentals of war from defense to assault, artillery imposed a new and multiple burden on urban populations: the building of far more complex systems of fortification, more difficult to design and far more expensive to build or modify than the old. In the initial phases, association with the noble art of warfare gave architects another resource in the conquest of social status: almost all the greatest architects of the sixteenth century could claim expertise in military design (Zerner, 1977: 138–9). But, by the seventeenth, the military engineer had become a specialized role, and in the second part of the sixteenth century, the separation of mathematics from geometry had signaled that the architect's abandonment of *techne* for *telos* was irreversible.[15]

Another set of powerful determinants of the architectural function came from the transformation of the city *prior* to industrial capitalism. The new fortifications became militarily useless before the nineteenth century, but they had had lasting effects on the fabric of growing cities: held in a "strait-jacket" by their walls and the no-man's-land beyond, capital cities were already overcrowded in the sixteenth century. The pressure for urban land begen to push up its value—and the height of poor people's housing as well (Mumford, 1961: 358–9). However, before the triumph of capitalism, the full effects of urban disorder and speculation could be physically contained by the baroque conception of spatial order (Mumford, 1961: chs. 12, 13).

The baroque city plan reflected both the practical and the symbolic needs of absolute power and the social structure it supported: the wide, straight, well-paved streets lent themselves to the display and the rapid deployment of armies, and to the use of artillery against external and, increasingly, internal enemies. At the same time, the city of the seventeenth and eighteenth centuries was an ideal theater for the palatial style of life and the daily dramatization of conspicuous consumption (Mumford, 1961: ch. 13).

The ancient relationship of monumental architecture to the city had always contained a conflictive core, for the urban environment is at the same time the context, the field of social resistance, *and the denial* of the architect's function: the anonymous architecture of the city is, indeed, "a monument to the production of competing builders," a constant reminder that architects cannot monopolize architecture (Lipstadt, 1979: 29). In the seventeenth and eighteenth centuries, the differentiation of both patronage and building types polarized this relationship between two extremes: the individual building, "submerged in urban tissue," and the regimented holistic environments built for the state by baroque planners—exact physical counterparts of the social polarization of the architect's role between private and public patronage.

Given their specialization in the *telos* of building, it was in stylistic, symbolic, and eminently *theoretical* terms that eighteenth century architects began to confront the crisis in their relations to construction and to the city. As the engineer consolidated his domain upon utility, architecture was increasingly reduced to ornamentation; but its scenographic freedom from constraints irremediably destroyed the stylistic remnants of the classic order. Archeological and historical exacitude—to which many architects turned in earnest—only exaggerated the conflict between imagination and historical "truth," as well as the controversy about which ancient style was the best model. In turn, the impossibility of stylistic unity inspired new scientific and functionalist approaches to the problem of finding symbolic expressions for the diversity of architectural types. Finally, for the problem of the city, three major kinds of "solution" had already emerged: the speculator's gridiron plan, improved transportation (which was the basic principle of the engineering approach to planning), and utopian schemes, proposed mainly by architects. The last of these were either total monumental conceptions, the integration of nature within the city, the rejection of the city through escape or reconstruction, or finally, an uneasy reconciliation of those three themes (Frampton, 1980; Tafuri, 1979: chs. 1-5). In the next two centuries, the contradictions of the architect's historical role became impossible to contain. The parts of these old-new utopian solutions that were, in fact, attempted, were almost inevitably doomed either to defeat or to isolation. In capitalist society, the motor of urban development is, indeed, the frequent alliance between the "speculator's" motives and the "engineer's" methods—between the one's exclusive concern with profit and the other's "bull-dozing habit of mind" (Mumford, 1961: 387).

Before we consider the disintegration of the architect's function under industrial capitalism and the strategies of reintegration that were attempted, the delineation of his historical role must be reviewed in order to grasp the strategic possibilities it already contains.

First, the possibility of architecture as a specialized occupational role depends on two sets of social relationships: the relationship between the *telos* and the *techne* of building, which becomes *social* as soon as the execution of construction is separated from its commission; and, second, the social relationship between patrons (or commissioners), who always define the *functions* of building, and "architects." As is commonly understood, the latter mediate between commissioners and executants.

Second, the *techne* is the competence of the executants, applied to the materials of construction. It is organized either by the executants themselves and their own delegates, or by the patrons and *their* delegates, among whom were the architects, at least before the Renaissance's redefinition of their role. The Renaissance may be schematically considered as a social and ideological turning point in the architect's history: architects used the possibilities of patronage to separate form from function in the *telos* of building and to appropriate conception, or the translation of function into form. The organization of construction was thus, in principle, more widely open than before to *other* delegates of the patron, or to other mediators.

Third, the appropriation of the aesthetic and symbolic part of the *telos* may be seen as a "dialectic of charisma." Architectural objects are special among other buildings because they embody charisma in one form or another. The historical appropriation of charisma by priests and warlords includes architecture among its means; appropriation implies that *the charisma of architecture is denied to the executants*. In turn, architects "borrow" the charisma of architecture from the church or the king. The sociopolitical and ideological configuration of the Renaissance allows artists to turn the tables on their patrons. Because the works of man are venerated as necessary to the manifestation of the divine, architects may now, *in ideology*, confer upon their patrons the charisma of their work. Architectural charisma has been reconstituted through the divinization of art, that is to say, through the specific ideological contribution of humanist intellectuals. The "dialectic of charisma" is now displaced to the theoretical and abstract level of *discourse about architecture*. Intellectual publics allow architects to appropriate the so-called pure *telos* of architecture autonomously and directly, but the appropriation is only symbolic, since the environment is affected only by what is built.

Fourth, in practice (and, until the emancipation of intellectual strata, in ideology as well) architects have been especially dependent on the patronage ;of church and state. Virtually until modern times, only they had the resources to commission monumental architecture. More important, monumentality can most visibly make an architectural object into an exemplar, by its scale, its site, its public uses. However, the multiplication of *private* patrons ties "artistic charisma" to *social stratification*; since charisma does not admit the logic of market consumption, it disappears, to become *mere status symbol*. The historical "dialectic of charisma" disappears in the increasing privatization of architects' production, although traces of the "dialectic" might perhaps be found in the ideology that surrounds public architectural works. In short, the artistic component of the architect's social role tends to lose its historical aura and becomes a status ideology.

Fifth, as all art objects become status symbols and all but architectural objects become commodities, art is desacralized. Artists' strategies, however, tend to affirm the special nature of their role and their production by denying their economic dimension (Bourdieu, 1977; 1979). On the other hand, the *special* support that humanist intellectuals had lent to the social elevation (and the economic valorization!) of artistic creativity is greatly restricted, if not cancelled, by the emergence of science as a competing intellectual activity, which vies for supremacy. After the fifteenth century, the links scientists seek to establish between theory and practice pass through technology, not art. The strategic approaches that architects could follow and combine are clear: they could assert the superiority of art over technology and mere utility; they could attempt to appropriate the legitimacy science confers on intellectual production; in practice, they could also attempt to become their own patrons, which is unlikely, given the deontology of professions; or they could attempt to become, once again, the directors of *techne*. Needless to say, this last approach was increasingly blocked by the engineer.

### Disintegration of the Architectural Function and Strategies of Reintegration

The problem the profession of architecture faced in the nineteenth century was not unique. However, the specific nature of the architectural object and the specific constraints that weigh on its production gave a distinctive cast to the multiple efforts applied to its resolution.[16] I have argued elsewhere (Larson, 1977) that the professionalization movements that followed the industrial revolution are best understood in terms of two interrelated lines of analysis. These lines of interpretation are seen to underlie the organizational efforts or projects, which express the individual and collective ambitions of the professional reformers and their constituencies. The first project is that of defining and controlling a protected market for professional services, which must be distinguished from competing services and convincingly defended in terms of the competence they represent and the benefits they can bring. The second project, inseparable from the first, is that of attaching social status and concrete economic and social privileges to the fact of membership in the corporate professional category. It is easy to see that the dual project necessarily points toward institutional means for self-definition and corporate defense, and toward the need to find adequate ideological legitimations for the monopolistic exclusion of competitors. The chief source of institutional support is the state, and the process of professionalization was different where the state promoted the establishment of professional corporations from what it was, most notably in the Anglo-Saxon countries, where the autonomous initiatives of professional reformers had to court the support of the state. In either case, however, professionalization both requires and implies the creation of relatively standardized competencies, so that services can be adequately distinguished from alternatives. Formal education and credentialism are the means for this task. A scientific base of knowledge helps the standardization of competencies and the exclusion of untrained competitors, while it gives a most powerful justification for the monopoly of competence. However, because science did not have either the clear links with practical technologies or the undisputed cognitive hegemony it has acquired in our time, professional reformers had to rely on moral, social, and political arguments as much as they did on practical demonstrations, when these could be mustered.

David Watkin (1977) argues that an unprecedented theoretical tradition had been developing since the eighteenth century in architectural writing. Its tendency was to "explain architecture away as a consequence or manifestation of something else" other than stylistic convention. The three predominant explanations that appeared in the nineteenth century were couched in terms of "religion, sociology and politics"; in terms of the Zeitgeist, or spirit of the times"; and in terms of rational or technical arguments (Watkin, 1977). A current of "romantic populism," emphasizing the vernacular as "an expression of the collective unconscious," crisscrossed the other three, gaining momentum in countries that were concerned with the national identity of their architecture. As Watkin notes, they were not theories *of* architecture: they could be used, and indeed they were, "to justify totally different architectural styles," although rational-technical theories came to predominate in the modern movement.

The background of the new theoretical tradition has already been mentioned: since the mid-eighteenth century, the multiplication of building types and of stylistic variations had greatly weakened the classical tradition. If it was difficult then to know with intuitive certainty what a building should look like, and the introduction of new materials—iron, glass, and, later, concrete—and new construction techniques destroyed forever the traditional arguments for the supremacy of the classic. As Benevolo points out, "The persistence of classical forms . . . now had to be justified in another way," either by seeking the "eternal laws" of beautiful form, or by appealing to the moral sentiments these forms evoked, or, simply, because they were there and they were traditional (Benevolo, 1971, vol. 1: 27 ff.).

Whatever explanation was chosen, the existence of an academy, charged by the state with the defense of official taste and the elaboration of architectural doctrine, was an undeniable institutional advantage for the defense of a chosen style. This advantage explains the head start that the French architectural profession appears to have had over other professional movements. Indeed, the continued support of the state preserved the influence of the academy on the corporate organization of the profession while, in turn, the presence of the academy influenced even its challengers and detractors. Moreover, in the latter part of the century, the classic coherence that it seemed to have protected emphasized the role of the Ecole des Beaux-Arts as both a professional and a stylistic model. It was followed even where, as in the United States, there was no centralized state apparatus and no corporate link between professional training and practice to sustain it. While the French model highlights the crucial role of the state in the constitution of professional monopolies, it also reveals the limits of professionalization in the case of architecture.

First of all, the French academy based the defense of its professional prerogatives on the traditional identity of the architect-as-artist: his function, however, was not protected, and it had been reduced to the mere embellishment of buildings constructed by means of different principles than those the academy upheld. If, through most of the nineteenth century, the Ecole des Beaux-Arts resisted all attempts to reform and modernize its purely theoretical teaching, it is in part because the practical teaching of construction had already been preempted by the rival schools of engineering. Preferred by the state even before Napoleon I, the corps of engineers did not even need to defend themselves from the attacks waged against their "miserable aesthetics" by a large part of the architectural press (Lipstadt, 1979).[17]

Second, the control that the academy exercised over the architectural profession was not based on the training it offered, but on its integral connection with the most prestigious forms of public architectural employment. As Charton, the author of the *Dictionnaire des Professions*, stated in 1880, "Architecture is not taught at the Ecole des Beaux-Arts; it only ascertains, by means of competitions, the progress [students] have made outside itself" (quoted by Lipstadt, 1979: 46, my trans.). Paradoxically, in a school so frankly oriented toward "pure art" and the theoretical, the possibility of elaborating the theoretical base of professional training was limited: apprenticeship was the real basis of training, and the dependence on the *ateliers* implies that the only effective mechanism of professional unification was the exclusivism of the controlling elite. Real as the exclusivism was, it was a severely restricted mechanism of control.[18]

The third point is an obvious consequence of the second: the built-in sociological limits of the state-academy model suggest that the situation of most French architects was not different, in fact, from that of their colleagues in other countries. The most significant way in which the Ecole influenced the profession was possibly not its defense of stylistic orthodoxy, but the frustration it bequeathed to its less successful products: the official rewards the Ecole could offer were available only to a small minority. The majority of its former students could not even accede to the second ranks of state employment; they were therefore destined to the sharp competitiveness of private practice, with no other protection—until the institution of a diploma in 1867—than the ambiguous title of "former student of the Ecole des Beaux-Arts;" or else they could work for others, among whom speculative builders were the largest source of employment (Lipstadt, 1979: 53 ff.). Thus, one possible difference between the average French architect and his counterpart elsewhere is that the former was barred from the only kind of professional practice the Ecole had taught him to respect; for him, the hope of public commissions from the state was far more unrealistic than it was in other countries. Below the official academic elite, itself stratified, French architects followed informally the strategy formalized by their English and American colleagues in the first stages of their professionalization: networks of "gentlemen" who shared not only a calling, but social status and social conventions, modeled after those of their most desirable clients, had declared themselves "the best of the profession"; on the basis, they struggled to transform social exclusivism into an institutional definition of the professional role (Kaye, 1960; Wright, 1980).

When superiority of competence could not be objectively demonstrated—as was true not only of architecture, but also of medicine before bacteriology, and of the Protestant ministry—shared cultural conventions directly defined the contents of the special knowledge professionals claimed to have. But the affluent and "genteel" clienteles of capitalist societies were culturally divided and no more culturally homogeneous in Europe than they were in America. In medicine, upper-class allegiances were divided between homeopaths and "regular" physicians; in architecture, private clients could choose among a variety of equally respectable, though not equally fashionable, styles. In the second half of the nineteenth century, public architecture received some outside help, even where there was no state-academic influence: associationism, as the predominant aesthetic theory, contributed to link building types to prevalent styles—Gothic for churches and Anglo-Saxon universities, Neoclassic for state buildings, banks and, most impressively, colonial cities.[19] In residential architecture, however, even if architects had been able to agree on a style as their professional trademark, they could have no hopes of imposing it as a dominant convention: as did the engineer in large-scale utilitarian projects, the contractor and the speculative builder reigned supreme in small-scale commercial and residential building. Before we consider how the architectural profession confronted the second and most threatening of its rivals in the field of building, we must pause to make an important, though perhaps obvious, point.

In capitalist societies, the economic imperatives of the market are the ultimate determinants of all social and political options. Following Karl Polanyi (1956), I would argue that the "radical utopia" of the self-regulating market evokes by its devastating effects on society a variety of defensive countermovements, defined by the particular historical formation and period in which they arise. All social countermovements have a hidden or overt economic dimension by the very fact that they attack the naked operation of market forces, and by this very fact they all have a political dimension. Beyond a purely local sphere, the attempts to counteract the market are addressed to the state; their success or failure is the outcome of political struggle. This allows us to identify a specifically modern component in the situation of nineteenth century architecture: besides technological innovation, the most important change lies, as often before in history, in the nature of political power. Capitalism and representative democracy are the new political factors that both limit and direct the intervention of the state in the built environment. As Polanyi points out, "*laissez faire* was enforced by the state . . . it was not the method to achieve a thing, it was the thing to be achieved" (Polanyi, 1956: 139-40). In the heyday of *laissez faire*, the state was still called upon to subsidize the public works that industrial capitalists needed but could not or would not pay for; similarly, it was called upon to provide for the collective social needs that the capitalist class would not meet. Only in the second half of the nineteenth century was popular housing finally recognized as a pressing need (Benevolo, 1971, vol. 1: 84-85).

Capitalism, however, demanded the defeat of baroque town planning. Under the absolute power of kings, building and planning—proceeding in concert—assured the unity of the whole; but planning now tended to become a statement, at times compelling, of the government's intentions. Indeed, the power of the state over real estate interests could only go as far as the configuration of political forces allowed.[20] First among these forces is the direct influence of private economic interests on the state (which have no reason to resist the building of sewers, water systems, transportation networks, or schools and parks). The second is the political and moral force of the groups who oppose capitalist power in general (the labor movement and socialist parties) or oppose particular capitalist abuses. The third force is the initiative and powers vested by tradition and by the form of government in the state apparatus. In any case, the limitations of state power mean that the architect tends to lose his traditional role of urban planner. Under capitalism, his opportunities to create order at any other level are limited and depend on the balance struck by state and market principles of social organization. This is true, in fact, for the practice and even the theory of every modern profession, which become, thus, *political* in a new sense and at many levels.[21]

To return, thus, to where we began: in capitalist societies, the definition of professional roles and the alternatives open to professionals depend neither on the state nor on the market, considered separately, but on the control of the one over the other and on the manner in which state control has been achieved—this is the political crucible in which professional differences among nations are formed. In the professions that create forms or technical devices, the political process that partly determines them and the political content of their practice are buried in the factual objectivity of their products; yet, in no other case are professional products more publicly or permanently exhibited.

Architects had traditionally designed the mansions of the rich. Since the Enlightenment, both utopian concerns and the fashion of idyllic cottages and rural retreats had given architectural dignity to the design of small houses (Rykwert, 1972; Wright, 1980: 52). Although the country home remains to this day a showcase of architectural ideas and innovations, it could not provide a model of urban residence for the expanding class of those not quite so rich. For them, nineteenth century architects designed grouped houses—antecedents for which had appeared in the residential squares of Paris and, above all, London since the seventeenth century (Mumford, 1961: 395-99)—and, increasingly, apartment houses in the fasion of Haussmann's Paris (Lipstadt, 1977) or in imitation of Vienna's *Ringstrasse* (Schorske, 1980: 54 ff.). In America, the suburban home—distinct from the palatial extravagances of multimillionaires— was a prevalent type through which architects could hope to guide the taste of their contemporaries. The hopes architects expressed, that they could influence the wider public's taste through their elegant achievements, seem either totally naive or painfully oblivious of the class reality on which their materialization depended. Yet, as we shall see, the popular as well as the specialist press could indeed diffuse ideas and model solutions to the broadest number. It is true that the problem of popular housing was largely untouched until our century, except in schemes that were acknowledgedly utopian. Collective solutions to the major problems of the built environment were in fact the purview of municipal engineers and public health reformers, not of residential builders, or even less of designers (Benevolo, I, 1971: chs. 2–3; Mumford, 1961: ch. 15). The middle-class dwelling was, on the other hand, a more promising channel of influence, especially when and where the availability of land and transportation allowed urban dwellers to escape in large numbers toward the ambiguous haven of the suburbs. There, indeed, in the new middle-class home, was an embodied symbol of the aspirations and fears of the new society; and it was a symbol that designers could help to shape through the plan, the forms and, importantly, the fixtures of the house. To understand how the market, traditional moral codes, and different aesthetic conceptions converged upon the middle-class home – and with the most power and significance on the American home—we must make a brief digression.

The logic of the market destroyed the cultural hegemony of aristocratic conventions; status striving alone could not direct the insatiable thirst for novel commodities on which consumers' markets rely. The ugliness and the poor quality of machine-made products for the bourgeois home became a public concern after the first world exhibition was held in London in 1851. Intelligent and farsighted civil servants, including its organizer, Henry Cole, emphasized the national interest in their campaigns for the reform of the applied arts. The universal exhibitions were, indeed, enormously popular showcases of national pride and intense competition: there were displayed, in the amazing new structures erected by engineers or in the architects' fantastic scenographies, the proliferation of merchandise, the increasingly varied products of the building industry, and the miracles of the machine (Benevolo, I, 1961: 96–118; Frampton, 1973; Giedion, 1948; Wright, 1980: 84 ff.). One point of view, consistently advocated by the *Deutscher Werkbund*, which Muthesius founded in 1907, was that only standardization could recreate order and this only if machine production was integrated with the artists' concerns. A deeper point of view, of which the former was one end point, was the immensely popular view of John Ruskin.[22] Linking morality and the redeeming virtues of the nuclear family to the very details of domestic architecture was one of Ruskin's signal achievements. It untapped a source of powerful ideological themes from which vast sectors of the public could abstract simple solutions to deep-seated fears and fix them on the house—a vision which in America, at least, it seemed possible to achieve and to own.

In America, the tremendous vigor of the house-building industry, together with the mechanical pattern adopted early by speculative planners, made "standardization a reality" underneath "the profuse ornaments of late nineteenth century houses,'' most fixtures of which were of course mass produced, in an endless variety of form and color (Wright, 1980: 26, 86 ff.). The forces that shaped the American middle-class house before the onset of architectural modernism are masterfully analyzed by Gwendolyn Wright (1980). In the vast domestic market of the United States, ideology played a role inferior only to that of the country's unique economic power. Thus, a vision of society which persistently submerged class divisions into the dream of a universal middle class could plausibly hold forth the promise of home ownership to industrial workers and immigrant masses. The image of the model home as the sign of respectability and middle-class status did not seem a totally unapproachable dream. What made the United States atypical, from a European standpoint, made its middle-class house archetypal: the rationalization and the mechanization of the moderately priced house are as American as collective popular housing in German and Austrian in the first part of our century (Giedion, 1948; Handlin, 1979; Wright, 1980).

Until the 1870s, there was little that could distinguish the architects' designs from those of the builders of better homes, if not the size and the quality of materials (see Wright, 1980: 22–23, 55 ff.). The fact that the former's clients were wealthier was not one to boast about, at least not in the Midwest. The builders were ready to denounce in the name of the populist and nationalist sentiment the elitism of architects who served the rich, imitated Europe, and pretended to keep the name of "architect" to themselves (Wright, 1980: 73 ff.). The dilemma was impossible to solve unless the traditional definition of the architect's role, imported from Europe and, more specifically, from the Ecole des Beaux-Arts by its former students, was entirely recast. From that narrow platform, professional architects had to acknowledge, in all but rhetoric, that builders and prototype designers dominated the aesthetics of the larger residential market. Indeed, in deploring their shoddy designs and the vulgarity of middle-class taste, elite architects only multiplied the number of their ideological adversaries: "builders, moderate-income clients, reform-minded women and building workers" (Wright, 1980: 74). How could they claim to be the true creators of the nation's architecture in the face of this array? One solution was to leave this mediocre domain and look elsewhere for the commissions that could manifest the best in the architect's vocation.

This is what the elite of the profession had generally done anyway: the public building, monumental in scale, was the true expression of what architects could do for the built environment of America. In Chicago, the particular pressures of rebuilding after the fire, the economic imperatives of the clients, and the concentration and rationalization of the building-materials industry combined with sheer engineering and architectural boldness to make the architects' self-defense into a prophetic reality. A major symbol of twentieth century architecture, as new in type as it was in stylistic expression, was born in the tall office buildings of the 1880s and 1890s.[23] The early aesthetics of the American skyscraper were to be rediscovered in the 1920s and 1930s, this time through the lens of European modernism.[24]

In the interlude, the triumph of academic classicism visibly aligned the symbolism of American monumental architecture with a traditional and formalistic interpretation of the teachings of the French Beaux-Arts. The impetus, as is known, came once again from Chicago. Its Columbian World Fair of 1893, the beginning year of a most severe depression, was, in the words of the eminent critic Montgomery Schuyler, "the most integral, the most extensive, the most illusive piece of scenic architecture that has ever been seen" (Schuyler, 1964: 291). It gave American architects a charismatic hero, in the person of its director of works, a man recognized in his time as a "resourceful and indomitable planner, the real Titan, the emperor of architecture, 'Uncle Dan Burnham' " (Burchard and Bush-Brown, 1966: 234).[25] At the Fair, American elite architects discovered the power and grandeur of baroque uniformity, and it was fitting, indeed, that Burnham should be the man who renewed L'Enfant's plan for Washington to make it a modern capital for a world power. "Make no little plans," Burnham said, "for they have no magic to stir man's blood" (quoted by Hines [1979: xvii]). The White City was a stirring experience for millions of Americans. The Fair did for the dominant wing of the profession what nothing else had yet done: it gave them a public identity on which to found their professional ambitions.

Thus, for American architects, a great stride in professionalization was made in a manner that confirmed all the traditional aspects of the European historical definition.[26] This included an intimate association with the elite, only accentuated by the collapse of the house-building industry in the depression of the 1890s; a taste for the monumental, which increasingly turned them to the government as the patron of patrons; in the private sector, the discovery of the corporation as the new *mecenas*; stylistically, a solution to eclecticism that tended to concentrate their attention on formal exercises in the classic mode, breaking the close association with structural engineering that had been the hallmark of the Chicago skyscraper style; and, in education, a cognitive base standardized far beyond anything Europe had produced, though based neither on theory nor on modern constructional principles, but on *academic style*. At this level, indeed, American architecture had become more French than France; as in Europe, the modernists would have their foil. If, however, modernism had to be imported to America in the 1930s, it was in large part because the architectural elite of the 1890s had been so successful. As credentialed expertise became the central theme of progressive reform, planning and rebuilding became one symbol of reform that magnified the architect's role and gave architectural professionalization a great incentive to proceed.

Architecture as well as progressivism had more than one side, however. It is true that, under the impact of the bitter class conflict of the 1880s and 1890s, the emphasis on centralized efficiency and scientific expert guidance increasingly superseded the current of democratic participation. But expertise, even architectural expertise, could be applied to urgent social problems. In the English garden city movement, in the planning laws and experiments conducted in England, in Holland, in Germany, in Austria, and even in Spain and the city of Lyons, Europe had other models to offer than those Burnham had chosen for his Chicago plan of 1909 with conspicuous neglect of popular housing (Benevolo, I, 1971: chs. 10, 11; Hines, 1979: ch. 14). In New York, few architects could emulate I. N. Phelps Stokes, turning both great wealth and a Beaux-Arts education into instruments of enlightened tenement reform (Lubove, 1964); but many in New York and elsewhere could place their expertise in the service of the settlement movement or of the many governmental and public agencies spawned by the progressive crusade for municipal reform (Davis, 1967; Lubove, 1962). The depression of the 1890s further moved architects to bring their interest in housing and their new ideas about domestic architecture to the forums provided by the reform movement (Brooks, 1972; Eaton, 1969; Wright, 1980: chs. 7–9). "In fact," says Wright,

> one motivation architects had for joining these organizations was an expanded search for private commissions. Yet, they were exploring architectural ideas then current *outside* their profession, discussing something very different from universal principles of beauty (1980: 222).

What they discussed, often with persistent ambivalence toward professional reorientation, was profoundly marked by the multifaceted influence of the women's movement. Better housing and the transformation of community through transformed home life were powerful themes in both the crusade for women's rights and progressivism at large. Popular women's journals became champions in this crusade, to which progressive social scientists and home economists added a voice from the universities. The focus on the model home and on rational home making emphasized physical design. As the initial thrust of egalitarian populism and enlarged democracy became blurred, the various interests of professional and middle-class reformers converged on a new image of moderate-cost housing. Not only at the level of the public city center, but at the level of the neighborhood, too, American architects were veering toward the social-planning function.[27] In different ways, American architecture had articulated both traditional and new responses to the problems of the industrial city. In 1922, Le Corbusier, in a country devastated by war, issued one of the signal cries of modernism: "Architecture or Revolution. Revolution can be avoided" (Le Corbusier, 1970: 169). In different ways, the cry had already been heard for decades by architects on both sides of the Atlantic.

The practice, the ideology, and the aesthetics of architectural modernism were resolutely based on machine production and industrial design. Thus, in a very real way, the modern movement was based—unavoidably and often unwillingly—on the ancient architectural denial of the executants' competence. Most notably in America, the vigorous struggle of the skilled building workers against the destruction of their skills had been defeated by industrial concentration and social repression before the turn of the century (Wright, 1980: ch. 6). In the new capitalist class structure, both in Europe and the United States, the professionalization movement had assured architects of positions that were always securely located in the middle class. Cutting across the internal stratification of the profession was the major difference among architectural commissions: domestic and monumental or, in empirical terms, housing and public buildings. This difference was already materialized in new architectural types, which absorbed and clearly expressed the insoluble contradictions and conflicts of the new capitalist era: the skyscraper, the suburban middle-class home, the *cite ouvriere*, the large housing project, and the superficially sanitized factory. In addressing the problems of finding modern aesthetic and symbolic expressions for these types, architects were obliged to confront the giant corporation, the industrial working class, the "new" middle class and, increasingly, the new functions of the capitalist state. The elements to be confronted and the methods of confrontation were differently combined in each country, although architectural responses necessarily reflected the contradictions of the architect's own social position.

### Modernism as a Professional Ideology: A Tentative Conclusion

A central theme has guided our journey through the long opposition between building, as that which anyone can do, and architecture, as that which only architects do. The historical constitution of the architect's social role condemned him to live this opposition, not as a matter of fact or an element of his specialized identity, but as a growing and insoluble conflict. The architect's function as a "conceptual" agent in special areas of the built environment could never be a *directive* one; yet, the illusion was and is tenacious, even though it lives today only as a frustrated and nostalgic ideology of total aesthetic control. It could arise because, *as buildings*, architectural objects are symbols of such great and immediate power. In the public domain, they are unavoidably present, and in the private, they are ubiquitous and indispensable. The illusion of "total aesthetic control" was nourished, moreover, by the historical association of the architect's role with the absolute power of the state and the cultural hegemony of the court over the classes that could provide patronage.[28]

As the nineteenth century advanced, the market expanded into new areas of social life, at the same time that it was controlled with different and not always incompatible intentions. The mandate, of the *ancien régime* to act upon the built environment was revised, though never obliterated; it was vested in new building types which served the old social functions, radically transformed and isolated from each other by the separation that capitalism effects between work and life, between public and private domains. The construction of department stores, railway stations, factories, exhibition halls, museums, hospitals, theaters, schools, universities—not to mention the varieties of planned housing—meant that architects' architecture could become directly relevant to larger sectors of society than ever before in history. Yet, wherever architects turned, they faced resistance to their ambitions and deep contradictions between the new opportunities and their inherited identity: the rivalry with engineers, the conflict with speculative builders, the rejection or indifference of the state, the arrogance or the conservatism of rich patrons, the status striving of the not-so-rich, the resentment of the middle class, the class antagonism of the workers, the rebellion or the contempt of other artists (including architects), the impossibility of imposing order on the city, their own insecurities as constructors or creators of style—the list need not be continued.

No single role could possibly have contained all these contradictory tensions nor confronted all these challenges. Increasingly, the historical definition of the architect as the organizer of construction and the conceiver of its form and symbolism tended to disintegrate. The pieces were taken over by different occupations which either were professions or, in many cases, tended to professionalize; within architecture itself, some of the lines of fracture coincided with the stratification effected by the types of commission. In general, the determination came from the increasing specialization of the built environment into antinomic components or dimensions: inside-outside, built space-green space; private-public, domestic-monumental, buildings-streets, work place-dwelling, housing-home, and, of course, structure-appearance and utilitarian-architectural.

Of the Vitruvian definition—architecture is the combination of "firmness, commodity and delight"—only delight was not claimed by credentialed or otherwise expert rivals. To concentrate on the aesthetic dimension of building was therefore an inevitable strategic choice. Not only has the formal definition of the role survived, the powerful ideological counterattack of modernist architecture has given a new face to the twentieth century cityscape, and a recognizable expression to social and political power. To architects, it has given an uncomfortable but undeniable social presence, if nothing else, as the scapegoats for what that power has wrought.

Rivers of ink have flowed to establish the principles of the modern movement, to propagate them—in manifestoes more effective by incantation than by analytical power—and to denounce them, then and now. I will limit myself to a few summary interpretations. The problems modernists confronted were prefigured in the preceding discussion: new building technologies, housing needs, new building types, urban problems, and the anachronistic tastes of academic elites and meretricious builders. Modernism was a movement of architectural minorities, but its radical opposition to the academy compelled them to speak prophetically, for the yet unborn majority of architects. At all the levels of its ideological and aesthetic battle, modernism sought an integration of architecture within the mainstream of industrial production. As Reyner Banham (1960) has argued, the aesthetics were derived from an *image* of machine-made objects; the premise of the ideology was the notion that art would conquer mass production by fusing with it.

Four key factors summarize the conditions in which architectural modernism was born as a movement with recognizable coherence: the existence of artistic *avant-gardes* in European capitals; the devastating experience of the first world war; the response to socialism and to the revolutionary movements of the brief interwar period; and the demonstration of immense productivity that large-scale industry had provided during the war effort.

The *avant-gardes* are linked to the academy. The academic system had, in fact, opened careers in the arts. The multiplication of aspiring artists made it impossible for the "academic machine" to absorb either innovators or innovations. Thus, in the second half of the nineteenth century, the permanent exclusion of a growing number of artists gave to the *Bohème* a semi-institutional existence: physically and economically close to the proletariat, yet ideologically and culturally different in that the *Bohème* functioned on the attractive premise that youth is a social, not a biological age. The ideology of the "unknown genius" and the diversity which the vast art market encouraged, however poorly, made this acceptable social limbo into a "reserve army" of the arts. Out of it, art dealers and critics were to fashion a substitute organization for the failing academic system (White and White, 1965: chs. 2-4). Since architects defined themselves primarily as artists, they had a natural place in these circles, although the realities of their practice pulled them away from the cultural entrepreneurs of the antiestablishment, toward the social connections that could give them work. The ideology of architectural modernism in Europe was thus sustained by this inclusive antiacademic *intelligentsia*, which gravitated toward a diffuse support for political radicalism. In the early period, the phenomenon of the architect known by his publications and not by his buildings is characteristic of countries with a strong academy, like France and Italy.

Secondly, the war had represented an experience of national mobilization and total devastation, most acutely in France and Germany. Catherine Bauer Wurster (1963) has perceptively remarked that the idea of a standardized "existence minimum" and of austere simplicity—symbolized by Mies van der Rohe's famous dictum "Less is More"—spoke exactly for a time of scarcity and fear. Even before the 1930s, social conflicts and fear of the Russian revolution fueled both the demand for housing and work and the state's response through public work programs. In Austria, in Holland, and most notably in Germany, new architects were given a chance by socialist mayors. In Germany, moreover, modernist architects participated in the Werkbund, which gave them a platform, commissions, and resources. The German experiment started, therefore, with the strongest institutional and organizational base; it was also the most brutally interrupted by Nazi repression. The vengeful return to neoclassic imperial architecture under Hitler clearly acknowledged the association of modern architecture with socialism under the Weimar Republic (Campbell, 1978; Lane, 1968).

Modernism in twentieth century architecture represented as total a departure from the immediate past as the Renaissance was from the Gothic. In both cases, ideology and aesthetic theory were the guiding principles, just as in both cases a social redefinition of the architect's role was being attempted. Only modernism, however, depended closely on new technologies of construction and new materials. Because the latter were means to achieve ideological goals, the buildings themselves must be considered ideological statements as much as the ceaseless flow of rhetorical discourse.

The first ideological intention was to destroy academicism and to bury both the academy and the historical allusions in which its stylistic identity was based. The new aesthetic was thus radically and purposefully antihistorical. Revolutionaries, however, must claim to speak for the largest number and to the largest number; the new architecture was thus presented as world-architecture and as an architecture for the masses. Its language appealed only to universals: Science, Geometry, Technology, the Machine, the Spirit of the Age, the Masses and, above all and always, Architecture. The generality of the language reiterated the universal antihistorical message: regionalism, nationality, traditionalism, particularism were abolished. As befitted a truly cosmopolitan elite of radical artist-intelletuals, Art was the new homeland proposed to all, but even artists needed architects in order to give unified meaning to the world order of science and the machine. The creation of a new future required active collaboration from the state, whenever the declarations veered toward anything resembling implementation.

The best way to make a surgical cut with the worn-out symbolism of the past was to demolish "artistically valueless monuments as well as all buildings whose artistic value is out of proportion to the value of their materials which could be put to other uses" (Conrads, 1970: 45). The best possible substitute for demolition (accomplished by the war, though not where it was needed) was to abolish the *signifiers* of the past—above all, ornament, denounced since Loos's famous pamphlet of 1908 as "crime," as "wasted labor power and wasted health," as a sad evolutionary lag (Conrads, 1970: 19–24). What would be left? Pure, efficient, useful Form, the embodiment of Function. Function—an image, not a concept—summarized all the mixed strands of the movement's ideology, for it could be invoked, and it was, in the organic-biological sense as much as in mathematical or in economic-utilitarian terms.

The machine, in Le Corbusier's poetic abstraction, was the source of all honest form and the guiding principle of organization for the built environment: "The house is a machine for living" just as "the town is a working tool" (Conrads, 1970: 60, 89). Inefficient and worn-out tools are replaced. The architect addresses directly the "businessmen, bankers and merchants," whose eyes do not see that they, indeed, are responsible for "creating throughout the whole world this accumulation of very beautiful things in which economic laws reign supreme, and mathematical exactness is joined to daring and imagination" (Le Corbusier, 1970: 22). The new architecture is, according to Le Corbusier, as much for the businessmen, bankers, and merchants as it is for "the various classes of workers" who "no longer have dwellings adapted to their needs" (Le Corbusier, 1970: 14). To resolve the antinomy between work and life, the new architecture would bring to the whole environment the "admirable order that reigns in the interior of markets and workshops," and "has dictated the structure of machines and governs their movements and conditions the gestures of each gang of workmen" (Le Corbusier, 1970: 52).

The social implications are too obvious to be even mentioned; they need not be taken too seriously, however, for they were not references to society but to aesthetic ideology. It is important to note, however, that the realizations of modernism, in abolishing all past stylistic signifiers, equated the new style with the *types* of objects that inspired the new forms: in Le Corbusier's inconography, the steamship, the locomotive, "the American grain elevators and *factories*, the magnificent first fruits of the new age" (Le Corbusier, 1970: 33; my italics). By association, the new architecture was indeed attempting to bridge the opposition between buildings where people work and buildings where they live, between utilitarian structures and architecture. Needless to say, few users approved of the result.

The antinomies of the built environment were confronted in other aspects as well. The new technologies and the new materials freed construction from load-bearing walls. The possibility of designing continuous spaces and "dematerialized" glass walls was vehemently seized by modernist architects for, as they repeated, it abolished the antinomy between outside and inside. The anonymous looks of mass-produced materials abolished even the symbolic traces of the executants' work: indeed, all the architectural object signified was the dominant conception of the form giver. It was, in this sense, a perfect ideological expression of monopolized expertise.

The theoretical complexities and obscurities by which the modern movement attempted to justify its aesthetic revolution gave architecture a rightful place among *academic* disciplines. There were now an esoteric language and esoteric meanings to elucidate. It would be unjust not to mention, however, that one of the lasting revolutions it accomplished was in the *practice* of academic teaching. While Le Corbusier appealed to the Renaissance fusion of art and incipient science into geometry, Gropius and the Bauhaus appealed to the pre-Renaissance union of all the artistic crafts (Gropius, 1965, 1968; Banham, 1960; Conrads, 1970: 46–53, 95–97). The principle of "designing from zero" was carried over to the design of industrial objects, partially achieving the ideological fusion with machine production and, more importantly, habituating the public to the new forms through mass consumption. When Gropius came to Harvard in 1937, the revolutionary principles of the new architecture and the new teaching came full circle: they had not revolutionized life, although they had appreciably changed its environment, but they had accomplished a revolution in the academic base of the profession (Jordy, 1964).

Architecture is an exceptional profession because it cannot, by definition, establish a monopoly; unlike other older professions, it does not succeed in establishing jurisdiction against either professional competitors or lay resistance. Its artistic component, however, need not seem exceptional. In the cultural situation of our time it is simply easier to resist and challenge than a demonstrably scientific base, such as medicine and engineering can claim, or an expertise ultimately based on the state's coercive powers, such as that possessed by lawyers. In all cases, expertise is established and justified by ideological persuasion and ritualization of uncertainty. What distinguishes architecture, therefore, is that cultural plurality is permissible in the arts, but not in science or in the law.

Thus, in its professional weakness and in its uncertain professional trajectory, architecture also reveals features common to all professionalization movements. The sphere of knowledge is abstracted from everyday life, and thereafter appropriated by specialists, who continue the abstracting process by their theoretical elaboration and the social authority vested in their roles. That the appropriation is resisted and the justifying ideologies are rejected by the layman is clearer in the case of architecture, because its products are not *functionally* different from nonarchitectural products; the superfluousness of its expertise can therefore always be invoked.

Tentatively, it may also be said that architects claim expertise in global terms in a domain too complex to be directed by a single function; the specialization process, which tends to disintegrate the theoretical unity of any profession, is, here, aggravated by the independent development of technology and by the external, largely economic, factors that "specialize" the built environment. Finally, architecture never escapes the initial relationship of patronage to create a controlled market. Its dependence on wealthy and powerful sponsors, be they private or public, is simply more accentuated than in other professions, which were able to *use* sponsorship for their project of market control. The architectural profession can thus be seen as a stark reminder that market-based professionalization in capitalist societies is a complex, though *subordinate* and *transient* phenomenon.

## NOTES

1. The interpretation of late nineteenth-century American society has produced an enormous literature. A few useful titles are Burton Bledstein, *The Culture of Professionalism*, New York, 1976; Paul Boyer, *Urban Masses and Moral Order in America, 1820–1920*, Cambridge, Mass., 1978; Samuel Haber, *Efficiency and Uplift*, Chicago, 1964; Richard Hofstadter, *The Age of Reform*, New York, 1955; Edwin T. Layton, Jr., *The Revolt of the Engineers*, Cleveland, 1971; Robert, Wiebe *The Search for Order, 1877–1920*, New York, 1967; and Gwendolyn Wright (1980).

2. On this point, see Larson (1977) and the different interpretation by Collins (1979) which deals more closely with American cultural pluralism than my own.

3. See Arthur Clason Weatherhead, *The History of Collegiate Education in Architecture in the U.S.*, Los Angeles, 1941, and Wright (1980: 332 fn. 30).

4. I discuss the White City briefly in the following pages; see note 25 below, and Hines (1979: 4–5) for a very complete historical account.

5. A useful summary of Mesopotamian urban history for the layman is given by Ruth Whitehouse, in *The First Cities*, New York, 1977. From a sophisticated architectural point of view, see Siegfried Giedion, *The Eternal Present, II: The Beginnings of Architecture*, New York, 1963.

6. Thus, "when Akhenaten founded his own religion, based on a form of solar monotheism, he had to train architects personally since there was no written tradition for the temples required by the new faith" (Kostof, 1977: 5). On the transformation of interior space in Mesopotamian temples following the consolidation of kingship, see Giedion (1971: 70).

7. The Roman constructional revolution rests on the development of the arch, the vault, and the dome, as well as on its materials: among these, concrete was not to be used again practically until the late nineteenth century (Giedion, 1971: 69, 259). More abstract, but perhaps even more important historically, is the Roman emphasis on *axiality* in urban design; the axial cross organizes the gridiron plan of Roman cities, superseding the Greek emphasis on "group design," which sought flexible spatial articulations between the volumes of free-standing buildings (Giedion: 1971, 9–10, 76).

8. Major problems must necessarily be ignored: first is the problem of the connections that may be discovered between cycles of economic development and phases of efflorescence or stagnation in nonutilitarian and artistic production. For a not too satisfactory interpretation, see Vytautas Kavolis, "Economic correlates of artistic creativity," *American Journal of Sociology*, November 1964. A second major problem that is ignored is that of the privileged relationships or "affinities" between segments of the ruling class and particular art styles in a given period.

9. For suggestive, though by no means conclusive, solutions to the problem of affinities, see Max Weber, "Religious Rejections of the World and their Directions," in Hans Gerth and C. W. Mills, *From Max Weber*, New York, 1958; Raymond Williams, *Marxism and Literature*, Oxford, 1977; and Jean Paul Sartre, *Questions de Methode*, Paris, 1967.

10. In Mesopotamia, the power of the kings arising in competition with that of the priests, tended to subsume under the king's name all the manifestations of building. Summaries of historical research do not report other examples of *individual* achievement, however (Whitehouse, *First Cities*).

11. Two qualifications must immediately be added: one is that the historical "dialectic of names," the patron's and the architect's, is based on expropriation. "Who built the seven gates of Thebes? asks Bertolt Brecht's worker, "The books are filled with names of kings . . ." (Brecht, 1959: 109). The patron, in fact and symbol, the architect in symbol only, appropriate the work of the real, *anonymous* producers. The other, related qualification is that individual social ascension for exceptional achievements is almost always possible, especially if the achievement adds to the glory of the monarch, as military victories and monuments do. Individual rewards, however, do not change the social defintion of the role, unless the exceptional architect remains sociologically connected to the occupational category, as the medieval master mason may have been in the free masons' guild. There is a fine line between exceptional architects whose renown is fully defined by architectural achievement and those who become great *because* of architecture, but *as* high-ranking servants of king or deity.

12. In the humanists' vision, the glorification of human creations was attuned

to both the triumphant mood of the new dynasts and the social ambitions of the artists. The veneration of art works for their own sake transformed the social reality of patronage and talent into a new ideological relationship: in the "symbiosis of greatness" of which we have such clear examples in the Italian sixteenth century and in the Counter Reformation (for instance, on the relationship between Pope Urban VIII and Bernini, see Haskell [1963: 36-37, 117-118]), the ideology of creative genius was a novel ingredient. To some extent, it protected the autonomy of the artist and it could be invoked by the not so great; it also enhanced the greatness of patrons, harnessing the "divine" aspect of creativity to their political and symbolic needs.

13. On the architectural treatises of the sixteenth century, see Zerner (1977: 149-154); Wittkower (1971: 62-69), 122-22); Rosenfeld (1977: 169-170). In France, where building guilds were much more powerful than in Italy, architectural writing could be an offensive move in a real conflict. See Zerner (1977: 125, 131 ff.) for a discussion of Philibert Delorme's attack on builders who were not, in his view, architects, in 1567. On the importance of publication for architects, see Lipstadt (1979: 41 ff.).

14. Palladio's architecture, destined for such lasting influence in the Anglo-Saxon world, is a most interesting case. The interpretation offered by G. C. Argan (1970) conflicts to some extent with that of Wittkower (1971), considered to be definitive. The empiricism Argan ascribes to Palladio's architecture "fits" with the latter's "professionalism," expressed in a work the main achievements of which are *"The Four Books of Architecture*, the villas, and exquisitely scenographic additions to the cityscapes of Venice and Vicenza. For Argan, earlier Renaissance architecture participated in a "weltanschauung" seeking to show "the truth of the supreme laws of the universe." Palladio's abstract classicism is different, "professionally" conscious of perspective as a mere technique, rather than a system of nature. Classicism here is pure image, says Argan, it becomes the culture "of a privileged and enlightened class." This transformation agrees with the position of Palladio's patrons: urban authorities in the context of declining Venetian power, and provincial landowning nobles, too provincial and too cultivated to follow stylistic fashion; hence the long Venetian resistance to Baroque penetration.

15. The exhibition *Potere e Spazio*, organized by Franco Borsi as part of the region-wide exhibition of the European Council for the Arts, "Florence and the Tuscany of the Medici in 16th Century Europe" (Spring and Summer 1980) was an almost inexhaustible source of detailed information and insights on this transitional period.

16. The most respected histories of modern architecture are Benevolo (1971), which I find most useful from a sociological point of view; Giedion (1973); Nikolaus Pevsner, *Pioneers of Modern Design*, London, 1960; Bruno Zevi, *Storia dell'Architettura Moderna*, Torino, 1961. Older but extremely detailed and interesting is Henry-Russell Hitchcock (1958). More recent examples are Frampton (1980) and Jencks (1976). For the U.S., see, in particular, Jordy (1976)

17. It has been argued that the survival of the classic approach in French architecture, through Perret and Garnier to Le Corbusier's *theories*, is due to the influence of J. L. N. Durand's teachings at the Ecole Polytechnique in the first part of the nineteenth century. Constructional rationalism tended to adopt the classic elements as the simplest and the most habitual to provide "suitable and economic" solutions. Another style would have done just as well: the Gothic, in fact, was the most obvious competitor, and it was extolled as such by Viollet le

Duc (Banham, 1960: 14–43; Benevolo, I, 1971: 3–37, 52–60). In what concerns training, academic architects often modeled their professional ambitions on the engineering corps of Ponts et Chaussees (the royal school of Ponts et Chaussees had been founded in 1747 and survived the Revolution); as a means toward the coveted status of the civil service engineer, they requested the formation of a ministry of architecture. The academy's detractors, on the other hand, from Cesar Daly to Le Corbusier, often found inspiration in the training of French engineers and even in their practical aesthetics (Lipstadt, 1979; Le Corbusier, 1970).

18. Students prepared themselves for the admission contest in the *atelier* of one of the members of the faculty, himself a winner of the coveted Grand Prix. As Lipstadt (1979: 51–52) notes, the *ateliers* developed such distinctive styles of drawing that the anonymous entries in the competitions could be easily recognized; the "dissident" *atelier* of Henri Labrouste was ostracized in this manner.) In the *ateliers*, the students learned through practice, helping senior students in their competitions and preparing themselves for their own: while they were held to enter a prescribed number of contests, they could also fail and try them over and over again before the limit of age thirty. The summit was the Grand Prix, which guaranteed to the laureates not only a period of study at the French Academy in Rome, but also, on returning, the position of "architects of the state," inspectors of works, expert consultants for the government, and, perhaps one day, members of the Academy of Fine Arts. Public commissions were either the direct purview of this official elite of civil servants or influenced by them, as members of juries or experts (Chafee, 1977; Draper, 1977; Lipstadt, 1979).

19. The associationism of the Gothic revivalists—most notably Pugin and Ruskin—belongs to Watkin's first category of explanation: aesthetic objects were considered as "signifiers of moral and social laws," which "evoked memories and emotions associated with that image through one's earlier education" (Wright, 1980: 51 ff.).

20. Wren's attempt to rebuild London according to baroque principles after the fire of 1670 was already "foiled by tenacious mercantile habits and jealous property rights" (Mumford, 1961: 386). Mumford attributes the failure of L'Enfant's Washington plan to the lack of control over public land: L'Enfant "overlooked the fact that he himself could not build the city he had planned, nor had the political leaders of his generation that power" (1961: 407). Conversely, the planning of the new Vienna could be controlled by the state because it owned "a sufficient area of public land in places relevant to the transformation of the town" (Benevolo, I, 1971: 84; Schorske, 1980: ch. 2). Thanks to the enormous profitability of the improvements and the exceptional powers of the executive under Napoleon III, Haussmann could keep partial control on his grandiose plan: while he did not even attempt, after a while, to curb speculation and could not prevent the privatization of what had been developed, he did prevent the total subversion of his scheme by private interests (Benevolo, I, 1971: 67–85).

21. On the political practice of other professions, see Luc Boltanski, *Prime Education et Morale de Classe*, Paris, 1977, on social workers and school teachers; Jacques Donzelot, *The Policing of Families*, New York, 1979, on psychologists and psychiatrists; Michel Foucault, *The Birth of the Clinic*, London, 1973, on medicine; and David F. Noble, *America by Design*, New York, 1979, on engineering. Professionalization movements are attempts to subtract certain areas of social life from the naked operation of market forces—self-interested, since they tend toward the corporate regulation of competition, and

disinterested at the same time, insofar as they propose a noneconomic vision of social needs. The totally self-interested movement of large-scale industry to regulate competition by eliminating competitors is also an attempt to protect profit against market uncertainty, although it is not intended to protect anything but profit.

22. On the *Deutscher Werkbund*, see Joan Campbell's (1978) excellent study. We cannot account here for the complex development of the Arts and Crafts Movement, but the differences between the origins and the following are worth noting briefly: from Ruskin's principles, William Morris derived a pointed rejection of machine production, not only because shoddy ornament was used to disguise the poor quality of the products, but chiefly because the mechanization of labor degraded the workers and destroyed their skills. The practical imperatives of his business imposed mechanized textile production on Morris, while the craft processes he favored condemned him to serve the elite public he detested. As he was to write: "Little by little I was driven to the conclusion that all these uglinesses are but the outward expression of the innate moral baseness into which we are forced by our present form of society, and that it is futile to deal with it from the outside" (Quoted by Benevolo, I, 1971: 181). As socialists, Morris and his followers were deeply concerned with working-class housing. It was left to his followers to carry what Morris had begun to realize to its logical conclusion: only by influencing *industrial* production could they hope to influence the quality of *mass* consumption; this, however, changed the movement's inspiration from production to consumption, from the causes of "barbarism" to the "vulgarities of civilization." See Gillian Naylor, *The Arts and Crafts Movement*, London, 1971, and Robert J. Clark, ed., *The Arts and Crafts Movement in the United States*, Princeton, N.J., 1972.

23. The literature on the Chicago skyscraper is voluminous. It is, first of all, treated in all the histories of modern architecture: Benevolo (I, 1971: 8); Burchard and Bush-Brown (1966); Jordy (III, 1976: ch. 1); and Giedion (1973 V). More specifically, see Carl Condit's authoritative work, *The Chicago School of Architecture*, Chicago, 1964; Hugh Dalzier Duncan, *Culture and Democracy*, Totowa, N.J., 1965; Hines (1979); and Mark Peisch, *The Chicago School of Architecture: Early Followers of Sullivan and Wright*, London, 1964. For a keen contemporary appreciation, see Schuyler (1964: pt. III).

24. The first manifestation of modernism in American skyscraper architecture (modernism European style, that is) was George Howe's significant PSFS building in Philadelphia, finished in 1931, as was the Empire State Building. Jordy (1976) compares them in vol. IV, ch. 1–2. On Howe, see Robert Stern's excellent biography, *George Howe*, New Haven, Conn.: Yale University Press, 1975.

25. On the White City, visited by twenty-one and a half million people, see Hines (1979: chs. 4–6) and Burchard and Bush-Brown (1966: pt. III) for the atmosphere of the period. See Schuyler (1964: 275–302) for an excellent contemporary analysis. On the domination of Eastern architects over Burnham, see Hugh Dalziel Duncan, *Culture and Democracy*, and Dimitri Tselos, "The Chicago Fair and the Myth of the Lost Cause," *Journal of the Society of Architectural Historians*, Dec. 1967. The main proponents of the "lost cause" version were Louis Sullivan, in *Autobiography of an Idea*, and Frank Lloyd Wright in his biography of Sullivan, *The Genius and the Mobocracy*; their objectivity may be doubted.

26. In the years following the Chicago Exhibition, formal education increasingly became a requirement for the draftsmen who would be architects: of the

twenty-eight programs in architecture founded before World War I, all but 7 were founded after the Columbian World Fair. Curriculum and methods of teaching were either directly controlled by "imported" French architects or dominated by Beaux-Arts programs. The Society of Beaux-Arts Architects, founded by former students of the Ecole, in New York, in 1893, became in 1916 the Beaux Arts Institute of Design, whose programs and awards dominated the teaching of architecture in America until the late 1930s. French teachers founded many of the major departments of architecture in American universities. The BAID programs—coupled with the Paris and Rome prizes it instituted—brought to American architectural teaching such standardization that the arrival of the " 'modern style' really took the character of a . . . palace revolution." See Draper and Joseph Esherick's personal *memoire* in Kostof (1977). See also Robert Stern, *George Howe.*

27. In the settlement movement of the 1890s, Wright already detects a growing conviction that the best home for the urban poor was in the suburbs: simple, standardized, but dignified and decent single-family houses (Wright, 1980: 114–22). By the 1920s, this image had been successfully extended to the middle class in the "studied simplicity" of an "architecture of visible health." With the standardization and also the prefabrication of the modest dwelling, reformers of all stripes then turned their attention to the planning of whole communities in the suburbs (Wright, 1980: chs. 8–9; Mumford, 1961: ch. 16; Mumford, 1972: pt. VI).

28. This royal road of architectural influence was not closed by industrial capitalism. But it should be noted that even in the most authoritarian regimes and in the most planned of cities, building always escapes the compass of architecture. Furthermore, if we conceive of the latter not as that which architects do, but as a vernacular art in which everyone engages, as he or she arranges the environment of his or her everyday life (Scruton, 1979: 16), the architectural function can even escape the domination of mass consumption.

# REFERENCES

Ackerman, J. S.
    1970    "Architectural practice in the Italian Renaissance." Chap. 7 in Gilbert, 1970, op. cit.

Argan, G. C.
    1970    "The importance of Sanmicheli in the formation of Palladio." Chap. 8 in Gilbert, 1970, op. cit.

Banham, R.
    1960    Theory and Design in the First Machine Age. New York: Praeger.

Benevolo, L.
    1971    History of Modern Architecture. 2 vols. Cambridge, Mass.: M.I.T. Press.

Boudon, P.
    1972    Lived-in Architecture: Le Corbusier's Pessac Revisited. Cambridge, Mass.: M.I.T. Press.

Bourdieu, P.
    1977    "La Production de la Croyance." Actes de la Recherche en Sciences Sociales, 13: 3–18.

1979    La Distinction: Critique Sociale du Jugement. Paris, France: Minuit.

Brecht, B.
1959    Selected Poems. Translated by H. R. Hays. New York: Harcourt, Brace, Jovanovich.

Brooks, H.
1972    The Prairie School. Toronto: University of Toronto Press.

Burchard, J. and A. Bush-Brown
1966    The Architecture of America: A Social and Cultural History. Boston: Little, Brown.

Campbell, J.
1978    The German Werkbund. Princeton: Princeton University Press.

Chafee, R.
1977    "The Teaching of Architecture in the Ecole des Beaux Arts." In A. Drexler, (ed.), The Architecture of the Ecole des Beaux Arts. New York: Museum of Modern Art.

Clagett, M., ed.
1969    Critical Problems in the History of Science. Madison, Wisc.: University of Wisconsin Press.

Collins, R.
1979    The Credential Society. New York: Academic Press.

Conrads, U.
1970    Programs and Manifestos on 20th Century Architecture. Cambridge, Mass.: M.I.T. Press.

Crombie, A. C.
1969    "Commentary." In Clagett, op. cit.

Davis, A.
1967    Spearheads of Reform: The Social Settlements and the Progressive Movement, 1890–1914. New York: Oxford University Press.

Draper, J.
1977    "The Ecole des Beaux Arts and the architectural profession in the United States: the case of John Galen Howard." Chap. 8 in Kostof, op. cit.

Du Colombier, P.
1973    Les Chantiers des Cathedrales. Paris, France: A. & J. Picard.

Eaton, L.
1969    Two Chicago Architects and Their Clients: Frank Lloyd Wright and Howard Van Doren Shaw. Cambridge, Mass.: M.I.T. Press.

Egbert, D. D.
1970    Social Radicalism and the Arts. New York: Alfred A. Knopf.

Elias, N.
1973    La Civilisation des Moeurs. Paris, France: Librairie Generale Francaise.

Ettlinger, L. D.
1977    "The emergence of the Italian architect during the 15th century." Chap. 4, in Kostof, op. cit.

Frampton, K.
  1973  "Industrialization and the crises in architecture." Oppositions 1: 57–82.

  1980  Modern Architecture: A Critical History. New York: Oxford University Press.

Giedion, S.
  1948  Mechanization Takes Command. New York: Oxford University Press.

  1971  Architecture and the Phenomena of Transition. Cambridge Mass.: Harvard University Press.

  1973  Space, Time, and Architecture. Cambridge, Mass.: Harvard University Press.

Gilbert, C., ed.
  1970  Renaissance Art. New York: Harper and Row.

Gropius, W.
  1965  The New Architecture and the Bauhaus. Cambridge, Mass.: M.I.T. Press.

  1968  Apollo in the Democracy. New York: McGraw-Hill.

Handlin, D.
  1979  The American Home: Architecture and Society, 1815–1915. Boston: Little, Brown.

Harvey, J. H.
  1971  The Master Builders. New York: McGraw-Hill.

Haskell, F.
  1963  Patrons and Painters. New York: Alfred A. Knopf.

Hauser, A.
  1960  The Social History of Art. 4 vols. New York: Vintage Books.

Hines, T. S.
  1979  Burnham of Chicago. Chicago: University of Chicago Press.

Hitchcock, H.
  1958  Architecture: Nineteenth and Twentieth Centuries. Baltimore: Penguin Books.

Jencks, C.
  1976  Modern Movements in Architecture. Garden City: Anchor Press.

Jenkins, A. D. F.
  1970  "Cosimo de Medici's patronage of architecture and the theory of magnificence." Journal of the Warburg and Courtauld Institutes, 33: 162–70.

Jordy, W. H.
  1964  "The aftermath of the Bauhaus in America: Gropius, Mies, and Brever." In H. Fleming and B. Baylin (eds.), The Atlantic Migration. Cambridge, Mass.: Harvard Univ. Press.

  1976  American Buildings and Their Architects, vols. 3 and 4. Garden City: Anchor Press.

Kaye, B.
1960 The Development of the Architectural Profession in Britain. London: Allen and Unwin.

Kopp, A.
1970 Town and Revolution: Soviet Architecture and Town Planning, 1917–1935. New York: G. Braziller.

Kostof, S.
1977 The Architect. New York: Oxford University Press.
1977 "The architect in the Middle Ages, East and West." Chap. 3 in Kostof (ed.), op. cit.

Lane, B. M.
1968 Architecture and Politics in Germany. Cambridge, Mass.: Harvard University Press.

Langer, S.
1953 Feeling and Form. New York: Charles Scribner.

Larson, M. S.
1977 The Rise of Professionalism. Berkeley: University of California Press.

Le Corbusier
1970 Towards A New Architecture. New York: Praeger.

Lipstadt, H.
1977 "Housing the bourgeoisie." Oppositions 8: 35–47.
1979 Polemique, Debat, Conflict: Architecte et Ingenieur dans la Presse. Paris, C.O.R.D.A.

Lubove, R.
1962 The Progressives and the Slums. Pittsburgh: University of Pittsburgh Press.
1964 "I. N. Phelps Stokes: tenement architect, economist planner." Journal of the Society of Architectural Historians. 1964: 23.2: 75.87.

MacDonald, W. L.
1977 "Roman architects." Chap. 2 in Kostof, op. cit.

Martines, L.
1980 Power and Imagination: City-States in Renaissance Italy. New York: Alfred A. Knopf.

Millon, H.
1970 "The architectural theory of Francesco di Giorgio." Chap. 6 in Gilbert, op cit.

Moulin, R. et al.
1973 Les Architectes. Paris, France: Calmann-Levy.

Mumford, L.
1961 The City in History. New York: Harcourt, Brace and World.
1972 Roots of Contemporary American Architecture. New York: Dover Publications.

Panofsky, E.
1957 Gothic Architecture and Scholasticism. New York: Meridian Books.

Pevsner, N.
1968   An Outline of European Architecture. Baltimore: Penguin.

Polanyi, K.
1956   The Great Transformation. Boston: Beacon Press.

Rattansi, P.
1972   "The social interpretation of science in the seventeenth century." In Peter Mathias, ed., Science and Society, 1600–1900. London: Cambridge University Press.

Rosenfeld, M. N.
1977   "The Royal Building Administration in France." Chap. 6 in Kostof, op. cit.

Rykwert, J.
1972   On Adam's House in Paradise: The Idea of the Hut in Architectural History. New York: Museum of Modern Art.

Santillana, G. de
1969   "The role of art in the scientific Renaissance." In Clagett, op. cit.

Sauer, W.
1972   "Weimar culture: experiments in modernism." Social Research 39: 254–284.

Schorske, K.
1980   Fin de Siecle Vienna. New York: A. Knopf.

Schuyler, M.
1964   American Architecture and Other Writings. Edited by W. Jordy and R. Coe. Abridged ed. New York: Atheneum.

Scruton, R.
1979   The Aesthetics of Architecture. Princeton: Princeton University Press.

Shapiro, T.
1976   Painters and Politics: The European Avant-Garde and Society, 1900–1925. New York: Elsevier.

Smith, C. S.
1971   "Art, science and technology: notes on their historical interaction." In D. H. D. Roller (ed.), Perspectives in the History of Science and Technology. Norman Okla.: University of Oklahoma Press.

Tafuri, M.
1979   Architecture and Utopia. Cambridge, Mass.: M.I.T. Press.

Van Rensselaer, M. G.
1972   "Client and architect." In Mumford, op. cit.

Vidler, A.
1977   "The idea of type: the transformation of the academic ideal, 1750–1830" Oppositions 8. 95–115.

Watkin, D.
1977   Morality and Architecture. Oxford, England: Oxford University Press.

Weber, M.
1978   Economy and Society. 2 vols. Berkeley: University of California Press.

White, H. and C. White
   1965    Canvasses and Careers: Institutional Change in the French Paining
           World. New York: Wiley.

Wilton-Ely, J.
   1977    "The rise of the professional architect in England." Chap. 7 in
           Kostof, op. cit.

Wittkower, R.
   1971    Architectural Principles in the Age of Humanism. New York: W. W.
           Norton.

Wright, G.
   1980    Moralism and the Model Home. Chicago: University of Chicago
           Press.

Wurster, C. B.
   1965    "The social front of modern architecture in the 1930s." Journal of
           the Society of Architectural Historians 24: 48-52.

Zerner, C. W.
   1977    "The new professionalism in the Renaissance." Chap. 6 in Kostof,
           op. cit.

# PART II

# Epistemology and Urban Design

## INTRODUCTION

*From cities of brick to cities in books to cities on maps is a path of increasing conceptualization.*
———Robert Harbison, *Eccentric Spaces*

Both among practitioners and academicians in planning and architecture there is growing interest in the epistemological foundations of urban design. Some of the intellectual themes and institutional ramifications are outlined briefly in the introduction to this volume. One central theme has been the ultimate inseparability of theory and practice. A dichotomy of theory and practice, with the "take it or leave it" attitude toward theorizing which that implies, is no more defensible than the separation of knowledge and action, or of description and explanation. Granting this, a first order of business has been to uncover the unscrutinized theoretical codes that pervade urban practice. Second, these codes must be studied in relationship to the goals of practice, and in relationship to codified knowledge in the social sciences. These themes have been extensively explored in the literature of planning theory. As suggested in the introduction, there have been several attempts to differentiate theory in design and in social science, for example, by appealing to dichotomies of facts and values, or of positive versus normative theory. The attempts to draw these distinctions and to elaborate apparently independent methodological positions have been motivated, in part, by the failure of the positivist program to provide a unified logic of explanation embracing natural and social science. Within social science, humanists,

*87*

positivists, realists, idealists, phenomenologists, Marxists, and pragmatists are developing positions in terms more exclusive than ecumenical. Each position has rather different things to say about theory in and of the design professions. The four papers in this section share a common conviction that current conceptualizations of theory are inadequate.

Miller attempts to translate for a planning audience, and to document with planning examples, a paradigm-based view of social practice. His concern is not with evolutionary aspects of paradigms in Kuhn's sense, that is, the processes by which one universally held view supersedes another. In contrast, Miller shows how divergent and largely unconscious modes of theorizing coexist in urban practice. Each of the five paradigms (evolutionary, physicalist, systems, conflict, and social construction) molds planners' conceptions of the urban reality and also implicitly constrains their sphere of action. For example, the evolutionary paradigm implies that urban structure unfolds with an inner logic that can be impeded or channeled, but not fundamentally changed.

Klosterman shows that recent attempts to fuse factual and ethical logics provide a basis for rational appraisal of planning proposals. This broadens the domain of planning theory to include (ethically justified) goals as well as (instrumentally justified) means. Such a fusion circumvents the problem inherent in the means-end conception of rationality, namely, that ends are not themselves accessible to rational debate. Klosterman's argument emphasizes the inadequacy of the standard nomological account of explanation for planning practice. Although he appeals to Rawls's theory of justice as an example of a highly developed and rationalistic treatment of value, Klosterman's case does not stand or fall by this analogy. There is broad consensus in the philosophy of social science that the logics of facts and values are less immiscible than once supposed.

Forester and Gale both focus on language as a principal means of generalizing theory and of showing its relationship to practice. Forester appeals to Habermas's critical theory, and in particular to his universal pragmatics, as a new means of understanding and combining theory and practice. Habermas's general program is predicated on the discovery of the meanings that constitute our understanding of social and cultural structures and that form a common basis for individual ontogeny, for social communication, and for a dialectical materialist reconstruction of history. Forester draws a clear distinction between instrumental and communicative action and suggests that planners' activities are best viewed as communicative (attention-shaping) activities. Habermas posits four bases for successful communication (truth, truthfulness, legitimacy, and comprehensibility). These enabling rules are conceived as pragmatics (in contrast to the usual linguistic preoccupation with syntax and semantics). Using these ideas, Forester provides numerous insights into the communicative process itself, while also illuminating the structural context of planners in the North American political system.

Gale's argument is the most ambitious in scope. He aims to forge a methodology appropriate to urban practice by reformulating the two components of traditional explanation: analytics (observation and description) and dialectics (argumentation). In each case the basic approach is linguistic. Analysis is conceived in terms of nonarithmomorphic structures capable of dealing with vagueness (e.g. multivalued logics and fuzzy set theory). Such tools are illustrated in the context of investment-decision making and partitioning geographic space. Dialectics are conceived in far broader terms than the familiar Hegelian triad. Despite the very wide-ranging philosophical justifications that Gale provides for his position, its import is sharply focused: substantively on the problems of urban planning, and procedurally on the linguistic features of interrogative systems.

# 3 Critical Theory and Planning Practice

## JOHN FORESTER

### PRACTICAL PLANNING THEORY

This paper introduces "critical theory" for use in planning contexts.[1] In particular, the "communications theory of society" developed by Jürgen Habermas will be applied to planning practice. To dramatize the case, it will be argued that a critical theory of planning practice can be not only empirical, interpretative, and normative in its content, but that it can be practical as well.[2] Why practical? Critical theory may help us anticipate and correct for (a) undeserved resentment and mistrust of planners (b) obstacles to effective design review and democratic planning processes, and (c) unintentionally counterproductive technical planning practice.

This work is based on eighteen months of regular observation of a metropolitan city planning department's office of environmental review, whose responsibility it was to assess building plans for the city, review them for "significant adverse environmental impact," and then issue either a "negative declaration" or a requirement of an environmental impact report. Some cases reviewed were obviously without significant impacts; a few others clearly required environmental impact reports. Most proposals, though, fell in between those two groups. In these cases, the planners had to check the likely impacts quite carefully and often negotiate then with the project sponsor or developer for design changes to assure minimal adverse environmental impacts. In such cases, the

Thanks for comments on this draft to Simon Neustein, Bruce Fink, Jim Dorris, and John Friedmann. This essay is an expanded and revised version of "Critical Theory and Planning Practice," prepared for the Cornell Conference on Planning Theory and Planning Practice, Cornell University, Ithaca, New York, April 26-29, 1979. Reprinted with permission from *Journal of the American Planning Association* 46, July 1980.

"review planner" was reviewing, to be sure, but he or she was also participating in project planning and redesign. By using simple examples from this context, it can be shown that a "critical theory of planning practice" may be at once practical, factual, economical, and ethically instructive as well.

In a nutshell, the argument is as follows; critical theory gives us a new way of understanding action, or what a planner does, as attention shaping (communicative action), rather than more narrowly as a means to a particular end (instrumental action).[3] If planners do not recognize how their ordinary actions may have subtle communicative effects, the planners may be well meaning but counterproductive nonetheless. They may be sincere but mistrusted, rigorous but unappreciated, reassuring yet resented. Where they intend to help, planners may create dependency; where they intend to express good faith, they may raise expectations unrealistically. These problems are not inevitable, though. By recognizing the practical, communicative character of planning actions, we can suggest strategies to avoid these problems and improve practice as well. In addition, we can understand structures of action, for example, the organizational and political contexts of planning practice, as structures of selective attention, and so systematically distorted communication. Developers and neighborhood residents are likely to withhold information, for example; access to information and the ability to act on it (i.e., expertise) are unequally distributed; the agendas of decision making (and planning department work programs as well) are politically and selectively structured; the ability of citizens to participate effectively is unequally distributed.[4]

Such a view leads us to ask a more specific set of questions of the planner than the ones we've always asked before about whose ends or interests are being served. Now we ask, how does the planner politically shape attention and communicate? How does the planner provide information about project alternatives to affected people, or withhold it? Does the planner speak in a way that people can understand, or are they mystified? Does the planner encourage people to act or rather discourage them with a (possibly implicit) "leave it to me"? What can planners do to prevent unnecessary, disabling distortions of communication: how can they work to enable learning, participation, and self-determination?

## THE CRITICAL COMMUNICATIONS THEORY OF SOCIETY: AN OVERVIEW

Only an overview of Habermas's communications theory of society can be presented here. In the remainder of the article, Habermas's arguments will be developed and applied in the context of planning practice. Significant other aspects of his work cannot be discussed in this brief paper though; such work treats, for example, the limits of instrumental rationality, the relationships between knowledge and interest, and the development of moral identity.[5]

Habermas's communications theory of society in effect treats social and politico-economic structures as operative communication structures. These relations of power and production not only transmit information, but they communicate political and moral meaning; they seek support, consent, trust, sacrifice, and so forth. The critical content of the theory is centered in the analysis of the systematically but unnecessarily distorted communications that shape the lives of citizens of advanced industrial societies. In the United States, citizens are faced with such influences when politicians or administrators pretend a political problem to be simply a technical one; when private, profit-seeking interests (such as the nuclear construction or pharmaceuticals industries) misrepresent benefits and dangers to the public; when professionals (such as physicians, planners, or social workers) create unnecessary dependency and unrealistic expectations in their clients; or when the established interests in a society avoid humanitarian social and economic policies (such as comprehensive health services) with misleading rhetoric and falsehood, for example "the public sector is always, inevitably, less efficient than the private sector." Such distortions of pretense, misrepresentation, dependency creation, and ideology are communicative influences with immobilizing, depoliticizing, and subtly but effectively disabling consequences. To isolate and reveal the debilitating power of such systematically distorted communications, Habermas seeks to contrast these with the ordinary common sense communication of mutual understanding and consensus which makes any shared knowledge possible in the first place.

The spinal element of Habermas's critical communications theory lies in this contradiction between the disabling communicative power of bureaucratic or capitalistic, undemocratic institutions on the one hand, and the collective enabling power of democratic political criticism, mutual understanding, and self-determined consensus on the other. By undertaking a detailed analysis of the requirements of the ordinary mutual understanding that makes any shared political criticism or technical analysis possible, Habermas establishes a critical reference point, the possibility of politically unobstructed discussion and common sense (technically, intersubjectivity), to which he can then contrast the distorting communicative influences of concrete productive relations and the structure and policies of the state. It is crucial to note, here, that some distortions of communication (e.g., imperfect information) are inevitable, necessarily present in the structure of any political economy; this is true of face-to-face communication as well. Nevertheless, many distortions are not inevitable; they are artificial, and thus the illusions they promote may be overcome. Such distortions are, for example, the deceptive legitimation of great inequalities of income and wealth, the consumer ideologies inherited and generated from the organization of capitalist productive relations, the manipulation of public ignorance in the defense of professional power, and the oppressive racial, ethnic, and sexual type casting to which vast segments of our population are subjected daily. Politically debilitating distortions of communication are political artifacts and not natural necessities. These are the target of Habermas's critical communications theory.[6]

Habermas thus sets the stage for an empirical political analysis exposing the subtle ways that a given structure of state and productive relations functions: (1) to legitimate and perpetuate itself while it seeks to extend its power; (2) to exclude systematically from decision-making processes affecting their lives particular groups defined along economic, racial, or sexual lines; (3) to promote the political and moral illusion that science and technology, through professionals and experts, can "solve" political problems; and so (4) to restrict public political argument, participation, and mobilization regarding a broad range of policy options and alternatives that are inconvenient to (incompatible with) the existing patterns of ownership, wealth, and power. Habermas assesses the problems of distorted communications not only at an interpersonal level but also at the level of social and politico-economic structure. In this way, he begins to fulfill the critical tasks of revealing how the citizens of advanced capitalistic societies may remain not only ignorant of their own democratic political traditions, but also oblivious to their own possibilities for corrective action—as they are harangued, pacified, mislead, and ultimately persuaded that inequality, poverty, and ill-health are either problems so "political" and "complex" that they can have nothing to say about them. Habermas argues that democratic politics or planning requires the consent that grows from processes of collective criticism, not from silence or a party line.

The critical impulse in Habermas's work, then, depends upon a two-pronged analysis. To show that the politico-economic structure, understood as a communications structure, is systematically but unnecessarily distorted, he must first develop an answer to the question, "distorted from what?" His theory of "universal pragmatics," discussed below, addresses this problem. Second, the critical communications theory must suggest how existing social and politico-economic relations actually operate as distorted communications, obscuring issues, manipulating trust and consent, twisting fact and possibility. Habermas has devoted less attention to this second problem (the empirical research into these systematic distortions of communication) than he has to preparing the groundwork for such research. Tables 1 and 2, though (presented and discussed later in this article), identify basic types of distorted communication that subvert understanding and knowledge at face-to-face, organizational, and politico-economic or structural levels of analysis. The power of Habermas's work is to carry forward the classical Marxian "critique of ideology" into a subtle and refined analysis of the structurally, systematically distorted communication expression in the concrete, historical social relations of production, politics, and culture. Although these paragraphs have provided only a simplified overview of Habermas's communications theory, some of the finer points can now be elaborated and applied to planning practice.

## PLANNING PRACTICE AS ATTENTION-SHAPING: COMMUNICATIVE ACTION

In practice any action works not only as a tool but also as a promise, shaping expectations. Planners may be effective not because they put words on paper, but because they may alter expectations by doing so. The planner's formality may tell a city resident more than the actual information provided. The quality of the communication counts; without it, technical information would never be trusted, and cooperation would be impossible. With no one listening, effective work in the planning office would grind to a halt.

Consider a local planner's description (to a neighborhood group) of a proposed shopping center project. If he or she describes the project in predominantly economic terms, the audience will see something different than if it is described in mostly political terms. And again, they would see something different if he or she describes the project in the simplest ordinary language—as if doing a Sunday supplement story about the proposed shopping center. But each of these descriptions would be about the same project. Which account should be given? Which account should be believed?[7] Choices must inevitably be made.

The problem is this: the planner's ordinary description of a project (or of a meeting, of what someone said, etc.) is a communicative action in itself. Like all action, it depends upon intentions and interests, and an audience. Without an audience, the description would be like a play on opening night when no one came, and it would be absolutely uninteresting and worthless, almost by definition, without intentions and interests setting it up. But with interests making something worth describing, intentions making the describing worth doing, and an audience to listen, the planner's description of a project may actually help get ordinary work done.

Planners do much more than describe, of course. They warn others of problems; they present information to other staff (and neighborhood residents, developers, and others); they suggest new ideas; they agree to perform certain tasks or meet at certain times; they argue for particular efforts; they report relevant events; they offer opinions; and they comment upon ideas and proposals for action. These are only a few of the minute, essentially pragmatic, communicative acts that planners perform all the time. These acts are the "atoms" out of which any bureaucratic, social, or political action is constructed. When they are verbal, we can call these acts "speech acts."[8] If these social acts were not possible, we couldn't even ask one another "what did the project sponsor say?" Precisely because such communicative acts are effective, the phrase "watch out—he doesn't like planners" has meaning. The pragmatic meaning is: you watch out.[9] Without these elementally communicative acts, the intelligibility and common sense of our ordinary social world could not exist. Planning problems would be inexpressible; pratical action would be impossible.[10]

These elementary communicative actions are at the heart of the possibility of any ordinary, cooperative working relationships—in everyday life, in planning, in political movements, and in society generally. Communicative acts are fundamental to practical life; they come first. Without them there is no understanding, no common sense, no shared basis even for disagreement or conflict.[11] Without shared, commonly structured communicative abilities (i.e., "communicative competence") we would not be able to say "Hello" and be understood. And the planner would not be able to say, "The meeting's Wednesday at 7:30—come prepared . . . " and be understood either. These communicative acts are ordinary, often just taken for granted, but they are politically potent as well.[12] The planners' speech acts perform both technical and political work.

## FROM ENABLING RULES TO ORGANIZING PRACTICES

### *Enabling Rules*

These essential communicative acts of ordinary planning practice don't just happen. They do not grow automatically from natural conditions. They are not biological. They are social actions, working through languages we can speak together. Words and noises don't just come from our mouths; we speak. We tell, or ask, or promise, or greet, or argue. We act. And when we speak, we don't just make noises, we participate in a structured form of social action, ordinary communicative action, which is already normative and rule-structured.[13] And it's not up to us to decide whether or not we want to follow the rules of ordinary language use—if we want someone else to understand what we say, what we promise, or warn of, or call attention to, or ask. If we want to tell someone that a project review meeting is likely to be especially important, we can't just make up a special world to get the point across—we must try hard to say what we mean, using the language, and whatever frame of reference we share. If we want to be understood when we speak practically, we must follow (or put into use, or work through) the rules structuring ordinary language—or what we really mean to say won't be what anyone listening thinks we mean. The rules here are not restrictions; they enable us to know what one another means.[14] They help me know that "please check out the proposal" isn't likely to mean "we're all done with it."[15] We can communicate pragmatically—though there are exceptions—because we presuppose and anticipate, when speaking, that a set of implicit rules will ordinarily be followed in real life.[16]

We ordinarily (but not always!) try to, and expect others:[17]

1. To *speak comprehensibly*; if we didn't ordinarily presuppose this norm to be in effect, we'd expect babble and never listen.
2. To *speak sincerely*; if we did not presuppose this norm, generally, we'd never trust anyone we listened to—or even trust that we could check with someone else to see what was really meant.[18]
3. To *speak legitimately*, in context; we don't expect building developers to give biblical interpretations in front of the Planning Commission or clergy to propose planned unit developments before their congregations.
4. To *speak the truth*; if we didn't generally presuppose this norm, we'd never believe anything we heard, even if we had no doubt of the speaker's sincerity, if we knew the best of intentions were involved. We'd never be able to check or test the truth of a story or hypothesis if we generally expected falsehood to pervade communication. Only by presupposing and mutually fostering this norm of "truth" do we make it possible for each other to tell the difference between reality and ideology, between fact and sheer fantasy. Those skeptical about this norm of truth might consider if they presume less when they speak of the realities of poverty, sexism, or cruelty. (Of course, exceptions to the generally presupposed norm exist. We can lie, but even the lie works only because the listener is ordinarily bound by the norm of expecting truthfulness in ordinary communication.)

These norms of pragmatic communication are usually taken for granted.

They are part of the subtle foundations of common sense. If we violate them, or when we do, we face puzzlement, mistrust, anger, and disbelief.[19] As these pragmatic norms are broken, our shared experience and our social and political world disintegrate.[20] These problems have special importance in planning for two reasons. First, since planners often have little formal power or authority, the effectiveness of their communicative acts becomes all the more important. Second, planners serving the public face particular special, private, or class interests (e.g., corporate development interests) which may work systematically to violate these norms of ordinary communication. Planners then face the results: a community group snowed by a developer's consultant, an inquisitive citizen confused by apparently "necessary" public works cutbacks, a working-class community organization led to accept delays as wealthier neighborhoods receive more attention from city government. Planning staff members need to anticipate the practical effects not only of the class-based communicative actions of others, but of their own communicative practices as well.

### Meaning More (in Practice) Than Intended

When planners tell a neighborhood group about a proposed project, they inevitably communicate more than they intend.[21] They may lapse into bureaucratic language and so confuse and mystify people.[22] They may present information but have no way of knowing what it will really mean to the audience. They may be trying to please, but their professional or formal manner may lead residents to doubt their sincerity. Pragmatically effective communication is never guaranteed.[23] The four norms of "universal pragmatics" are just that: they are pragmatic guides and standards for practice.[23] As they are violated, mutual understanding, trust, and cooperation will suffer. We can take these four norms of ordinary communication, our universally presupposed pragmatic abilities, and pose them, then, as practical questions for planning practice.

1. Is the planner's communication *comprehensible*, so others can understand what in fact is happening around them or to them?
2. Is the planner's communication offered *sincerely* and uttered in good faith, or are the listeners being manipulated, misled, fooled or misguided?
3. Is the planner's communication *legitimate*, given the planner's role and the participation of other interested parties, or is the planner taking advantage of professional status unfairly? (If a planner tells a developer or community organization member, "You'll have to live with this design, there's nothing you can do," this may be, for example, a personal judgment in professional clothes.)

4. Is the planner's communication *true*? Can we believe it, bet on it? Is there evidence supporting it? What do other accounts of the situation say? Are the listeners being offered information upon which they can act, or are they being misinformed, however unintentionally?

## *Practical Distortions of Communication: Political Costs and Corrective Strategies*

In bargaining or other adversarial situations, for example, planners won't be expected to "tell the whole truth, and nothing but the truth." When planners must present arguments as advocates for a particular proposal, or when they must argue for budgetary needs, others may expect the ordinary norms of communication discussed above to be violated by the planners, but they will also expect (in order to compensate) to be able to check what the planners say with others, for example, friends or contacts in other agencies whom they expect *not* to violate these basic norms.[25] This latter expectation makes any checking possible.[26] Thus, in those conventional situations when bargaining or adversarial behavior is expected to result in exaggeration, untruth, or misrepresentation, the ordinary pragmatic norms nevertheless make possible compensating checking strategies that protect us from being mislead, from "being snowed." In these situations, the four questions of comprehensibility, sincerity, legitimacy, and truth become more, rather than less, important. If we are generally to trust and rely upon planners as responsible public servants, it will be crucial to know not only when and why insincerity and falsehood may at times be justified, but also to know what results such practices have.[27] These questions are particularly important because of the bureaucratic and political pressures operating upon planners.[28] Planners will often feel compelled to be less frank or open than they might wish, but then they should not be surprised when they find members of the public at times suspicious, resentful, or angry.

These four questions ask how the four norms of ordinary communication are met or violated in planning practice, but this is only a slight beginning. The planners' distortions are certainly no more important or influential than the systematic structural distortions of communication which planners and their clients both face. Consider: the politically selective channeling of information; the unequally distributed ability to engage in political and planning processes (of citizens to engage in political and planning processes (of citizens with or for whom the planning staff work); the professional status (or stigma) of the planner's deeds; conflicting interpretations of cases and significance; scarce information and fluid networks of contacts; and a maze of bureaucratic rules for the uninitiated to navigate. We are led to ask of the organizational structure of private interests and public agencies how they foster or retard open, unmanipulated communication (and so participation) by affected persons. When ordinary communication is structurally but unnecessarily or deliberately distorted, responsible political action will be crippled.[29]

The socially and politically structured distortions of communication we face every day—as citizens and as planners—can now begin to be recognized and assessed (table 3.1). For each entry in table 3.1, we can ask a practical question: "How can planners work with others to prevent such distortions of communication?" Table 3.2 suggests strategies of response, "exposing" or correcting the distortions of table 3.1.

TABLE 3.1

*How We Experience Distortions of Communication*

| PRACTICAL LEVEL | COMPRE-HENSIBILITY | NORMS OF PRAGMATIC COMMUNICATION | | |
| | | Sincerity | Legitimacy | Truth |
| --- | --- | --- | --- | --- |
| Face to face | Lack of sense, ambiguity, confusion | Deceit, insincerity | Meaning out of context | Misinformation |
| | "What?" | "Can I trust him?" | "Is this right?" | "Is this true?" |
| Organizational (e.g., hospital proposing expansion) | Public exclusion by jargon | Rhetorical reassurances, expression of false concern, hiding of motives | Unresponsiveness, assertion of rationalizations, professional dominance | Information withheld, responsibility obscured, need misrepresented |
| | "What's this mean?" | "Can we trust?" | "Is this justified?" | "Is this true?" |
| Politico-economic structure | Mystification complexity | Misrepresentation of the public good | Lack of accountability by line—not by active participation | Policy possibilities obscured, withheld, or misrepresented; ideology as: public ownership is always inefficient |
| | "Do you think *they* understand what that means?" | "That's their line." | "Who are they to say?" | "What they never tell us about is . . . " |

These strategies of response are varied, but they can be summarized in one word—"organizing." This is the planner's pragmatic response to a political reality of effectively disabling distortions of ordinary communication: the careful, political organization of attention and action that corrects or seeks to eliminate these distortions.[36] Not only do these strategies address the basic obstacles to an open democratic political process, they are pragmatic as well. They seek concretely to marshal information, to cultivate support, to work through informal channels, to use expertise discriminately, and so forth.[37] Thus, the analysis of the distor-

TABLE 3.2

*Responses Correcting Distortions of Communication*
*Organizing Practices of Planners*

| PRACTICAL LEVEL | COMPRE-HENSIBILITY | DISTORTION TYPE (PRAGMATIC NORM VIOLATED) | | |
| --- | --- | --- | --- | --- |
| | | Sincerity | Legitimacy | Truth |
| Face to face[30] | Revealing meaning | Checking intentions | Determining roles and contexts[31] | Checking evidence |
| | "What does that mean?" | "Does she mean that?" | "I don't need to accept that . . . " | "I'll check to see if this is really true." |
| Organizational[32] | Minimizing jargon; creating public review committees | Organizing counter advocates; checking with contacts, networks | Making decisions participatory; checking with affected persons | Utilizing independent/critical third-party expertise |
| | "Clean up the language so people can understand it." | "Check with Stu to see if we can trust them on this." | "What's the neighborhood association had to say about this?" | "Check the data and calculations to see if these figures are really correct." |
| Politico-economic structure[33] | Demystification; counter-skills | Exposing unexpressed interests | Democratizing the state; politicizing planning[34] | Institutionalizing debate, political criticism |
| | 'All this really means is . . .'' | "Of course they say that! They're the big winners if no one speaks up." | "Without political pressure, the bureaucracy will continue to serve itself. . . . " | Democratizing inquiry; politicizing planning[35]: "We have to show what can be done here." |

tion or violation of the norms of ordinary communication leads logically to questions of response.

## ON PRACTICE: ENABLING (ORGANIZING) AND DISABLING PRACTICE

Now, what of local planning practice? Where's the practical payoff for planners? As we broaden our understanding of the planner's action (from technical to communicative), we come to understand the practical organization problems planners face a little differently. We come to understand that problems will be solved not by one expert, but by pooling expertise and nonprofessional contributions as well; not by formal procedure alone, but by informal consultation and involvement; not predominantly by strict reliance on data bases, but by careful use of trusted "resources," "contacts," "friends"; not through formally rational management procedures, but by internal politics and the development of a working consensus; not by solving an engineering equation, but by complementing technical performance with political sophistication, support building, liaison work, and, finally, intuition and luck. Only in the most isolated or most routine cases will future-oriented planning proceed "one, two, three."[38]

The planner's technical acts may be instrumentally skilled, but nevertheless politically inept. A formal economic calculation may be impeccably performed, but the planner's client may "not really trust the numbers." Any technical action (calculating a solution, making a demographic prediction, reviewing architectural plans for flaws) communicates to those it serves, "this solution (etc.) serves your needs" or "now, this much done, you may still wish to . . . (change this parameter, devise another scenario, look and see for yourself)." In planning contexts, this metacommunicative character of technical action has often been overlooked.[39] Its practical implications, particularly its costs, have often been neglected. The most well-meaning professional activities of planning staffs have at times communicated, if unintentionally, "leave the analysis to me; I'll give you all the results when I'm through; you can depend on me." At times this has reflected an agreed-upon division of labor. At other times the political and practical consequences of such (often implicit) communication has been to separate planners and planned-for, to reduce the accessibility to information of those affected by plans, to minimize the planner's capability to learn from design review criticism, to engender public mistrust for planning staff, and to reinforce the planner's apprehensions of what seems to be necessarily disruptive public participation. As long as this practical communicative dimension of (even the most technical) planning is ignored, planners will pay such costs.[40]

This practical communicative dimension of planning practice involves much more than how clearly the planner writes or speaks.[41] *What* the planner chooses to say—and not to say—is pragmatically, and politically, crucial. If the planner, for example, takes the role of the "informed technocrat" and chooses to emphasize the technical aspects of a problem while ignoring its political dimensions, the planner's own understanding of his or her appropriate role may lead to a serious misrepresentation of that problem. Ideologies, of course, are distortions of communication in precisely this sense. They are distortions not because they are unclear, but because they are indeed clear; but they so misrepresent social and political reality that they may obscure alternatives, cover up responsibility, encourage passivity and fatalism, and justify the perpetuation of inequity and suffering.

Echoing the work of Karl Mannheim and John Dewey, Habermas's argument implies that such distortions are increasingly likely in planning if planners become more removed from a democratic planning process which encourages political debate, the criticism of alternative problem definitions, and the collective construction of new design and policy proposals.[42] Thus, the sensitivity to distorted communication by planners leads not only to attention to matters of clarity, "cleaning up communications," but also to the appropriate, inevitably political roles of planning staff: do they foster or thwart informed public participation; do they pre-empt or enable public debate and argument; do they encourage or discourage design and policy review and criticism?

Planning organizations may—against all their best intentions—immobilize or disable responsible public political participation and action. By ignoring the effects of bureaucratic language, planning organizations may perpetuate the exclusion of all but those who already "know the language." If they are not perceived to speak truthfully, planning organizations will breed distrust, suspicion, and a growing hostility to professional public servants—to say little of the possible cooperation that will be poisoned. More subtly, if planning organizations pre-empt community involvement by defining problems as overly technical or as too complex for nonprofessionals to understand, they may, again against their best intentions, engender political passivity, dependency, and ignorance.[43] And if they do not systematically search for design alternatives and possible political solutions through regular processes of community consultation, expertise pooling, and project reviews, running from "brainstorming" to "collective criticism," planning organizations are likely to "satisfice" too quickly or inefficiently, and miss real program or design opportunities.

Ironically, then, technically oriented planning may effectively but unintentionally communicate to the public, "You can depend on me; you needn't get involved. I'll consult you when appropriate." This message may simplify practice in the short-run, but it may also lead to inefficiency and waste in general. It counterproductively may separate planners from the political constituency they serve, weakening them both before the designs and agendas of powerful economic forces in their neighborhoods and cities.[44] It may subvert the accountability of planners and serve to keep affected publics uninformed rather than politically educated about events and local decisions affecting their lives. Planning which is predominantly technical in focus may also neglect its political friends. When action is at stake—not to mention the planners' jobs themselves, of course—this can be costly. We may find opportunities to improve planning productivity and efficiency, then, not simply by appealing to community involvement, but by calling attention to the minute, practical communications which function either to discourage or alternatively encourage cooperative, constructive, trusting, supportive organizational and community bases for the actions of planners. Technical work should not be seen in a vacuum, then. To avoid the counterproductive "leave it to us" messages that these acts may metacommunicate, planners have several options, as indicated in table 3.3.

The statement "Planning is political" need not be the end of discussion; it may be a fruitful beginning. By anticipating the interests and commitments of affected groups, planners may build political support in addition to producing technically sound documents. To be effective, rigorous analysis must be used (if not always appreciated) by politically influential groups or the staff of other agencies; technical analysis in planning cannot stand alone. Numerous studies show that the "technician" role of planning analysis is often frustrating and ineffectual if divorced from the pragmatic considerations of political communication: lobbying, maintaining trust and "an ear," addressing the specific concerns of the decision-making audiences as well as those inherent in the projects themselves, and so on.[45] Paying attention to the practical communications that structure the planning process can save wasted time and effort; otherwise, technical reports may be destined to end up on the shelf.

Nevertheless, the strategies indicated above are not without their problems. How much information should be given to which groups, and when? What can planners do to prevent such information from being ignored, misinterpreted, or manipulated? What organizational and political forms of community planning, widespread participation, and design review might be both democratic and efficient? These are not new questions for planners—but the analysis of systematically distorted com-

TABLE 3.3
*Communicative Strategies Complementing Planners' Technical Work*

Complementing their technical work, planners can:

1   Cultivate community networks of liaisons and contacts, rather than depending on the power of documents, both to provide and disseminate information

2   Listen carefully to gauge the concerns and interests of all participants in the planning process to anticipate likely political obstacles, struggles, and opportunities

3   Notify less-organized interests early in any planning process affecting them (the more organized groups, whose business it is to have such information, won't need the same attention)

4   Educate citizens and community organizations about the planning process and the "rules of the game"

5   Supply technical and political information to citizens to enable informed, effective political participation

6   Work to see that community and neighborhood, nonprofessional organizations have ready access to public planning information, local codes, plans, and notices of relevant meetings, and consultations with agency contacts, "specialists" supplementing their own "in-house" expertise

7   Encourage community-based groups to press for open, full information about proposed projects and design possibilities

8   Develop skills to work with groups and conflict situations, rather than expecting progress to stem mainly from isolated technical work

9   Emphasize to community interests the importance of effective participation in informal processes of project review, and take steps to make such design-change negotiation meetings equitable to professionally unsophisticated groups

10   Encourage independent, community-based project reviews and investigations

11   Anticipate external politico-economic pressures shaping design decisions and compensate for them — soliciting "pressure we can use" (e.g., countering vested antipublic interests) rather than minimizing external pressure altogether

NOTE: These actions are all elements of "organizing" practices, practically mobilizing concerned and affected persons, in addition to technically calculating problem solutions.

munication provided by critical theory allows these questions to be asked and answered in new ways. In particular, these ways include: (1) clarifying the ordinary norms of practical communication; (2) identifying the essential types of disabling distortions to be corrected; (3) clarifying the planner's role in perpetuating or seeking to correct such distortions; and (4) locating within a politico-economic structure of power and ideology—treated as a structure of systematically distorted communication of assurance, threat, promise, and legitimation—the pragmatic and political communicative character of planning practice. Each of the entries in tables 3.1, 3.2 and 3.3 ought to be regarded as an illustration pointing to practical, political research questions. Such quesions are *empirical* as they question the forms and effects of disabling or enabling communication; they are *interpretative* as they question the meanings and myths generated by alternative organizational forms and professional practices; and they are *normative* as they question the political and moral responsibilities of professionals, bureaucrats, and citizens alike. If the organizing strategies listed in table 3.3 are considered as isolated ideas, they are nothing new. Only if they are understood and carried out in the context of the structural analysis of systematically distorted communication illustrated in tables 3.1 and 3.2, can they be seen in a new light, focused upon new goals and objectives, and put into practice in increasingly sensitive and effective ways.

## CONCLUSION

Practical organizing strategies (suggested in table 3.3) may provide options for planners seeking to improve local planning practice and avoid the disruptive, frustration-producing problems of organizationally distorted communications (suggested in table 3.1). Planning actions are not only technical, they are also communicative: they shape attention and expectations. These communicative effects are often unintentional, but they are pragmatic nevertheless; they make a difference. Presenting technical information to a community organization, a planner's manner may communicate as much as his or her words.

These practical communicative effects can be counterproductive for planners if they are ignored. Alternatively, if they are recognized, planners can complement their technical activities with strategies (suggested in table 3.2) designed to open effective communication to those persons and groups affected by proposed projects and plans. These practical communication strategies may be organizationally economical as they reduce the unnecessary disruption of the planning process, as they cultivate support for planner's actions, and as they reduce the likelihood that planners' efforts will be washed away by the larger political process in which any planning is embedded. Finally, the focus on the pragmatic aspects of such communicative planning actions can be rooted in the recent literature of critical theory, especially as developed in the writings of Jürgen Habermas. Significantly, a critical theory of planning practice, barely indicated here, calls our attention (a) *empirically* to concrete communicative actions and organizational and politico-economic structures, (b) *interpretatively* to the meanings and experiences of persons performing or facing those communicative actions, and (c) *normatively* to the respect or violation of fundamental social norms of language use, norms making possible the very intelligibility and common sense of our social world. By recognizing planning practice as normatively rule-structured, communicative action that distorts, covers up, or reveals to the public the prospects and possibilities they face, a critical theory of planning aids us practically and ethically as well. This is the contribution of critical theory to planning: pragmatics with vision—to reveal true alternatives, to correct false expectations, to counter cynicism, to foster inquiry, to spread political responsibility, engagement, and action. Critical planning practice, technically skilled and politically sensitive, is an organizing and democratizing practice.

## NOTES

1. By "critical theory" I refer predominantly to the work of Jürgen Habermas and the interpreters of his recent work (1970; 1971; 1973; 1975; and 1979). Excellent interpreters of Habermas's critical theory are Richard Bernstein (1976), Thomas McCarthy (1978), and Trent Schroyer (1973)

2. Bernstein completes his review of the apparent restructuring of modern social and political theory with the challenge: "An adequate social and political theory must be *empirical, interpretative,* and *critical*" (1976: 235).

3. For one distinction between instrumental and communicative action, see Habermas (1970: 91ff). Weber's concept of "meaningful social action" can be understood as communicative action, as Schutz has shown (1970). Also important for an understanding of the concepts of systematic structuring of attention (e.g., distortions of communication) is Berger and Luckmann (1966).

4. See Steven Lukes (1974) for the treatment of the structural distortions of communications and information considered by E.E. Schattschneider, Peter Bachrach, and Morton Baratz; Murray Edelman's work (1971, 1978) provides another view of distorted communications. Schroyer (1973) and Claus Mueller (1973) are attempts to bridge Habermas's analysis of communicative action and its distortions (on the one side) and the more traditional treatments of power and political structure (on the other side). See also, for example, the lengthy introduction to Habermas (1973). Cf. Alvin Gouldner's very narrow reading of systematic distortions of communication as "censorship," (1976). Cf. also Paulo Freire's powerful and moving *Pedagogy of the Oppressed* (1970) which provides many fascinating parallels with Habermas's work.

5. See note 1, above.

6. Such distorted communications mediate, in Marxist terms, the contradictions between working and ruling classes, between the means of production and the social relations of production, between labor and capital. In ordinary terms, these distortions hide from citizens the end results of their labor, the possibilities of collective improvement now existing in modern cooperative organization and technology, and the social costs of the private control of investment and labor.

7. This question is especially important to the extent that the listener has no opportunity to engage the speaker and question the given description—thus enabling a richer account to be given. But when the listener is uninformed and trusting, even the recourse to conversation and interaction may not change matters. The offered account, selective as it must be, will effectively stand (e.g., the planner may say to the community organizatin member/developer. "There's just

nothing much you can do.''). It's helpful to remember, of course, that planners are not omniscient, and that such statements, like others, may or may not be actually true.

8. The classic analysis of "speech acts" appears in the work of John Austin (1961), and more recently, John Searle (1969).

9. Nonverbal communication counts, too, but must be developed in another paper. In face-to-face interaction, nonverbal communication takes the form of tone, gesture, deadpan or lively facial expressions. At the organizational level, nonverbal communication is effective in the structuring of agendas, meetings, work-programs, and the character (e.g., more or less formal, comprehensible, encouraging) of the planning or policy formulation process. At both levels, what remains unsaid may be as important, and effective, as what is said. See, for example, Paul Watzlawick et al. (1967). See also note 39.

10. Habermas calls the theory of these speech acts "the theory of universal pragmatics": universal because all social communication seems to depend on the structure and possibility of such acts, and pragmatic because these acts are concretely practical—they make a difference in our lives. See his (1979) "What is Universal Pragmatics?" See also note 9, above.

11. See, for example, Karl Otto Apel's "The Priori of Communication and the Foundation of the Humanities" in Dallmayr and McCarthy (1977).

12. Paul Watzlawick shows that even a threat depends upon effective communication; the minimal conditions for a successful threat are that it must "get through" and be believable (1976: 107ff).

13. See, for example, Cavell (1969), especially the essay "Must We Mean What We Say?" Cf. Pitkin (1972).

14. See Searle (1969) for the difference between *regulative* and *constitutive* rules. Charles Taylor develops some of the political implications of these differences for politics and the study of politics in his "Interpretation and the Sciences of Man," in Dallmayr and McCarthy (1977).

15. "Please check out the proposal" may have many nonliteral practical meanings too, of course. It may mean, "this proposal isn't documented properly," for example. But our understanding of such nonliteral meanings presupposes we know how to apply the ordinary rules of language-use. Otherwise, we wouldn't, at the first level, be able to recognize the literal meaning, its possible implications, and then at the second level, its fit or possible mis-fit with the context of its use (i.e., whether or not we should take it literally).

16. Extended analysis of such presupposition and anticipation of the "universal pragmatic" norms of speech can be found in McCarthy (1978). Jeremy Shapiro (1976) is also helpful.

17. See Habermas's "What is Universal Pragmatics," (1979: 2).

18. This "sincerity" condition differs from the "truth" condition, which follows. Sincerity refers to the genuine expression of the speaker's intentions; truth refers to the fit or misfit of statements or representations of reality with the reality supposedly represented. A speaker may be sincere or insincere; a statement may be true or false. (One might say that an expression, as an indication of a speaker's intentions, is sincere or insincere.) A physician may be utterly sincere in prescribing a medication to alleviate certain symptoms, but the medication may nevertheless not work; a planner may be wholly sincere in saying that a certain widening of a street will draw twice the existing traffic flow, but the widening may not actually have those consequences. In each case, the speaker is sincere, but what is said is not true. Insincerity threatens and subverts trust; untruth weakens

and subverts knowledge. Consider as examples fads in political movements, popular psychology, or the misuse of the women's movement in commercial advertising.

19. "Since our ability to cope with life depends upon our making sense of what happens to us, anything which threatens to invalidate our conceptual structures of interpretation is profoundly disruptive" (Marris 1975: 13).

20. Fred Dallmayr argues that the violation of and respect for these universal pragmatic norms of communication may be taken to ground a "communicative ethics" and a normative political vision (1974). Forester develops the implications of a "communicative ethics" for planning (1778a). See also, Trent Schroyer (1973: 162–63), for the argument that Habermas's critique of systematically distorted communications is a refined form of the classical critique of ideology.

21. Cavell distinguishes the semantic meaning of an uttered sentence from the pragmatic meaning of the same utterance, and he argues that as speakers and actors we are responsible for both. Good intentions are not enough; pragmatics count (1969).

22. From the journal of a young planner in California:
> Sitting in Environmental Review Committee meetings, I notice how the applicants interact with the Committee—the "slickies" know the genre. They speak with professional language, e.g., "that's correct" for "that's right." Others come in and get bounced around by the strange terminology and the unfamiliar process. What a humiliating experience for them. . . (Personal correspondence, Fall, 1978).

23. Cf. a public health department director, facing a planning commissioner's proposal of additional formal interagency meetings: "What you're proposing is a formal structure that'll look great on paper, but won't be operational. What we need is ongoing informal consultation and communication so we know what each other's doing—that's what works!" (K.G., Tompkins County Comprehensive Health Planning Subarea Council, 21 March 1979).

24. "The normative foundation of a critical theory is implicit in the very structure of social action that it analyzes" (Bernstein 1976: 213).

25. To the extent that neither of these two expectations (first, that the situation at hand is one in which the norms of communication are likely to be broken, and second, that methods and means of checking, to compensate, are available) exists in the listener, a planner's (or any speaker's) violation of the ordinary norms of communication will be particularly dangerous and oppressive.

26. It is important to make clear, especially to those holding that conflict is everpresent in social and political life, that the proposition, $P$, that all interactions are so conflictual as to be untrustworthy sources of misrepresentation, is untenable, for then not only would checking the truth of any one position be impossible, but it would be impossible for the proposition $P$ itself to be credible, that is, for any consensus that $P$ was trustworthy or true. Compare the discussion of the "norm of truth" in the text.

27. See Sissela Bok (1978), for an extended discussion.

28. Assessing the distorted communications prevalent in modern bureaucracies, Ralph Hummel argues that bureaucratic organizations are characterized not by two-way communication, but by one-way information. "Bureaucracy separates man from his language. . . . The 'language' through which a bureaucracy speaks to us is not a language designed for problem solving. Bureaucratic language is a language for passing on solutions. . ." (1977: 157–59).

29. See, for example, Mueller (1973).

30. Forester treats the problems of distorted communication and political response at the level of face-to-face interaction in "Listening: The Social Policy of Everyday Life (Critical Theory and Hermeneutics in Practice)" (1978b).

31. R.R. McGuire writes, " . . . insofar as systems of rules and norms contribute to systematically distorted communication, insofar as they exist as systematic barriers to discursive will formation, they are irrational. . . . And insofar as (communication structures) create a fiction of reciprocal accountability, concomitantly creating ideologies by sustaining the 'legitimacy' of these very structures they are irrational . . . and hence illegitimate—involving no moral obligation" (1977).

32. Several sources provide insight and suggestions for those seeking to correct distortions of communication at the organizational level: Harold Wilensky (1967), Needleman (1974), Saul Alinsky (1971); also helpful may be Guy Benveniste (1977) and Paulo Freire (1974, 1970).

33. The politico-economic ethic or vision of "opening communications" is the ethic of the critique of ideology. Embodied in actions seeking to correct distorted communication, the distortion of attention to actual possibilities, this is a call for political organizing, for democratizing public policy. Cf. note 20 above.

34. To politicize planning does not mean to "make trouble," to grind planning to a halt. This is the poisonous misreading of politics that perpetuates a narrow, technically focused, politically inept planning practice. To politicize planning along the lines called for by critical theory means to broaden the basis of consideration of alternatives, to foster participation and spread responsibility to nonprofessional citizens; to balance the reliance upon technique with the attention to regular political debate and criticism. See Pitkin (1972).

35. "The ultimate objective of repoliticization . . . should be to resurrect the notion of democracy, which is far too important an ideal to be sacrificed to capitalism. . . . . The problem is not that capitalist societies accumulate, but the way in which they do it. In order for the beneficiaries of accumulation to remain a narrow group, a boundary is established beyond which democracy is not allowed to intrude. . . . [T]he time has come to think, not about demolishing accumulation, but about democratizing it. The way to eliminate the contradictions between accumulation and legitimation is to apply the principles of democracy to both—to give people the same voice in making investment and allocation decisions as they theoretically have in more directly political decisions" (Wolfe 1977: 346).

36. The normative goal or ideal of organizing and opening communications ought not be dismissed as romantic or utopian, a call for infinite gentleness or listening forever—for it is a practical call to prevent noise, misinformation, unnecessary ambiguity, the misleading elevation or lowering of citizens' expectations. See Forester (1979).

37. We must beware, when we speak of opening communications, that this is not understood so narrowly as "getting more citizen input," getting more bodies to meetings. This is precisely how "input" misleads us, for it is not input, but responsibility and constructively critical political participation that are at issue.

38. See for example, Benveniste (1977).

39. When the context of a planner's description or evaluation is technical, that description or evaluation may have a pragmatic political effect in addition to that of its technical message. Paul Watzlawick writes, "The paramount communicational significance of context is all too easily overlooked in the analysis of human communication, and yet anyone who brushed his teeth in a busy street rather than

in his bathroom might be quickly carted off to a police station or a lunatic asylum—to give just one example of the pragmatic effects of nonverbal communication'' (1967: 62).

40. Ivan Illich argues, "Paradoxically, the more attention is focused on the technical mastery of disease, the larger becomes the symbolic and non-technical function performed by medical technology" (1977: 106).

41. Such a "clarity criterion" falls under only the first of the four universal pragmatic norms discussed above: comprehensibility, sincerity, legitimacy, and truth.

42. See, for example, Karl Mannheim (1950, 1949), and John Dewey (1927).

43. Jeffry Galper (1975) writes of professional social work practices: "In every interaction in which we engage, we encourage certain responses in others and discourage other responses. Workers who are themselves politicized . . . will offer suggestions and interpretations from this perspective . . . [These interpretations] must clearly be offered in service to the client and not in service of political ends that are somehow separate from the situation and well-being of the client."

44. Cf. Galper: "In one sense, the virtual death of a formal welfare state organizing role is a benefit because it forces us to develop the organizing role for persons in all service-delivery positions" (1975: 217). In the face of fiscal conservatism and austerity budgets, planners, too, must work as organizers. See Clavel, Forester, Goldsmith, eds., (1980).

45. See, for example, Arnold Meltsner (1976), and Norman Krumholz et al. (1975); cf. the analysis of interviews with local planners in Baltimore by Howell Baum, School of Social Work and Community Planning, University of Maryland, Baltimore, Maryland 21201. (Cf. note 32; Needleman [1974]; Wilensky [1967]; Alinsky [1971].)

# REFERENCES

Alinski, S.
  1971 Rules for Radicals. New York: Vintage Press.

Austin, J.
  1961 How To Do Things with Words. London: Oxford University Press.

Benveniste, G.
  1977 The Politics of Expertise, 2nd ed. San Francisco: Boyd and Fraser.

Berger, P. and T. Luckmann
  1966 The Social Construction of Reality. New York: Anchor Press.

Bernstein, R.
  1976 The Reconstructing of Social and Political Theory. Philadelphia: University of Pennsylvania Press.

Bok, S.
  1978 Lying. New York: Pantheon.

Clavel, P., J. Forester and W. Goldsmith, eds.
  1980 Urban and Regional Planning in an Age of Austerity. New York: Pergamon Press.

Cavell, Stanley
  1969 Must we Mean What We Say? New York: Scribners.

Dallmayr, F.
1974   "Toward a critical reconstruction of ethics and politics." Journal of Politics 37: 926–57.

Dallmayr, F. and T. McCarthy
1977   Understanding and Social Inquiry. Notre Dame, Indiana: Notre Dame Press.

Dewey, J.
1927   The Public and Its Problems. Denver: Henry Holt.

Edelman, M.
1978   Political Language. New York: Academic Press.
1971   Politics as Symbolic Action. New York: Academic Press.

Forester, J.
1979   What are Planners Up Against? Planning in the Face of Power. Working Paper 33. Ithaca, N. Y.: Cornell University Department of City and Regional Planning.
1978a  What do Planning Analysts Do? Planning and Policy Analysis as Organising. Working Paper 8. Ithaca, N. Y.: Cornell University Department of City and Regional Planning.
1978b  Listening: The Social Policy of Everyday Life (Critical Theory and Hermeneutics in Practice). Working Paper 6. Ithaca, N. Y.: Cornell University Department of City and Regional Planning.

Freire, P.
1974   Education for Critical Consciousness. New York: Seabury Press.
1970   Pedagogy of the Oppressed. New York: Seabury Press.

Galper, J.
1975   The Politics of Social Services. Englewood Cliffs: Prentice Hall.

Gouldner, A.
1976   Dialectic of Ideology and Technology. New York: Seabury Press.

Habermas, J.
1979   Communication and the Evolution of Society. Boston: Beacon Press.
1975   Legitimation Crisis. Boston: Beacon Press.
1973   Theory and Practice. Boston: Beacon Press.
1971   Knowledge and Human Interests. Boston: Beacon Press.
1970   Toward a Rational Society. Boston: Beacon Press.

Hummel, R.
1977   The Bureaucratic Experience. New York: St. Martin's Press.

Illich, I.
1977   Medical Nemesis. New York: Bantam Books.

Krumholz, N. et al.
1975   "The Cleveland policy planning report." Journal of the American Institute of Planners 41: 298–304.

Lukes, S.
1974   Power: A Radical View. London: Macmillan.

Mannheim, K.
1950   Freedom, Planning and Democratic Planning. New York: Oxford University Press.

1949    Man and Society in an Age of Reconstruction. Boston: Routledge & Kegan Paul.

Marris, P.
1975    Loss and Change. New York: Anchor Press.

McCarthy, T.
1978    The Critical Theory of Jürgen Habermas. Boston: M.I.T. Press.

McGuire, R. R.
1977    Speech acts, communicative competence, and the paradox of authority." Philosophy and Rhetoric 10: 30–45.

Meltsner, A.
1976    Policy Analysts in the Bureaucracy. Berkeley: University of California Press.

Mueller, C.
1973    The Politics of Communication. New York: Oxford University Press.

Needleman, C. and M. Needleman
1974    Guerrillas in the Bureaucracy. New York: Wiley.

Pitkin, H.
1972    Wittgenstein and Justice. Berkeley: University of California Press.

Schroyer, T.
1973    The Critique of Domination. Boston: Beacon Press.

Schutz, A.
1970    Phenomenology and Social Relations. Edited by H. Wagner. Chicago: University of Chicago Press.

Searle, J.
1969    Speech Acts. London: Cambridge University Press.

Shapiro, J.
1976    "Reply to Miller's review of Habermas's 'legitimation crisis'." Telos 27: 170–76.

Watzlawick, P.
1976    How Real Is Real? New York: Vintage Press.

Watzlawick, P. et al.
1967    Pragmatics of Human Communication. New York: Norton Press.

Wilenski, H.
1967    Organizational Intelligence. New York: Basic Books.

Wolfe, A.
1977    Limits of Legitimacy. New York: Free Press.

# 4 Foundations for Normative Planning

## RICHARD E. KLOSTERMAN

The planning profession in the United States and England grew out of and has been in large part shaped by two very important intellectual traditions. Most obvious in this regard is the widespread Western faith in rationality and science, which has viewed planning as the institutionalized application of the methods and findings of science to social affairs. Equally important, however, has been the great tradition of middle-class reform, which has seen planning as a means for improving government and society (see Lubove, 1967; Eversley, 1973: 43–84).

A recurring problem for planning, both practice and theory, has been the fact that these traditions suggest somewhat conflicting roles for the planning profession and the practicing planner. The rationalist tradition suggests that the planner, as an applied scientist, must be dedicated to objectivity, careful collection and analysis of data, and rigorous adherence to the canons of the scientific method. The reform tradition, on the other hand, suggests that the planners must be committed to change and to ensuring that their proposals promote the best interests of their clients or the population at large. These two roles can conflict not only in planning practice (e.g., when a planner's commitment analyze impartially all possible courses of action conflicts with a commitment to promote only those alternatives that favor his clients), but also in the definition of the planning profession and planning education (e.g., to

The author gratefully acknowledges the assistance and encouragement of Pierre Clavel, of Cornell University's Department of City and Regional Planning, and David Lyons, of the Sage School of Philosophy at Cornell.

Reprinted with permission from *Journal of the American Institute of Planners*, vol. 44, no. 1, January 1978. Copyright 1978 by the American Institute of Planners (now the American Planning Association).

emphasize a scientific approach to problem analysis or, perhaps, a commitment to social change).

## EVOLUTION OF INSTRUMENTAL PLANNING

Early planning practice and education were shaped primarily by the profession's roots in the reform tradition. Planning problems—unregulated urban growth, poor sanitation, inadequate transportation and public facilities—were relatively clear-cut. As a result, the profession's early substantive theories were unsophisticated, and its methodologies were straightforward applications of the "design standards" approach of the more established professions, such as engineering, architecture, and public health (Webber, 1969). Guided by a rather naïve form of environmental determinism, planners assumed a professional responsibility for improving society through changes in the physical environment and saw themselves protecting the public interest from the self-interested and uninformed actions of politicians and private individuals (Tugwell, 1940). Planning education reflected this reform emphasis in its neglect of analytic planning methods and social science theory and its consideration of utopian plans that might define professional ideals.

In the last two decades, however, planning ideology and education have increasingly emphasized the planner's role as an applied scientist. The simplistic assumptions of the early profession have been replaced by an increased reliance on the theories and models of the social sciences. More dramatic has been the replacement of the early design approach by a variety of highly sophisticated, computer-assisted planning tools and techniques from large-scale urban simulation models to linear programming and regression analysis. Contemporary planning education reflects this conception of the planner-as-scientist in its emphasis on statistics, planning methods, and the substantive theories of economics, sociology, regional science, and the other positive social sciences.

With this increased theoretical and methodological sophistication has come a neglect of the profession's reform heritage. That is, implicit in the emphasis on analytic techniques and social science theory is a view of the planner as a "value-free means technician" who collects and analyzes "factual" data concerning the means for achieving public policy objectives but avoids the "value" questions of defining these objectives.

For example, a recurring local public policy of question is whether public, low-income (and often minority) housing developments should be located in middle-class residential areas. It seems planners can help communities deal with issues like this in a variety of ways including:

estimating the most probable effects of locating a development in a particular area, surveying the experience in other communities, identifying community sentiments on the issue, and determining the least costly way to implement whatever public policy is established. Academic planners, as positive social scientists, may likewise consider the general question of mixed residential neighborhoods by, for example, building predictive models of changes in residential patterns or developing theories of the social and psychological effects of mixed housing.

Under the widely assumed view of planners as technicians, this is all planners can and must do—collect and provide information that will make for more informed policy making. That is, it is assumed planners can help determine the relative costs and benefits of alternative public policies and the most appropriate means for achieving public policy objectives, but must leave the determination of these objectives to the public and its elected and appointed representatives.

## THE CALL FOR NORMATIVE PLANNING

This "instrumental" concept of planning has been increasingly questioned by both planners and nonplanners (Fromm 1972; Kreiger 1974; and Long 1975b). Most radical have been the calls by Friedmann (1966), Faludi (1973), and others for "normative" planning in which planners subject both the ends and means of public policy to rational consideration. These proposals are of particular interest because they suggest that the planning profession can combine scientific analysis with reform and change and thus be true to both of its intellectual roots.

However, none of the calls for normative planning has outlined the procedures by which planners are rationally to evaluate public policy ends. More fundamentally, they have not developed the logical foundation for rational consideration of ethical issues in public policy—an activity that runs counter to some of the most fundamental and widely shared assumptions of the positive social sciences.

This article attempts to provide this intellectual foundation for normative planning, the rational consideration of both factual questions of public policy means and ethical questions of public policy ends. First, it argues, planners cannot consider factual questions of alternative means alone, but must also deal with substantive ethical questions—implicitly if not explicitly. Current attempts to deal with the ethical issues of public policy planning by claims to professionalism and by pragmatic politics are review and judged inadequate. More fundamentally, the "logical-positivist" foundation for the instrumental view is examined and found to be deficient. Further, the "post-logical-positivist" views of such contemporary philosophers as John Rawls are found to suggest that ethical issues can be rationally considered in ways similar to those of the empirical sciences. These views, finally, suggest the foundations for a normative yet rational approach to planning, and the implications of that approach for planning practice and theory are briefly considered.

## THE IMPOSSIBILITY OF
## VALUE-FREE PLANNING

A dominant theme underlying much of the planning literature is the view that planners can and should avoid the consideration of substantive ethical questions. Traditional land-use planning was seen by many as a purely technical activity directed by statements of land-use goals and objectives that had been approved by the community or were self-evident and needed no approval. Planning in this view, was political only in that planners might have to convince public officials to accept and act on their final plans. "Process" approaches to planning utilizing decision theory, linear programming, and operations research have similarly been seen as avoiding substantive ethical questions by limiting the planner's role to identifying the optimal or most efficient means for achieving the objectives of elected and appointed public officials.

While these approaches have been criticized on a variety of grounds, the relevant point here is that neither eliminates the need for planning to deal (implicitly, if not explicitly) with the ethical issues implicit in questions of public policy. Altshuler (1965), Banfield (1959), and others have observed that, for a variety of good reasons, communities and public organizations are reluctant to establish the long-range goals that are presumed to guide planning practice. Goals, when established, are vague and often conflicting; as a result planners and administrators must make substantive decisions in preparing detailed plans and evaluating specific government actions (Appleby, 1949).

These traditional approaches have been supplemented by proposals for advocacy planning in which planners promote the interests of community groups (Davidoff, 1965) and for limiting planning's role to providing information to existing multicentered policy-making processes (Webber, 1965; Rondinelli, 1971). However, neither of these approaches eliminates the need for planners to deal in some way with substantive ethical issues. Advocate planners must select the interests that are (and are not) to be represented in the policy-making process, because not all groups will be homogeneous in all relevant respects[1] Even providing additional information to existing market and policy-making processes requires a determination of (among other things) which studies are to be conducted, which data collected, and what findings provided to which community groups (Webber, 1965). Because the answers given to each of these questions affect the final policy that is adopted, they necessarily involve substantive ethical issues that must be resolved, either explicitly or implicitly, by planners (Tribe, 1972).

More fundamentally, public policy planning without the explicit consideration of substantive ethical or political issues seems impossible because planning is itself *essentially* political. As Norton Long pointed out in 1959,

> The question is not whether planning will reflect politics, but whose politics will it reflect. . . . Plans are in reality political programs. . . . In the broad sense they represent political philosophies, ways of implementing different conceptions of the good life (p. 168).

To the extent that planners are successful in influencing the policies and actions of government, they are acting politically in the most fundamental sense of the word because their actions help determine "who gets what, when, how, (Laswell, 1936) and thus affect the members of society, positively and negatively. As a result, their decisions and actions *necessarily* involve ethical issues of, for example, balancing the conflicting interests of the members of society, and it seems impossible both in practice and in principle to limit planning to only the factual consideration of means.

## ATTEMPTING TO DEAL WITH
## NORMATIVE ISSUES

It has, of course, been widely recognized by both planning academics and practitioners that value-free planning is impossible (Davidoff and Reiner, 1962; Altshuler, 1965; Benveniste, 1972). In fact, planners often have strongly felt personal or widely shared professional views on such public issues as the desirability of mixed housing and regularly attempt to get their views enacted at the local, state, or even national level.

Early planners assumed that their views corresponded to an enlightened public interest and saw their attempts to help define public policy objectives as merely the application of their professional judgment to narrow technical issues within their unique competence with issues within their unique competence with issues of land use and related public facilities. Thus, like the professional opinions of doctors and lawyers, planning prescriptions were presumed to be justified by the practitioners' expertise with the relevant issues and their membership in a moral community guided by a well-defined set of professional norms. This emphasis on professionalism is reflected in the repeated attempts to demonstrate that planning is a profession and to develop professional and personal "philosophies" that could guide individual planners (see, e.g., Howard, 1954, 1955).

However, planners' claims to professional competence have never been widely accepted by others involved in defining public policy (see, e.g., Altshuler, 1965: especially pp. 17–83). In addition, the norms presumed to guide professional practice have been found to be not only unclear and rarely enforced but often conflicting (see, e.g., Marcuse 1976). More importantly, planning issues are now recognized to be important political questions involving the interests of a wide range of actors, and planners' prescriptions have been found to reflect the often unrecognized bias of the profession's middle-class members (see, e.g., Davidoff and Reiner, 1962; Davidoff, 1965).

## DUAL BASES FOR CONTEMPORARY PRACTICE

With the recognition of planning's political nature and the questioning of its professional heritage has come a fundamental uncertainty about the way in which planners are to deal with the ethical aspects of their work. For technical or "scientific" issues of understanding the operation of nature and society (the way the world *is*), planners receive relatively clear guidance from the empirical sciences and the loosely defined norms of the scientific method. Thus, it seems, planners should attempt to collect all available data, generalize from particular observations to general theories, laws, and models, and test these by comparing them to reality. However, for political or ethical issues of determining what policies should be enacted (the way the world *ought to be*), no such guidance seems to be available. There may be a variety of opinions about what ought to be done in a particular case, and it is often not clear how these alternative positions can be evaluated or even what information is relevant for comparing them.

Thus, perhaps inevitably, practicing and acdemic planners are left with a feeling that ethical positions are mere relative matters of individual taste and preference (such as a preference for one color over another) and that planners' views can only compete with many conflicting and equally valid political opinions. Motivated by this belief, contemporary planners have generally adopted two conflicting perspectives on the ethical issues of public policy planning. Some, emphasizing planning's scientific nature and adopting the perspective of the positive social sciences, attempt to avoid all ethical questions by collecting and providing decision makers with factual information on the probable effects of alternative policies. The implicit belief here is simply that better information will lead to better public policy decisions. Others, emphasizing planning's political nature and downgrading policy analysis, just assume their political positions to be "correct" and engage in pragmatic politics in order perhaps, to promote the interests of underrepresented groups or, more generally to improve their political effectiveness. The implicit belief here is that, by acting politically, planners can improve the political process and its representatives and, thus, public policy decisions.[2]

However, by emphasizing either the information on which public decisions are made or the decision process and the groups involved, both approaches ignore the inevitable ethical issues of public policy planning, both avoid direct consideration of the *substance* of public policy objectives.[3] In addition, by separating scientific analysis from political action, neither approach reflects the profession's traditional concerns with both rationality and reform. To determine whether, in fact, these two concerns can be combined in the rational consideration of substantive questions of public policy it is necessary to examine the intellectual foundation of the instrumental approach.

## FOUNDATIONS OF INSTRUMENTAL PLANNING

The assumption that planning should be limited to the factual consideration of means reflects, if unconsciously, the long-standing and extremely influential positivist view that the empirically based sciences provide the only means for obtaining systematic and reliable knowledge. In particular, it has been motivated by two important aspects of this tradition: the logical-positivist conception of ethics, developed by the Vienna Circle at the turn of the century, and the means-end conception of rationality.[4]

### Logical-Positivist Conception of Ethics

The logical-positivist position is based on an assumed distinction between factual sentences that are "cognitively meaningful" (i.e., can be proved to be correct or incorrect) and nonfactual sentences such as questions, requests, and exclamations that are neither true nor false and thus cannot provide the basis for systematic knowledge. Further, the logical positivists assumed, sentences can be cognitively meaningful in only two ways. First, they argued, sentences can be cognitively meaningful if they express statements that are "analytic," that is, true or false just by virtue of the meaning of the words used. For example, the sentence "A U.S. census standard metropolitan statistical area consists of a county containing at least one city of 50,000 or more inhabitants and any adjacent metropolitan counties" is an analytical truth or tautology, true by the meanings of the English terms *U.S. census, standard metropolitan statistical area, county,* and so on. Similarly, the sentence, "A U.S. census standard metropolitan statistical area consists of only one county containing a city of 50,000 or more inhabitants" is analytically false or self-contradictory on the same grounds, that is, because of the meanings of the English words *U.S. Census, standard metropolitan statistical area,* and so on.

Second, in their famous "verifiability principle," the logical positivists argued that "synthetic" (i.e., nonanalytic) sentences can be cognitively meaningful only if they express statements that can be empirically verified, that is, confirmed or disconfirmed by empirical observations. For example, the sentence "The present population of the New York metropolitan area is thirteen million" is cognitively meaningful under this criterion because it is possible to imagine ways in which it could be empirically confirmed or disconfirmed—using, perhaps, standard census enumeration and sampling techniques.

In the logical-positivist view, sentences that are neither true (or false) by virtue of the meanings of the words they contain nor empirically testable (at least in principle) are cognitively meaningless and, therefore, neither true nor false. In particular, the logical positivists viewed "ethical" sentences (stating that an action is good or bad, right or wrong, etc.) as neither analytic nor empirically verifiable and, thus, cognitively meaningless and neither true nor false. Thus, it was assumed, a clear distinction can be drawn between factual and ethical statements and a "logical gap" separates the two, that is, that no set of factual statements entails an ethical statement (and the reverse). Disagreements about ethical questions were seen as not resolvable on rational grounds because, in this view, they can reflect differing value systems and the choice between these is itself an ethical decision that cannot be made on rational grounds. (For an earlier version of this position see Ayer, [1952: 102–119].)

## Means-End Conception of Rationality

Closely related to the logical-positivist position is the means-end conception of practical reason revealed in the works of both contemporary writers such as Herbert Simon (1957) and classical writers such as Max Weber (1949) and David Hume (see, e.g., the selections in Raphael [1969: pp. 8–14, 83–90]). In this view, actions can be justified only as providing a means for achieving a person's ends and can be rationally evaluated only on this ground (e.g., as providing an adequate means for achieving those ends). An end that guides the selection of one set of means may, of course, provide a means for achieving "higher" or more valued ends and be rationally evaluated with respect to those ends. However, in this view, the chain of means and ends must stop with an "ultimate" end the selection of which is a mere matter of individual taste or preference that cannot be justified on rational grounds. For example, it is assumed, planners may justify placing public housing projects in the middle-class neighborhoods as a means for reducing racial and class discrimination, but they cannot justify reducing discrimination because they merely dislike or prefer to reduce discrimination.

## Implications for Planning

Together the logical-positivist conception of ethics and the means-end conception of rationality imply the instrumental view that public policy planning must be limited to the factual consideration of means toward ends established outside of the planning process. That is, if, as is generally assumed, planning is the application of rationality to public policy making, planners must restrict their attention to questions that can be considered rationally. In the means-end view, the rational consideration of courses of action can consist only of the selection of appropriate means for achieving designated ends. While a given end may be justified as a means for achieving a higher end, ultimately the chain of means and ends must stop with an ethical judgment that, under both positions, cannot be justified on rational grounds. Thus, it appears, if planners are to deal only with rational issues, they can only attempt to identify the most appropriate means for achieving ends or goals established by others (e.g., elected officials or client groups). If, however, these two views are mistaken, this widely, if implicitly, assumed argument for limiting planning to the consideration of only public policy means is likewise mistaken.

## EXAMINATION OF THE INTELLECTUAL FOUNDATION

As was pointed out above, the logical positivists assumed that ethical issues cannot be rationally discussed because, under their verifiability principle, ethical statements were not meaningful. As they recognized (Ayer, 1952), however, any statement of their verifiability principle would *itself* satisfy neither of these criteria for identifying meaningful sentences. It could not be a tautology, true by virtue of the meaning of the words, because the crucial word *meaningful* is used in a variety of ways, including several that do not correspond to that implied by the verifiability principle. (For example, the ethical sentence "Stealing is wrong" is *in some sense* meaningful, i.e., different from "Stealing isn't wrong.") It also could not be a synthetic claim or assertion of fact that could be tested empirically because, as a philosophical claim *about meaningfulness*, it is a claim of an entirely different order.

Evading the issue, the logical positivists viewed the verifiability principle as a verbal recommendation that would promote clarity in the discussion of ethical questions. As merely a *recommendation*, however, it can be either rejected or accepted. If it is rejected, the logical-positivist position on which it is based must likewise be rejected. And if it is accepted, even though *by its own criteria* meaningless, there is no reason to believe that ethical statements should not also be accepted even though they are also meaningless under these criteria. In either case, the logical positivists' assumption that ethical issues cannot be rationally discussed is highly questionable.[5]

## The Basis for Scientific Discourse

More fundamentally, philosophers now recognize that ethical reasoning is much more like scientific reasoning than the logical positivists recognized. That is, while the logical positivists were correct in pointing out that empirical evidence alone cannot entail an ethical belief, this is also true for scientific laws and theories that also cannot be conclusively supported by observational evidence alone. As philosophers and historians of science have demonstrated repeatedly (e.g., Kuhn [1970] and Hempel [1966]), there is always more than one theoretical explanation for any set of observational data, and a degree of choice is involved in the selection of one theory or paradigm over another.

However, the choice between competing theories is not arbitrary; it is regulated by the loosely defined norms and procedural requirements of the scientific method, and reliance on these criteria can itself be justified. For example, while two different explanations (e.g., a sociological one and a psychological one) may be offered for an observed social phenomenon, the procedural norms of the scientific method suggest several criteria for choosing between them: Which more completely accounts for available empirical data? Which relies on fewer unmeasurable variables? Which is more parsimonious? and so on. And, if pressed, one could justify reliance on these criteria (e.g., argue that it is reasonable to assume that nature is simple rather than complex and thus that parsimonious explanations are preferred over less simple ones) (Rudner, 1961).

As Gerwirth (1968) has pointed out, the logical positivists and others, who assumed that science was an entirely cognitive and rational process while ethics was not, failed to recognize the problem of justifying the norms and criteria of the scientific method. Their conception of science included only activities that satisfied these criteria (e.g., neurology, physiology, and astronomy) and ignored those that did not (e.g., Christian Science, phrenology, and astrology). Their conception of ethics, however, included not only the views of Albert Schweitzer, missionaries, and democrats but also those of Al Capone, cannibals, and Nazis. If their conception of science had been as broad as their conception of ethics (to include, for example, a "scientific" dispute betwen a Christian Scientist and a neurologist), they would have observed fundamental disagreements in "preference" or "attitude" (concerning, perhaps, the type of evidence to be accepted) similar to those in an "ethical" dispute between say, a missionary and a cannibal.

## The Basis for Rational Discourse

It is now generally recognized that this pattern of reasoning (i.e., with respect to criteria that must themselves be justified) underlies not only scientific reasoning but all rational discourse (Feigel, 1952: 672–80). Consider, for example, a purely empirical claim that a healthy individual is mortal. This claim cannot conclusively be proven because, until that person dies, it is at least logically possible that the individual in question will live forever. However, it can be given a great deal of support by an inductive argument pointing out that everyone who has lived to date has been mortal, which makes it *very* likely that the individual in question will also die. A complete justification for the original claim must, however, include a justification for reliance on the rules of inductive logic.

In a similar way the ultimate justification for claims to nonempirical knowledge (e.g., those of mathematics) lies in the rules of inference and substitution of deductive logic. Rational argument, either inductive or deductive, presupposes the reference to one or both sets of principles which are at least implicitly agree upon. While knowledge claims of either type can be supported by demonstrating that their derivation was in accordance with the relevant set of principles, a complete justification for the original claims must include a justification for reliance on those principles.

Reliance on the rules of deductive inference is easily justified on pragmatic grounds because only reasoning that accords with them can insure the transition from true propositions to other true propositions. Similarly, reliance on the rules of inductive logic is pragmatically justified for all attempts to make true inductive inferences because only these rules can be shown (deductively) to provide a self-corrective means for disclosing any underlying order to nature.[6]

## The Basis for Means-End Discourse

In addition, contrary to the means-end conception of rationality, a similar two-stage process underlies the rational evaluation not only of means with respect to ends, but of ends themselves. This is best illustrated by graphic, if somewhat unrealistic, examples such as a proposal to collect all the children in a community at their neighborhood schools, load them onto school buses, drive them to a nearby airport, and fly them to a remote mountain region in order to isolate them from the rest of the population. Here is a perfect example of means-end reasoning; and on the means-end conception of rationality the policy is rational because, we can assume, it outlines the most efficient means for achieving the end of isolating the community's children. However, as this example illustrates, a means-end justification is inadequate because the important question is not whether the most appropriate means were selected to achieve the chosen objectives but whether the objective is appropriate. That is, contrary to the means-end view, a complete justification for an action must consider not only the means chosen for achieving selected ends but also the ends themselves.

For example, a community that implemented the public policy outlined above would *seem* to be acting irrationally even if its elected officials preferred to implement it (which, in the instrumental view of planning, is all that is required to justify a policy). The policy would be rational and justified only if there were good reasons for its implementation (e.g., that it provided the only mechanism for protecting the children from an extremely dangerous epidemic). That is, as was true for scientific, inductive, and deductive reasoning, the justification for actions is not dependent on mere irrational preference or taste but, rather, on considerations and criteria. These can, in turn, be rationally justified (in principle) by reference to fundamental empirical characteristics of human beings and the world in which they live (e.g., the fact that, in Hart's words, public policy deals with "social arrangements for continued existence, not with those of a suicide club" [1961: p. 183], which are not mere matters of individual taste but are reflected in the whole structure of our thought and language (Hart, 1961: 181–95).

*Richard E. Klosterman*

# ALTERNATIVE FOUNDATIONS

As has been pointed out above, scientific reasoning and indeed all rational discourse is ultimately supported by criteria which, while usually only implicitly assumed, can be rationally justified. Recognizing this, contemporary philosophers (e.g., Rawls [1968, 1971] and Brandt [1959: 241–70]) suggest that the question of the rationality of ethical discourse turns simply on whether similar sets of rationally defensible criteria exist for validating (and invalidating) ethical principles and decisions. That is, as we have seen, scientific reasoning is accepted as rational only because there exist widely accepted and rationally defensible criteria for evaluating scientific observations and theories. Thus, these philosophers argue, if similar sets of criteria for evaluating ethical positions and principles were developed and justified, then ethical discourse could likewise be accepted as a rational activity. From this contemporary perspective, moral philosophy is an attempt to formulate rationally defensible principles and criteria that match our considered moral judgment just as the philosophy of science attempts to develop systematic principles that agree with accepted scientific practice.

## An Example

While the formulation and defense of moral principles has been a continuing concern of philosophers from Plato to the present, these "post-logical-positivist" views have dramatically revived interest in social and political philosophy (Germino, 1967). The most important example of this contemporary interest and one that best illustrates its implications for planning practice and theory is John Rawls's *A Theory of Justice* (1971).

In *A Theory of Justice* Rawls develops two "principles of justice" to be used to evaluate the major political, economic, and social institutions of society.[7] The first, "the greatest equal liberty principle," holds that each person is to have an equal right to the most extensive basic liberty compatible with an equal liberty for others. The second holds that social and economic inequalities are to be arranged so that they are (1) reasonably expected to be to everyone's advantage, particularly that of the least well off ("the difference principle"); and (2) attached to social positions that are open to all ("the fair equality of opportunity principle").

Rawls (1971: 11:22, 46–53) defends his principles with two separate, but closely related, arguments. The first, his so-called "contract argument," suggests that his principles are the solution to a hypothetical problem of rational choice under constraints (most importantly, fairness and impartiality) which, he argues, are appropriate for selecting principles of justice. The second, which might be called a "congruence argument," suggests that his principles more nearly match our considered moral judgments than do the alternatives (e.g., unlike classical utilitarianism, his principles would not approve of the institution of slavery even if it benefitted the majority (Lyons, 1974).

## Implications of the Example

The details of Rawls's arguments are too complex to be considered here and have, in fact, been subject to a great deal of criticism (see, e.g., the selections in Daniels [1975]). In addition, the importance of Rawls's work for the present discussion lies not in its details but rather in providing an example of the contemporary approach to the consideration of ethical principles (and particular ethical questions). The example is especially appropriate because it clearly illustrates the parallels with the more traditional consideration of the principles of the scientific method (and particular "scientific" questions) referred to above. In intent, the two approaches are similar in that Rawls's principles are to be used to evaluate the major institutions of society just as the principles of the scientific method are to be used to evaluate the hypotheses and theories of the empirical sciences. In structure, the two are similar in that Rawls's first argument corresponds to placing general restrictions on the selection of the principles that are to guide scientific practice (e.g., requiring that they not be biased toward any particular theory); his second corresponds to requiring that these principles agree with accepted scientific practice.

More importantly, Rawls's work suggests one way in which planners can practice normative planning, rationally evaluating both the means and the ends of public policy. That is, it suggests planners can argue that social institutions with redistributive effects benefiting the least well off are just and can rely on Rawls's principles (and his arguments in their defense) to support their position.[8] In this way the planners' ethical positions would not reflect mere preference or taste but would be supported in a way similar to that of their scientific positions (which are likewise based on principles which must be rationally defended). Other groups could of course pursue other objectives, but under this approach to normative planning, would have to justify *their* perspectives, allowing the bases for the conflicting positions to be rationally evaluated.[9] Thus, while not eliminating the inevitable conflicts over public policy objectives and the groups they favor, this approach would provide a framework within which these conflicts can be rationally considered.

127

## Implications of Normative Planning

Not only would this approach provide a rational basis for planners' ethical positions, it would also unite planners' political and scientific roles, expanding the scope of the latter. Under this approach planners would no longer rely merely on pragmatic politics and claims to professionalism to promote their proposals, but rather, would attempt to defend them on rational grounds. Once they did so it would soon be recognized that their ethical positions (e.g., promoting mixed residential neighborhoods) were largely dependent on numerous empirical and thus researchable assumptions. That is, in this case the desirability of mixed housing seems largely dependent on the *empirical* issues of its aggregative and distributive effects under particular circumstances, for example, whether there is an identifiable tipping point, whether it will reduce property values and increase crime rates or, more positively, will increase racial understanding. While determining these effects may be extremely difficult, they are clearly suitable subjects for empirical research, and information such as this seems essential for adequately supporting recommendations on the advisability of mixed housing (see Long, 1975a). A particularly important new avenue for planning analysis, which would seem to follow from a normative, yet rational, approach, would be the determination of the *distributive* effects of public policies (i.e., the determination of not merely whether total project benefits exceed total project costs, but also of which groups in society reaped the benefits and which bore the costs).

More generally, Rawls's work points to a need for rationally defensible, normative criteria for evaluating and justifying particular public policies and actions. While Rawls's criteria are applicable only to the evaluation of the major social institutions, it seems that similar criteria could be developed for considering specific government policies and actions. Once developed and (at least provisionally) defended, these criteria would provide a rationally defensible basis for the evaluation of public policies comparable to that which the criteria of the scientific method provide for the evaluation of scientific theories (see Klosterman, 1976).

These criteria would also provide the basis for the rational evaluation of alternative approaches to planning—which is itself a second order policy decision. Many planning theorists (e.g., Faludi 1973) attempt to avoid all ethical questions by developing predictive hypotheses identifying which of a number of alternative approaches will, in fact, be used in a given situation. However, by merely describing present planning practice, these descriptive hypotheses provide little guidance to practitioners attempting to determine which approach *ought* to be used under particular conditions, or to the profession's continuing effort to improve public policy decisions and the processes by which they are made. Given rationally defensible criteria for evaluating these alternative approaches, planning theorists could abandon their present value-neutral approach and evaluate these alternatives as more or less likely to improve existing policy-making processes and, consequently, the community as a whole. Thus, for example, it might be argued that even though a narrowly defined technician role may most effectively get planning proposals implemented in a cohesive political system, a less effective role of advocacy planning may better educate the public and, in the long run, be a more appropriate strategy.

The work of Rawls and the other critics of instrumental planning's positivist foundations is, of course, only suggestive and does not provide detailed guidance for conducting normative planning. However, it seems the most important implications that would follow from a rejection of value-free instrumental planning lie, not in the development of new planning techniques, but rather in fundamentally changing the way individual planners and the profession as a whole view their role in society. The above analysis suggests that planners need not (in fact, cannot) separate planning analysis from planning politics by focusing only on technical questions of public policy means. Rather, it argues, planners can go further and combine their dual commitments to scientific analysis and social reform in the rational consideration of the difficult but important questions of defining public policy objectives. If this does, in fact, happen and the rational evaluation and justification of public policy ends joins the scientific analysis of public policy means as a guiding ideal of the profession, the implications for both theory and practice will certainly be far reaching.

## NOTES

1. This has been explicitly recognized in Davidoff's call for "ideological advocacy" in which the advocate planner works with available groups to promote *his own* views (Davidoff, Davidoff, and Gold, 1970) and Peattie's (1970) call for planners to choose as clients those groups that seem *to the planner* to be developing issues worthy of support.

2. The clearest examples of the second approach are, of course, the calls for advocacy planning by Davidoff (1965), Peattie (1970), and others; it is also reflected in the attempt by Bolan (1967), Rabinovitz (1969), and others to identify roles and strategies that will increase planners' political effectiveness, on the implicit assumption that whatever a planner wants is what ought to be done.

3. This emphasis on the policy-making process and the groups involved in that process rather than on the *substance* of public policy reflects a similar perspective which dominates both political science and public decision making (see, e.g., Cochran, 1973; Lowi, 1967).

4. While revealed only implicitly in the work of practitioners, these intellectual roots are explicitly revealed in arguments for the instrumental approach in Herbert Simon's influential *Administrative Behavior* (1957: especially chs. 1–4) and Davidoff and Reiner's "A Choice Theory of Planning" (1962). For brief histories of the positivist tradition and development of logical positivism see Abbagnano (1967) and Passmore (1967).

5. This aspect of the logical-positivist position was pointed out to the author by David Lyons. In fact the logical positivists never succeeded in stating their verifiability principle in a way that rejected as meaningless the transcendental claims of metaphysics while retaining as meaningful the hypotheses and theories of the empirical sciences (see Ashby, 1967).

6. Interestingly, as is true for the development of a rationally defensible basis for ethical decision making discussed here, developing a rigorous system of inductive logic that agrees with common sense and accepted scientific practice is exceedingly difficult (see Skyrms, 1966).

7. That is, contrary to the impressions of some (e.g., Berry and Steiker, 1974), Rawls does not suggest that these principles be used to evaluate specific governmental actions and policies but, rather, limits their use to more fundamental decisions concerning the nature of major social institutions.

8. An example of this approach in contemporary planning practice is the work of the Cleveland Planning Commission, which has pursued an explicit normative position of "promoting a wider range of choices for these Cleveland residents who have few, if any, choices." Unlike other advocacy groups, however, the commission has not merely adopted this position but has attempted to justify it on rational grounds, relying in part on Rawls's arguments (see Krumholz, Coggen, and Linner, 1975; Cleveland City Planning Commission, 1975).

9. For an attempt to defend an alternative to Rawls's principles of justice (in the form of an extreme "libertarian" state, dedicated only to protecting persons against force, fraud, theft, and breach of contract) see Nozick (1974).

# REFERENCES

Abbagnano, N.
  1967    "Positivism." The Encyclopedia of Philosophy. Vol. 6. New York: Macmillan.

Altshuler, A. A.
  1965    The City Planning Process: A Political Analysis. Ithaca: Cornell University Press.

Appleby, P. H.
  1949    Policy and Administration. Alabama: University of Alabama Press.

Ashby, R. W.
  1967    "Verifiability principle." The Encyclopedia of Philosophy. Vol. 8. New York: Macmillan.

Ayer, A. J.
  1952    Language, Truth and Logic. New York: Dover.

Banfield, E. C.
  1959    "Ends and means in planning." International Social Science Journal 11: 361–68.

Benveniste, G.
  1972    The Politics of Expertise. Berkeley: Glendessary Press.

Berry, D. and G. Steiker
  1974    "The concept of justice in regional planning: justice as fairness."
          Journal of the American Institute of Planners 40: 414-21.

Bolan, R. S.
  1967    "Emerging views of planning." Journal of the American Institute of
          Planners 33: 234-46.

Brandt, R. B.
  1959    Ethical Theory. Englewood Cliffs: Prentice-Hall.

Cleveland City Planning Commission
  1975    Cleveland Policy Planning Report: Vol. 1. Cleveland: The Commis-
          sion.

Cochran, C. E.
  1973    "The politics of interest: philosophy and the limitations of the
          science of politics." American Journal of Political Science 17:
          745-66.

Daniels, N. ed.
  1975    Reading Rawls. New York: Basic Books.

Davidoff, P.
  1965    "Advocacy and pluralism in planning." Journal of the American In-
          stitute of Planners 31: 331-37.

Davidoff, P. and T. A. Reiner
  1962    "A choice theory of planning." Journal of the American Institute of
          Planners 27: 103-15.

Davidoff, P., L. Davidoff, and N. N. Gold
  1970    "Suburban action: advocate planning for an open society." Journal
          of the American Institute of Planners 36: 12-21.

Eversley, D.
  1973    The Planner in Society: The Changing Role of a Profession. Lon-
          don: Faber and Faber.

Faludi, A.
  1973    Planning Theory. Oxford: Pergamon.

Feigel, H.
  1952    "Validation and vindication: an analysis of the nature and limits of
          ethical arguments." In W. Sellars and J. Hospers (eds.), Readings in
          Ethical Theory. New York: Appleton-Century-Crofts.

Friedmann, J.
  1966    "Planning as a vocation." Plan Canada 6: 99-124; 7 :8-26.

Fromm, E.
  1972    "Humanistic planning." Journal of the American Institute of Plan-
          ners 38: 67-71.

Germino. D.
  1967    Beyond Ideology: The Revival of Political Theory. New York:
          Harper and Row.

Gerwirth, A.
  1968    "Positive 'ethics' and normative 'science.' " In J. J. Thompson and
          G. Dworkin (eds.), Ethics. New York: Harper and Row.

Hart, H. L. A.
1961    The Concept of Law. London: Oxford University Press.

Hempel, C. G.
1966    Philosophy of Natural Science. Englewood Cliffs: Prentice-Hall.

Howard, J. T.
1954    "Planning as a profession." Journal of the American Institute of Planners 20: 58-59.

1955    "The planner in a democratic society—a credo." Journal of the American Institute of Planners 21: 62-66.

Klosterman, E.
1976    Toward a Normative Theory of Planning. Ph.D. dissertation, Cornell University.

Kreiger, M. H.
1974    "Some new directions for planning theory." Journal of the American Institute of Planners 40: 156-63.

Krumholz, N. J. M. Coggen, and J. H. Linner
1975    "The Cleveland policy planning report." Journal of the American Institute of Planners 41: 298-304.

Kuhn, T. S.
1970    The Structure of Scientific Revolutions. 2d ed. Chicago: University of Chicago Press.

Laswell, H. D.
1936    Politics: Who Gets What, When, How. New York: P. Smith.

Long, N. E.
1959    "Planning and politics in urban development." Journal of the American Institute of Planners 25: 167-69.

1975a   "Making urban policy useful and corrigible." Urban Affairs Quarterly 10: 379-97.

1975b   "Another view of responsible planning." Journal of the American Institute of Planners 41: 311-16.

Lowi, T.
1967    "The public philosophy: interest-group liberalism." American Political Science Review 61: 5-24.

Lubove, R.
1967    "The roots of urban planning." In R. Lubove (ed.), The Urban Community: Housing and Planning in the Progressive Era. Englewood Cliffs: Prentice-Hall.

Lyons, D.
1974    "The nature of the contract argument." Cornell Law Review 59: 1064-76.

Marcuse, P.
1976    "Professional ethics and beyond." Journal of the American Institute of Planners 42: 264-74.

Nozick, R.
1974    Anarchy, State and Utopia. New York: Basic Books.

Passmore, J.
  1967    "Logical positivism." The Encyclopedia of Philosophy. vol. 5. New
          York: Macmillan.

Peattie, L. R.
  1970    "Drama and advocacy planning." Journal of the American Institute
          of Planners 36: 405-10.

Rabinovitz, F. F.
  1969    City Politics and Planning. Chicago: Aldine.

Raphael, D. D.
  1969    British Moralists: 1650-1800. vol. 2. London: Oxford University
          Press.

Rawls, J.
  1971    A Theory of Justice. Cambridge, Mass.: Harvard University Press.

  1968    "Outline of a decision procedure for ethics." In J. J. Thompson and
          G. Dworkin (eds.), Ethics. New York: Harper and Row.

Rondinelli, D. A.
  1971    "Adjunctive planning and urban development policy." Urban Af-
          fairs Quarterly 7: 13-39.

Rudner, Richard
  1961    "An introduction to simplicity." Philosophy of Science 28: 109-19.

Simon, Herbert A.
  1957    Administrative Behavior: A study of Decision-making Processes in
          Administrative Organizations. 2nd ed. New York: Free Press.

Skyrms, B.
  1966    Choice and Chance: An Introduction to Inductive Logic. Belmont,
          Calif.: Dickenson.

Tribe, L. H.
  1972    "Policy science: analysis or ideology?" Philosophy and Public Af-
          fairs 2: 66-110.

Tugwell, R. G.
  1940    "Implementing the general interest." Public Administration Review
          1: 32-49.

Webber, M. W.
  1965    "The roles of intelligence systems in urban-systems planning." Jour-
          nal of the American Institute of Planners 31: 289-96.

  1969    "Planning in an environment of change." Town Planning Review
          39: 277-96.

Weber, M.
  1949    "Objectivity in social science and social policy." In E. G. Shils and
          H. A. Finch (trans. and eds.) Methodology of the Social Sciences.
          New York: Free Press.

# 5 Theory, Paradigms, And Planning

## DAVID K. MILLER

Stimulated by Kuhn's *Structure of Scientific Revolutions* (1970) and Berger and Luckman's *Social Construction of Reality* (1967), social scientists have become more aware of the relativistic nature of their theories. We have come to recognize how the paradigm, or world view, with which we approach a substantive problem limits the set of explanations we might have for social behavior, affects the methods by which we test the validity of our explanations, and even constrains the way we define the research problem.

Although social scientists may have come to recognize the relativistic nature of their work, most professionals who make use of social science knowledge have not. This is especially true when the knowledge used is "folk" knowledge, information that "everyone knows." By not recognizing alternative paradigms, professionals unwittingly constrain the range of explanations they can apply to behavior and thereby constrain the range of proposed actions.

In his book, *Social Theory for Planning*, Joe Bailey (1975) applies Kuhn's notion of paradigm to the sociological knowledge used by planners. He delineates four major paradigms that are and could be used to explain social behavior relevant to the planning process. He labels these paradigms: evolutionary, systems or functional, conflict, and interpretative.

While Bailey's book shows remarkable insight into the theoretical approaches that characterize urban planning, his writing style makes the book virtually inaccessible to nonsociologists. To redress that deficiency,

An earlier version of this paper was read at a conference, "Theory and Practice: The Contribution of the Social Sciences to Urban Planning," held at the State University of New York, Albany, 1978.

this paper will utilize many of the arguments presented in Bailey's book, illustrating them with statements from actual planning documents. By so doing I hope to begin a dialogue with planners to make them aware of the relativity of their theoretical knowledge just as social scientists have come to recognize the relativity of their own work, and to make them aware of the implications for action involved in operating under one or another paradigm.

In this paper I present five paradigms, or theoretical approaches, which are often adopted by practitioners in order to explain the behavior of urban components. They are evolutionary, physicalist, systems, conflict, and social construction. Although this list may not exhaust the paradigms in social science, its elements provide sufficient breadth to illustrate for planners the implications of the relativity of knowledge in social science.

In the illustrations I provide, I selectively quote phrases and paragraphs that display a given paradigm. Such a presentation gives the impression that a planner utilizes a single paradigm. That is not the case with any of the plans or documents discussed in this paper. Planners operate under a mixture of paradigms, and their plans reflect that mixture.

Many discussions of social science theory imply that theories and paradigms are either correct or incorrect. I propose that they are either useful or not. Using a particular paradigm is like using a particular filter or lens to film a scene; different lenses or filters bring out different aspects of the same scene.

## EVOLUTIONARY PARADIGM

Most planners are familiar with theories proposed by Robert E. Park and his students, at the University of Chicago, concerning ecological processes in cities. Those theories arise from and illustrate what I call the "evolutionary" paradigm whereby the city is conceived as an environment inhabited by a variety of individual decision makers whose decisions have implications for their own "survival" in the city.

Given a technological order that sets constraints on the resources available from the environment and an economic system that determines how those resources are distributed, the paradigm implies that land use and social relations in the city will evolve to efficient forms (since inefficient forms will tend to be selected out). In the city, for example, these processes take the form of invasion into and succession within what Park called "natural areas."

The use of this paradigm by planners is widespread. In a plan submitted by the Mayor's Advisory Commission on Small Business in Baltimore, the Commission begins with a quote from an earlier Department of Planning and Traffic Engineering report:

> The general excess of retail area in the inner city, difficult to eliminate, indicates a chaotic condition which can be alleviated only by the application of urban renewal techniques. . . . In the meantime, neighborhoods will deteriorate more rapidly; the unneeded vacant stores will be filled by less desirable non-residential uses or forsaken to marginal residential uses. . . . Soon the last remaining untapped market for the new merchandising techniques will be the more densely populated area of the City, where the older shopping districts are located. Nothing stands in the way of this exploitation but an obsolete, congested and mixed-use retail structure (1970: 1).

This quote reflects an action implication of the paradigm, namely, that planners should assist in getting rid of the "obsolete" to make room for the more "efficient." The planner's role seems to be to make us aware of what is going to happen so that we can make the best of it. A quote from *San Francisco Business* could easily have come from the San Francisco planning office.

> BART will also transform the residential profile of the Bay Area. Land values which are rising rapidly are spurring landowners to maximize economic use of their land. Single-family dwellings are being replaced by multi-family units . . . because (San Francisco) has only 6% of the land (in the Bay Area) and 16% of the population, it logically is the first to undergo extensive demolition of its single-family housing stock into multi-family highrise units (Sletteland, 1971: 17).

The implication is that bankers, land developers, and politicians should prepare themselves for a city of multifamily highrise buildings rather than single-family dwellings because that's how the city is going to evolve.

The paradigm implies an inevitability; change can be delayed or accelerated but never stopped. A comment by the president of an apartment owner's association in San Francisco minces no words in asserting this implication.

> If San Franciscans don't want their city converted into Manhattan, then let 'em go someplace else. But don't keep complaining about it, because that's what's going to happen and nobody can stop it (Sletteland, 1971: 18).

Not all planners base their work on such a simple version of an evolutionary paradigm, though. Moshe Safdie (1975), in a plan for Park

Heights in Baltimore, recognizes the critical role transportation plays in altering sustenance possibilities from the environment. He proposes focusing effort on transforming the transportation system in order to have an impact on the evolution of the community.

> Inherent in the foregoing brief history of Park Heights is the premise that the physical structure of the community has resulted almost directly from, and been principally affected by, the urban transportation routes that have evolved over time within the limitations of the existing topography of the area. . . . If it can be assumed that the new transportation pattern will have a continuing effect on the evolution of the community, then it is apparent that construction of highways that bypass residential areas and rapid transit systems that provide convenient access to the metropolitan region are opportunities for the revitalization of the community that must be considered in the plan (1975: 18).

Thus, a second implication of the evolutionary paradigm is that only by modifying the economic system or technologies which affect transfer of sustenance and information can planners have any effect on the evolutionary drift of a city.

A third implication which persists from the early twentieth century is that what has survived to the present must be somehow the most efficient. As Bailey (1975: 50) says, "Evolution is the retrospective interpretation of what is believed desirable in the present." Planners often use this paradigm to justify maintaining the status quo.

Basically, by adopting an evolutionary paradigm, planners take a more conservative stance toward social change. Change is out of the hands of the planners and in the long run will select out the fittest adaptors to the environment anyway. It is the role of planners to discern which structures are fittest, then to encourage those structures to minimize failures of unfit ones.

## PHYSICALIST PARADIGM

A second paradigm used frequently by planners is what I call the "physicalist" paradigm. As does the evolutionary paradigm, it views social relations in the city as determined by processes of a higher order than occur between individual human beings. For the physicalist planners, physical features of the city and its major institutional forms, such as schools or hospitals, shape urban life. Consistent with this approach is the planner who claims that deteriorated housing stock, overutilized thoroughfares, and a paucity of parks are responsible for the wretched conditions in many of our urban ghettos. When Jane Jacobs (1961) writes about the need for short blocks to stimulate community life, she approaches the problem of social interaction from a physicalist paradigm.

This paradigm minimizes the perceived effects of social groupings, racism, and other social relations and concentrates on traffic flow, communication systems, local subcenters, a capital web, plazas, parks, and so on. "The General Plan for the City of Boston," for example, reflects an overwhelming conception of Boston as an organism composed of traffic flows, regional action corridors, frontage street groups, and so on. The report describes streets as "containers of activities," as "channels of visual communication," and as "builders of private development and architectural potential."

> A street system designed to improve the relationship between pedestrian and vehicular uses, to promote the proper density and architectural quality of abutting land uses, and to improve visual communication will be that much more efficient as a carrier of traffic (Boston Redevelopment Authority, 1965: 24).

To be fair to the plan, the authors do mention the importance of neighborhood group support, but that treatment occupies only one half-page out of the sixty-page report.

Planners who view the city from a physicalist perspective tend to see human beings as reasonably malleable and affected strongly by the physical features of their environment. To these planners, signs of physical decay imply impending social problems. Solutions to urban problems concentrate on buildings, land-use practices, traffic corridors, and physical features of the environment rather than on problems or deficiencies within the economic system or the community's social structure.

## SYSTEMS PARADIGM

A third paradigm widely used by planners can be labelled a "systems" paradigm. The city is seen as a complex organism composed of many levels of subsystems. One attempts to understand the larger system. Whenever a subsystem is not adequately performing its function or whenever it is not sufficiently tuned to the system as a whole, social disorder will occur.

Plans incorporating medical imagery usually stem from a systems approach. A Denver Urban Renewal Authority pamphlet (1965) describes run-down areas as "cancer cells feeding on the body of the city." They propose "treatments" involving both "preventive" and "corrective" cures, invoking a structure of urban renewal activities much as a doctor would prescribe a medicine.

Under a systems paradigm everything is seen to be related to everything else in such a manner that any changes in one subsystem cause ripple effects in all other systems until the whole system reaches equilibrium again. A familiar example of this approach is Forrester's (1969) *Urban Dynamics* model. He models the city as a system comprised of three major sectors: population, industry, and housing. His computer simulations predict nonintuitive results from sincere actions to solve social problems because of the highly interconnected nature of the systems within the city.

A new town plan for the Washington, D.C., area (Menco O'Leary and Associates, 1972) prides itself on its emphasis on urban systems. A large part of the plan describes ways to integrate the communication systems, the educational system, the health care system, the transit system, the public safety system (police and fire), and even the recreational system of carefully designed bike paths, pools, gymnasiums, and exercise rings.

The systems paradigm most probably filtered into planning from management approaches such as those adopted for the aerospace industry. It implies that any problem, no matter how complex, can be solved by dividing it into manageable subsystems. The Washington plan was conceived by members of a subsidiary of Westinghouse; their approach to planning a complex social entity is reminiscent of corporate management strategies and is imbued with the same kind of optimism that managers use in reporting to stockholders.

While proponents of the systems paradigm may be optimistic about success, their approach also raises significant cautions: (1) problems are more complex than they appear on the surface; (2) caution should be exercised in making changes since the effects of those changes might be quite nonintuitive and may ripple out to affect a large number of subsystems; (3) since the system is so complex, a great deal of information about individuals and institutions, massive computer models, and highly trained specialists are needed to advise planners and the public on policy decisions; an (4) subsystems not in tune with the larger system must either be insulated from the system or be modified so that the survival of the whole system is not endangered. Bailey sums up these implications when he writes:

> There is no getting away from the fact that what makes a system a system is stability and the maintenance of a pattern; that is, the very lack of change. This passivism and conservatism is the price systems theory has paid for its obsession with the world as more than anything else a *complex* place, so

complex that science concentrating on tinkering with only a few factors at a time could not deliver the goods (1975: 62–63).

## CONFLICT PARADIGM

In contrast to the systems image of a city as a well-oiled machine with parts working in harmony, the conflict paradigm has the image of a society in which various social groups are vying for power and privilege and laying claim to scarce resources. This view is less common in American planning. Most American planners and even many American social scientists view the world essentially as one in which consensus about basic values and goals can be reached. Moshe Safdie's (1975) plan for Park Heights, for instance, assumes throughout that, with the appropriate mechanisms for community involvement, Park Heights residents will come to agreement with the city and among themselves concerning the rehabilitation of their community. Safdie mentions initial distrust among community groups concerning each others' motives but then writes a history of the development of the plan which implies that the differences were eventually resolved, resulting in an amicable Community Development Corporation.

Safdie's consensual view of society can be contrasted with that of Robert Goodman (1972) in *After the Planners* and with that of the writers of a series of *Bay Guardian* articles on highrises in San Francisco. In a *Bay Guardian* article Greggar Sletteland (1971) describes the "secret plan" of the Chamber of Commerce to "blitz SF neighborhoods." He describes how the Chamber first invited fifty leading bankers to the Bohemian Club to gain financial backing for high-rise luxury apartments in ten San Francisco neighborhoods, then consulted the politicians to work out deals.

> The planning process: first, the Chamber comes up with a blockbuster plan, then to the bankers, then to their politicians. The people who live here, the people who will subsidize the plan, haven't been consulted, and until they read this, won't know about it. . . . They'll know only when it's a fait accompli (1971: 20).

The conflict is set between the Chamber of Commerce and owners of high-rise buildings on one side and the general public on the other. Sletteland implies that at best a standoff between the two groups will be reached.

Planners such as Robert Moses of New York and Justin Herman of the San Francisco Redevelopment Agency undoubtedly viewed the city from a conflict perspective and used astute political maneuvering and power to get their way. (Perhaps one of the reasons they got their way so often was that the general public and planning staffs viewed the city from a consensual perspective, essentially ignoring power and its consequences, expecting that the democratic process would insure that the goals of "public servants" would be the same as those of the public they served.)

Planners who work under this paradigm are likely to disavow their role as disinterested technical consultants and to treat planning as a political activity in which one expects conflict and mobilizes political support for some policies and against some others. The contrast between Robert Goodman and Robert Moses is instructive: it shows how the same paradigm can be adopted both by people in the seat of power and by those outside it. Such critics of planning as Goodman (1972) urge us to be wary of claims for general benefits since benefits to some usually occur at cost to others. The paradigm implies a conflict over scarce resources. The paradigm also implies that planning may be ineffective if it expects consensus among large groups of people. Planners from this perspective may urge more decentralized decision making.

## SOCIAL CONSTRUCTION PARADIGM

A fifth paradigm, not yet widely used, is based on Berger and Luckman's (1967) *Social Construction of Reality* and on Erving Goffman's (1959) *Presentation of Self in Everyday Life*. This perspective is the "social construction" paradigm. It sees the social world as constructed and also alterable by human beings. The meanings we attribute to objects, the roles we define for ourselves and others, the institutions we have to assist our communal existence and our patterned behavior with each other are all potentially under our control since we, as a society with a human culture, fabricated them in the first place.

Planners working from this paradigm recognize the inertia for change within our institutions and attempt to create new institutions, new role relations, and new meaning structures in order to achieve the goals we as a public demand. Nothing is taken for granted. Meanings attributed to physical features of the city can have a substantial effect on social life but can also be altered with a new coat of paint, media campaigns or local community action. The planners' role is essentially one of empowering individuals within a culture to reassert their responsibility in creating their own worlds. The planner works with people and communities rather than with physical plans, buildings, traffic arteries, or zoning laws.

While only a few planners have explicitly adopted this paradigm, it does appear in many plans. Planners involved in the development of midtown Manhattan (New York Department of City Planning, 1980) recognize that the image of the area west of Broadway has been so tarnished that developers avoid it despite low land costs and accessibility to mass transit. They have proposed a series of city development programs and face-lifting to alter unpleasant memories of the area.

A strong feature of the social construction paradigm is its emphasis on empowerment of people. Nothing about the city is inevitable. Moshe Safdie's plan for Park Heights, for instance, concludes with an upbeat assertion of the power of Park Heights residents to build an acceptable social world in spite of an "indifferent outside world."

> The answers to all the questions listed above lie with the community. The strength which it can generate within itself, the determination which it can exhibit towards an indifferent outside world, the unity, cohesion and above all hope and optimism which it can raise will generate community power that can bend the bureaucracy, produce the resources and in time make life in Park Heights such as few dare dream today (1975: 137).

While Safdie's comments may sound excessively optimistic, the report reflects a great deal of work to make it happen. It is as if Safdie and his associates really do believe they can change the world.

## CONCLUSION

Using a paradigm approach to inform planning is at the same time frustrating and rewarding. Being able to state the subtleties and implications of a particular paradigm is difficult even for social scientists immersed in social science theory. While some users may be perceptive because of their emotional and intellectual distance from the paradigm, we cannot expect most practitioners of planning to be perceptive of paradigmatic differences and the implications for action of different approaches. We need additional comparative treatments such as Bailey's, which analyze and contrast complex paradigms underlying large bodies of social science theory. Such analyses are needed by wider public than simply the social science theorists.

However, examining a situation from several different perspectives allows a planner to discover subtle biases that may affect the success of a plan and to discover alternative solutions that may be more effective and less costly than the original solution. Seeing from a variety of perspectives may also make the planner more capable of interpreting and acting on requests and criticisms from politicians and public, since he or she may be better able to understand the paradigm under which the criticisms or requests are made.

While operating from a physicalist perspective may still be the most effective because physical solutions are visible, because they can easily be incorporated into laws and regulations, and because the public has come to expect physical solutions, planners need to be free to choose alternative paradigms. Instead of demolishing and rebuilding they may be able to achieve similar results by changing the meaning structures associated with a given area. Instead of expecting that a single building will change a neighborhood, they may look toward other agencies and social institutions which, when acting as a system, can achieve results no individual agency could accomplish. Instead of being hurt or angry when they are unable to achieve consensus on what they consider an excellent solution, they may be able to forge a more acceptable solution by working with the many groups vying for political and economic power in order to understand the basis for their views.

Planners as well as social scientists are quite often unaware of the world views that guide their interpretation of social reactions. Given this lack of awareness, it is understandable that neither planners nor social scientists are always aware of what paradigm they are using, nor do they choose a paradigm for its usefulness and applicability. We need to be able to adopt or reject a given paradigm, depending on its ability to explain relevant social phenomena and on its implications for action.

Because social scientists and planners working together can develop theoretical and practical understanding that neither could develop alone, we need further discussions of paradigms in a language accessible to both groups. Social scientists need to rephrase their theoretical work to make it understandable to planners. Planners need to examine their own work as case studies of the effect of operating from a given paradigm or mixture of paradigms.

When we are able to recognize the implications of a paradigm for defining what is problematic, for determining the most appropriate evaluation tools, and for limiting the range of conceivable solutions, we become free to move toward the ends for which we plan.

# REFERENCES

Bailey, J.
　　1975　Social Theory for Planning. Boston: Routledge and Kegan Paul.
Berger, P. and T. Luckman
　　1967　Social Construction of Reality. Garden City: Anchor.
Boston Redevelopment Authority
　　1965　"1965/1975 general plan for the city of Boston, March 1965".
Denver Urban Renewal Authority
　　(n. d.)　"Urban renewal goes forward in Denver."

Forrester, J.
1969    Urban Dynamics. Cambridge, Mass.: M.I.T. Press.

Goffman E.
1959    The Presentation of Self in Everyday Life. New York: Doubleday-Anchor.

Goodman, R.
1972    After the Planners. London: Pelican.

Jacobs, J.
1961    The Death and Life of Great American Cities. New York: Random House.

Kuhn, T.
1970    Structure of Scientific Revolutions. Chicago: University of Chicago Press.

Mayor's Advisory Commission on Small Businesses
1970    "A program for older business districts—Baltimore".

Menco O'Leary and Associates
1972    "Fort Lincoln, new town." Washington, D. C.: Menco O'Leary and Associates.

New York Department of City Planning
1980    "Midtown development project." New York: Department of City Planning.

New York Planning Foundation
1980    "Remarks delivered by Garrett Thelander." New York: Planning News 44:6.

Safdie, M. and Associates, Montreal, Canada
1975    "A new life for Park Heights." Prepared for Commissioner of Housing and Community Development.

Sletteland, G.
1971    "A city of skyscrapers." In The Ultimate Highrise. San Francisco: San Francisco Bay Guardian Books.

# 6 Thoughts on the Separability of Theory and Practice

## Analytic and Dialectic Approaches to Planning in a Nonstationary World

### STEPHEN GALE

The past several decades have witnessed a movement within the natural and social sciences toward a view of inquiry and action in which language plays a central role: a view in which observations, concepts, and methods of reasoning are understood as being directly dependent on their linguistic presuppositions.[1] To some extent this development can be traced to debates within philosophy itself, but for the most part it seems to be a response to the practical problems of inquiry. How are the observer and the observed related? How are concepts formed and used? What is the relationship between inference procedures and problem types? How are praxis and action connected to understanding? Thus, even as the logicians' sanguine ideals of a unified language and methodology of science have faded, the need for a more diversified perspective on inquiry has become manifest. At the center of this change, language stands as the principal motivation and instrumental force.

In this essay, I shall outline an argument for a language-based approach to social inquiry that provides the grounds for the integration of methods of analytical representation and dialectical argument. Thus, although the substantive motivation for my argument can be recog-

The partial support of the National Science Foundation (Grant No.SOC76-12358) and the U.S. Department of Transportation (Grant No.DOT-TSC-1459) are gratefully acknowledged as are helpful comments and criticisms given by Mr. Michael Atkinson.

This paper was presented at a conference, "Theory and Practice: The Contribution of the Social Sciences to Urban Planning," The State University of New York at Albany, 1978.

nized as a dissatisfaction with the current separation of theory and practice in social planning in particular, it is also rooted in what I see as a misconstruction of the roles of analysis and dialectics in inquiry as a whole. And, since I am ultimately concerned with the development of practical, institutionally alive procedures for an evolving world characterized by vague concepts and ideals, I will hold that inquiry must be directly linked to viable procedures of observation, explanation, prescription, and evaluation that are based on commonly understood patterns of linguistic representation and argument.

## INTRODUCTION

Historically, the concept 'analytic' has been identified with different grammatical categories and meanings. In reference to 'laws of thought,' for example, it has indicated (a) the general activity of thinking or reasoning, (b) norms for correct reasoning, and (c) formal laws of truth (Körner, 1966: 414–17). In mathematics, it has come to mean anything that exploits what Georgescu-Roegen (1966) has called "arithmomorphic" concepts and the related modes of argument (e.g., proof theory).[2] And in philosophy the concept has come to be closely associated with the perspective developed by Russell, Moore, Carnap, and the Wittgenstein of the *Tractatus* (Weitz, 1964: 97–105). Obviously, the concept 'dialectic' has historically had a similar variation of meaning (Hall, 1967).

These ambiguities notwithstanding, for the purposes of my argument a clearer, more specific definition is required; a definition that does not combine these diverse meanings, but reflects what I see as the essence of the debate between the use of analytical and dialectical methods in the study of change.[3] In particular, I will employ Georgescu-Roegen's (1966, 1971) comments on the differences between arithmomorphic and dialectic concepts as the characterization of the general dimensions of the debate. First, it is important to recall that, although there is a need to provide clear representations of meaning, meaning often cannot be given by references to the types of discrete, distinct categories that underlie the usual forms of mathematical entities and descriptions. At the same time, however, I will also maintain that simply asserting that a concept is vague does not preclude its being defined and expressed in an analytical manner; it may, of course, mean that the rules of the language of definition and representation must be changed to enable us to accommodate such statements, but it does not dismiss the idea that we can be analytical about such concepts.

Equally significantly, it should be noted that giving 'analytic' this broader meaning does not force us into an arbitrary distinction between 'analytic' and 'dialectic': it does not, in effect, force us to accept Georgescu-Roegen's broader conclusions that dialectics must carry the whole weight of the argument against arithmomorphic representations. In distinction from the spirit of both Georgescu-Roegen's arguments and the Hegelian-Marxist conception, dialectics will not be characterized here by the triad of 'unity of opposites/negation of negation/quality and quantity' (which was designed to treat questions of ideological dispute and the explanation of *sudden* transformations of concepts, purposes, and actions). Dialectics, as I use the term here, is simply a relation-ship — a means of reasoning and argument — between different represen-tations of reality, plan and action, possibility and actuality, and so on. Opposites are not required; neither is a strong negation thesis; nor is an a priori distinction between quantity and quality needed. These, I main-tain, are functions of the problem of giving analytic representation to concepts. Dialectics simply refers to a process of reasoning and rhetoric, and it should be equated neither with Hegelian-Marxist conceptualiza-tions nor with the kind of Gestalt therapy inherent in the ideas of hermeneutics (Gadamer, 1976).

Though the discussion thus far may appear abstruse, it is actually quite hard-headed. If the social understanding and praxis in an evolving world are to be anything more than ambiguously related forms of intellectual sculpture and criticism, if there is to be an integrated approach to the understanding and design of programs for social change that can offer insight into planning and practice, than scientific inquiry must offer more than descriptions and explanations of patterns of past behavior or simplistic, normative programs based on idealized optimal or ethical selection rules. In effect, it must be constituted as a heterodox methodology that integrates (i) description and explanation; (ii) projec-tions of potential consequences; (iii) understanding the roles of prescrip-tive and normative judgments; (iv) operational procedures that translate prescriptive analyses into practice; and (v) experimental modes of valida-tion and evaluation. My claim is that this process must be built on a general understanding of the role of language and argument in different situations and the development of specific *rules* of (a) observation and measurement (what I am calling 'analytics') and (b) dialogue and argu-ment (what I am calling 'dialectics').

The discussion is presented in four parts. First I will outline some of the philosophical and substantive motivations for my approach. Next, I will summarize the main points of a perspective on the methodology of social inquiry — a theory based on a question-answering process — which integrates analytics and dialectics. Third, I will identify several elements of a program for the use of an 'analytic/dialectic' mode of inquiry on problems concerning planning in an evolving (nonstationary) world.

Finally, I will describe some of the issues involved in developing a workable program of inquiry. Note that although I expect that my treatment will ultimately result in specific rules and procedures for relating inquiry and practice, at this point I am able to offer only a sketch of its rationale and structure.

# A WEB OF MOTIVATION:
# PHILOSOPHIC AND SUBSTANTIVE

The motivations for the argument of this essay form a web of fibers linked to a variety of philosophical pragmatic, and methodological concerns. Nevertheless, they form a single web: they are connected by way of common intersections, structural relations, and, ultimately, purpose. Though to do justice to this web is beyond the scope of my discussion here, it is appropriate to trace briefly a few of its strands and indicate how they are related to the theme of the argument. Note, however, that throughout my discussion I will employ the terms 'analytic' and 'dialectic' in the senses described above; this point is central to my general thesis that a reasonable approach to social inquiry and action must be based on a concept of methodology that integrates analytics and dialectics.

## *Two Philosophical Motivations*

Triads are never far below the surface of philosophical attitudes and arguments. Indeed, two such triads provide important philosophical examples of the motivation for my perspective: (i) that of Naming, Knowing, and Judging; and (ii) that of Mechanism, Adaptation, and Rule Following. Each is also an integral part of the debates on the nature of social inquiry and, therefore, should serve to illustrate the importance of integrating analytic and dialectic approaches in a general method of social inquiry.

Naming, Knowing and Judging (a paraphrase of W. H. Auden's (1948) well-known essay, "Making, Knowing and Judging") can be regarded as characterizing three central philosophical activities. Equally important, they are central themes in the problem of explicating the case for methodological heterodoxy. How is it that we classify, typify, distinguish, and categorize—Name—thoughts, objects, beliefs, and so on? What is it that constitutes understanding—Knowledge—of the world? Ho do we make inferences about—Judge—what ought to be? And what is the relationship among the three? From Plato and Aristotle to Kant to Hume to Russell, these issues have been, and remain, of central concern in both philosophy and science, as well as practice.

As I will point out in greater detail further on, much of contemporary Anglo-American social science has followed the lead of the natural sciences, abstracting one theme from this triad and treating it as the singular aim of science. Inquiry is, in effect, reduced to one specialized form: the world is seen (categorized, defined, and measured) in terms of arithmomorphic analytical expressions, and the corresponding dialectics of knowledge is identified with methods of giving answers to 'Why' questions about the occurrence of events. Now whether or not this strategy is useful for some purposes, it has some obvious limitations as a paradigm for inquiry in general. Consider, for example, the other two elements of the triad. Naming, as a process, is the basic operation for prescribing and setting conceptual distinctions and boundaries — of giving (or imposing) structure. Here analysis amounts to a choice of classification (or measurement) schemes, and dialectics is concerned with the argument that relates these classifications to specific purposes. Judging, on the other hand, refers to the process of distinguishing among states of affairs, not only in terms of what they are, but also what they *should be*. It is a means of selection, but selection taken as derived from concepts of 'ought' rather than 'is.' Analysis, here, amounts to a description and explication of possible states of affairs and social norms and rules; dialectics, on the other hand, is concerned with relationships between the range of possible worlds and the selection of procedures for prescribing optimality, efficiency, rule conformity, and so on. (The latter is what Perelman and Olbrechts-Tyteca [1969], for example, mean when they speak about dialectics and legal reasoning, cf. Booth [1974] and Weitz [1964].) But even knowledge systems must be regarded as being more broadly defined. 'Why' questions, for example, are only one very special class of inquiries. 'How,' taken in the sense of strategic operations; 'What,' taken in the sense of identification; 'Which,' taken in the sense of specification; and so on; all are forms of knowledge, based on quite different interpretations of analytics and dialectics in inquiry.

Aside from the obvious implications concerning the limitations of contemporary logical empiricist philosophy of science, what should be apparent from this example is that analytical and dialectical approaches are jointly part of the process of inquiry. Naming, for example, is a means for being clear about the categories of reference and types of membership; and whether or not the name itself is vague, one can still provide an analytical structure to the categories. Dialectics, on the other hand, provides the means for reasoning about application of a particular set of entities or ideas to the categories of, say, a specific assignment procedure. In the case of arithmomorphic languages, this process reduces to the specification of a set of entities and Boolean categories (by virtue of the application of the Comprehension Axiom) and the use of an assignment rule specified in terms of the set (or class) membership relation. Note, however, that the rejection of this form of representation and assignment does *not* dismiss the importance of integrating analytical and dialectical approaches to the Naming process, but rather illustrates the weaknesses inherent in the singular, orthodox view of the linguistic and reasoning presuppositions of inquiry.

Though even a cursory review of the characteristics of the ideas underlying the second triad—(physical) Mechanism, (biological) Adaptation, and (social) Rule Following—is beyond the scope of this essay, it is useful to make a few general remarks. As has been noted by, for example, Georgescu-Roegen (1966, 1971) and Commons (1950), each of these approaches to theory is characteristic of the operation of particular kinds of systems: Mechanistic theories have been appropriate for middle-scale physical systems; theories of Adaptation have been useful for representing certain kinds of evolutionary processes; and Rule Following has been central to the nature of social systems. But in saying this, once again I claim that there is no basis for a parallel inference to the effect that one or another of these theories is analytic or dialectic. Each requires a specific analytical representation (for example, a system of differential equations or list of specific laws, rules, or mores), and each involves some type of dialectical process that *relates*, say, observations to models or acts to laws. What we *may* take issue with is the argument that only one type of representation or process of reasoning is viable because there is only one true form of expression and reasoning (say, mathematics and mathematical reasoning). But, as before, this is a question about the nature of the language chosen and the acceptable modes of reasoning rather than of 'analytic' versus 'dialectic.'

## Two Substantive Motivations

As the above examples illustrate, the debate between 'analytics' and 'dialectics' is, in some very real senses, a straw man: 'analytic' and 'dialectic' are simply two sides of the same inquiry coin. Two substantive issues should serve as further illustrations of this point: (a) that of accounting for time in investment decisions; and (b) that of the identification and specification of geographic boundaries.

One of the most striking observations about the work of such unorthodox economists as Keynes, Georgescu-Roegen, Lowe, and Shackle is the central, nonneutral role that time plays. As distinct from its position as a backdrop in the equlibrium-oriented theories of neoclassical economics, time is viewed not only as imposing finiteness on resources (say through the operation of the law of entropy), but also as the reason that necessitates specifying horizons in capital investment and other forms of planning. Just as time cannot be used again, events are not repeatable, and resources are not replenished; and just as time changes the conditions of demand and supply, in accounting for the effects of time we must be aware of the exogenous nature of the horizons we use to specify the period of investment and planning.

Though this point is conceivably well known to economists, it is rarely taken very seriously.[4] Following from the use of the usual accounting procedures and functional representations of patterns of exchange and investment, economists have typically assumed that (a) conditions of stationarity obtain, (b) events and resource conditions are continuously replicated, and (c) planning horizons can be specified with a special (usually mathematically based) form of analytic representation; dialectics is asumed to follow directly from the analytic assumptions (e.g., as a process of deductive reasoning). As with the philosophical examples discussed above, however, it should be clear that the difficulties in this approach are not solely the result of the failures of analytic representation. It is true that analysis, in the sense of being clear about the representation of possible time-paths of investment or planning, commonly uses arithmomorphic linguistic methods of representation that are far too restrictive to represent the qualities of complex, fuzzy systems. But by virtue of the peculiar association between representation and reasoning that is characteristic of mathematical expression, it is also true that dialectics is thereby reduced to either the usual proof form, or arguments by formal analogy.

The final example is in some ways more directly related to the relationship between analysis and mathematical representation. Consider the problem of identifying the appropriate spatial partitions for representing and reasoning about social and political conflicts (Gale, 1975a, 1976a). These may occur at any scale: within the family, neighborhood, community, city, nation, and so on. The analytic representations of spatial delineations are, in turn, often used as the instrumental bases of proposals for prescriptive changes in political and social organization (e.g., world government, weighted voting in the United Nations, territorial reorganization). Notice, however, that in the usual case these models are largely reifications of the kinds of formal linguistic structures provided by classical geometric concepts of a real delineation and set membership that arose along with Greek conceptions of the city-state. As Tarski (1959) has shown, however, models of geometry with set membership are anything but categorical; and more to the point, it can also be shown that the use of alternative analytic structures as the basis of models of spatial partitions gives rise to a multiplicity of classes of use-specific meanings, each with its own criteria of dialectical argument (Gale, 1975a). Again, this is a very complex issue which is not simplified by ignoring the presuppositions of language and, as such, it is another example of the importance of developing and using a form of inquiry that explicitly recognizes the relationships between analytics and dialectics.

## ANALYSIS AND DIALECTICS IN INQUIRY

It is one of the peculiarities of current practice in science that, in the study of 'analytical methods,' far less attention has been given to questions concerning the nature of the analytical part than to the development of methods. Analysis is assumed, roughly, to have something to do with numbers, numerically distinguished constructs, or to measure spaces in general; and on this assumption, a variety of numerically based methods are simply adopted from one or another area of application. Indeed, since the Second World War, the invocation of the phrase 'analytical methods' was enough to ensure the acceptance of the validity of almost any measurement procedure so long as the methods, per se, were correctly employed. Little scrutiny was made of the appropriateness of measurement scales or, more important, of the meaning and implications of using various kinds of representations of measurement and classification. And although there has recently been some attention directed at problems of developing representation theorems for measurement models (Krantz, Luce, Suppes, and Tversky, 1971), as yet there has been very little by way of an examination of the foundations and general implications of the use of formal methods of analytic representation.

While a general theory of the appropriate uses of formal methods and their (respective) dialectical relationships is still in its formative stages, recent developments in logic, mathematics, and linguistics are beginning to have a number of important impacts on our understanding of the structure and process of representation and reasoning. Thus, as Carnap's (1973 ed.: 51) "Principle of Tolerance" and Perelman and Olbrecht-Tyteca's (1969) "New Rhetoric" have become (implicitly) serious philosophical considerations, we have begun to re-examine the foundations of measurement (analysis) and inference (dialectic) procedures and, in general, to reassess the role of formal languages in the modelling process. In part the moves in this direction have been adoptive: new languages and inference procedures are available and, for experimental purposes, they are used in a variety of contexts (Körner, 1966; 1976). More important, however, several of the changes in orientation have been motivated by failures of existing analytical and dialectical procedures to account for specific classes of questions.

One additional point should be made at this juncture. though much of this part of my argument is philosophically based, it should nevertheless be regarded primarily as a means for comparing the relative efficacy of various language-based strategies for representation and reasoning in practical circumstances. In itself, the discussion is not designed to provide direct clarification of any philosophical disputes (though it may do this). The intent is simply to provide a means for characterizing some of the linguistic issues concerning the roles of analytics and dialectics in social inquiry.

Though current social science lore has emphasized the development and testing of analytic models for explanation and prediction (in an effort to discern 'social laws'), there have recently been strong counterarguments to the effect that these goals are, if not misplaced, certainly of limited scope.[5] To be sure, these claims have often been ideologically based, but they have at lest provided a methodological conscience to what often are regarded as philosophical truisms. At heart, however, there is the view that a gap exists between two perspectives: on one side there is a tradition of what has come to be viewed as scientific orthodoxy based on analytically motivated forms of model building, using mathematical criteria of description and inference; and on the other side, there is a heterodox dialectical tradition (often) combining historical, philosophical, and critical methods. The first is based largely on extensions of physical science paradigms of analysis while the second appears grounded in predominantly humanistic perspectives and ideals.

Contemporary social research programs appear to be clustered around two sides of this conceptual gap. The analytic, models-oriented, theory-testing crowd is on one side proclaiming that the true path has been found; the humanists, on the other side, have sought mainly to preserve the integrity of less formalized reasoning methods, to remind us that even truth is relative, and that there are important classes of questions that have been ignored by their opposite numbers. In a sense, it is a kind of dialectic in which there are neither commonly recognized grounds of dispute (i.e., in terms of the delineation and character of the conceptual gaps), nor even a reasonably good idea of what kinds of arguments would resolve them.

What appears to have been ignored in this intellectual face-off is that there are more pragmatically related conceptions of inquiry which can (potentially) give some structure to the ground between these seemingly disparate perspectives — at least insofar as they can delineate approaches that are appropriate for specific classes of questions. For example, I have recently written a paper on the logic of questions and answers (i.e., an erotetic logic) and its relation to inquiry.[6] The argument is quite simple and is the basis for my proposed integration of analysis and dialectics: If we view science as a general question-answering process then, by virtue of the (say, linguistically determined) class of questions that are asked (e.g., about formation of names, definitions and measurements, alethic issues, value-based problems, rule conformity), different methods of analysis and argument can (in general) be delineated for each such class. In this view, the gap between the positions described above is not so much one of differences 'in principle', as a claim for the heterodoxy of methodology and the need for an understanding of the appropriateness of specific strategies of inquiry in specific circumstances. In other words, there appear to be grounds for considering these seemingly different approaches in terms of a richer conception of what we may call the modeling process which does not regard truth (in the analytical sense) and arithmomorphic representation and reasoning as the only basis of inquiry.

The term 'model' has come to have about as many different meanings as there are people doing modeling.[7] Quite apart from the various functions (e.g., simplification and partitioning of problems), however, at its root a model is simply an expression in a given language: there are linguistic models of thought (e.g., various natural languages), mathematical models of entification and relations (e.g., various set theories), physical models (e.g., reduced-scale representations of streams, airfoils, etc.), and so on. Within the framework of a given language, a model provides a (usually simplified) representation of some fragment of concepts or phenomena, or both. Of course, except for special abstract cases (e.g., those arising in connection with classical model theory, representation rules are rarely complete; they simply form conditions for satisfaction which (under some circumstances) provide the basis for successively better approximations.

More specifically, the modeling process may be (heuristically) conceived of as a question-answering system $Z = (Q, M, G)$, consisting of a question (Q), an answer (or model M), and a generalized dialectical procedure (G) that describes (or prescribes) the relations between Q and M.[8] In particular

$$Q = D <(?)S, P, L >$$

and

$$M = D << L, A, T >, < U, R_1,...,R_n >>$$

where *(?)S* is an interrogative sentence (or proposition), $L$ is a given (formal or natural) language, $P$ is a set of presuppositions, $A$ is a set of axioms (consisting specifically of some representation axioms), $T$ is a set of potential answers to (i.e., theories about) Q (as allowed by $P$), $U$ is the (nonempty) universe of discourse, and $R_1,...,R_n$ are relations on $U$.[9] G may be regarded as a characterization of a context-dependent dialectical (argumentation) procedure which describes, say, (a) the inference strategy for the recursive elimination and substitution of unsatisfactory elements $t_j \ \varepsilon \ T$, (b) the identification of homomorphic representations, (c) a general consequence relation, and so on. A more thoroughgoing specification of G would involve a number of complex issues that cannot be treated adequately here; for the present, the designation of rules of consequence, satisfaction, and partial satisfaction is regarded as a metatheoretical issue, the solution to which is dependent (at least) on the nature of G and the properties of $L$.

Clearly, this very abstract perspective on inquiry processes needs much more flesh than has been given here. For the present purposes, however, two points are of special importance. First, it should be noticed that the structure of z is dependent on its specification on a language, $L$. Questions, for example, arise and are phrased in (i.e., presuppose) a language; the language of answers (or models) must be conformable (in the sense that a response in some other language is not intelligible without explicit translation rules); and the dialectical relationships between Q and M, that is, G, must be sufficiently rich to be able to represent (at least) the syntactic and semantic relationships of all sentences (propositions) within the inquiry process. Language, taken in a broad sense, is the concept which carries the principal epistemic force. The representation (i.e., analytic structure) of ideas and the object world itself are treated as *linguistically based* entities (within a question-answering process); the reconstruction of ideas and the addition of new concepts (e.g., value-based propositions) are similarly regarded as being predicated on the reformulation of the underlying linguistic (e.g., representational) structure.

The second point amends the first. Though we may agree that all thinking and communicating takes place in language, as Suppes (1970) and others have pointed out, models that are expressed solely in terms of even standard analytic languages become not only impossible to axiomatize in many cases, but also operationally intractable. Thus, as a way of providing a fixed set of operational procedures, z also includes axioms for a set theory that is conformable with the structure of $L$. Notice that only in special cases does this provide a sufficient basis for the use of the usual methods of analysis which depend on mathematical operations and inferential methods.

The world pictured in this view of the process of inquiry is thus a structured, language-based world: entities, their relations, and theories about them are all stated in and reasoned about in a particular, formalizable language (with a related set theory and mode of argumentation). Ontologically, epistemologically, and operationally, the analytic and dialectic structure of events and plans is treated as a function of its linguistic characterization. Note, however, that although the language must be fixed for specific operational purposes, no *particular* language (i.e., form of analytic representation or mode of argumentation) is presupposed. As was noted above, this is in keeping with Carnap's (1973 ed.: xv) "Principle of Tolerance":

> The view will be maintained that we have in every respect complete liberty with regard to the forms of language; that both the forms of construction for sentences and the rules of transformation (the latter are usually designated as "postulates and rules of inference") may be chosen quite arbitrarily. Up to now, in constructing a language, the procedure has usually been, first to assign a meaning to the fundamental mathematico-logical symbols, and then to consider what sentences or inferences are seen to be logically correct in accordance with this meaning. . . . The connection will only become clear when approached from the opposite direction: let any postulates and rules of inference be chosen arbitrarily; then this choice whatever it may be will determine what meaning is to be assigned to the fundamental logical symbols.

Clearly, the choice made with respect to the analytic structure of inquiry, that is, $L$, influences not only the ideas we have about the world (say, in the sense that "the elements of the theories of $T$ are predicated on $L$"), but also the very structure of the universe of discourse, its relations, and the mode of argument: in effect, whether or not $U, R_1,...,R_n$, and $G$ have independent existence (which is obviously a knotty philosophical problem), pragmatically they are treated (structured, reasoned about, and understood) in terms of the overall linguistic character of the inquiry process.[10]

Now, this kind of transformation of the modeling process into a more general framework oriented toward the understanding of language-based structures may appear artificial or even extraneous. For a number of decades, the linguistic foundations of analysis in science have been almost universally treated as being equivalent to that of mathematics. (This is the so-called "mathematics is the language of science" argument reified by the logical-empiricist movement.) But it is precisely the sort of intellectual move proposed here that has been successful in the history of physics (e.g., quantum mechanics and, to a lesser degree, relativity theory), where developments in new forms of mathematical analysis and argument have generally gone hand-in-hand with the development of substantive theories.[11] The same has been true in other areas (e.g., ethics[12]), but the results have engendered far less general agreement. The point is quite simple, however, and amounts to a paraphrase of Nuel Belnap's reply to Herbert Simon's claim for the singular efficacy of existing arithmomorphic structures: it may be that when it comes to fundamental questions, there is no point asking the applied scientist *which* foundational questions are not worth asking, but from the point of view of the scientist asking *new* classes of questions, it may also be that there are no questions *other than* foundational questions!

## ANALYSIS AND DIALECTICS IN PLANNING IN A NONSTATIONARY WORLD

Thus far the discussion has concentrated principally on abstractions: abstractions about the nature of the concepts of 'analytic' and 'dialectic' and their roles in inquiry. The point, of course, has been to give a brief characterization of the concepts and to provide an intellectual setting for their use and interpretation in specific contexts. I will now attempt to provide such an interpretation in terms of some of the problems of planning in an evolving (nonstationary) world; following this, I will attempt to indicate some of the ways in which a theory of inquiry based on an integration of analysis and dialectics can help to structure problems in planning. In particular, I will suggest that, for most tasks that lie outside the realm of day-to-day crisis problem solving, the development of decision-making strategies is really part of a modeling process that combines analytic and dialectic elements in much the same manner suggested by such disparate authors as Braybrooke and Lindblom (1963) and Korner (1976). As was noted above, the interactions in this process are among the processes of describing, understanding, and prescription; or, more specifically, in terms of the relations among the representation of information, decision makers' understanding of present (and potential) conditions, and the ways in which we selectively choose amongst goals, planning horizons, and alternative futures. Each integrates means of analytical representation and dialectical reasoning; each can be expressed in terms of question-answering scheme; and each will ultimately provide indications for the development of a language-based integration of analysis and dialectics.

Though 'planning' is difficult to characterize in general (cf. Gale, 1976b, 1976b), we might take Georgescu-Roegen's (1971) lead and use time in an abstract sense (say, as entropy) as the principal conceptual force in the argument. Time imposes limitations on resource availability; it changes a deterministic, stationary world into a stochastic, nonstationary one; it forces us to select the boundaries of our planning horizons and, therefore, the ways in which the future influences the present. But how do we approach any particular planning decision-making task, that is, what are the roles of analysis and dialectics in planning inquiry? How do we select amongst alternative planning periods and decision-making rules? How do we treat the problem of selecting a means for describing future events? And what are the relationships among description, prescription, and evalution in an evolving world? Note that while these questions articulate some of the fundamental problems in the relationship between understanding and action, we must take a more concrete approach in order to see just how analysis and dialectics provide complementary perspectives in planning inquiry.

Now, at the outset we must be clear about two points: first that empirical models are, in some sense, always models of data (Suppes, 1960; Moore and Gale, 1973); and second, that a theory is, most often, an answer to a (very specific and probably quite limited) question. As I indicated above, however, social theory and modeling are much broader and complicated than analogies to explanation-oriented physical science paradigms would have us believe (cf. Bromberger, 1966; Körner, 1966, 1976; Toulmin, 1969 ed., 1977; Gale, 1977a). Management strategies and jurisprudence are, for example, integral to concepts of planning and decision making; and just as institutions influence the structure of models of data (say, through the collection procedures and the organization of modes of analytic representation), so too do institutions affect the nature of dialectical procedures such as social laws, organizational behavior, and individual decisions (Dunn, 1974).

Paraphrasing the Sapir-Whorf thesis, we can say that we see what institutions allow us to see, we think what institutions allow us to think, and we act as institutions allow us to act. This is, of course, a very strong claim—which has more than its share of critics even when restricted to its normal linguistic context. At the same time, however, its merits are often just as inescapable. To 'see' the world of planning problems and decisions, for example, we can say that we use the 'filters' shaped by those existing social institutions that are responsible for analytical frameworks as those connected with information collection and organization. And to think about processes of decision making, we employ dialectical representations of individual choice and modes of social organization. Far from being watered-down Marxism, however, each of these claims speaks to a pragmatic thesis: that both the structure of information (analysis) and social and individual decisions (dialectics) are direct functions of the interactions among these concepts in a generalized inquiry scheme.

Ideology notwithstanding, then, the perspective I will develop here presupposes a pragmatic approach to understanding planning in an evolving world, an understanding based on an explicit recognition of the influence of the roles of analysis and dialectics in structuring observations and the rules that organize social institutions.

To fix ideas, consider the following schematic diagram (fig. 6.1) of the sequence of analytic and dialectic relationships that take place in a general planning, policy development, and evaluation process.[13] Suppose, for example, that as a result of the implementation of a new housing program (say, the construction of an integrated apartment complex consisting of 2,000 units for the working poor and the elderly), there is a perceived need to plan for (i.e., develop and/or reorganize) the related social services (e.g., schools, libraries, bus routes and schedules, etc.).[14] The proposed change in the availability of dwelling units will obviously affect specific segments of the population in different ways and, in turn, will have differential effects on the composition of the population in the various subareas of the locale. A reasonable (though obviously complex) question, then, is, "What effects will the proposed construction program have on the population's composition and distribution and how will they affect the distribution, organization, and provision of services?"

Traditional approaches to this type of problem have, for the most part, attempted to separate the question into a number of subparts—usually organized according to disciplinary interests: one part addressing, say, the politics of publicly sponsored housing and others addressing the relation between population composition and level and kind of service provision and the dynamics of residential mobility. Sidestepping the knotty issue of 'problem fragmentation,' it is useful to consider in greater detail the ways in which the investigation of this planning question is treated.

Given the dominant perspective on the separation of analysis and dialectics in inquiry, the question posed above has generally been translated into something like the following framework:

1.  Planning and design goals are treated as either (a) optimization schemes based on analytical representations of preferences for housing (with prespecified budget constraints) and a prescribed social welfare allocation scheme, or (b) weak extrapolations of dialectical assignment and selection procedures which are identified through the comparisons of prior instances of analagous programs.

2.  The identification of the relevant system's attributes is normally determined solely by prescribed analytic models for (a) information organization, (b) the use of surveys to elicit more detailed data on residential preferences, family structure, income, and so forth, and (c) the construction of theoretical indicators that conform to specific, idealized decision procedures (e.g., utility for accessibility).

3.  The alternative futures are those distributions of population derived from either (a) analytically based economic models of economic investment in public housing services, or (b) again weak extrapolations of existing (or analogous) patterns of selection.

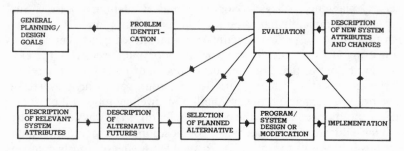

**Fig. 6.1.** Planning and Decision Making

In general, little attention is given to such problems as how planning alternatives are selected or to questions of program design, implementation, and evaluation. An explicit separability between analysis and dialectics is also presumed, which relegates planning problems either to a program that synthesizes existing data within the framework of specific types of analytic models or involves the application of specific program rules. Analytic methodology, in effect, is taken as primary and the results of the inquiry follow directly from its limited presuppositions.

The related and perhaps more fundamental problem of the role of dialectics in an integrated program of inquiry also arises in connection with the general orientation of schematic representations such as figure 6.1. By virtue of their design, thinking about flow chart diagrams tends to focus on the boxes (i.e., specific states and activities) rather than on the arrows (i.e., the *processes* by which the observations and activities are carried out). In a sense, the usual approaches to inquiry obviate the need for independent consideration of processes: the way in which an activity is carried out is regarded as a direct function of its analytical representation.

An illustration of this point is provided by reference to the arrow connecting the boxes labeled "description of alternative futures" and "selection of planned alternative." The intuition is that, once we are given some kind of list of possible futures (as states and/or as actions), some *dialectical procedure* is used for determining which item (or items) on the list will be treated as the selected alternative (i.e., for subsequent examination or implementation). If, for example, the procedure is treated as a purely technical issue (say, as part of a market-based exchange paradigm) and subject to a particular type of mathematical characterization, we would expect that the argument (the dialectics) would be based on the use of some form of optimization strategy. Or, if the procedure is regarded in essentially political terms, some institutionalized form of voting may be employed as the (dialectics of the) decision procedure.

Underlying any such procedure, however, is an explicit recognition that the arrows—the dialectical relationships—must, themselves, constitute part of the design and selection of the overall inquiry strategy, and that the analytical structure of the information base must be, in turn, designed to facilitate the use of alternative procedural criteria.

The point here thus reinforces and extends the previous discussion: not only has contemporary social science tended to isolate the analytic aspects of methodology as the principal means for identifying and approaching problems, but the selection of a methodology has itself been isolated from considerations of the nature of the *rules of argument*. Planning for an evolving world thus becomes translated into a problem of analytical representation and the statistical manipulation of data—both which are several steps removed from the dialectical presuppositions of (a) the data classification and organization procedures and (b) the procedures that employ analytic results as part of the larger planning and policy-making process. The microcosm of analytically based explanatory theories thus becomes the macrocosm of social practice: theory and practice are linked, almost by fiat, with little regard to the substance of the links or the type of chain that has been forged.

Extending this example a bit further, consider the central role the box labeled "evaluation" plays in figure 6.1[15] Evaluation, in its broadest sense, serves as a generic term for a monitoring and comparison procedure within a general learning system (e.g., a system concerned with guiding changes). Where the veracity of a causal model is under scrutiny, for example, the evaluation *procedure* may be something on the order of the dialectics of a Popperian falsificationist paradigm or a Carnapian inductivist principle. Or, where the rules for selection of a particular planning alternative are at issue, the evaluation scheme might consist of a dialectical system for comparing alternative (numerical and ethical) choice procedures. The point here, however, is not that there is (or can be) a unified theory and methodology of evaluation, but that the nature of our data, models, and institutionalized decision procedures must explicitly address some relevant monitoring and learning scheme—and that this presupposes consideration of an integrated approach to analytics and dialectics in inquiry.

Unfortunately, there are pragmatic tensions involved in describing the planning process in terms of an integrated characterization of inquiry. Social institutions, for example, often have vested interests in using certain forms of analytical representations and specific dialetical relationships (say, in terms of particular types of programs and in the structure of the evaluation processes). It is inevitable, then, that if we make strong attempts to develop analytical representations that are sufficiently flexible to be used as the basis for learning, we will be led to reformulate these

*161*

same problems and therefore to modify the institutions and dialectical relations we employ to deal with them. Such changes will, in turn, generate a shift in both the analytical and dialectical bases for inquiry and, most likely, in the distribution of economic and political power as well.

If, however, this type of problem is inherent in a nonstationary, evolving world, then the consequences of failing to recognize the need to shift the analytical and dialectical frameworks will be even more disturbing. Programs designed with little regard to the process of change in analytical and dialectical relationships are likely to be inflexible and generally of little value. (Often, for example, they generate unexpected — or even expected — windfall profits for certain groups at the expense of others who fall progressively further behind in their ability to obtain adequate standards of education, housing, health, or other social goods and amenities.) Of course we are always faced with problems of allocating limited resources within a particular value structure and political framework. It should be clear, however, that, from the point of view of the proposed inquiry system, there is really no justification for basing decisions on a monotheistic view of either analytical form or dialectical relationships.

## THE LINGUISTIC INTEGRATION
## OF ANALYSIS AND DIALECTICS

The intent of the preceding discussion has been to illustrate different (though not unrelated) aspects of the problem of developing a general approach to an integrated 'analytic/dialectic' perspective on inquiry: to propose, in effect, the development of a question-answering approach to inquiry that would be appropriate for treating planning problems. What should be apparent at this point is that this approach is directly analogous to the problem of translation among natural and formal languages and sociolinguistic properties of dialogue structure (Steiner, 1975; Körner, 1976). What is needed, now, is (a) an interpretation of some of the linguistic characteristics of the planning process and (b) an itemized list of the elements of languages, both formal and natural, and dialogue types that could provide the analytical and dialectical building blocks for such a theory. This is no small order: it not only requires resolution of the problems engendered by translation (say, in terms of the question-answering process described above), but a fairly complete categorization of the elementary features of languages and their relationships. And, as we recognize from current work on both formal languages and sociolinguistics, there is no unified treatment as yet. It is as if to say that we need a method for undoing Babel *without* relying on a conjecture concerning the efficacy of a universal language; for no matter what analytical structure is employed, the basis for communication must recognize the import of the mind set and the variability of grammatical, semantic, and dialogue rules.

We begin by using the idea of an integrated 'analytic/dialectic' conceptualization of methodology to provide the basis for the identification of a scheme for relating types of planning issues (i.e., the "purposes" described in fig. 6.1) to forms of analytical representation (i.e., data organization). Note that the underlying motivation of such a typology is *not* to give a definitive characterization of all aspects of this relationship, but to propose a scheme that will allow us to recognize the presuppositions and relationships among types of questions and the associated types of analytical data structures — and, thereby, to provide the grounds for selecting the kinds of reasoning (dialectic) methods that are appropriate for inquiry.

More specifically, as was indicated with respect to the discussion of figure 6.1, the selection of methodological strategy is directly linked to the purposes being served. There are, in fact, a variety of complementary approaches to inquiry, each related to different analytical and dialectical functions. What is needed is to make explicit the connections among these functions, the associated (analytical) data requirements, and the kinds of arguments appropriate in each case: in effect, to provide a typology of questions, data, and methods.[16]

The identification and specification of typologies is often regarded as a 'no lose game' since typologies can neither be validated nor falsified in any of the usual ways. Though this point is obvious sophistry (since it presupposes the universal applicability of a very specialized concept of evaluation), it nevertheless brings up an important question: Just how should a typology be understood and how can it be used as a framework for guiding practical inquiry?

As with classification procedure in general, typologies serve to structure the meaning of the common properties of a set of ideas or observations. Typologies, however, begin with the selection of the major dimensions of interest (and their respective partitions) and ask how these elements (and combinations of elements) are related to some specific conceptual and operational problem. The practical consequence of my earlier remarks, for example, is that prior to any study of an inquiry system for planning there needs to be both a clear identification of the classes of questions that are of importance and the relevant analytic representations and dialectic procedures. Indeed, it is the relationships among these elements that will eventually form the basis for understanding the presuppositions of specific models and theories and the relative efficacy of different analytical and dialectical approaches. Note that although this latter issue will not be discussed in detail here, it should be regarded as the underlying motivation for the remainder of the discussion.

Again, to fix ideas, consider figure 6.1 and the related typology depicted in table 6.1. Recall that the idea of the former is to present a schematic picture of a series of functions which could be regarded as integral to the general planning and policy process. Each of these functions can, I contend, be treated as elements of the typology presented in table 6.1. Note, however, that what I have earlier called "functions" (in the interest of generality), will now be called "purposes" (as a way of suggesting the link between the typology and the linguistic character of analytical representations and dialectical procedures).

More specifically, for illustrative purposes we can translate several of the elements of figure 6.1 directly into the following categories of table 6.1.

1.  The "description of the relevant system attributes" can be identified with three types of purposes: "classification and measurement," "accounting," and "explanation."

2.  The "description of alternative futures" is associated with the "projection" (of the future consequences of the present state of affairs, conditioned on a range of possible modifications of these states by present decisions such as capital investment, changes in legal jurisdictions, etc.).

3.  The "selection of planned alternative" corresponds to the idea of "prescription."

4.  The "program/system design or modification" function can be identified with the concept of "rule" or "program" design in which institutionalized procedures are selected to bring about the prescribed changes.

5.  The "implementation" function is translated directly into the idea of an administrative "implementation" operation for effecting and maintaining the proposed program.

6.  And the "evaluation" function is related directly to the two operational categories of "monitoring" and "evaluation."[17]

In effect, I propose that the use of these functionally designated categories as one dimension of the typology provides a basis for understanding the relationships among (a) the purposes of planning and policy design, (b) the analytical form of the data employed to answer

TABLE 6.1

*Types of Inquiry and Data*

| TYPES OF DATA | TYPES OF INQUIRY | | |
|---|---|---|---|
| Purpose | State | Activity | Programmatic |
| Classification and Measurement | What are the entities in a classification scheme? | What are the classes of transactions? | What are the classes of institutions and rules relevant to the entities and their transactions? |
| Accounting | What is the distribution of the entities? | What is the distribution of the transactions? | What are operational details of these rules, precedents, etc.? |
| Explanation | Why are these entities distributed as they are? | Why are these transactions distributed as they are? | How did these rules affect the distribution of the entities and their transactions? |
| Projection | What will the distribution of entities be? | What will the distribution of transactions be? | How will the rules affect the future distributions of the entities and their transactions? |
| Prescription | What should distribution of entities be? | What should distribution of transactions be? | What types of rules should be used to influence the distributions? |
| Program Design | | | What specific rules should be used to achieve particular distributions? |
| Implementation | | | What procedures should be used to organize and maintain these rules? |
| Monitoring | What is the change in the indicators of distribution of the entities? | What is the change in indicators of the distribution of the transactions? | How have the rules been applied? |
| Evaluation | | | How effective has the application of rules been? |

specific classes of questions, and (c) the linguistic characterization of the respective dialectical (reasoning) procedures.

The second dimension of the proposed typology, which represents the idea of analytical structure in terms of "type of data," draws directly on Dunn's idea of organized statistical systems as classes of "entity representations." As Dunn (1974: 91–92) puts it, the problem of the design of social data systems is

. . . a problem in system design and development, guided by two kinds of information. (1) We need a representation of the kinds of data elements that can perform a variety of representational tasks and can, therefore, be justified as components of a multiple-purpose record. This requires a representation of the ways in which observational fields and adaptive situations of the principal classes of information processors overlap. Some such image is not only essential to designate the scope and content of multiple-use archives, it is essential in indicating the ways in which the observations must be symbolized to facilitate their multiple use. Such a representation is essential to guide the appropriate organization of statistical records. (2) We need a set of images to guide the organization of the administrative and technical systems necessary to provide the flexible access to data elements essential for their use in a variety of entity representations.

The idea here is simply that the uses to which records are put should be directly related to the ways in which information is represented, organized, and assessed: that is, that it is important explicitly to recognize the importance of an integrated 'analytic/dialectic' approach to inquiry.

Clearly, there are a variety of ways of identifying a typology that includes 'type of entity representation' as the principle dimension of the analytical structure. One approach, for example, would be to simply identify and organize the available data sets with respect to a particular analytical characterization (such as a Boolean structure). For the present purposes, however, I have employed the first three elements of Dunn's (1974: 77–85) four-part classification:[18]

1.  State descriptions. Representations of this type depict the status, the results of the performance, of systems and include five structural characteristics: "the name of the entity being represented, a time descriptor that specifies the time of the observation, a space or place descriptor, a descriptor that names the attribute under observation, and a quantifier or quality description which specifies the unit of measurement, count, or attribute quality" (Dunn, 1974: 78). Such representations give static descriptions of the traits that an entity possesses, the extent to which it is possessed, and where and what time the observation is made. In general, no indication is provided concerning the sequence of changes that preceded the specific observations, nor is there necessarily a self-conscious characterization of either the observational procedure or the model of measurement, classification, and definition (Moore and Gale, 1973). Furthermore, only under conditions where the general structure of the transaction processes is known and the processes are stationary can inferences be made concerning the process of change.

2.  Activity descriptions. Representations of this type depict state conditions as well as the *kinds* of performance (or activities or

developmental sequences) that give rise to them. To the five structural characteristics of state descriptions are thus added: "a description of the nature of the act, the description of the relevant pre-act and post-act states of the entity, and the specification of the time span or duration of the act" (Dunn, 1974: 82). Such a representation is thus a description of the state of a system, the observed sequences of change, *and* the acts that led to the changes. Note, however, that the use of the term "process" here does not refer directly to information on the properties of the institutions that structure the performance patterns.

3. Programmatic descriptions. Representations of this type depict, in addition to state and activity descriptions, the structure of the programs (e.g., the social institutions) that govern the sequence of actions and the selection of the type of actions. Sequences of acts are treated here as functions of programs that structure choices and provide rules and norms for behavior. The programs, however, are regarded as fixed.

Though all of this is admittedly abstract, at the core there is a concept of a 'hierarchy of information' which recognizes that, for different purposes (to answer particular classes of questions) there are specific types of analytical prerequisites. Thus, when a question refers to an arithmomorphic property (such as numbers of families in each census tract in the United States in 1970), state descriptions can often provide a characterization of the relevant analytic qualities of the information base. But where questions refer to the processes that give rise to these observations, their patterns of temporal change, and the rules governing these changes, then a higher level of information is required which presupposes an association with richer forms of dialectical structures in the inquiry process.

The resultant typology (table 6.1) thus refers to the kinds of questions that arise at different stages of the policy and planning processes, the type of analytical representation (data organization) available, and some of the principal linguistic properties of the underlying dialectical processes.[19] Notice that even this very rough account emphasizes the importance of focusing on an integrated view of analysis and dialectics. The typology is, in effect, a claim for the context dependency of questions and, in particular, for the need to reorient contemporary methodological paradigms to account for the diversity of questions, their presuppositions, and the associated forms of argument.

Thus far, my discussion of the idea of an integrated 'analytic/dialectic' perspective on inquiry has focused primarily on the presuppositions imposed by the analytical representation. From the types of questions developed in connection with the explication of table 6.1, however, it should now be apparent that the concept 'dialectic' is directly related to the linguistic form of the question itself. In particular, I contend that the idea of dialectics (in the sense which I have used it in this discussion, i.e., as 'form of argument') is capable of being characterized in terms of certain properties of the linguistic structure of the questions themselves. This, of course, was the purpose of developing the notion of a general inquiry program, but it is now possible to be more concrete about the nature of these aspects of language. With this in mind, I will thus simply outline what I regard as the main substantive features of language that are integral to the development of an integrated analytic/dialectic theory of inquiry. Notice, however, that once we reject the singular efficacy of arithmomorphic representations, we open a virtual Pandora's Box.

1. *The use of modalities in various languages.* Though "truth," in the sense of aletheism (Hiz, 1962), conceivably has universal properties and interpretation in all formal and natural languages (and this is certainly open to question), the ways in which modal verbs are employed and interpreted possess no such universal quality. Verbs such as "will," "shall," "can," "may," "must," "ought," "need," "prefer," and "believe" perform different roles and functions in different languages: they *mean* different things. However, at the heart of the analysis of any planning issue are questions that use such terms: "How many housing units are *needed* to provide adequate housing for the elderly?" "What *should* we do to resolve racial imbalances in the school system?" "What *must* we do to provide a good faith gesture of peaceful intentions?" And so on. Following the strategy proposed by Rescher (1969), White (1970), and others, the most straightforward approach to this problem is through the detailed examination of the formal grammatical properties of the occurrence of each of these terms (and their synonyms): that is, by representing the uses of the terms in alternative (and comparable) axiomatic (logical) systems, their consequences (theorems) can be compared and used as the basis for indicating differences, designing translation rules, and explicating context-specific dialectical procedures.

2. *Rules of argumentation.* As Hamblin (1970) has demonstrated, the most easily recognizable point of consistency in argumentation is the nature of the textual rules (and, in particular of the fallacies and the manner in which fallacies are identified). From the point of view of the present discussion, this issue is obviously critical since the idea of representation and argument is based on the identification of those principles that discern effective principles of reasoning within a given language. A related problem is the need to identify the rules by which dialogues (e.g., paragraphs, texts) are structured.

3. *Vagueness and ambiguity.* All languages contain vague terms and ambiguous grammatical representations. Indeed, as Georgescu-Roegen has pointed out, it can be argued that communication is impossible without vagueness and ambiguity. At the same time, we have seen that vagueness does not preclude analysis and, in fact, we can expect that different languages will treat vagueness and ambiguity in different ways. (This point has been discussed at some length by, e.g., Lakoff [1973] and Zadeh [1971] with respect to the explication of natural language semantics by means of fuzzy sets.) However, conflicts often arise where vague and ambiguous texts are used in argumentation and, though this is to be expected, it should be recognized that an integrated approach to inquiry presupposes rules that both codify the substance of these differences and provide a basis for mapping one analytical usage into another.

4. *The use of presuppositions.* Presuppositions are used in many ways in language: there are ideological, formal, lexical, grammatical, substantive, causal, and many other kinds. Each language employs presuppositions in different ways and, as has been noted above in the explication of the general question-based inquiry structure, these differences strongly influence both the choice of analytical form of propositions and the sequence of utterances (dialectics). Again, explicit rules (say, in terms of "grammars of presupposition") are required for translation, that is, for a dialectics that links one analytic representation with another.

Much more can be said about each of these issues; and thorough research must be done before the program we have outlined yields any results that can be applied in pragmatic contexts. But at least in terms of the current status of the theory, I believe there is a great deal to be said for the approach proposed here: at the least, it can help to clarify the roles of analysis and dialectics — independently of the personalities and ideologies engaged in the debate.

# CONCLUSIONS

The moral of the story is actually quite short. The history of the concepts of 'analytic' and 'dialectic' has, at least in recent times, promoted an image of the development of analytic representation models aimed solely at 'Why?' questions and other forms of questions concerned with causation. The counterimage I have attempted to present here is that this limited type and form of inquiry has unnecessarily narrowed the range of relevant issues and that, with a broader class of pragmatic purposes in mind, a far more heterodox set of orientations and approaches would emerge. In effect, I have tried to counter the image of methodological

Stephen Gale

neatness with one based on an integrated approach to inquiry that focuses on the centrality of questions, the context dependency of method, and the joint roles of analysis and dialectics. As an interpretation of the importance of this integration, I have presented a sketch of the role of analysis and dialectics in planning in nonstationary (time-dependent) situations. The upshot of my argument thus closely parallels Georgescu-Roegen's earlier suggestions: (i) that methodology as much influences the classes of questions that can be regarded as meaningful as it provides guidelines for their solution; and (ii) that the greatest fallacy of inquiry is that of misplaced concreteness—and that this fallacy is all the more serious if it is methodology itself that is taken as concrete.

# NOTES

1. This point stands in distinction to much of the recent literature in the philosophy of science, which emphasizes the logical unity of method and the singular (and symmetric) roles of explanation and prediction in science. Though it is not at all clear that scientists do what philosophers say they do, there appears to be a strong core of belief that the language of science should be treated as fixed, that the aim of science is explanation (via inference from universal laws), and that methodology and observation must conform to these presuppositions..

2. Note that this use of the term 'analytic' is itself ambiguous since, "while the cardinal numbers of the systems studied in arithmetic or number theory are (or sometimes finite); *analysis* on the other hand deals with the real numbers and other systems of objects having the cardinal 2 (or sometimes a higher cardinal)" (Kleene, 1952: 29).

3. Clearly, as with every definitional argument, there is a strong element of circularity in reasoning from 'purpose of use' to 'meaning'; needless to say, it is also unavoidable without resorting to some equally unsatisfactory metaphysical or empirical theses.

4. There are, of course, a number of exceptions: see, for example, Shackle (1969) and Georgescu-Roegen (1972).

5. The literature relating to this point is far too extensive to document here. For the record, and with no attempt at comprehensiveness, I note just a few ready examples from several different fields: Braybrooke and Lindblom (1963), Lörner (1966), Galtung (1967), Goguen (1968), Toulmin (1969), Bromberger (1971), Churchman (1971), Olsson (1975), Targ (1971), von Wright (1971), Ackoff and Emery (1972), van Dijk (1972), Gale (1972), Georgescu-Roegen (1972), Habermas (1972), Morgenstern (1972a, b), McCarthy (1973), Gottinger (1974), and Suppes (1974).

6. Gale (1977a). Also see Belnap (1963, 1966, 1969), Bromberger (1963, 1965, 1966, 1971), Harrah (1963, 1969a, 1969b, 1971), Aquist (1965, 1972), and Keenan and Hull (1973).

7. See Suppes (1960) for a discussion of some of this variety of meanings. Note, however, that in Suppes's view all the uses are regarded as effectively equivalent to the model-theoretical conception developed with respect to the semantics of mathematical logic.

8. The symbol " = D" indicates "is by definition."

9. More generally, we can conceive of $R_1,...,R_n$ as being a function of: $L \rightarrow U$ which specifies the reference in U, of each element of the language L.

10. See Körner (1966, 1970, 1976) and Zinov'ev (1973) for related discussions. Note also that this perspective is not all that different from the so-called radical meaning variance position taken by, e.g., Feyerabend (1965, 1970a, 1970b).

11. See, for example, Reichenbach (1944), Watanabe (1969), Heelan (1970), Sneed (1971), and Hooker (1973).

12. See, for example, the collections by Rescher (1969) and Hilpinen (1971).

13. Figure 6.1 and table 6.1 are the result of several intensive discussions with Eric Moore on the proper characterization and interpretation of this (and related) flowchart type diagrams and typologies. I am sure that neither he nor I would defend them in detail, but they provide reasonably representative schema of the relations between the main elements of the decision-making process and the types of information employed at each step.

14. Figure 6.1 refers to this stage as "problem identification."

15. Note that evaluation, per se, takes place throughout any learning, planning, and decision-making process. The arrows in figure 6.1 simply describe the major evaluative steps often associated with planning studies.

16. This strategy follows from earlier papers (Gale, 1977a,b; Moore and Gale, 1973) and, in fact, builds on a suggestion of Dunn's (1974: 134) by indicating the range of connections between typological elements and linguistic entities.

17. Note that in the interest of clarity in the argument I will not treat the "general planning/design goals" and "problem identification" functions in this paper. These issues depend, of course, on the related concepts of social values and social learning, and their discussion in the present context would be prohibitively lengthy.

18. Note that particularly with respect to Dunn's classifications (iii) and (iv), I have given Dunn's formulation a substantial reinterpretation. I hope, however, that this will not result in any misinterpretation.

19. The empty cells in table 6.1 indicate areas in which questions cannot be associated directly with either of the dimensions of the typology.

# REFERENCES

Ackoff, R. L. and F. E. Emery
    1972   On Purposeful Systems. Chicago: Aldine.

Aqvist, L.
    1965   A New Approach to the Logical Theory of Interrogatives, Pt. 1: Analysis. Uppsala: The Philosophical Society Series.

    1972   "On the analysis and logic of questions." In R. E. Olson and A. M. Paul (eds.), Contemporary Philosophy in Scandinavia. Baltimore: The Johns Hopkins Press.

Auden, W. H.
    1948   "Making, knowing and judging." In the Dyer's Hand. New York: Random House.

Belnap, N. D., Jr.
    1963   An Analysis of Questions: Preliminary Report. Technical Memoran-

dum, Santa Monica, California: Systems Development Corporation.

1969    "Questions: their presuppositions, and how they can fail to arise." In K. Lambert (ed.), The Logical Way of Doing Things. New Haven: Yale University Press.

1966    "Questions, answers, and presuppositions." The Journal of Philosophy 63: 609–611.

Booth, W. C.
1974    Modern Dogma and the Rhetoric of Assent. Chicago: University of Chicago Press.

Braybrooke, D. and C. E. Lindblom
1963    A Strategy of Decision. Glencoe: The Free Press.

Bromberger, S.
1963    "A theory about the theory of theory and about the theory of theories." In B. Baumrin (ed.), Philosophy of Science, The Delaware Seminar, vol. 2. New York: John Wiley.

1965    "An approach to explanation." In R. J. Butler (ed.), Analytical Philosophy. Oxford: Blackwell.

1966    "Why-questions." In R. G. Colodny (ed.), Mind and Cosmos. Pittsburgh: University of Pittsburgh Press.

1971    "Science and the forms of ignorance." In E. Nagel, S. Bromberger and A. Grunbaum (eds.), Observation and Theory in Science. Baltimore: The Johns Hopkins Press.

Carnap, R.
1973    The Logical Syntax of Language. London: Routledge and Kegan Paul.

Churchman, C. W.
1971    The Design of Inquiring Systems. New York: Basic Books.

Commons, J. R.
1950    The Economics of Collective Action. New York: MacMillan.

Dunn, E. S., Jr.
1974    Information Processing and Statistical Systems-Change and Reform. New York: John Wiley.

Feyerabend, P.
1965    "Problems of empiricism." In R. G. Colodny (ed.), Beyond the Edge of Certainty. Englewood Cliffs: Prentice Hall.

1970a   "Problems of empiricism, Part 2." In R. G. Colodny (ed.), The Nature and Function of Scientific Theories. Englewood Cliffs: Prentice Hall.

1970b   "Against method: outline of an anarchist theory of knowledge." In M. Radner and S. Winokur (eds.), Analysis of Theories and Methods of Physics and Psychology. Minneapolis: University of Minnesota Press.

Gadamer, H. G.
1976    Hegel's Dialectic: Five Hermeneutical Studies. New Haven: Yale University Press.

Gale S.
  1972    "Stochastic stationarity and the analysis of geographic mobility." In
          W. P. Adams and F. M. Helleiner (eds.), International Geography
          1972. Toronto: University of Toronto Press.

  1975a   "Boundaries, tolerance spaces, and criteria for conflict resolution."
          Journal of Peace Science 1: 95–115.

  1975b   "On a metatheory of planning theory." In R. H. Wilson and T.
          Noyelle (eds.), 1975 Symposium on Planning Theory, Papers in
          Planning No. 1. Philadelphia: University of Pennsylvania, Depart-
          ment of City and Regional Planning.

  1976a   "A resolution of the regionalization problem and its implications for
          political geography and social justice." Geografiska Annaler 5B:
          1–16.

  1976b   "Paradigms and counterparadigms: or does neatness count in plan-
          ning theory." Paper presented at the 1976 Symposium on Planning
          Theory, University of Pennsylvania, Philadelphia.

  1977a   "A prolegomenon to an interrogative theory of scientific inquiry." In
          H. Hiz (ed.), Questions. Dordrecht: D. Reidel.

  1977b   "Remarks on information needs for the study of geographic mobility."
          In W. A. V. Clark (ed.), Models of Georgraphic Mobility. Evanston:
          Department of Geography, Northwestern University.

Galtung, J.
  1967    "On the future of the international system." Journal of Peace Science
          4: 305–333.

Georgescu-Roegen, N.
  1966    Analytical Economics. Cambridge: Harvard University Press.

  1972    The Entropy Law and the Economic Process. Cambridge: Harvard
          University Press.

Goguen, J. A.
  1968    "The logic of inexact concepts." Synthese 19: 325–73.

Gottinger, H. W.
  1974    "Toward fuzzy reasoning in the behavioral sciences." In W.
          Leinfellner and E. Kohler (eds.), Developments in the Methodology
          of Social Science. Dordrecht: D. Reidel.

Habermas, J.
  1972    Knowledge and Human Interest. Translated by J. Shapiro. Boston:
          Beacon Press.

Hall, R.
  1967    "Dialectic." Pp. 385–89 in P. Edwards (ed.), The Encyclopedia of
          Philosophy, vol. 2. New York: Macmillan.

Hamblin, C. L.
  1970    Fallacies. London: Methuen.

Harrah, D.
  1963    Communication: a Logical Model. Cambridge: M.I.T. Press.

  1969a   "On completeness in the logic of questions." American Philosophical

Quarterly 6: 158-64.

1969b   "Erotetic logistics." Pp. 3-21 in K. Lambert (ed.), The Logical Way of Doing Things. New Haven: Yale University Press.

1971   "Formal message theory." Pp. 69-83 in Y. Bar-Hillel (ed.), Pragmatics of Natural Languages. Dordrecht: D. Reidel.

Heelan, P. A.
1970   "Complementarity, context dependence, and quantum logic." Foundations of Physics 1: 95-110.

Hempel, C. G.
1965   Aspects of Scientific Explanation. New York: The Free Press.

Hilpinen, R.
1971   Deontic Logic: Introductory and Systematic Readings. Dordrecht: D. Reidel.

Hiz, H.
1962   "Questions and answers." Journal of Philosophy 59: 253-65.

Hooker, C. A. (ed.)
1973   "Editor's introduction." In The Is/Ought Question. London: Macmillan.

Keenan, E. and Hull, R.
1973   "The logical presuppositions of questions and answers." In J. S. Petofi and D. Franck (eds.), Presuppositions in der Philosophie und Linguistik. New York: Atheneum.

Kleene, S. C.
1952   Introduction to Metamathematics. Princeton: VanNostrand.

Körner, S.
1966   Experience and Theory. New York: Humanities Press.

1970   Categorial Frameworks. Oxford: Blackwell.

1976   Experience and Conduct. Cambridge: Cambridge University Press.

Krantz, D. H. et al.
1971   Foundations of Measurement, vol. 1. New York: Academic Press.

Lakoff, R.
1973   "Questionable answers and answerable questions." Pp. 456-67 in B. B. Kachru et.al. (eds.), Issues in Linguistics: Papers in Honor of Henry and Renee Kahane. Urbana: University of Illinois Press.

Lowe, A.
1969   On Economic Knowledge: Toward a Science of Political Economics, vol. 35. R. N. Anshen (ed.), World Perspectives. New York: Harper and Row.

McCarthy, T.
1973   "On misunderstanding 'understanding'." Theory and Decision 3: 351-70.

Mishan, E. J.
1976   Cost-Benefit Analysis. New York: Praeger.

Moore, E. G. and S. Gale
1973   "Comments on models of occupancy patterns and neighborhood change." Pp 135-73 in E. G. Moore (ed.), Models of Residential

Location and Relocation in the City, Study #20. Evanston, Illinois: Department of Geography, Northwestern University.

Morgenstern, O.
1972a "Descriptive, predictive and normative theory." Kyklos 2: 699–714.

1972b "Thirteen critical points in contemporary economic theory: an interpretation." Journal of Economic Literature 4: 1163–89.

Olsson, G.
1975 Birds in Egg. Ann Arbor: Department of Geography, University of Michigan Press.

Perelman, C. and L. Olbrechts-Tyteca
1969 The New Rhetoric: A Treatise on Argumentation. Notre Dame, Indiana: University of Notre Dame.

Popper, K. R.
1972 Objective Knowledge. Oxford: The Clarendon Press.

Reichenbach, H.
1944 Philosophical Foundations of Quantum Mechanics. Berkeley: University of California Press.

Rescher, N.
1969 Many-valued Logic. New York: McGraw-Hill.

1970 Scientific Explanation. New York: The Free Press.

Shackle, G. L. S.
1969 Decision, Order and Time in Human Affairs. Cambridge: Cambridge University Press.

1972 Epistemics and Economics. Cambridge: Cambridge University Press.

Sneed, J. D.
1971 The Logical Structure of Mathematical Physics. Dordrecht: D. Reidel.

Steiner, G.
1975 After Babel. New York: Oxford University Press.

Suppes, P.
1960 Axiomatic Set Theory. Princeton: Princeton University Press.

1970 Set Theoretic Structure in Science. Stanford: Institute for Mathematical Studies in the Social Sciences.

Targ, H.
1971 "Social science and a new social order." Journal of Peace Research 8: 207–220.

Tarski, A.
1959 "What is elementary geometry." In L. Henkin, P. Suppes, and A. Tarski (eds.), The Axiomatic Method. Amsterdam: North Holland.

Toulmin, S.
1969 The Uses of Argument. Cambridge: Cambridge University Press.

van Dijk, T. A.
1972 Some Aspects of Text Grammars. The Hague: Mouton.

vonWright, G. H.
1971 Explanation and Understanding. Ithaca: Cornell University Press.

Watanabe, S.
  1969    Knowing and Guessing. New York: John Wiley.
Weitz, M.
  1964    Hamlet and the Philosophy of Literary Criticism. New York: World
          Publishing Company.
White, H.
  1970    Chains of Opportunity. Cambridge: Harvard University Press.
Zadeh, L. A.
  1971    "Comparative fuzzy semantics." Information Science 3: 159–76.
Zinov'ev, A. A.
  1973    Foundations of the Logical Theory of Scientific Knowledge. Boston
          Studies in the Philosophy of Science 9. Dordrecht: D. Reidel.

# PART III

# Professions and Practice

## INTRODUCTION

*The most disturbing aspect of life in the United States today is the widening discrepancy between privatized luxury and public amenity. . . . Nor does all the architectural and urbanistic activity of recent years seem to halt this tendency. It often appears, on the contrary, to accelerate it.*
— —James Marston Fitch, *American Building*

An occupation attains recognition as a profession when its claims to a monopoly over an esoteric and unique service receive public acknowledgment. Because of the expertise involved and because of the profession's avowed concern for the benefits it offers clients—indeed, the entire society—it obtains, when successful, the exclusive right to carry out a particular set of tasks, to control training, and to supervise the activities of auxilliary occupations (Hughes, 1958; Freidson, 1970). Not only is a profession represented by a set of techniques and skills, it is also represented by a culture embodied in professional associations and in networks of colleagues (Goode, 1957). It is particularly significant that, when a profession is successful in its claims to a mandate and accompanying jurisdiction, that the profession acquires the right to tell the members of society what is in their interest, or, "what is good for them and what is bad for them" (Hughes, 1958: 79). In return for this "moral" responsibility, the profession is simultaneously protected and patronized by political and economic elites.

While the model just described is helpful in accounting for the patterns observed for the "established" professions—medicine, law, dentistry, and the clergy—it serves more to highlight a series of discrepancies between the objectives of planning and architecture and their actual positions in society. Both are professions in the sense that relatively high levels of education and training are required for their members and both serve clients, yet they have attained neither the influence of the established professions nor a monopoly over a given set of services.

The differences between the established professions, on the one hand, and the design professions on the other, relate largely to the way in which the professional-client relationship is structured. An aura of the sacred surrounds the private, one-to-one relationship that exists between patient and physician, clergy and parishioner, and lawyer and client. (To be sure, this relationship is changing in the context of bureaucratic medicine, corporate law, and churches in which the laity is more informally related to the clergy; yet the power of these professionals was fully institutionalized before such changes occurred.)

Architects and planners have very different kinds of relations with clients than do these other professionals. Planners serve a diffuse collectivity; indeed, their activities center on the provision and allocation of public goods. Nor do planners control the day-to-day decisions that bear on the allocation of public goods, for they must accommodate themselves to conflicting interest groups, and more important, to political and economic elites. Architects, as individuals, serve more diversified clients than do planners, but even in their relations with private clients they share responsibilities with other professionals, such as engineers and interior designers, which inevitably weakens their authority, if not their charisma. Moreover, in contrast to the historical model of sole practitioner in the established professions, planners have always worked in organizations, and this is increasingly so for architects as well. The implications of organizational practice for the reduction in professional autonomy, fragmentation of work, subordination to bureaucratic authority, and problems of coordination, are fairly clear. Another difference between the established professions and the design professions is that neither architects nor planners have such a single paradigm as germ theory or the Constitution, which serves to integrate, respectively, members of the medical and legal professions.

From these very reasons for the failure of the design professions to conform to the model of the established professions, it can be argued that architecture and planning may provide a model for the direction in which the established professions appear to be moving. For one thing, all professional work is becoming increasingly organized in large bureaucratic settings, and planners in particular have already evolved requisite models for organization-based practice (see, for example, Burchell and Sternlieb, 1978); this remains a problematic area for physicians (Blau, 1983). The accommodation to clients' and users' expressed needs and interests has always been part of the designer's ethical responsibilities; the public is increasingly insisting that medicine and health care resources now be brought under public scrutiny. This, however, sidesteps the issue of whether planners and architects ought to use the model of the established professions in attempting to attain greater control over a domain of work and public legitimation of that control. More light can be shed on this issue by just considering the differences between architecture and planning.

In blunt terms, Colbert distinguishes the two: "It appears that the planner *serves the public at the expense of the individual* while the architect *serves the individual at the expense of the public* (1966: 227; Colbert's emphasis). The point, of course, is that both deal with the built environment, yet the architect has failed to justify projects in other than individualistic and artistic terms, and the planner has emphasized continuity and overall order at the expense of human scale. There is clear evidence that this gap is beginning to be bridged by collaboration in urban design projects, historical renovations in downtown areas, and joint efforts in large-scale energy conservation projects (see Ferguson, 1975; Holliday, 1977; Dubeck and Miller, 1980).

In spite of converging interests and collaboration, architects and planners can be distinguished from one another in a number of important dimensions. Planners tend to work in the public sector, architects in the private sector. The very fact that most planners work for a salary, and architects, whether salaried or not, depend on fees for their economic well-being means that architects are particularly subject to conflicts between their professional commitments to clients and their business objectives, notably profitability. A strong reference for architects is aesthetic theory, whereas planners have a wider range, including geography, sociology, economics, and public administration. Yet another differentiation is that planners are chiefly concerned with process (for example, of urban growth, political dynamics, and economic changes), architects with product.

Given their different institutional base and types of relations with clients, planners and architects differ with respect to their professional roles. Kirk (1980) summarizes the four main roles of professional planners as follows: manager, advocate, reformist, and state agent. The manager role and its limitations are dealt with in this book by Miller (chapter 5). The difference between the advocate and reformist roles is analyzed by Genovese (chapter 13). The Marxist conceptualization of the planner as state agent is elaborated in chapter 7 by Beauregard, who views planners as operatives within a dominant class, under the control of a repressive and controlling institution. Thus dominated, planners unwittingly promote the interests of capitalism and the accumulatand

*179*

legitimation functions of the state. The parallels to architects, who in a more direct way serve the needs of corporate elites, are quite obvious. It is in the final section of the book that the full ramifications of Beauregard's analysis are explored as various authors propose radical alternatives for the roles of architects and planners.

However conceived, the individual planner's role tends to be fairly stable, given the particular status of the planner in a work organization. In contrast, when we discuss the situation of the architect, we must recognize that the architect may fill a variety of roles simultaneously. In fact the profession of architecture can be analyzed in terms of the dilemmas that arise from the incompatible expectations surrounding the four roles of artist, technician, entrepreneur, and client advocate. These dilemmas are considered in this section by Gutman, by Blau and Lieben, and by Larson, Leon, and Bolick.

Gutman analyzes an important consequence of the fact that architects have never had a monopoly over the design market, namely, that the strategies pursued by architects to secure a larger share of this market may be inconsistent with one professional norm — quality design — while consistent with another — responsiveness to client needs on a mass scale. This strategy, which consists of participation in the production of stock plans and the operation of local plan shops, serves to diminish the prestige and autonomy of architects while paradoxically expanding their domain of influence and improving the quality of housing for the average home buyer.

Two chapters deal with aspects of office practice and organization. The one by Blau and Lieben is concerned with the variety of dimensions of organizational effectiveness and the conditions of failure. The dimensions of organizational effectiveness are: productivity, profits, design quality, and growth. One question deals with firm changes over a five-year period on each of these dimensions, a second with the reasons why architectural firms fail. The findings suggest that the very factors that serve to maximize success on one dimension may promote failure on another, highlighting the dilemma of a profession that has multiple goals.

The title of the chapter by Larson, Leon, and Bolick, "The Professional Supply of Design," implies two ironies. First, it underscores the point made by Gutman that architects supply only a minor part of the market for design services despite their prestige and historical prominence. Second, their analysis reveals that the most significant suppliers are those that are in fact marginal to the profession: the economic giants and the struggling entrepreneurial firms. Using national survey data, the authors examine a great variety of questions about architectural firms: their geographical distribution, structural characteristics, and variation in the quality of design. They conclude by speculating on future trends in the practice of architecture.

All these authors deal in a variety of ways with the question of whether the design occupations are indeed fully professionalized. Cullen provides reasons why in fact they ought *not* to be. He argues that professionalization of architecture would require such a high degree of centralization that the very autonomy of professionals, university departments, and professional associations would be seriously undermined. Such autonomy is particularly important to architecture because of the intrinsically creative nature of work of high quality and the diversity of the professional role. A similar case might be made for planning.

There is another reason to question how wise it is for the design professions to see the kind of power that the established professions have enjoyed in the past. Admittedly we now have rampant pluralism rather than rational control in decisions that shape the urban environment. Engineers, lawyers, developers, politicians, speculators, and private interest groups all have a say in decisions. Although we may wish for a more fully participatory process than we now have, the existing arrangement is more consistent with democratic values than would be the centralized control suggested as desirable by some segments of the design professions. As Arrow (1974) has pointed out, there ought to be a difference in the locus of control when services are provided to the general public in contrast to single individuals. The provision and allocation of public goods and the decisions involving the built environment probably should not be under the central control of any single profession, but rather should reside in the hands of a plurality of competing interest groups.

## REFERENCES

Arrow, K. J.
   1974   The Limits of Organization. New York: W. W. Norton.

Blau, J. R.
   1983   "The organization of hospitals." In John Talbott and Seymour Kaplan (eds.), The Handbook of Administrative Psychiatry. New York: Grune and Stratton.

Burchell, R. W. and G. Sternlieb, eds.
   1978   Planning Theory in the 1980's. New Brunswick, New Jersey: Center for Urban Policy Research.

Colbert, C.
   1966   "Naked utility and visual chorea." Pp. 214–35 in Laurence B. Holland (ed.), Who Designs America? Garden City, New York: Anchor.

Dubeck, P. and Z. L. Miller, eds.
1980     Urban Professionals and the Future of the Metropolis. Port Washington, N. Y.: Kennikat Press.

Ferguson, F.
1975     Architecture, Cities and the Systems Approach. New York: Braziller.

Freidson, E.
1970     Profession of Medicine. New York: Dodd, Mead.

Goode, W. J.
1957     "Community within a community." American Sociological Review 20: 194–200.

Holliday, J.
1977     Design for Environment. London: Charles Knight.

Hughes, E. C.
1958     Men and Their Work. Glencoe: Free Press.

Kirk, G.
1980     Urban Planning in a Capitalist Society. London: Croom Helm.

# 7  Planners As Workers:
# A Marxist Perspective

## ROBERT A. BEAUREGARD

Viewing their occupation through the distorting lens of professionalism, planners distinguish the practice of planning from the work of other laborers. Planners are not workers, they are professionals. Their tasks are seemingly qualitatively advanced over the manual activities associated with the great majority of the labor force (Altshuler, 1965: 392–405; Marcuse, 1976; Rabinovitz, 1969: 132–8). The attainment of professional status has, in fact, been a major goal since the emergence of this occupation. However, this desire to differentiate planners from labor in general has resulted in the neglect of those characteristics they share with labor.

Certainly, any analysis of planners' practice must recognize that there is a professionalism, justified or not, which affects planning ideology and practice. Nonetheless, planners are workers. As part of the laboring class they are affected by the forces that shape the role of labor under advanced capitalism and by the position they occupy within this laboring class. To describe planners as professionals fails to explain the basic dimensions of their practice. Only an analysis that positions planners within the class structure and pinpoints the functions they serve for key institutions can accomplish this.

The objective of this paper is to identify certain constraints and opportunities facing planning practice in the United States by analyzing the position of governmental planners within the class structure, particularly as that position is articulated at the workplace. [1] Planning practice is conceptualized as abstract labor (i.e., as work in general) rather than in its concrete and ideological manifestations (e.g., professionalism). [2] This allows planners to be placed directly within the larger political economy. While the practice of planning is affected by individual initiative and personality, by planning education, and by the bureaucratic and social dynamics peculiar to the communities in which planners work, it is the abstract nature of their work, the structure of the political economy, and the position of planners' within that structure which shape their practice. These latter forces establish the context and set the limits on planners' activities. Structure transcends the peculiarities of people and place. The structural perspective utilized herein, moreover, is Marxist.[3] Planners within advanced capitalism are conceived as a fraction of labor whose work is molded by the forces of capital and class struggle, and mediated through the State.[4] To this extent, a secondary objective of this paper is to explore the relevance and utility of Marxist analysis for planning behavior.

In order to achieve these objectives, three tasks must be undertaken. First, planning practice and the occupation of planning must be identified in a purely descriptive fashion. Such identification delimits this fraction of labor and the work it performs, thus focusing the discussion. Using this characterization, the occupation of planning is then analyzed from a Marxist perspective. The abstract characteristics of planning as labor within the context of advanced capitalism are delineated. The functions planners serve for capital, labor, and the State are then articulated, and the position of planners within the class structure is explored. The resultant analytical portrait contains various clues as to the constraints upon, and the potentialities within, planning practice. These are investigated in terms of three dimensions of practice: the technical, the social, and the political.

## THE PRACTICE AND
## OCCUPATION OF PLANNING

While planning itself is a general activity that can be performed in a variety of spheres ranging from household finances to animal husbandry to space exploration, the activity considered here is considerably narrower. The analysis is limited to urban and regional planners whose historical antecedents are in the land-use and housing reform movements of the early part of the twentieth century and whose present orientations focus primarily on modifications in and control over the built environment (Altshuler, 1965; Gans, 1968; Scott, 1969). These planners analyze the interaction between socioeconomic processes and the physical environment, and develop plans and regulations for controlling the resultant consequences. Among other activities, they engage in the manipulation of land uses, the development and deployment of housing, the protection of the natural environment, the location and design of transportation systems, the rehabilitation of neighborhoods, the revitalization of central business districts, and the spatial allocation of health services.

In performing these tasks, planners act primarily as technical experts, and as governmental employees. In the role of technical experts, planners undertake the collection and analysis of data (Benveniste, 1977). Their objectives are to determine the nature of the problem, identify the forces that shape it, and then devise a plan or set of procedures for preventing or reacting to that problem. They pursue these objectives through the scientific and ostensibly value-free analysis of factual (usually quantitative) information and the derivation from that information of a set of alternative solutions or paths of action.[5] Thus, their expert knowledge is used to devise a rational response that best achieves the intended results. The selection of the preferred alternative is left to the employer (in most cases, elected officials) and its implementation to other occupations. While this general description of planners as technical experts has many nuances and exceptions, it captures the historical essence of the contribution that planners view themselves as making toward the betterment of society.[6]

Generally, the practice of this type of planning takes place within the government. At the turn of the century, planners emerged as part of a reform movement. The private sector was despoiling the built and natural environments and oppressing the new mass of industrial workers. Many city neighborhoods were overcrowded, prone to the rampant spread of fire and disease, and without adequate housing. Government was pressured by reformers to become more active in regulating private-sector activity, protecting the citizenry and providing services. The progressive movement called for good government and municipal reform based on expertise and a quest for the efficient provision of services. Government enmeshed in personal politics and ethnic affiliations was to be replaced by scientific procedures. Experts were hired to manage the city. Those who regulated the built environment were eventually labeled 'planners.'

These early planners believed they could and should act in a nonpolitical fashion to prevent the excesses of unfettered competition and individual greed. Essentially they were (and still are) reform liberals who accepted the need for government to curtail the negative externalities generated by the market and to act positively in areas (e.g., low-income housing) that the private sector had abandoned. The work of planners is ostensibly performed in the public interest; it is assumed to be nonpartisan, favoring neither one group nor another. Instead, the best plans and proposals are developed for the community as a whole (Klosterman, 1980).

This orientation to the built and natural environments, the dominance of the role of the nonpolitical technical expert, and the involvement in government (with the reformist and public interest biases which this implies) all delineate key aspects of the practice and occupation of planning. Using this general characterization, the occupation can be described quantitatively in order to learn more about the individuals who comprise it.

## Quantitative Dimensions

Quantitatively, planners do not constitute a significant percentage of the labor force. In 1970, fewer than 10,000 people — 9,214 to be exact — were identified as planners by the Bureau of the Census (Beauregard, 1976). This is an extremely small number when compared with the more than 83 million people in the labor force during that same year. An estimate for 1979 places the size of this occupation somewhere between 20,000 and 25,000 individuals (Leavitt, 1980a: S227). But even this doubling of the occupation, if real, does not significantly increase the relative size of this group when compared to the labor force as a whole, or to other professional-technical occupations. Architects are between three and four times more numerous, lawyers and judges twenty times more numerous, and social workers fourteen times greater in number.

Relative to its size, however, the occupation is expanding rapidly. From 1960 to 1970, it grew more than tenfold, and during the seventies it may have doubled.[7] Moreover, this trend will likely continue, although somewhat abated. While, in 1970, there were approximately 4,000 graduate students enrolled in planning schools throughout the United States, by 1977 this had increased to slightly more than 5,100 (Corby and So, 1974; Hamlin, 1978). People continue to enter the occupation in relatively large numbers.

The great majority of these planners work for the government. Almost 80 percent of all planners recorded by the Bureau of the Census in 1970 were governmental workers, with slightly over 80 percent (80.9) of these employed by local (i.e., municipal and county) governments. The remaining governmental planners were working for state and federal agencies (10.6 percent and 8.5 percent respectively). The American Institute of City Planning (AICP), in a survey of its roster during the latter months of 1979, found that 46.2 percent of those who responded were governmental employees.[8] Of those, 79 percent worked for city, county, metropolitan, or regional agencies. These latter data, however, are biased by the professional nature of this organization, which is more oriented, and more useful, to private consultants than to governmental workers. Even so, governmental employment, particularly in local government, is important to the occupation of planning.

Those planners not employed by government are mostly involved in private consulting firms. The 1970 Census estimated this percentage of the occupation at 18.4, with the remaining planners (1.8 percent) either self-employed or unpaid family workers. The AICP survey identified 32.5 percent of its respondents as private consultants. This far high figure, again, is probably a result of the professional nature of the organization itself. The remaining 21.3 percent of its respondents were either employed by industry or business, colleges or universities, research foundations, nonprofit planning agencies, or other similar entities.

Various surveys have also gathered information on the yearly incomes, educational attainment, and personal characteristics (i.e., sex, race, and age) of urban and regional planners. In 1970, the median yearly earnings for male planners was $11,544, whereas that for female planners was $6,726. These figures were significantly higher than the similar median yearly earnings for the labor force as a whole, but only slightly higher than the median for professional, technical, and kindred workers (Beauregard, 1976: 190). A survey conducted by the American Society of Planning Officials found that in 1977 the median yearly earnings for males was approximately $20,000 and that for females approximately $16,000 (Leavitt, 1980b: 224). These planners earned significantly more than the median money income of all full-time, year-round workers in 1977: $15,070 for males and $8,814 for females (United States Bureau of the Census, 1979: 460).

As for educational attainment, the major credential that marks a person as a professional planner, and that is generally required for most planning positions, is the master's degree. Neither the bachelor's degree nor the doctorate are appropriate for professional planning practice. In 1970, 49.7 percent of all planners had one or more years of graduate education, and 89.2 percent of the total had one or more years of college education, either undergraduate or graduate. A survey of planners conducted in 1979 found that 73.4 percent of its respondents held master's degrees, with another 12.4 percent having education beyond the master's (Leavitt, 1980c: 41–2).

As for personal characteristics, the occupation of planning is predominantly male and Caucasian, and most planners are under the age of 45. The Bureau of the Census analysis from 1970 estimated that 89.5 percent of all urban and regional planners were male and 91.0 percent were Caucasian. The median age for male planners was 35.9 years and for female planners, 28.1 years. The AICP roster survey of 1979 included 93.6 percent male respondents and 97.9 percent Caucasian respondents. In addition, 58 percent of those respondents were under 45 years of age.

*187*

Again, one would expect this survey to discover somewhat lower proportions of female, nonwhite, and younger planners, since members of this organization are fairly advanced in their careers. Within planning, such people are usually male, Caucasian, and older.

Overall, then, the occupation of planning is a relatively small portion of the labor force as a whole and even of the subcategory of professional and technical workers. Employment is dominated by the government, primarily with city and county agencies. The yearly incomes earned by planners are generally above those for the labor force as a whole, placing them somewhere among middle-income wage earners. Their education consists of graduate training in professional schools. In terms of personal characteristics, most of the occupation is male and Caucasian, and its median age is under 45. This brief description of planners, their qualitative characteristics as governmental, technical experts, and the quantitative characteristics of the occupation itself, delineates the basic dimensions of this fraction of labor.

## PLANNERS AS A FRACTION OF LABOR

Any analysis of planners must embed their work within the structural forces of a given historical moment. To avoid this would be to impute to these workers a fully determinative control over their practice and its consequences, which they do not possess. The relation of an occupation to basic economic, political and cultural forces is important not only for the work that occupation can legitimately undertake but also for its very existence (Braverman, 1974). Moreover, through work, society is produced and reproduced (Peet, 1975). Work and occupation are not isolated from social structure (Parston, 1980: 157-76). Thus work is at the core of collective and individual existence. Nor is *practice* distinct from work.[9] Practice is the work an individual performs, and the practice in which one engages is partially determined by the class to which one belongs and the fraction of labor in which one participates.

In addition, the Marxist perspective considers practice as having various qualitative manifestations (Lefebvre, 1968: 25-28; Vazquez, 1977). Using a simple formulation, there are three interrelated dimensions of practice: the technical, the social, and the political. The technical dimension involves the performance of tasks that lead directly to the production of either a good or service. For a planner this might include the collection of data and their translation into tables and graphs, which then comprise a plan. Work also has a dimension that emanates from the social relations involved. Along this dimension, one's practice directs, and is subject to, the interactions among people participating in the production of goods and services. The presentation of a plan to a citizens' advisory board, the interviewing of local merchants to determine the problems facing a neighborhood's commercial district, and negotiations with other governmental experts to better coordinate programs are examples of this social dimension of planning practice.

Lastly, practice has a political dimension. Here, the individual's work involves either the support and perpetuation of, or challenge to and destruction of, existing patterns of power and privilege within and without the workplace. It usually consists of both actual behaviors and ideological pronouncements. When planners devise plans that favor local business elites and allow them to maintain their control over local politics, the political nature of their practice emerges. When they redistribute funds to lower-class neighborhoods and strengthen them politically through greater access to program decisions, they are again undertaking political practice. Their public claims that central business district redevelopment is in the public interest is just one example of the ideological element of their work. In almost every planning activity, the three aspects of practice are present. Planners emphasize the technical, but they cannot avoid the social and the political.

To understand how these various dimensions of planning practice are molded by larger, politico-economic and ideological structures, planners must be placed within them. In this rudimentary analysis, three structural aspects of the occupation of planning will be assessed: first, the characteristics of planners' work; second, the basic functions they perform within the present stage of advanced capitalism; and, third, their position within the class structure itself. The resultant interpretation can then be used to draw forth implications for the three dimensions of planning practice.

### Planners' Characteristics

The most general and important determinant of the structural attributes of an occupation is whether or not the individuals within that occupation own the means of production used in their work. If they do not, then they must sell their labor power in order to obtain income by which to live.[10] To be in a position in which one must sell one's labor power is to be forced to put oneself under the control of those who own the means of production, that is, the capitalists. This general distinction is at the core of Marxist theory and creates the delineation between the two major, abstract classes: labor (the proletariat) and capital (the bourgeoisie). In this scheme, planners are part of the working class.[11] The majority of planners do not own the means of production for the work they do, but must instead practice in the employ of capital or of the State.[12]

A second important distinction involves the extent to which planners are productive or unproductive labor within the context of advanced capitalism (Gough, 1972). Productive labor produces commodities (either goods or services) that are exchanged in markets for money. Capitalist production occurs in such a way that the capitalist is able to capture an increment of value over and above both the wages paid to the laborers and the cost of inputs and fixed capital (i.e., raw materials, machines). This increment is labeled the 'surplus value' and is a measure of the degree to which labor is exploited by capital (Marx, 1967: 177–230). It is realized or captured by the capitalist only through the sale of the commodity. Unproductive labor, on the other hand, makes a commodity which has use-value, but that commodity is not exchanged, and thus surplus value is not realized. This kind of labor may help the capitalist to generate or realize surplus value more efficiently or effectively, but it does not itself create surplus value. Thus, a worker on an automotive assembly line is a productive worker and a cashier in a supermarket is an unproductive worker. The former is producing a commodity (i.e., an automobile) which will be purchased (i.e., exchanged in a cash transaction), whereas the latter is producing a service (i.e., the billing of the consumer) which is not directly exchanged in a market.[13]

From this perspective, planners are unproductive workers. The commodities (e.g., plans, research reports, regulations) that they produce are not exchanged.[14] Even though the products of their work are used to enhance the conditions for capital accumulation and to lower the costs of production (e.g., by constructing more efficient transportation systems), no new surplus value is realized directly from these products. The benefits of planning accrue to the State in the form of lower public service costs or higher tax revenues, and to those capitalists assisted by the State programs in which planners are involved. This increased fiscal capacity gained by the State as a result of planning, however, is not realized through the sale of products or services produced by its planners but through the enhancement of the economic base or the prevention of threats to that base.[15] Planners' work, then, is related to production only in the sense that it enhances the conditions for capital accumulation. In addition to these technical contributions, planners offer an ideology to explain their work and to legitimate capitalism as well as State policies and programs. This is also unproductive work. For these reasons, planners are unproductive workers.

A third important characteristic of planners' work is that the commodities they produce take the form of intermediate services. That is, they are neither material commodities nor the final product of the planning process. Even though a material commodity (e.g., a planning report) often flows from planning practice, it is seldom considered the ultimate objective (Beauregard, 1980a: 320-1). The final product is the actual manipulation of the environment, a manipulation that is not performed by planners but by other governmental agencies, nonprofit organizations (e.g., a neighborhood housing agency) or capitalist enterprises (e.g., a developer). Thus the major thrust of planners' work is in directing and controlling material production performed by others, not in themselves producing material commodities. Their output is rules, regulations, approvals or disapprovals, and grants.[16] Planners, in effect, provide a service. Rather than being manual workers, though some manual work is involved, planners are primarily 'mental' workers (Wright, 1976: 9). Admittedly, this is a gross distinction. But it does direct attention to the intermediate nature of planners' commodities, and reinforces the point that these commodities have no exchange value.

The workplace for most planners is the governmental agency, and their employer is the State, not a capitalist (Friedman, et al., 1980). The commodities produced by planners for the State are not exchanged for money, and thus surplus value is not realized. Nonetheless, this does not mean that State planners are not alienated, exploited, or subject to the forces of capitalism. To the extent that planners do not control their work or its products, they are alienated (Beauregard, 1980a). The problems to which planners apply their expertise, the rules and regulations that guide their analyses, and the resultant products are generally determined outside of the planners' workplace. Executive and legislative decisions create the work of planners and circumscribe legitimate planning activities.[17] On the other hand, the work of planners is not wholly susceptible to standardization, thus making it difficult to separate the immediate direction of planning from its performance (Braverman, 1974: 59-152). This provides planners with some autonomy in their practice. In addition, few planners manage other labor, that is, work for the State in controlling the social relations of production. While there are planners in administrative positions, the great majority of planners perform planning in a technical rather than a managerial capacity. Except for barriers to standardization, each of these factors diminishes planners' control over their work, alienates them, and also hinders the drive to professionalization.

If planners produce value for the State that is not fully compensated by the wages paid, then they are also exploited.[18] Under conditions of fiscal austerity, one might expect the State—under pressure from both workers and capitalists—to reduce taxes (the money out of which planners are paid) and to cut State expenditures by eliminating programs and making the remaining programs more efficient (i.e., less costly). State workers might then be expected to be more "productive" without a corresponding wage increase. The point is that planners are not immune to the forces of capital and may suffer alienation and wage exploitation.

In general, then, planners produce commodities for the State that are mostly nonmaterial, are intermediate in the larger process of facilitating the interests of the State and of capital, which are not exchanged for money, and are independent of the realization of surplus value. In this sense, planners are unproductive workers. But this analysis is incomplete. Planners do produce use-value for capital and the State. To understand this, we need to look closely at the general functions they perform.

## Functions

The functions of planners can be characterized by first delineating the major functions of capitalism — production and reproduction — and then exploring the more specific functions of the advanced capitalist State — accumulation and legitimation (O'Connor, 1973). Production, in this context, refers to the creation of commodities that can be used in exchange and, concomitantly, for the generation of surplus value. Reproduction, on the other hand, involves the perpetuation of the relations of production, the class structure that supports capitalism, and the laboring class itself. It requires the maintenance of the political, economic, and ideological relationships that define advanced capitalism, and subsumes the sphere of circulation in which capital flows between and among capitalists and through financial intermediaries. Production and reproduction, moreover, are overlapping spheres of activity. The production of commodities reinforces capitalist relations by enhancing capital accumulation and by reasserting capital's control over labor. Thus, within the production process, reproduction occurs. What is important for this analysis is the degree to which these two functions are engaged in by planners.

The State does not produce commodities for exchange, but is not simply and solely in the sphere of reproduction. On the one hand, the State — through the provision of infrastructure (e.g., roads), the enforcement of contracts, and the granting of subsidies (e.g., accelerated depreciation allowances), among other activities — enhances the conditions that facilitate production and capital accumulation. This has been labeled its "accumulation function." On the other hand, the State also functions to amass and sustain political support for itself and for the economic structures with which it is entwined. This is its "legitimation function." It includes not only the allocation of material goods to individuals to assure their support (e.g., oil depletion allowances and food stamps) but also the development of ideological structures (e.g., 'democratic' voting procedures, citizen participation) that are meant to achieve a symbolic identification with the extant political economy. The overall role of the State is to serve, in a relatively autonomous fashion, the long-run interests of capital. To accomplish this it must bolster capital accumulation and also provide for the reproduction of labor and the prevention of political conflict that would interfere with those processes.

Planners are involved in both the accumulation and legitimation functions of the State (Beauregard, 1978a). They engage in numerous tasks that enhance the production process for capitalists. The arrangement of land use to increase transportation accessibility to industrial sites; the design and allocation of tax abatements to reduce the costs of new construction in redeveloping areas; the attainment of land write-downs and low-interest industrial development loans; the disbursal of construction grants; and the undertaking of market analyses for local merchants are only a few examples of planners' indirect contribution to production. Most noteworthy is planners' protection of the privilege of private property through zoning and other land-use regulations.

Planners are also engaged in the legitimation function (Harvey, 1978). They develop plans for allocating health services and facilities to protect the labor force from disease. They institute citizen participation procedures that channel political discontent into acceptable and nonthreatening activities. They develop plans and proposals that demonstrate the State's interest in redeveloping distress areas, and they add to those plans arguments that point out how all citizens, both capital and labor, will benefit. Moreover, just through their role as technical experts within the State they create an impression that the State is operating rationally to produce public services and programs that are in the public interest.

Planners, then, can be placed primarily in the sphere of reproduction.[19] Their contribution to production is decidedly indirect; it enhances the environmental, social, and ideological relationships that facilitate capital accumulation. Their work has little direct material import for capital. It functions mainly to convey an ideology of technical expertise which masks the underlying orientation of the State toward capital. To this extent, planning is ideological; it is definitely a legitimation device and part of reproduction. Planning helps to overcome some of the destructive consequences of competition. Its environmental contributions facilitate capital accumulation, and its ideology reinforces capital relations. Thus planners serve both the accumulation and legitimation functions, but do so from the sphere of reproduction.

*Robert A. Beauregard*

## Structural Position

The structural position of any individual or group within capitalism is initially determined by that individual's or group's relationship to the means of production, that is, whether they own capital or must sell their labor power. Using this abstract scheme, planners are a fraction of labor. However, the real class structure within advanced capitalism is far more complex.[20] These gross structural positions require articulation in both concrete and historical terms. Class analysis must consider not only the relationship to the means of production but also other criteria (e.g., amount of control over work, common ideology). Of particular concern are those 'professional' occupations that have arisen in the era of advanced capitalism.

The structural position of planners, managers, scientists, engineers, teachers, and other professional and administrative fractions of labor has generally perplexed Marxist analysts of class structure within advanced capitalism (Giddens, 1973: 82–98; Walker, 1979; Wright, 1976). These fractions seem to belong to neither capital nor labor, nor even to the petty bourgeoisie.[21] Of the many interpretations of these fractions of labor, three can be usefully surveyed to construct a rough approximation of the structural position of planners. They are the Professional-Managerial Class (PMC) argument developed by Barbara and John Ehrenreich, the new petty bourgeoisie as interpreted by Nicos Poulantzas, and the objectively contradictory location of 'managers' as presented by Eric Olin Wright.

The Ehrenreichs argue that professionals and managers within the United States constitute a distinct class, the PMC (Ehrenreich and Ehrenreich, 1979). The Professional-Managerial Class is comprised of salaried workers who do not own the means of production and who perform primarily mental activities. Their major function is to reproduce capitalist culture and capitalist class relations through such social control activities as education, management, and the propogation of ideology. Because of this, the PMC contains essentially unproductive labor. In fact, their salaries are paid out of the surplus value created by the working class. Thus they dissipate the mass of surplus value in society and benefit from the exploitation of productive labor. Lastly, the PMC has a common culture and ideology. Of particular importance is the confluence of reform liberalism and the orientation to technical solutions for social problems, both of which have their roots in the Progressive Era.

Obviously, many of these characteristics fit the occupation of planners, and the Ehrenreichs explicitly mention planners as part of the PMC. However, the claim that such workers are oriented solely toward the reproduction of culture and class relations deserves scrutiny. The reproduction activities of planners are not focused mainly on cultural elements. Rather, their contribution to reproduction includes the perpetuation of productive capacities, on the one hand, and the spatial articulation of class relations on the other (Peet, 1975). The former serves capital and, as a result, maintains capital's dominance. The latter differentiates spatially between capital and labor, and amongst fractions of labor in order to maintain the class structure. Thus planners do contribute to production. To separate production functions from reproduction functions in such an unambiguous and narrow fashion, as the Ehrenreichs do, is empirically and theoretically problematic. To this extent, the concept of the PMC requires modification before planners can be placed unequivocally within it. Still, in terms of this brief analysis, the congruence is strong.

A second approach is to place planners within the 'new petty bourgeoisie' as interpreted by Nicos Poulantzas (Wright, 1976: 3-15). Simply stated, this class comprises unproductive wage earners who are involved in the political domination of capital over the working class and whose labor is primarily mental. As experts, workers within the new petty bourgeoisie have knowledge of production. They use this knowledge within the social relations of production in order to dominate workers ideologically. But rather than claiming this group as a 'new' class, as was done by the Ehrenreichs, Poulantzas argues instead that this group of white-collar employees, technicians, supervisors, and civil servants has replaced the traditional petty bourgeoisie as the marginal class between capital and labor.

Since the work of planners is essentially unproductive and is more mental than manual, the idea of a new petty bourgeoisie might be useful for locating planners within the class structure. However, a problem arises when considering the extent to which planners are involved in the political domination of capital over labor. Only a few planners are engaged in the management of workers. Their political domination at the point of production (or nonproduction, in this case) is minimal. To the extent that they help fragment the working class through land-use and housing policies that segregate fractions of labor across space, they are indirectly involved in political domination which occurs outside the workplace. For planners, it is their ideological domination that is more important. Here their expertise and technical objectivity is used to depoliticize issues and garner support for policies and programs that reproduce capital (Beauregard, 1978b). At times, planners do oppose capital, both politically and ideologically. But in the long run, as employees of the State, one would expect their work to serve the interests of capital. Further analysis of the work of planners and of the occupational distribution of the new petty bourgeoisie is needed if planners are to be placed unequivocally in this class.

Wright has developed a third version of this group of professional and managerial occupations. He rejects both the PMC and new petty bourgeoisie interpretations, positing instead the existence of objectively contradictory locations within the class structure of advanced capitalism. These "represent positions which are torn between the basic contradictory class relations of capitalist society" (Wright, 1976: 26): bourgeoisie, proletariat and petty bourgeoisie. In effect, they are doubly contradictory. Of interest here is that contradictory location between the bourgeoisie and the proletariat—the managers. This grouping includes top and middle managers, technocrats, and foreman or line supervisors who have some autonomy over their work, limited control over subordinates, and no command over the productive apparatus. But when Wright considers technocrats, his attention is directed primarily to those technicians and professionals within the corporate hierarchy, rather than those employed by the State.

While planners would seem to fit most of Wright's characteristics for this contradictory class location, their placement in the corporate hierarchy and between the proletariat and the bourgeoisie is bothersome. Planners are generally State employees. Their role is not simply to mediate between these two classes but also to mediate between the State and these classes, between the State and the petty bourgeoisie, among fractions of capital, and among the three classes themselves. Certainly if the State is viewed as basically the instrument of capital, then planners "sit" between capital and labor. But to the extent that in concrete situations and in the short run the State is relatively autonomous from capital and susceptible to both bourgeoisie and petty bourgeoisie interests, then the class location of State employees in general and planners in particular is less definite.

While none of these perspectives provides an adequate interpretation of the structural position of planners, each suggests much about planning practice that is not yet fully understood. More investigations must be directed at the relative importance of the various functions in which planners might engage, for example, the reproduction of culture, social control, the reproduction of class relations, the facilitation of capital accumulation, and the perpetuation of the State. In exploring these functions, attention must be given to the extent to which planners enhance the domination of labor by capital. Certainly planners are involved in the spatial fragmentation of labor and the depoliticization of issues that threaten the stability of the political economy. But how is this translated into political domination, and how are planners implicated? Lastly, more research has to be focused on the position of planners within the

State. As State employees, they develop multiple relationships with various fractions of capital and labor, and with various components of the State. The fragmented nature of the State, its relative autonomy, and the relative autonomy of State employees do not so much position planners between classes but among and within them.[22] An understanding of these facets of planning practice will clarify another question: the degree to which planners are conscious of their role in advanced capitalism. Such consciousness is necessary if planners are to engage in political action and advance their own practice.

# IMPLICATIONS FOR PRACTICE

At this time it is neither possible nor appropriate to present a thorough and definitive analysis of the multitudinous ways in which the structural attributes, functions, and position of planners shape the practice of planning. However, certain key relationships can be sketched in order to convey the potential of this approach for elucidating the constraints upon planning practice and the possibilities of changing it. To focus the discussion, three dimensions of planning practice will be highlighted: the technical, the social, and the political.

## *Technical Practice*

The fact that planners are State employees sets limits on the techniques they use.[23] The State must impress labor with its neutrality in the struggle between capital and labor. Thus its experts must utilize techniques that are ostensibly value-free and devoid of political analysis, and that do not uncover underlying contradictions, or point out the State's bias toward capital's long-run interests. The technical practice of planners is therefore most appropriate to the State's interests when it claims to derive solutions in the public interest and focuses on the efficient allocation of State outputs, a rational criterion that conserves State resources. Even when these techniques incorporate equity considerations, they must retain a focus on distributional results rather than their productive causes; the latter would strike at the root of inequality in a capitalist society and thus at the contradictions themselves.

In addition, planning techniques must not unveil the ideological aspects of State programs. They must reinforce the supposedly unbiased and nonpartisan nature of State outputs. The benefits to capital must not be made too obvious. Any truly objective analysis would expose the ways in which planning is often supportive of capital to the detriment of labor. Planners must use their techniques to avoid this. These techniques must also be effective at resolving tensions relatively quickly, before they evolve into conflict, and at disbursing State outputs in a timely and acceptable fashion. Failure in this would create a crisis within the State (Habermas, 1975: 61–8). The State would be unable to respond efficiently and effectively to demands and would thus lose legitimacy and political support.

Despite these constraints, there are also opportunities for changing the technical practice of planners. Planners are not without some control over their work. Moreover, their involvement with both accumulation and legitimation places them in a position to analyze technically the linkage between these functions. To the extent that planners act ideologically to enhance accumulation through State programs, there is the potential for their techniques to reflect and even make explicit the underlying tensions. For example, an analysis that points out the overall benefits of tax abatement to a developer, the direct costs to citizens, and the uncertain and problematic benefits that might accrue to labor will have difficulty reconciling this distribution of costs and benefits with the ostensible public interest orientation of planners and the State. This may lead planners to become more critical, or to mystify further, both the planning process and the consequences of State programs.[24]

The development of plans with a specific future orientation also has the potential for directing planners' techniques toward a more structural analysis of capitalism and the role of the State. Existing techniques of plan development tend to hold constant the political economy and to avoid political issues. As planners understand better how the future unfolds in material terms, they may also begin to analyze the role of different fractions of capital and labor in producing that future. This might lead to historical analysis and the unearthing of the long-run interests of capital, labor, and the State. Of course, the class position of planners may limit the extent to which they can perform such analyses. Throughout each of these dimensions of practice, in fact, the class interests of planners influence their behavior. They may accept the constraints of the State because, simply stated, it assures them of employment. Or, they may exploit the potential for change because that route promises less alienation and wage exploitation, as well as greater influence for their work.

### Social Practice

Employment by the State constrains the social relations of planners' practice. In their 'official' capacity, they are allowed to interact only with groups that have 'legitimate' business with the State. Planning activities are confined to those groups who follow proper procedures and make requests that correspond to State outputs. To become involved with groups who are antagonistic to State policies and programs is unacceptable. Any advocacy on the part of State planners is extremely difficult and might lead to loss of employment (Needleman and Needleman, 1974). Additionally, as planners interact with citizens, they must channel this participation away from accumulation issues (Friedland et al., 1977) and treat participation as ideological rather than substantive. Both responses limit the social dimension of planning practice: the first by disallowing citizen-planner interaction on economic development issues and the second by preventing the experiential knowledge and political support of citizens from explicit use in the planning process. In the latter case, planners retain their claim to expertise and act as professionals. This weakens their social practice, but it may serve their class interests.

Because the State needs to separate its accumulation and legitimation functions and to fragment the citizenry through a multitude of agencies, planners are also prevented from a truly comprehensive involvement with all aspects of State activity.[25] Planners are confined to certain policy areas. They must plan for transportation independently of State actions on employment and industrial development, for example. Each function is normally in a different agency, and no overall planning function exists. To establish such a function, the State would risk either exposing its bias toward capital or allowing the planning function to debate the contradictions within the political economy. Though this planning might be captured by capital, ideologically it is unacceptable and materially it might strengthen the reformist and liberal elements in the planning occupation.

Within this social dimension of planning practice there are opportunities for overcoming these limitations. In the interests of its own legitimacy, the State needs citizen participation and democratic procedures as well as a relatively open planning process. Thus planners have the capability and the opportunity to demythologize planning and the actions of the State (Forester, 1980). They can interact with citizens in such a way as to clarify State actions and to allow more critical debate. Moreover, they can use the political support so engendered to bolster their own critical analyses. Such changes in this dimension of planning practice require more than the unilateral actions of planners. Planners need the support of anticapitalist constituencies to help them to understand their class interest as labor and to modify accordingly the practice of planning.

## Political Practice

Obviously, the constraints and potentialities inherent in the dimensions of planning practice described above have political causes and political implications. Both technical and social practices affect the distribution of power and privilege and are, in turn, affected by them. In addition, certain aspects of planning practice are explicitly and primarily political. On the one hand, direct involvement of planners in political behavior has been suppressed by the State and by the ideology of planners (Needleman and Needleman, 1974). Yet, this nonpartisan stance allows planners to gain entrance to the State employment structure. Planners are granted certain reformist behaviors (e.g., environmental pollution controls). Beyond such reform, however, planners would have to confront the political, economic, and ideological contradictions in capitalist society. This is not permitted.

Planners' employment by the State and their guise of professionalism, moreover, have not engendered strong ties to the working class. In fact, when client groups (e.g., neighborhoods) are identified as part of an advocacy strategy, those groups are usually not structural in nature, that is, they are not class groups with a consciousness linked to revolutionary politics. Indeed, it is questionable whether client groups harbor the potential for progressive political action with planners, or whether planners must instead organize themselves at the workplace (Adams and Freeman, 1979). More to the point, the imposition of socialism might make planning more of a political reality, but it would also entail the dismantling of the isolated technical expertise of planners by forcing them to confront the political nature of their work. Revolutionary action on the part of planners is thus fraught with uncertainties. For this reason, and because employment and research opportunities are linked predominantly to the State, planners have not developed a model of revolutionary practice. The political dimension of their work remains reformist.

Certainly, the potential for a more political and progressive practice exists (Clavel et al., 1980: 1–9). The knowledge of State actions and capitalists' behaviors can be very useful in developing political strategies. The transition from one historical form of capitalism to another, toward socialism, requires the technical analysis for which planners' work is noted. Planners often deal with goods and services which are not commodified, that is, which are provided in a public fashion outside of the market. Moreover, under socialism, planners would benefit from a larger State sector and from public ownership. Their influence would be more widespread and their access to key aspects of social and environmental change less tenuous. In these various ways, then, planners would expand their influence and be useful in directing and solidifying the transition to socialism. The conservative argument for using planning to dismantle the present welfare State is less favorable to planners. This would clearly result in a loss of employment. Planners, given this choice, are most likely to opt for a perpetuation of advanced capitalism.

# CONCLUSIONS

In the technical, social, and political dimensions of planning practice constraints are imposed by the structural attributes, functions, and position of planners. But in addition there are opportunities for planners to redirect their work. Both exist simultaneously, and flow from the same source. Yet, there is much more to be written. The nature of planners' work — their practice — has not been fully assessed. While we know a good deal about what planners do, and can describe their behavior extensively, these data are less useful in ascertaining the work of planners from a structural perspective. Moreover, future theoretical work needs to be focused on the relationship between occupational characteristics, occupational function, and class position. Of particular importance are those fractions of labor employed by the State, a category which has been neither conceptualized nor researched to an adequate degree.

These observations clearly show that structural analysis, particularly Marxist analysis, is both useful and important. It is useful because it probes beyond the professionalism and ideology which clothe planners' work, and it penetrates to the essential nature of that work within a given historical stage of the political economy. It is important because such analysis uncovers implications for the practice of planning. The ways in which the work of planners is shaped to fit the economic, political, and ideological needs of the State can be contrasted with the potentialities for breaking out of these constraints, criticizing that practice, and modifying planning activities. To the extent that Marxist analysis enables planners to understand, critically evaluate and redirect their practice, it deserves our attention.[26] It provides an alternative to casting planners simply as professionals, and underlines the fact that, despite their pretensions, planners are workers.

# NOTES

1. Planners employed or self-employed as consultants are excluded from this analysis. In part, this is to simplify the presentation. Additionally, such planners constitute a relatively small portion of the occupation. As will be obvious later, planning consultants do have different characteristics, slightly different functions, and possibly a different class location than governmental planners. An extended theoretical interpretation of planners as workers would have to include them.

Robert A. Beauregard

2. The term 'abstract' denotes the *general* relation of labor to capital and differentiates this approach from one that probes the complexity and heterogeneity of the working class (Schaffer and Weinstein, 1979: 148-9). This does not mean that planners are treated as part of an undifferentiated mass of labor. Rather, it means that distinguishing planners from other groupings, or fractions, of labor is done on the basis of material characteristics that change planners' essential relationships to capital, the State, and other fractions of labor.

3. The label 'structural perspective' refers to the identification of relatively enduring and essential patterns of relationships within a given historical stage of a society and their use in developing explanations for relevant phenomena. The Marxist structural perspective, among other attributes, gives primacy to economic relationships within capitalism and views political, cultural, social, and ideological relationships and phenomena as delimited — but not fully determined — by the economic base (Beauregard, forthcoming; Castells and de Ipola, 1976). Obviously, other structural perspectives are possible.

4. A 'fraction of labor' is simply a grouping of labor in terms of nonstructural criteria; e.g., occupation, ethnicity, residential location, income homogeneity. The term is used to circumvent the more difficult issue of the degree of consciousness of this grouping and its potential for linkages to other fractions and for revolutionary action. The 'State' is the multitude of authoritative executive, legislative, judicial, administrative, military, and police functions that comprise the government of a nation. See Miliband (1969).

5. For an important discussion of the possibility of a normative planning (i.e., one that incorporates values) see Klosterman (1978).

6. This, of course, is an idealized description, a description that grows out of a highly rational and normative approach to planning practice. See Beauregard (1980b).

7. In 1960, the Bureau of the Census estimated that there were 865 planners in the United States, and in 1970 the estimate was 9,214. For 1980, the estimate may approach 20,000.

8. These data are from a one-page tabulation obtained from the AICP. The AICP is part of the American Planning Association (APA), the result of a merger in 1978 between the American Institute of Planning (AIP) and the American Society of Planning Officials (ASPO).

9. "Practice" is a term used by professionals to distinguish their work from that engaged in by other occupations with less status. But, the term is also used in Marxist analysis to refer to the larger notion of 'praxis'; i.e., a person's work plus his or her ethical and political life (Bernstein, 1978: 11-83).

10. The worker sells his or her capacity for labor (i.e., labor power) to the capitalist in terms of the time spent at the workplace. The capitalist must manage this labor power to extract the maximum surplus value. See Marx (1967: 167-76).

11. Those planners who are self-employed are more accurately positioned within the petty bourgeoisie; those who are owners of firms within the bourgeoisie. To repeat, the focus herein is not on these planners but on planners employed by the State. An historical analysis would point out how and why the composition of the occupation of planning has changed. In its early years, self-employed planners and owners of firms were relatively more numerous. Different issues were considered by planners and they mediated among different fractions of capital and labor more frequently than they do now.

12. The advanced capitalist State is primarily an instrument of capital. However, it also represents labor in the sense that the long-run interests of capital

are served by the maintenance of labor's general well-being (O'Connor, 1973). The State can thus be considered as relatively autonomous.

13. A good deal of disagreement surrounds the interpretation of these two types of labor and the allocation of occupations into these categories. Gough (1972) would support the statements in the text, whereas Noble (1979) would not. O'Connor (1975) would opine that unproductive labor does not create surplus value but, more importantly, is labor that undermines capitalism. Baran (1957) characterizes unproductive labor as that which produces for nonessential (i.e., luxury) consumption, regardless of whether the commodity is exchanged.

14. Planners employed by consulting firms do produce commodities that are exchanged. Thus they are productive workers.

15. A thorough analysis of these relationships would have to consider the fragmented nature of the State and the competition among 'local' States and 'state' States for investment and middle-class consumers (Goodman, 1979).

16. To the extent that planners allocate money (e.g., rent subsidies), there is a material output to their work. Still, it is intermediate, since the final product has yet to be produced.

17. In effect, planners operate under bureaucratic control; i.e., control embedded in the social relations of the workplace (Edwards, 1979: 130-62).

18. Since State planners do not produce commodities that are exchanged in the market, no surplus is realized. Theoretically, without the existence of surplus value, no capitalist wage exploitation occurs. However, State planners do create use-value and thus, in theory, there may or may not be a discrepency between that use-value and the use-value which can be realized by the planners through the spending of their wages. Obviously, this is too complex an issue to resolve here.

19. An important issue in a more intensive analysis would be the role of planners in perpetuating the bureaucracies within which they are employed, and in expanding their sphere of influence within the State.

20. This class analysis is strictly Marxist. There are other perspectives most of which reject the Marxist formulation (Giddens, 1973: 13-138). Because their basic epistemology and categories differ from those of Marxism, they are likely to position planners within a different class structure, thus making it difficult to compare their argument with the one presented here.

21. The petty bourgeoisie, the small property owners, were sometimes referred to by Marx as the 'middle class' in capitalism (Giddens, 1973: 31). Marx hypothesized that they would eventually be eliminated as monopoly capital extended its control. The petty bourgeoisie would then become part of the proletariat.

22. One would expect that these dimensions of planning practice would vary across capitalist countries and between capitalist and noncapitalist countries. The emphasis here is on the United States. Few national comparisons of planning have been undertaken.

23. It is not being argued that planners are aware of these consequences. That must be determined in practice.

24. Certainly, planners might respond to these possibilities by becoming more radical, or more reactionary. The political direction they take depends on their class position and class consciousness, their awareness of workplace alienation, and the types of political fractions outside the State who provide support for these changes (Fainstein and Fainstein, 1979: 384-8).

25. This, of course, is contrary to much of the ideology of planning: if planning is to be successful, comprehensiveness is required. Planning should include all

substantive aspects of public policy relevant to the planning problem, and spatially it should encompass the full dynamics of these problems.

26. Its primary contribution, however, may be in pointing out to planners the various fractions of labor with which they have common interests, thus providing the encouragement for organizing both within and beyond the workplace.

# REFERENCES

Adams, P. and G. Freeman
1979　"On the political character of social service work." Social Service Review 53: 560–72.

Altshuler, A.
1965　The City Planning Process. Ithaca, N.Y.: Cornell University Press.

Baran, P. A.
1957　"The concept of the economic surplus." Pp. 22–43 in Paul A. Baran, The Political Economy of Growth. New York: Monthly Review Press.

Beauregard, R. A.
1976　"The occupation of planning: a view from the census." Journal of the American Institute of Planning 42: 187–92.

1978a　"Planning in an advanced capitalist state." Pp. 235–54 in R. Burchell and G. Sternlieb, op. cit.

1978b　"Resolving tensions: planning theory about and for local planners." Pp. 84–98 in H. A. Goldstein and S. Rosenberry (eds.), The Structural Crisis of the 1970's and Beyond. Blacksburg, Va.: Virginia Polytechnic Institute.

1980a　"Thinking about practicing planning." Pp. 308–25 in P. Clavel et al., op. cit.

1980b　"Teaching planning theory: dilemmas beyond the rational model." Bulletin of the Association of Collegiate Schools of Planning 28: 1–4.

Forth-　"Structural analysis and urban redevelopment." Comparative Urban
coming　Research.

Benveniste, G.
1977　The Politics of Expertise. San Francisco: Boyd and Fraser.

Bernstein, R. J.
1978　Praxis and Action. Philadelphia: University of Pennsylvania Press.

Braverman, H.
1974　Labor and Monopoly Capital. New York: Monthly Review Press.

Burchell, R. W. and G. Sternlieb
1978　Planning Theory in the 1980's. New Brunswick, N.J.: Center for Urban Policy Research.

Castells, M. and E. de Ipola
1976　"Epistemological practice and the social sciences." Economy and Society 5: 111–44.

Clavel, P. et al.
1980    Urban and Regional Planning in an Age of Austerity. New York: Pergamon.

Corby, L. L. and F. S. So
1974    "Annual ASPO school survey." Planning 40: 20-5.

Edwards, R.
1979    Contested Terrain. New York: Basic Books.

Ehrenreich, B. and J. Ehrenreich
1979    "The professional-managerial class." Pp. 5-45 in P. Walker, op. cit.

Fainstein, N. I. and S. S. Fainstein
1979    "New debates in urban planning: the impact of marxist theory within the United States." International Journal of Urban and Regional Research 3: 381-403.

Forester, J.
1980    "Critical theory and planning practice." Pp. 326-42 in P. Clavel et al., op. cit.

Friedland, R. et al.
1977    "Political conflict, urban structure and the fiscal crisis." International Journal of Urban and Regional Research 1: 447-73.

Friedman, J. et al.
1980    "Working within the state: the role of the progressive planner." Pp. 251-78, in P. Clavel et al., op. cit.

Gans, H.
1968    "City planning in America: a sociological analysis." Pp. 57-77 in H. Gans, People and Plans. New York: Basic Books.

Giddens, A.
1973    The Class Structure of the Advanced Societies. New York: Harper and Row.

Goodman, R.
1979    The Last Entrepreneurs. New York: Simon and Schuster.

Gough, I.
1972    "Marx's theory of productive and unproductive labor." New Left Review 77: 47-72.

Habermas, J.
1975    Legitimation Crisis. Boston: Beacon Press.

Hamlin, R. E.
1978    Guide to Graduate Education in Urban and Regional Planning. Chicago: American Society of Planning Officials.

Harvey, D.
1978    "On planning the ideology of planning." Pp. 213-33 in R. W. Burchell and G. Sternlieb, op. cit.

Klosterman, R. E.
1978    "Foundations for a normative planning." Journal of the American Institute of Planning 44: 37-46.

1980    "A public interest criterion." Journal of the American Planning Association 46: 323-33.

Robert A. Beauregard

Leavitt, J.
  1980a  "The history, status, and concerns of women planners." Signs 5: S226–S230.

  1980b  "Women in planning: there's more to affirmative action than gaining access." Pp. 219–34 in G. R. Wekerle et al. (eds.), New Space for Women. Boulder, Colo.: Westview Press.

  1980c  Planning and Women, Women in Planning. Ph.D. dissertation. New York: Columbia University.

Lefebvre, H.
  1968  The Sociology of Marx. New York: Random House.

Marcuse, P.
  1976  "Professional ethics and beyond." Journal of the American Institute of Planners 42:264–74.

Marx, K.
  1967  Capital. Vol. 1. New York: International Publishers.

Miliband, R.
  1969  The State in Capitalist Society. New York: Basic Books.

Needleman, M. and C. Needleman.
  1974  Guerrillas in the Bureaucracy. New York: John Wiley.

Noble, D.
  1979  "The PMC: a critique." Pp. 121–42 in P. Walker, op. cit.

O'Connor, J.
  1973  The Fiscal Crisis of the State. New York: St. Martin's Press.

  1975  "Productive and unproductive labor." Politics and Society 5: 297–336.

Parston, G.
  1980  Planners, Politics and Health Services. London: Croom Helm.

Peet, R.
  1975  "Inequality and poverty: a marxist-geographic perspective." Annals of the Association of American Geographers 65: 564–71.

Rabinovitz, F. F.
  1969  City Politics and Planning. New York: Atherton Press.

Schaffer, R. and J. Weinstein.
  1979  "Between the lines." Pp. 143–72 in P. Walker, op. cit.

Scott, M.
  1969  American City Planning. Berkeley: University of California Press.

U. S. Bureau of the Census
  1979  Statistical Abstract of the United States: 1979. Washington, D.C.: U. S. Government Printing Office.

Vazquez, A. S.
  1977  The Philosophy of Praxis. Atlantic Highlands, New Jersey: Humanities Press.

Walker, P.
  1979  Between Labor and Capital. Boston: South End Press.

Wright, E. O.
1976    "Class boundaries in advanced capitalist societies." New Left Review
98: 3–41.

1978    "Intellectuals and the working class." The Insurgent Sociologist 8:
5–18.

# 8 Architects in the Home-Building Industry

## ROBERT GUTMAN

Practicing architects often model themselves on physicians and lawyers, the two most prestigious and influential professions in the United States. The comparison is justified in many respects. All three professions have roots in ancient civilization, acknowledge the importance of theory and research as a guide to practice, require advanced education as a condition for admission to their ranks, and utilize a structure of professional associations to promulgate their ideas and values. However, there are also important social differences between architecture, on the one hand, and law and medicine, on the other. Probably the most significant difference for understanding their relative power and status is that architects do not possess the monopoly over the market for design services that physicians enjoy over health care or lawyers over the system for administering justice.[1] Under the registration laws adopted by state governments, the title of "architect" is protected, but other designers are allowed to prepare plans and supervise building construction. The privilege is shared by engineers and by various unlicensed occupations, including so-called building designers and employees of construction and contracting firms who possess limited design training (Fitch, 1965). In the field of home building, the regulations are even more relaxes than for other fields of construction. In most towns, suburbs, and rural areas, prospective homeowners are allowed to develop plans for their houses. The key decision maker in the building

I am grateful to the Design Arts Program of the National Endowment of the Arts for a Design Project Fellowship that enabled me to conduct the research on which this paper is based; to the Director of the Design Arts Program, Michael Pittas, and to the Assistant Director, Charles Zucker, for their guidance and advice during the execution of the project; and to Ms. Mason Andrews and Ms. Daral Dankervoet for their assistance in interviewing and analyzing the data.

process is the local building inspector. If he approves a plan, building can go ahead, whoever the author of that plan may be (Gutman, 1982).

Because their practice is not protected, architects have had to develop strategies other than the acquisition of a monopoly position in order to assure themselves a place in the market for design, especially in the field of housing.[2] Three-quarters of the American housing market consists of the production of single-family dwellings (Meeks, 1980). The plan of a single-family house is a relatively simple design problem. Once a specific house type is selected, it is easy for a home builder to construct it over and over again. Between 40 and 50 percent of the single-family units constructed during the post-World War II period have been produced by builders who construct 100 or more units each year (Sumichrast, 1970); and 10 to 15 percent of the production has been the work of builders who regularly construct more than 1,000 units annually (Grebler, 1973).[3] With this volume under their command, the housing industry is able to dictate the designs they prefer and the fee at which they will renumerate architects. If licensed professionals refuse to design under these conditions, the absence of protective legislation enables the builder to hire other designers, or to purchase stock plans. The power of the home builders is enhanced by the advanced degree of standardization in the U.S. housing industry. Although few single-family dwellings, with the exception of mobile homes, are fully manufactured away from the building site, most units use parts and materials, including roof trusses, doors, partitions, and kitchen, bathroom, and utility components that are available ready-made from factories and local suppliers (Great Britain, 1966; Kelly, 1959).

The strategies architects have developed for dealing with the home-building industry represent, for the most part, some form of accommodation to the requirements imposed by the client. Two of the most important standard strategies are discussed in this paper: participation in the production of stock plans and the organization and operation of what we call "plan shops,"[4] which are really another version of stock plan services but oriented to a local rather than a national market.

One characteristic of these accommodative measures should be kept in mind when considering the profession's recommended standards of practice. It is important to realize that the terms under which architects are expected to contribute their designs often do not conform to the profession's recommended standards of practice. For example, stock plan architects often work under a royalty arrangement instead of receiving a fee based on a percentage of the total cost of the project; many of them are not self-employed practitioners; usually they are not consulted about the siting of the units; nor do they supervise their construction. It is these conditions that lie behind the common assertion in the architectural literature that architects design only 5 to 10 percent of American housing (Fitch, 1965; Frampton, 1971). This assertion reflects the opinion within the architectural community that architects should have control of projects throughout the building process, and unless they do, should not be regarded as designers of the project.[5] This view is understandable in terms of the profession's aspirations to take complete charge of the domain in which architects function, but it contradicts the actual experience of the profession during most periods in the history of building. Before the industrialization of the building process in the nineteenth century, architects had very little to do with the design of housing, except for the great houses of aristocrats and the upper classes. Almost immediately upon the development of the mass housing movement in response to urbanization, architects of housing were forced to share responsibility with other experts, including structural and mechanical engineers, surveyors, urban planners, and landscape architects (Pawley, 1971). We emphasize this divergence between the architect's expectations and practice because it partly accounts for the adversary relationship of the profession to the home-building industry, and it also helps to explain the profession's embarrassment over the way its members must operate in order to maintain a foothold in the housing field.

## STOCK PLAN SERVICES

The development of designs for stock plan services is the principal method through which the architectural profession participates in the American home-building industry today. Stock plan services conduct their business in much the same way as do the pattern services that sell designs to women who sew their own clothing. The home builder or prospective homeowner looks through a catalog of floor plans and renderings of completed houses. He or she selects the most appealing design, sends a check or money order for the plans and related documentation to the service, and in return receives by mail a set of the drawings needed to construct the house. The price for a single set of drawings is currently between $50 and $80, up from $10 twenty years ago (Kelly, 1959). The typical purchaser orders four or five sets, for which the total price is between $80 and $135. One set is for the homeowner, another for the builder, and the remainder are used by subcontractors and the local building inspector.

There are about 100 stock plan services operating in the nation at the present time.[6] They range in size from services that may sell 100 or 200 plans a year to the very largest organizations that mail out 1,000 to 2,000 *each month.* Most of the services have been in business only since the

1950s, starting up in response to the boom in single-family housing construction that followed World War II. The companies still operating are the survivors of a far larger number of services that were organized by individual architects or by small architectural firms, but being unable to find a market, went out of business or merged with other services. Only one of the existing services, Garlinghouse, in Topeka, Kansas, has an extended record of activity. It was set up in 1907 by a Topeka builder who recognized the potential market after the display of his houses in the window of a local bank brought many requests for his plans.

Today's plan services are the equivalent of the pattern books that carpenters and builders in Europe used in erecting houses for the bourgeoisie toward the end of the eighteenth century. Many English examples of these books were imported into this country and became the source for the Georgian style of domestic architecture that was the model for elegant single-family housing in the colonies and during the pre-Federalist period. The availability of cheap land, low-density urban settlement, a large middle-class population, and a climate and natural landscape different from Europe soon generated an indigenous literature on house design, much of which included plans that were widely copied. It was this literature that helped establish the vernacular forms of the Cape Cod and American farmhouse styles (Scully, 1949). By the 1840s, this country had produced its first authentic philosopher of the tradition of the single-family house, the architect Andrew Jackson Downing. Downing's book, *Cottage Residences*, first published in 1842, went through four editions; it contained 321 illustrations that served as models (Johnson, 1969). Copious collections of floor plans were also a common feature of the many books that began to be published around the same time. These became more numerous later in the nineteenth century, dealing with child rearing, family life, and household management (Wright, 1980). There was even a stock plan service functioning during this period, run by the publishers of *Godey's Lady Book*, the leading magazine addressed to a specifically feminine audience. Between 1846 and 1898, Godey's printed 450 model home designs, the drawings for which could be obtained free of charge by writing to the offices of the journal. Wright (1980) reports that these designs were the model for more than 4,000 homes built in the 1850s alone. Around the time when Godey's magazine ceased publication, free house plans began to be made available by lumber companies, building supply dealers, and, in the early decades of this century, by such large mail-order catalog stores as Sears (Kelly, 1959; Wright, 1980). During the 1920s, eighty-five small architectural offices on the Eastern Seaboard and in the Midwest organized a unique, limited dividend corporation under professional sponsorship to publish a plan magazine, *Small Home*, and to sell stock plans (Holden,

211

1925). Except for Garlinghouse, all these sources had more or less disappeared by the time of the great suburban expansion following World War II.

The stock plan services that flourish today are more specialized than were most of the extinct ventures. Contemporary organizations in the business of making and distributing plans do nothing else in the design and home-building fields, although they may have financial links to other kinds of practices and enterprises. One result of such specialization is that their plan documents offer more detailed information about construction than even the plans sold by the architects' group in the 1920s. Plans now available indicate the preferred building techniques, show the location of utilities and plumbing, provide information useful in constructing foundations or slabs, and are easily usable as working drawings. With only minor adjustments, they usually qualify for building permission. For a small additional fee, many of the services also provide cost estimates. The plans sold by *Better Homes and Gardens*, a leading popular magazine addressed to homeowners, even project labor and material costs in the specific region in which the purchaser intends to build.

Architects get involved in stock plan work in three different ways. Some own stock plan services themselves. We estimate that 10 percent of architects who do stock plan work operate as owners, although probably no more than one-half the total number of services are owned by members of the profession. The discrepancy between the two figures reflects the fact that the services owned by architects are smaller on the average, that is, they have fewer plans to sell. On the other hand, two services owned by architects are among the biggest in the nation. John Bloodgood, an architect in Des Moines, Iowa, runs a service that specializes in modern and contemporary house designs. Many of his plans are published in *Professional Builder*, a magazine with offices in Chicago that is addressed to medium-sized and large home-building firms. For many years Bloodgood was building editor of *Better Homes and Gardens*, and also served as chairman of the Committee on Housing of the American Institute of Architects, in 1979. Herman York, an architect with a firm on Long Island who has run a service for more than thirty years, is reputed to be the originator of the split-level home design that was common in the New York region during the 1950s.

The architects who own stock plan services design many of the plans they sell, although they also employ other architects and unlicensed designers for design work, to draw details, to do renderings, and to prepare the working drawings and specifications. Such owners frequently conduct a standard professional practice on a limited scale, often under a consulting arrangement, to large home builders and land developers.

Herman York, for example, was one of the Levitt corporation's principal design consultants in the construction of Levitt communities in Pennsylvania and New Jersey, and Bloodgood is currently an active consultant to developers.

The largest number of licensed architects who engage in stock plan design occupy salaried positions in the services, or work for them part-time, to obtain extra income. Some of the part-timers work on a retainer, others as independent consultants paid only for the specific jobs they do. In addition to architects, these services employ industrial designers, interior designers, "building designers," and "delineators" to produce the plans they sell.[7] The services employing architects under these various arrangements include some of the largest in the business, such as Home Planners, in Farmington, Michigan; Master Plan Service, in Mineola, New York; and National Plan Service, in Elmhurst, Illinois. These services are independent commercial organizations, but similar services are subsidiaries of publishers and distributers of books and magazines dealing with other aspects of home building or home ownership, such as the plan service of Davis Publications, with offices in New York City. Davis publishes magazines and books on consumer electronics and home repair. The major magazines in the home decorating and gardening field, the so-called shelter magazines, also run stock plan services, as do some of the magazines to which builders subscribe to. One shelter magazine that provides plan services has already been mentioned, *Better Homes and Gardens*; among the others are *House and Garden, House Beautiful,* and *Family Circle*. The leading magazine for builders is *Professional Builder*.

These two types of stock plan services—the firms run by architects and the firms that employ them—dominate the stock plan field. But individual architects can also participate in selling stock plans if their designs are chosen for publication by the few home-plan guides and magazines that accept submissions on a competitive basis. Best known among the guides are those issued by Hudson Publications, Inc. in Menlo Park, California. They appear monthly in magazine form or are issued quarterly as pocket-sized paperback books. Hudson receives hundreds of designs annually from architects all over the country, selecting the plans the editors believe are most likely to appeal to a national audience. Some are submitted by well-known designers in the stock plan field, including Bloodgood and William Thompson, an architect in Princeton, New Jersey, known for his authentic reproductions of colonial houses. Many are sent in by young architects, fresh out of graduate school, who hope to achieve visibility quickly and also to earn some additional income. Interested readers order their sets of plans from the company that publishes the guide; the company sends the order to the architect-author, who then forwards the documents directly to the purchaser. Under the arrangement, the fee for the plan is divided between the guide publisher and the architect.[8]

How does the consumer gain access to information about the stock plan services? The plan guides are available at book stores and at the regular outlets of news dealers, such as grocery stores, and newstands in airports, bus stations, and railroad terminals. The news dealers also distribute the plan books and magazines issued by some of the large stock plan services. These guides, plan books, and magazines sell for between one and three dollars, and contain from 50 to 200 designs each, including a rendering of each house and a basic floor layout. The individual family that contemplates building or buying a house can thus easily get a good deal of needed information without great effort.

A second major source of information about the services is the advertisements they place in the monthly issues of shelter magazines. Almost all stock plan services use this channel to communicate with potential customers. The ads generally include a coupon to be filled out and returned directly to the office of the service, along with a check or money order for the plan book. Books distributed by this method are more expensive than those sold through news dealers outlets, but the advantage to the consumer is that these books are targeted to specific requirements and tastes: log houses, vacation homes, houses in contemporary style or traditional style, houses under 1500 square feet, or large houses. The Scholz company, one of the big prefab home builders, offers a similar volume, and charges $20 for it. Unlike the other plan services, Scholz and other prefab companies provide the full set of plans and documents only through their franchised builders.

Still another source of information about stock plans are newspaper articles. Two national press services, the Associated Press and Kings Features, distribute a weekly column on house plans to their subscribers. The columns appear regularly in about 500 newspapers across the nation and produce an excellent response for the services or architects who are lucky enough to have their plans chosen as "the house of the week." Interested individuals can obtain their plan documents by addressing an inquiry to the architect or service shown in the article, sent care of the local newspaper. Again, the plan service or the designer splits the purchase price of the documents with the publisher. Newspapers in this country have been printing similar articles at least since the end of World War I. They were, for example, a major outlet for the plans of the Architects' Small Home Service Bureau, the limited dividend corporation of professionals that was operating during the 1920s. During this very prosperous decade for the American housing market, the Bureau distributed information every week about its designs and services to seventy five newspapers with a total circulation of five million readers (Holden, 1925).

Small local building firms of the sort that produce five houses in an ordinary year and as many as twenty-five in a good market get much information about stock plans from the same sources as do prospective homeowners. However, the larger builders who order stock plans through the mail are more likely to get their plans through services they hear about at meetings of local chapters of the National Association of Home Builders (NAHB) or from publications that report on trends in the housing market, such as *Professional Builder* and *Housing* (formerly *House and Home*). The latter, a McGraw-Hill publication, has the largest circulation of any journal in the housing field.

In many but not in all states and local jurisdictions, the documents purchased from the plan services meet the standards of the building code. In New Jersey, however, a state known for its rigorous controls over urban development, the documents cannot be used for building purposes unless they are stamped by an architect registered in the state. Some of the architects whose plans are distributed by the services are registered in New Jersey, even when they are not residents, in which case their stamp qualifies the document. If the designer is not registered, the builder or developer must have the plans redrawn and stamped by an architect who is.[9] As has already been noted, in New Jersey and other states where a similar rule is in force, persons building their own houses are not subject to this requirement. This is a major reason why stock plans are so attractive to owner-builders. Somewhere between 10 and 20 percent of single-family, detached housing built in this country since World War II has been built by owners themselves, helped by friends, relatives and subcontractors (Kelly, 1959; Turner and Fichter, 1972).

Stock plan services will rarely provide additional services to the client. Even if consumers approach the designer directly with a request to site a house or modify the plan documents, the designer usually turns them down. During the 1950s, it was more common for the services to provide advice about siting and construction, using written instructions, but with the increasing fear among the design professions about liability, this service has been stopped (Coplan, 1978). The only exception we found to this rule was an architect in the Midwest who runs his own plan service and sells plans to developers. If this architect is passing through the region where a developer to whom he has sold plans operates, he will sometimes make a side trip to consult, at no extra fee.

Plans issued by the services vary in design quality and in the completeness of their documentation. Architects themselves admit that the plans turned out by some of the national services are often superior to custom work by small, local firms. Many of the owners and employees of the services are well trained, have worked for prestigious firms during some portion of their career, and are more familiar with the problems of mass housing than the average practitioner whose experience has been confined to work on small projects and building additions. We should note in this context that, according to the most recent estimate, one-half the registered architects in this country are still solo practitioners whose total annual receipts are under $10,000.[10] This situation does not provide much opportunity to become an expert in housing production, a field oriented to consumer needs and preferences that also demands special knowledge of the market and the methods for saving money through a series of small revisions in design and construction. The dearth of local talent in many parts of the country, along with the sophistication of the product available from the services, is a major reason for professional builders' continued reliance on stock plans.

## "PLAN SHOPS"

The sales of the stock plan services have not kept pace with the growth in the volume of housing production over the last decade. The decline in their market is the result of several factors, including the diminution in the proportion of owner-built homes, the increase in mobile home production, and the passage of legislation requiring builders to use plans stamped by local architects, as well as the gradual shift away from single-family housing to town house projects and garden apartments (Meeks, 1980). Of course, some of the stock plan services still return large profits to their owners, but they are mainly the services run by architects whose plans are marketed with the support of the professional building community.

A further condition that has contributed to the declining market for the services is the emergence throughout the country, but especially in large metropolitan regions, of small one- or two-person architectural offices that serve local builders, and sometimes prospective home owners, by selling stock plans across the counter. These offices, or "plan shops," are run by several types of architects. Some have regular jobs in large design firms or in government agencies, who then earn extra income by preparing or selling plans. This kind of moonlighting is not uncommon in the architectural profession, but only recently have so many architects specialized in offering stock plans. Other plan shops are run as adjuncts to practices engaged in the standard range of small building jobs, and also serve the housing industry by providing stock plans. A third type are small practices dealing with a range of demands that arise in the building process, including land speculation and feasibility studies, which also sell stock plans.

In all three types of offices, the pattern is similar: the plan shop contains several file drawers containing stock plans. The individual or developer comes in, goes through the drawers, identifies the desired plans, and comes back a few days later to collect the documents — often without ever having met the architect in charge. It is not unusual for the architect to have obtained the original documents from one of the stock plan services. In this case, the plan shop usually redraws the documents and then adds its stamp so the plans meet the requirements of the local jurisdiction. Architects who practice according to this formula charge double the amount of the stock plan services, usually $300 to $400 for the first set of plans. If further copies are needed to erect the same house on another lot, an additional royalty is charged, at one-quarter to one-third of the fee for the original (*House and Home*, 1967).

Plan shops developed during the 1930s in many of the Northeastern states as a measure intended to keep small firms solvent during the Depression, and they became more common during the suburban expansion after World War II. From the builder's point of view, the plan shops are a decided advantage over the stock plan services. Even when builders have no personal contact with the architect who runs the shop, they know something of his reputation through his work for other builders in the region. Furthermore, using an architect who is known to the local building inspectors and planning and zoning boards, insures that there will be fewer delays in receiving building approval. Perhaps most important of all, if the builder requires additional advice or documentation, the plan shops can provide these services. Indeed, as has been indicated, many of the architects who conduct plan shops do perform other work for builders. They have information about where good buildable land is located and about going price. They know which house types and styles are popular and what small extra features make houses more saleable. Many of these shops also have good contacts with local banks and mortgage companies and can assist the builder in obtaining cheaper terms on construction loans. The expertise of the architects in this field stems from their experience in contracting,[11] and many help to make up the 3 percent of the membership of the National Association of Home Builders who are registered architects.[12] In our interviews, we encountered one architect who established such a good reputation as a home designer through his success as a builder that he eventually was able to give up his building business and concentrate on providing architectural services only.

The attitude of members of the profession regarding the participation of their colleagues in preparing and selling stock plans is a mixture of contempt for the way in which it violates the ideal definition of the architect's role, embarrassment that registered architects are forced to operate in this fashion in order to earn income, and secret admiration for the profits this type of business generates. Stock plan work can be very remunerative for those architects whose plans are purchased in large quantities, or whose services or shops are patronized by developers. Architects who own their own services or who run plan shops collect the full amount of the royalty paid for plan documents. Those whose plans are sold through the plan guides, magazines, and newspapers, as we noted, receive one-half the sum paid by purchasers, but are relieved of the expense of advertising their work. The most successful designers are the owners of services and shops. Stock plan work carries a very low overhead, so that when the home-building industry is flourishing, an owner can easily net as much as one hundred thousand dollars annually from his business.

Architects who argue that stock plan production compromises the norms of professional conduct are not supported in their conviction by the AIA code of ethics, or by the licensing regulations of the state boards that examine and register architects. Nowhere does the code explicitly forbid any of the activities in which architects engage who own services, sell designs through them, or work for them. The sentiments of disdain and embarrassment reflect informal norms that have developed in the profession during the last century. These norms express the ambition of professionals to differentiate themselves from the acknowledged mercenaries in the building industry, such as contractors and "jerry-builders" (Burnett, 1978), and thus justify the claims for monopoly privilege that architects have never fully achieved (Kaye, 1960; Saylor, 1957). Indeed, one could argue that the abashed feeling some architects display toward their colleagues involved with stock plans is magnified by the lack of a clear mandate from the public and clients in support of their desire to be recognized as professionals rather than as businessmen. In our interviews it became apparent that stock plan architects are fully aware of their reputation and have internalized the profession's ambivalent view of their activities. Many respondents were anxious to convince us that their designs did not necessarily reflect personal standards, but were a necessary accommodation to the preferences of developers, builders, and housing consumers. Several sought to divert the conversation from their stock plans to other work they did, citing examples of projects over which they had been able to exert the greater degree of control associated with professional autonomy. Some architects made comments that they felt sure would impress a researcher from an architectural school, for example, the plan shop owner who mentioned that he always referred to Bannister Fletcher's (1931) classic history of architecture and sent us to photograph a development which, by its use of an unusually wide range of historic styles, confirmed his design method. Another stock plan service owner resisted our efforts to get him to talk about his business and, instead, spent most of the interview recounting his days in graduate school when he was a student in Louis Kahn's master class.

## CONCLUSION

It is standard in the architectural profession today to bemoan the crisis in architecture (MacEwen, 1974). Many examples of the conditions that contribute to this judgment are illustrated by the responses of architects to the home-building industry. The profession is divided against itself, with many architects adopting accommodative strategies which their colleagues condemn. Offices form, then dissolve, then their partners and employees regroup and start up practice again, with a frequency that confounds the idea of a professional career. The AIA occupies an ambiguous position within the architectural community. Only 50 percent of registered architects are enrolled. The Institute tries to mandate particular rules for practice, but then, as happened in 1981, it suddenly relinquishes its moral authority by making its code of ethics purely voluntary for members. The control of the market for services is constantly threatened, as architects contest the legal rights of other design professions, and as they try to compensate for the power of an increasingly centralized housing industry. Within the profession, as in the building industry as a whole, large comprehensive offices are supplanting the solo practices and small firms. Architects are losing their autonomy by taking jobs as "captive" professionals in client organizations. Commercialization and entrepreneurial ambitions are running rampant (Gutman, 1980).

These trends cannot be disputed, but the conclusion that a crisis exists is subject to one important qualification. The conditions that constitute a crisis with respect to the norms, aspirations, and self-image of architects may, from the point of view of the needs of clients, represent a solution. It is very hard to demonstrate that home builders and homeowners are ill-served because architects design stock plans or run plan shops. There may be better techniques than these for integrating the theory and skills of architects into the housing process, but it is surely not self-evident that such techniques must necessarily include granting more authority to design professionals or reducing the market power of home builders.

We confront an issue here that extends beyond architecture, namely, the problem of the proper structure for professional services generally. In the case of law and medicine, for example, there is substantial support for the judgment that advances in health care and the administration of justice demand reduced, rather than increased, control by lawyers and physicians. Because architects model their claims for authority on the position of lawyers and doctors, they tend to assume that architecture is retrograde in its lack of comparable privileges. However, the present situation of architecture is perhaps closer to the future status of the professions in general than are these fields that architects admire with such fervor.[13] The requirement imposed on architects, that they share authority and responsibility with clients and users, probably represents the progressive model that most disciplines and professions will be forced to imitate in coming decades.

# NOTES

1. The perspective developed in this paper for understanding the problems of the profession of architecture has benefited from the interpretation of the history of professionalism set forth in the work of Abbott (1981), Berlant (1975), Johnson (1972) and Larson (1977).

2. Unless another source is mentioned, the discussion of the manner in which the profession of architecture participates in the home-building industry is based on an analysis of stock plan books and interviews conducted in person and by telephone, in 1979 and 1980. The respondents included owners and employees of stock plan services, architects who submit designs to services, plan shop owners and employees, home builders and developers, representatives of the American Institute of Architects and the National Association of Home Builders, officers of local chapters, editors of housing magazines, and officials in federal, state and local government agencies that oversee building and planning.

3. The concentration of single-family housing production in the hands of firms that produce 100 or more units annually partly reflects the enormous increase in the number of trailers or mobile homes as a percentage of total single-family units that are started each year. By the end of the 1970s these manufactured units represented as much as 25 percent of all single-family units produced (Meeks, 1980: 235).

4. The additional strategies that the profession is now pursuing to maintain a foothold in the housing industry are discussed in a report on this subject prepared for the National Endowment for the Arts (Gutman, 1980).

5. The advertisements for most single-family housing developments never mention the name of the designer. Purchasers tend to base their decision on the reputation of the builders. Expensive housing is sometimes advertised as "architect-designed," but even in these cases specific architects are seldom identified as authors of the plans.

6. Stock plans are also used in the construction of gasoline stations and chain stores, but these are usually distributed by the national organizations that own these facilities (Fitch, 1965: 235).

7. "Building designer" is a quasi-professional label adopted by self-taught designers and architects with professional training but who are not registered. In California, building designers have tried without success to achieve recognition

from the registration boards. They do, however, have their own association, the American Institute of Building Design, with offices in Sacramento. It has seventeen chapters in the states of the Far West, and 500 members. This, compared with 60,000 registered architects in the country as a whole, of whom about 30,000 are members of the American Institute of Architects. "Delineators" are people who sketch plans but are not qualified to make the drawings required for building permission. When names are listed with the house designs included in the plan books of the large commercial services, the author is sometimes identified as delineator.

8. A similar division of proceeds takes place whenever a magazine or newspaper is the source from which a prospective purchaser learns about a stock plan service.

9. The work of preparing house plans for approval by the building inspector is a regular source of income for solo practitioners and for architects employed in larger offices and in government agencies. These architects are among the 50 percent of licensed professionals whose annual billings totaled less than $10,000 in the early 1970s (Gutman, 1977).

10. No architect could possibly survive financially on such a low volume of annual receipts, which suggests that many of the one-person firms are run by men and women whose principal income comes from other sources, such as teaching or salaried employment in large firms and government agencies. This version of "moonlighting" is a well-established practice in the history of the profession (Gutman, 1977).

11. The American Institute of Architects has traditionally frowned upon its members having any financial stake in constructon companies, but it altered its code of ethics in 1978 to remove the official prohibition. Many smaller firms had been ignoring the prohibition for decades, which explains why many licensed professionals were able to acquire extensive experience in homebuilding (American Institute of Architects, 1981).

12. The National Association of Home Builders (NAHB) is the trade association of the home-building industry. Its membership of 120,000 includes almost all the contractors and developers in the U.S. who produce more than a handful of houses annually. Architects are eligible for associate membership in the organization, and in 1980 they constituted 2.7 percent (3,200 architects) of total NAHB membership.

13. The admiration of architects for the legal profession has been tempered somewhat by the increase in malpractice suits against architects. The greater frequency of these suits is often attributed to the rise in litigiousness among consumers, a trend for which architects believe lawyers are partly responsible. Along with other professions suffering under the rapid increase in premiums for professional liability insurance, the AIA is advocating that architects support the Liability Insurance Supplement Act, sponsored by Sen. Charles Percy (MEMO, 1981).

# REFERENCES

Abbott, A.
    1981    "Status and status strain in the professions." American Journal of Sociology 86: 819–35.

American Institute of Architects
1981    Design-Build Contracting Monitoring Task Force Report, May 1981. Washington, D.C.: American Institute of Architects.

Berlant, J.
1975    Professions and Monopoly. Berkeley: University of California Press.

Burnett, J. C.
1978    A Social History of Housing 1815–1970. Newton Abbott, England: David and Charles.

Coplan, N.
1978    "Negligence, not human error decides liability." Progressive Architecture 59: 136.

Fitch, J. M.
1965    "The profession of architecture." Pp. 231–41 in Kenneth Lynn (ed.), The Professions in America. Boston: Beacon Press.

Fletcher, B.
1931    A History of Architecture on the Comparative Method. New York: Scribner's.

Frampton, K.
1971    "Polemical notes on architectural education." Mimeo. New York: Institute of Architecture and Urban Studies.

Great Britain, Ministry of Housing and Local Government.
1966    House building in the USA. London: H.M. Stationery Office.

Grebler, L.
1973    Large Scale Housing and Real Estate Firms. New York: Praeger.

Gutman, R.
1977    "Architecture: the entrepreneurial profession." Progressive Architecture 58: 55–58.

1980    Who Designs American Housing. Report to the National Endowment for the Arts, October 1980. Available from the author, School of Architecture, Princeton University, Princeton, N.J. 08544.

1982    "Architecture as a service industry." Casabella, 475/476: 28–32; 108–109.

Holden, A.
1925    "Outside buisness factors as competitors of the architect." Journal of the American Institute of Architects 8: 308–310.

House and Home
1967    "When does a merchant builder have to have an architect?" 32: 58–65.

Johnson, J. S.
1969    "Introduction." Pp. v–xv in A. J. Downing, The Architecture of Country Houses. New York: Dover.

Johnson, T. J.
1972    Professions and Power. London: Macmillan.

Kaye, B.
1960    The Development of the Architectural Profession in Britain. London: G. Allen and Unwin.

222

Kelly, B.
1959    Design and the Production of Houses. New York: McGraw-Hill.

Larson, M. S.
1977    The Rise of Professionalism. Berkeley: University of California Press.

MacEwen, M.
1974    Crisis in Architecture. London: RIBA Publications.

Meeks, C.
1980    Housing. Englewood Cliffs: Prentice-Hall.

Memo
1981    "Professional Liability Bills Gain Support in Congress." May 28, 1981: 7.

Pawley, M.
1971    Architecture versus Housing. New York: Praeger.

Saylor, H.
1957    "The AIA's first hundred years." Journal of the American Institute of Architects 28, pt. 2: 1–184.

Scully, V.
1949    "The Cape Cod cottage: A design analysis." Architectural Forum 90: 88–94; 90: 100–6.

Sumichrast, M.
1970    Profile of the Builder and His Industry. Washington, D.C.: National Association of Home Builders.

Turner, J. F. C. and R. Fichter
1972    Freedom to Build. New York: Macmillan.

Wright, G.
1980    Moralism and the Model Home. Chicago: University of Chicago Press.

# 9 Growth, Decline, and Death: A Panel Study of Architectural Firms

JUDITH R. BLAU and KATHARYN L. LIEBEN

The main interest in studies of organizational change and development has been growth, and very few studies focus on the decline and failure of organizations. Indeed, many authors (Hannan and Freeman, 1977a; Aldrich, 1979: 118; Pennings, 1980; Whetten, 180; Miles, 1980) have recently called attention to the need for research on organizational death. As Miles in particular emphasizes, this is no longer an era of expansion and abundance, but rather one of recession and scarcity, and the effects of these conditions on organizational outcomes are not well understood. This research is based on a longitudinal study of architectural firms over a five-year period marked by a severe economic recession. The simple dichotomy of death versus survival is expanded by distinguishing the degree to which survival is meager or is accompanied by genuine expansion along each of several dimensions of effectiveness.

## BACKGROUND

The general economic decline in New York City, beginning in about 1974 and aggravated by the fiscal crisis in 1976,[1] created for most organizations located in Manhattan an environment of uncertainty and the threat of decline or ruin. Some organizations were less dependent on

An earlier version of this paper was presented at the 1981 American Sociological Association meetings. The research was supported by grants from the Research Foundation of the State University of New York and The Research Foundation of the City University of New York. We acknowledge the research assistance of Jeffrey Kallan. The authors are particularly grateful to M. Craig Brown, who provided helpful advice in the initial stage of the study, and also wish to thank Richard H. Hall, Francis C. Lees, and Peter M. Blau for their comments on an initial draft.

224

the city and the resources it had (and has) to offer, and for many of them relocation was a reasonable option. But many organizations were too closely tied to this particular metropolitan environment, and staying in New York City after 1974 was the Hobson's choice, though it meant a high risk of failure.

Among organizations especially dependent on Manhattan's resources are architectural firms. Those who were initially attracted to the city were among the most prestigious design firms in the country. Manhattan is important for architects partly for symbolic reasons: it is the undisputed center for creative and artistic enterprise in the nation, if not the world. But also important are the special resources upon which architectural firms depend: the many schools of design and architecture that provide recruits; specialized consulting firms located in the city; a discriminating (and wealthy) clientele. Architecture critic Paul Goldberger (1975: 43) wrote, in one of the leanest years, "Somehow, in spite of the fact that the building business is in a genuine depression in New York, none of the New York-based architecture firms seem to have given a thought to moving away. Many of them are doing their buildings elsewhere, of course . . . but this remains the city in which most architects want to be based. . . ." Although no government or private agency maintains records on the failure rate of professional offices, surveys by architectural associations indicate many firm failures as well as high rates of unemployment among the city's architects, beginning in 1973 and continuing through 1977.[2]

## OBJECTIVES

The initial study, based on a random sample of 152 Manhattan firms, was carried out in 1974, just prior to the onset of the economic recession, and the second panel study was carried out in 1979. Our purpose is to compare firms that did not survive with those that barely survived and those that actually flourished during this five-year period.

The distinction between failure and survival is not altogether clear, as Kaufman (1976: 27) and Davis (1961: 3) point out. We define organizational failure for these firms as the inability to survive in Manhattan's declining economic environment. There is considerable evidence, from discussions with architects and with officers of the New York City Chapter of the American Institute of Architects, that firms that no longer existed in Manhattan in 1979 had simply closed, although a few might have moved.[3] But it is exceedingly difficult to relocate an entire professional staff, attract new clients, and become integrated in the networks of contractors, engineers, interior designers, and other specialists in another metropolitan area. In short, all available evidence suggests that most firms no longer in existence by 1979 had disbanded, their professional members having scattered to find jobs in other firms, and even the few exceptions that might have survived outside New York City can be considered failures in the struggle for survival in the most desirable location for an architectural firm.

While failure in all cases is thus lack of survival in Manhattan, each of the trichotomous outcome variables incorporates as the two remaining categories a different parameter of organizational effectiveness. These parameters are: productivity, profits, design quality, and size. To illustrate, the outcome variable of size change has the following three categories: demise; a decline or no increase in firm size from 1974 to 1979; and an increase in firm size over the five-year period. Thus, each variable is an exhaustive and mutually exclusive classification of qualitative states of change. The technique employed is discriminant function analysis, which permits us to determine what conditions measured at a prior time best discriminate among the three categories of each outcome variable. It should be pointed out that components of some outcome variables — size change, for example — are also predictors for other effectiveness measures; thus, its 1974 size is expected to influence a firm's profitability in 1979. Accordingly, separate analyses of the four change variables permit testing all plausible impacts of earlier conditions on later outcomes without being bound to an unrealistic set of causal assumptions.

## EXPLANATIONS OF CHANGE AND EFFECTIVENESS

As Hodgkinson (1978: 180–82) wrote, "The first law of organization is survival. The organization must maintain itself. . . . The second [law] is growth. Organizations seek to expand; their dynamic finds form in extension. Merely to survive and maintain the status quo is not enough." A variety of approaches can be used in explaining survival, change, and expansion: models of entrepreneurship, bankruptcy, the organization as open system, the organization as structure, and population ecology.

### *Entrepreneurship*

The emphasis on the role of the entrepreneur in affecting the fate of the organization is particularly important in two research traditions: the economics of the small firm, and the social psychology of leadership.

In the economic literature the stress is on the entrepreneurial role that encompasses a variety of functions different from those of the manager. The entrepreneur is the risk-taker, interested in short-term rather than long-term profit objectives, and in innovation rather than efficiency (Mayer and Goldstein, 1961; McGuire, 1964; Deeks, 1976). From a somewhat different perspective, social psychologists have focused on the personal characteristics of entrepreneurs (Pickle, 1964) and styles of leadership (Braybrooke, 1963/64). In this tradition considerable attention is given to the decision-making process and the locus of authority.

Several specific predictions from both research traditions can be tested with the data on architectural firms, which, while not all headed by a sole entrepreneur, are generally not large corporations but relatively small firms that place a high premium on innovation. Many report that such small firms are the most vulnerable, particularly when there is much environmental turbulence (Hazel and Reed, 1973; Deeks, 1976). It has been suggested (Schon, 1971; Peterson and Berger, 1971) that under such conditions strong centralized leadership is required. Other studies conclude just the opposite, namely, that during periods of uncertainty, a flexible democratic leadership (Miller, 1965) and decentralized authority (Thompson, 1967; Lawrence and Lorsch, 1967) are most effective. It is interesting to note that the 1974 study found the more decentralized architectural firms to be more effective than others on a variety of measures.[4] The question, then, is, Does the degree of decentralization in 1974 affect later outcomes?

One of the most important debates in the entrepreneurship literature concerns the ability of small firms to survive, given the tendency toward increasing scale, mergers, and incorporation (see Starbuck, 1965; Pfeffer, 1972; Deeks, 1976). There is a strong tradition in professional offices to resist much growth, for small size is thought to benefit collegiality, and incorporation is suspected of undermining professional autonomy. Nevertheless, there are probably economies of scale that give large firms competitive advantages, and incorporation protects personal assets under adverse economic conditions, in architecture as in other industries.

Implications of entrepreneurship theory can be tested by determining the effects of type of ownership (sole proprietor or other more complex forms), 1974 size, and the degree of centralization on the likelihood of failure or survival. Analysis of the influences of such conditions as type of ownership and innovation on changes in size over time are also relevant for testing entrepreneurship theory.

### Bankruptcy

Modern economics has developed empirical models that successfully distinguish between firms that go bankrupt and those that do not, based on extremely detailed financial data (for reviews see Foster, 1978; Scott, 1979). Since profit maximization is not the prime objective of professional organizations, and because their finances are less complex than those of the corporations studied by economists, overall indicators of financial health are sufficient in this analysis.

Two outcome measures reflect changes in economic health. Profit change is indicated by the differences among three groups—firms that failed, survivors for which profits did not increase, and those that experienced increased profitability. Productivity change divides firms into groups consisting of nonsurvivors, those declining or not increasing with respect to annual completed projects, and those that completed more projects in the latter, compared with the earlier, period. A widely accepted assumption is that large organizations can produce at lesser costs per unit than small ones can (see Starbuck, 1965: 457-60), and we shall test with these data whether or not economies of scale are attained in professional offices. Productivity and profits are also used as independent variables in the analysis of size change and quality change in order to determine the effects of earlier economic health on the subsequent fate of architectural firms.

## Open Systems Model

Many aspects of the environment are important in the open systems model (Pennings and Goodman, 1977), but this model's particular emphasis is on the nature and number of other organizations with which the focal organization maintains exchanges (Osborn and Hunt, 1974; Hirsch, 1975; Evan, 1971; Katz and Kahn, 1966). An important assumption is that the way to reduce uncertainty is to establish diverse and beneficial linkages with other organizations and that the motivation for establishing them is highest in periods of scarce or declining resources (Pfeffer and Nowak, 1976; Aiken and Hage, 1968). Data from the 1974 survey are available for the following types of linkages: joint ventures, use of engineering consultants, and whether or not the firm is an affiliate.

It can be hypothesized on the basis of earlier work (Aiken and Hage, 1968; Paulson, 1974) that engaging in joint ventures contributes to survival and effectiveness. Similar results are expected for the use of consultants because this broadens expertise with no expansion of staff or overhead costs. Affiliation with another firm, on the other hand, may hamper the autonomy and flexibility of the office, as Osborn and Hunt (1974) and Kaufman (1976) indicate, and thereby probably has negative consequences for survival and effectiveness.

In one sense, the economic environment for these firms was constant in 1974 — they were all located in Manhattan — but in another sense their environments differed for they were more or less tied to the city's economy depending on the extent to which their buildings were constructed there or elsewhere. In 1973, about 50 percent of the average firm's projects were commissioned for a location in the metropolitan area. It is not unreasonable to assume that the more a firm depended on the local economy in the earlier period, the less its chances of survival over the next five years. This dependence is operationalized by the percentage of all 1973 projects that were built within the New York City metropolitan area.

## Structural Model

The approach of the structural model views the organization as a complex formal structure with a variety of mechanisms of coordination and integration. The emphasis, which can be traced to Weber, is that organizational rationality governs processes and outcomes (Simon, 1957; Thompson, 1967; P. M. Blau and Schoenherr, 1971). While a main feature of the structuralist tradition has been an interest in internal differentiation, in small professional offices, structure in the sense of subdivisions (levels, divisions, branches) is less important than size itself, task structure, mechanisms of control and routinization, and staff composition.

From the perspective of economic models of both entrepreneurship and bankruptcy, size is important for mostly financial reasons, but from the structuralist perspective, size has other consequences as well. In particular, size has implications for the likelihood of innovation, which we view as manifest in design work of high originality and quality. A variety of investigators (Mahoney et al., 1972; Zaltman et al., 1973: 137; Wilson, 1966) report that large organizations are more flexible and innovative than small ones. In professional organizations, specifically, the greater differentiation made possible by large size is expected to improve quality by offering greater opportunities for social interaction with diverse individuals (Ben-David, 1972; J. Blau, 1976).

The task structure of a firm has been conceptualized as operational goals (Perrow, 1961), the organization's purpose (Barnard, 1938), or the program of activity (Caplow, 1964). It is assumed by Wilson (1966) and Hage and Aiken (1970: 74-77) that a complex goal structure protects the organization in an uncertain environment. Two aspects of the task structure of architectural firms are used in this analysis: the range of services provided by the firm and the degree to which the firm designs diverse projects or specializes in only a few. Closely related to the task structure is the type of technology employed in the organization (Perrow, 1972). For architectural firms the relevant office technology is the computer, which is typically used for design and engineering purposes as well as for administration.

Central to the structuralist approach is the assumption that predictability and rationality are achieved through formal mechanisms of control and of routinization (P. M. Blau, 1968). Formal mechanisms of control, most notably regulations and rules, may be most elaborate in large bureaucratic or industrial organizations, though they are not unimportant in small, professional organizations, because they help achieve coordination. Whatever their function, the proliferation of rules can bring about rigidity, and thus may reduce survival chances or the ability to adapt to environmental changes. A distinction is made between operating rules, which dictate the work process and are designed to routinize design and production phases, and personnel rules, which specify such conditions as promotion qualifications and often improve, rather than hinder, the autonomy of staff. Routinization in professional organizations is also achieved through the delegation of work to semiprofessionals, and the extent of such routinization is measured by the relative size of the technical component, which includes draftspeople, specification writers, and cost estimators.

An important component in the division of labor in a professional office are those staff members who carry out basic tasks. In this case these are the registered architects. A relatively large architectural staff indicates an orientation to design rather than to routine production and thereby reflects a high degree of professionalism. While some (Price, 1968; Hall, 1968) report that such an orientation in an organization promotes effectiveness and innovation, it cannot be ruled out that under adverse economic conditions firms with a large component of highly paid architects would be less able to effect substantial cuts and thus more adversely affected than their less professional counterparts.

## Population Ecology Model

Although organizational age has long been viewed as important in the literature on organizational effectiveness (see Mayer and Goldstein, 1961; Stinchcombe, 1965), population ecology models extend general considerations of organizational age to more complex ones, such as the specific benefits of age, cohort effects, and changes over time. For example, Meyer (1979: 194) reports that one advantage of the old organization is that it can "block or redirect the environment most effectively." In examining the effects of age on survival chances and effectiveness for architectural firms we will want not only to determine whether older organizations are more effective in a turbulent environment than younger ones but also to test Campbell's (1969) notion that the oldest organizations change least. A prior history of internal stability or persistence is assumed, in the population ecology model, to protect the organization during periods of external change (Aldrich, 197: 195-99). A measure of the degree of internal stability is the relative amount of staff fluctuation during 1973.

According to the ecological model, organizations that can exploit the distinctive resources available in an ecological niche are most likely to be successful (Hannan and Freeman, 1977b; Aldrich, 1979: 28). Such successful exploitation of special environmental opportunities is defined here, first, by the firm's ability to attract valued clients and, second, by its ability to succeed as a design firm as evident in design awards and its reputation. In a market economy, valued clients are those having stable economic resources and prospects of future commissions. For these reasons, architects tend to prefer corporate clients; this was particularly the case after 1976 when there was a virtual halt in public construction in New York City. Corporate clients, unlike private individuals or small businesses, have long-term building plans, routines for negotiating contracts, and in many instances, an interest in translating corporate identity into a visual image to enhance public relations.

The successful attainment of an objective implied by organizational values is increasingly recognized as fundamental in the understanding of organizational structure and activities (see Ranson et al., 1980; J. Blau, 1980). For architectural firms, original design of high quality represents that objective, and recognition of it secures for the office a unique environmental niche. The question is, however, What role does quality play in a declining economy? Innovation and risk taking may be rewarded by more commissions in a stable economy, but not during a severe recession. The implications of the population ecology model suggest that the following conditions affect the chances of success and failure: age of the firm, prior internal flux, client type, and the quality of the firm's work.

# METHODS

Organizational effectiveness is a multidimensional concept (Yuchtman and Seashore, 1967), and the attempt is made here to encompass the variety of dimensions that are germane to architectural firms. There are four dimensions of effectiveness and failure; merely to survive is the minimal indicator of success. Productivity change divides firms into those that have failed, those that have had neither increase nor decline in the number of completed projects between 1973 and 1978, and those that completed more projects in 1978 than they did in 1973. Profit change is indicated by failure, no increase or a decline in the proportion of projects for which construction costs were at least one million dollars in the middle 1970s (1974 through 1978) compared with the early 1970s (1969 through 1973), and an increase in the proportion of such projects in the latter over the earlier period.[5] Quality change is measured by failure by 1979, not winning any awards in the period of 1974 through 1978, and winning at least one award in the same period. Size change is indicated by demise by 1979, no growth or decline from 1974 to 1979, and growth over the five-year period.

Although using the same lowest category for all four dependent variables is redundant, these dimensions, as we shall see, reveal quite different patterns of influence, notwithstanding their having one category in common. Correlations among the components of the outcome measures indicate that the dimensions of effectiveness are not highly correlated for either time period, but that the magnitudes of association are roughly the same for 1974 and 1979 (table 9.1, top left and bottom right). Comparing 1974 and 1979 measures, the autocorrelations are substantial, except for that of productivity (bottom left, diagonal), though the 1974 measures of effectiveness are not highly associated with survival chances (bottom row).

All independent variables have been referred to earlier; definitions, means, and number of missing cases are reported in the appendix. Because the literature deals for the most part with effectiveness rather than survival and failure, preliminary analysis was carried out using techniques of analysis of variance and cross-tabulation. This led to a set of independent variables that were included as candidates in the analysis of group differences for each dimension in the discriminant function analyses; in each instance some of the candidates that the preliminary analysis indicated were important contributed little to the linear function and were excluded, as indicated in the tables.

### Data Collection

Data were collected in the spring of 1974 from a random sample of one-third of the 540 architectural firms listed in the Manhattan telephone directory. About four-fifths of the principals contacted agreed to provide information, and the 1974 data set is based on a total of 152 firms. (See J. Blau and McKinley, 1979, for details of the study.) Five years later, in the spring of 1979, an attempt was made to contact all 152 firms, the main objective being to determine the impact of the economy on the firms' organization and activities. A careful search of address changes,

TABLE 9.1
*Correlations Among Components of Effectiveness Dimensions*

| 1974 Study Variables | 1974 STUDY VARIABLES | | | | 1979 STUDY VARIABLES | | | |
|---|---|---|---|---|---|---|---|---|
| | Productivity | Profits | Award | Size | Productivity | Profits | Award | Size |
| Productivity[a] | — | | | | | | | |
| Profits[b] | – .01 | — | | | | | | |
| Award[c] | .12 | .30 | — | | | | | |
| Size[d] | .24 | .37 | .32 | — | | | | |
| **1979 Study Variables** | | | | | | | | |
| Productivity[e] | .21 | – .00 | – .04 | – .02 | — | | | |
| Profits[f] | .11 | .58 | .42 | .51 | .11 | — | | |
| Award[g] | – .05 | .30 | .55 | .22 | .05 | .48 | — | |
| Size[h] | .04 | .35 | .24 | .80 | .05 | .52 | .18 | — |
| Survive (dummy) | .10 | .02 | .19 | .18 | | | | |

[a]Number of projects completed in 1973; N = 151.
[b]Percentage of 1969-73 projects having at least one million dollars in construct costs; N = 152.
[c]Won award(s) during 1969-73 (dummy); N = 152.
[d]Size (raw); full-time equivalents as of 4/1/74; N = 152.
[e]Number of projects completed in 1978; N = 92.
[f]Percentage of 1974-78 projects having at least one million dollars in construction costs; N = 71.
[g]Won award(s) during 1974-78 (dummy); N = 81.
[h]Size (raw): full-time equivalents as of 4/1/79; N = 92.

by telephone calls and letters, indicated that 60 had closed their offices and 92 still existed in Manhattan. From the 92 survivors, information was collected, primarily by telephone interviews and, in a few cases, by a mail questionnaire. The response rate was 100 percent although some information is missing on nearly all variables.

## Technique of Analysis

Discriminant analysis is the procedure employed. It provides a means for deriving one or more functions, each of which maximally diffentiates among several groups—in this study, the three categories of each outcome variable. A function is a linear combination of a set of differentially weighted independent variables. That is, discriminant analysis weights and combines variables so that the categories of the groups are as statistically distinct as possible. (For detailed discussions see Cooley and Lohnes, 1971: 243-57; Morrison, 1974; Tatsouka, 1970.)

Each organization's unit score on a derived function is defined as a weighted linear combination in the form:

$$D_i = d_{i1}Z_1 + \ldots d_{ip}Z_p,$$

where $D_i$ is the score on the function $i$, the $d_i$'s are the weighted coefficients, and the $Z_p$'s are the standardized values of the $p$ discriminating (independent) variables (Nie et al., 1975: 435)[6] The number of discriminating variables ($Z_p$) used in the derivation of a function in these analyses is determined by a stepwise procedure that is based on the minimization of Wilks' lambda, which can be described in terms of the partial F-ratio that tests for the statistical separation of groups. The criterion employed for the inclusion of a variable is a partial F-ratio of at least 1.0.

The degree to which the function discriminates among the original categories of the dependent variable is assessed by the configuration of the group centroids. These represent group means that are transformed in terms of the linear function and can be conceptualized as the peaks of dispersion with respect to that function. The degree of separation among centroids, or the raw differences among them, is an indication of the function's power of discrimination among the original categories. One test of significance for the function is the canonical correlation, which is a measure of association between the function and the categories of the dependent variables. It is a PRE measure and is similar, for the purpose of interpretation, to the analysis of variance statistic eta. The second test of significance for a function is the chi-square.

One advantage of discriminant analysis over conventional statistical techniques is that there need be no assumption of interval level measures. Moreover, it can reveal patterns among the independent variables that are other than linear, which is problematic in regression type analyses (Morrison, 1974). One particular use of discriminant analysis is as a classification procedure to assign existing or new cases to groups. Thus, the value "percent correctly classified" is employed for predictive purposes, but it is also useful in that it reflects the degree of separation among centroids and within-category homogeneity in the original data.

In the tables presented here, variable coefficients and centroid values are reported. The coefficients are analagous to these in factor analysis with respect to the range of values they take (from $-1.00$ to $+1.00$) and to the typical situation in which values on a function are both negative and positive. Centroid values also range from $-1.00$ to $+1.00$. Thus, the association between a given independent variable and a category of the outcome measure is reflected in the product of the coefficient of that variable and the centroid value of the category.

# FINDINGS

## *Productivity Change*

It is large size and computer use that best discriminate among the categories of productivity change, though the coefficients for age and personnel rules are also substantial (table 9.2, top panel).[7] What is most interesting is that the two extreme groups—firms that fail and firms that have become productive in the later period—have more similar prior characteristics than the middle category—firms that merely survived without experiencing any increase in productivity (table 2, bottom panel). That is, nonsurvivors as well as the most successful firms were relatively small in 1974, tended not to use consultants, were unlikely to have a computer, and are on the average older than firms in the middle category.

Our interpretation of these findings rests on the market strategies probably employed during this period. A content analysis of the *Journal of the American Institute of Architects* reveals a marked increase in articles about renovation and utilization of energy-saving technology. Although nothing is known about energy-saving technology in the 1974 study, only a very small number report doing any restoration projects in 1973 (the average number is 0.05), whereas in the question asked in 1979 concern-

TABLE 9.2
*Standardized Discriminant Function Coefficients for Productivity Change;
Group Centroids and Number of Cases*

A. STANDARDIZED DISCRIMINANT FUNCTION COEFFICIENTS*

| Variables** | |
|---|---|
| Size (log) | − .57 |
| Use of consultants | − .41 |
| Personnel rules | − .28 |
| Computer | − .45 |
| Age | .41 |

B. GROUP CENTROIDS AND NUMBER OF CASES

| *Productivity Change Groups* | *Centroid* | *N* |
|---|---|---|
| Nonsurvivors | .28 | 60 |
| Constant or declined | − .39 | 55 |
| Increased | .13 | 37 |

*Canonical correlation = .29; $X^2$ = 19.0 ($p <.04$).
**Variables excluded: Sole Ownership, Project Specialization, Percent Technicians, Average Rating.

ing changes, 70 percent mentioned that they had commissions for renovations, and 53 percent said that they had incorporated energy-saving technology into their design practice. Since the results indicate that small size is a critical variable, we suspect that some small firms were highly vulnerable, but others were able to employ flexible strategies with respect to the market, namely, to adopt such innovations as solar heating or to respond to opportunities for renovation work. Whether or not it is the superior ability of the small firm to capture new markets during an economic recession, it is clear that, with respect to the productivity dimension of effectiveness, small size can be either a great liability or a great asset, whereas large size is merely a buffer against failure.

Moreover, firms in the two extreme categories are similar in other ways that help to bolster this interpretation. Specifically, in contrast with more survivors, they are unlikely to use computer technology, rely little on outside consultants, and are less likely to have formal personnel rules. It is suggested that these factors are a manifestation of organizational autonomy that can either benefit flexibility, or create vulnerability. For example, using the organization's own personnel rather than outside consultants for particular problems frees the firm to build greater flexibility into scheduling and design, while simultaneously decreasing overhead costs. But such practices are apparently risky, probably because they ignore the superior expertise of specialized consulting firms. Age, too, can be an asset, but it appears that an uncertain economy can hasten the demise of older firms if they are vulnerable in other respects.

### Profit Change

It is a general principle for industrial and commercial establishments that productivity and profits are highly correlated, but this does not hold for architectural firms (nor, perhaps, for other small professional offices), as reflected in the lack of association between the indicators of productivity and profits: the correlations for the 1974 and 1979 measures are $-.01$ and $.11$, respectively (table 9.1). Consistent with the conclusion that these are independent forms of effectiveness, the variables that best discriminate among firms with different profit trends (table 9.3, top panel) are quite different from those that discriminate among firms with different productivity trends. Three variables—ownership, complexity, relative size of the architectural staff, and private clients—are significant in the linear function, and a series of variables that were included in the earlier exploratory analyses were excluded from the equation by the criterion measure, including, notably, size and productivity.[8]

The group centroids reveal transitivity (table 9.3, bottom panel), with

TABLE 9.3

*Standardized Discriminant Function Coefficients for
Profit Change; Group Centroids and Numbers of Cases*

A. STANDARDIZED DISCRIMINANT FUNCTION COEFFICIENTS*

*Variables***
Complex ownership     −.60
Percent architects     .51
Private clients     .42

B. GROUP CENTROIDS AND NUMBER OF CASES

| Profit Change Groups | Centroid | N |
| --- | --- | --- |
| Nonsurvivors | .30 | 60 |
| Constant or declined | −.01 | 39 |
| Increased | −.55 | 32 |

*Canonical correlation = .32; $X^2$ = 15.0 ($p < .02$).

**Variables excluded: Size (log), Centralization, Productivity, Operating Rules, Outstanding Ratings.

failing firms at one extreme and increasingly profitable ones at the other. The most profitable firms in 1979 had relatively few private clients (who, by and large, commission residences), employed a fairly small number of architects relative to their total size, and tended to have a complex ownership status. At the other extreme, those most likely to fail were firms that relied on commissions from private clients, had a central interest in original and creative work, as indicated by the large component of architects, and were also of the simplest ownership type.

Contrasting the two sets of results presented, it is clear that what means vulnerability on one dimension has little in common with vulnerability on the other dimension. In the case of productivity, it is notably small size that paradoxically increases the chances of failure, while at the same time increasing the chances of success, depending, we assume, on whether a firm is able to innovate and quickly move to capture new markets. The results for the dimension of profitability are more clear-cut; three factors make a substantial difference for success or failure on this dimension, namely, firm ownership, clients, and a strong design orientation. The results indicate that it is the traditional entrepreneur—the sole owner with high professional standards engaged in small-scale work for private individuals—who is the most vulnerable with respect to profits and most likely to go bankrupt.

Also, these conclusions, together with the results on productivity, qualify economic assumptions of scale and strongly suggest that whatever economies of scale there are in these professional offices, large size is not of great advantage in their overall economic health as reflected in both profits and productivity.

## Quality Change

Deeply embedded in professional organizations are the ideologies and values of the professional group (Beyer, 1981; Satow, 1975). As Ranson and associates (1980) state, "Organizational members create *provinces of meaning* which incorporate interpretive schemes, intermittently articulated as values and interests, that form the basis of their orientation and strategic purposes within organizations" (Ranson's italics). The provinces of meaning in architectural offices clearly evolve around innovative design and high quality work. It is important to understand what conditions best distinguish those firms that were able to produce high quality work, through the years between 1974 and 1979, from those that did not.

The function reveals that size, use of consultants, and computer technology are positively related to quality change, whereas profits and age are negatively related to it (table 4, top panel). They comprise a better set of predictor variables compared with the analyses for productivity and profit change as indicated by the higher value for the canonical correlation and a chi-square that is significant beyond the .01 level.[9] At one extreme are those architectural firms that won an award between 1974 and 1978; compared with others they were larger, had lower profits, were more likely to use consultants and computers, and were younger (table 9.4, bottom panel). Apparently, large size and technological sophistication (as revealed by computer technology and the use of engineering consultants) promote improvements in creative design, a conclusion somewhat at odds with artistic stereotypes, but which replicates earlier findings (J. Blau and McKinley, 1979). And although newness is a liability for productivity, as Stinchcombe (1965) suggests, it is an asset for quality. Young firms are mostly apt to win awards. The most obvious reason is that the young firm is working in the most current design style. Of interest, too, is the lesser profitability of the high-quality firms, which suggests that different criteria of sucess are not merely independent of one another but may actually be incompatible alternatives. Firms much concerned with profit, and hence with minimizing cost, are not likely to design outstanding buildings that bring awards.

## Size Change

Size, as we have seen, has contradictory implications for other measures of effectiveness. Now the focus is on the conditions that affect

TABLE 9.4

*Standardized Discriminant Function Coefficients for*
*Quality Change; Group Centroids and Numbers of Cases*

A. STANDARDIZED DISCRIMINANT FUNCTION COEFFICIENTS*

| *Variables*** | |
|---|---|
| Size (log) | − .98 |
| Profits | .27 |
| Use of consultants | − .43 |
| Computer | − .33 |
| Age | .65 |

B. GROUP CENTROIDS AND NUMBER OF CASES

| *Quality Change Groups* | *Centroid* | *N* |
|---|---|---|
| Nonsurvivors | .40 | 60 |
| No Award | .18 | 41 |
| Won award(s) | − .78 | 40 |

*Canonical correlation = .45; $X^2$ = 33.5 ($p < .01$).

**Variables excluded: Sole Ownership, Joint Venture, Diverse Services, Project Specialization, Percent Technicians.

the likelihood of growth or decline in size by distinguishing among failures, those becoming smaller or remaining constant, and those increasing in size. Given the highly uncertain environment, the capability to expand is probably the best overall indicator of organizational health. Four variables make up the discriminant function, with percentage of architects and project specialization yielding the highest coefficients, and percentage of corporate clients and affiliation somewhat lower ones (table 9.5, top panel). The function is significant beyond the .01 level.[10] It is interesting to note that, among other variables that make no difference in discriminating among groups, are sole ownership, percentage of New York City projects, age, and a quality measure.

A comparison of group means yields a curvilinear pattern in which declining firms are most different from both failures and successes. (table 9.5, bottom panel). Both firms that have failed and, particularly, those that have expanded tend to have a sizable architectural component, much project specialization, a disproportionate number of corporate clients, and usually no affiliate. Firms that just barely survive exhibit the opposite characteristics, notably a relatively small architectural staff and little project specialization.

The finding that these group means do not exhibit transitivity suggests again the existence of a set of critical factors that have contradictory implications. In the case of growth, this set consists primarily of the relative

*239*

TABLE 9.5

*Standardized Discriminant Function Coefficients for*
*Size Change; Group Centroids and Numbers of Cases*

A. STANDARDIZED DISCRIMINANT FUNCTION COEFFICIENTS*

| *Variables*** | |
|---|---|
| Affiliate | −.22 |
| Project specialization | .62 |
| Percent architects | .88 |
| Corporate clients | .46 |

B. GROUP CENTROIDS AND NUMBER OF CASES

| *Size Change Groups* | *Centroid* | *N* |
|---|---|---|
| Nonsurvivors | .13 | 60 |
| Constant or declined | −.53 | 44 |
| Increased | .32 | 48 |

*Canonical correlation = .33; $X^2$ = 20.9 ($p$ <.01).

**Variables excluded: Sole Ownership, Use of Consultants, N.Y.C. Projects, Percent Technicians, Age, Outstanding Ratings.

size of the architectural staff, project specialization, and corporate clients. Together they make up the crucial difference between failure and expansion. A large architectural staff is expensive; if the firm is flexible and can adapt to changing conditions, this staff can be an asset; it not, it will be a liability. Similarly, having captured specialized markets in 1973—as indicated by project specialization, may have long-term benefits if early specialization meets changing markets, but may be disastrous if it does not. And if corporabe clients themselves go bankrupt or cut down on building programs, the firm is vulnerable; on the other hand, if these wealthy clients continue to do well, the firm will prosper. In short, these factors create conditions of high risk during periods of uncertainty.

## SUMMARY

Recognizing that the study of what Perrow (1977: 98) terms the "gross malfunction" of organizations is long overdue, we have focused attention on a variety of conditions that influence the likelihood of demise, as well as that of relative effectiveness on four dimensions for a sample of architectural offices over a five-year period, incorporating, whenever possible, data over a longer period of time. The results can be briefly summarized in terms of the models discussed earlier, none of which are completely supported by the findings, though all are partially supported.

The data do not confirm the assumption of theories of entrepreneurship, namely, that the sole owner is most effective in an uncertain environment by virtue of flexibility and innovativeness (Deeks, 1976: 250); in fact, corporate status offers some advantages with respect to financial success (table 9.3). Nor do the data support the idea that entrepreneurial leadership is a crucial factor, as Peterson and Berger (1971) argue, since centralized control has no influence on effectiveness. Moreover, profits and productivity are not found to be affected by economies of scale; in fact, the firms experiencing increased productivity tend to be small (table 9.2). As independent predictors, economic variables play a minor role, and what role they do play is also contrary to the predictions of economic models. In addition, profit maximization objectives, as realized in high profits, impair the ability of firms to produce high-quality work (table 9.4).

It is suggested in the open system model that ties with other organizations are advantageous, particularly during a period of much uncertainty (Aiken and Hage, 1968). But this is only partially supported by our findings. Whereas the use of consultants is a feature of high-quality firms (table 9.4), it is also a feature of the least productive surviving firms (table 9.2). These results lend limited support to the idea that linkages prevent a firm from slipping over the threshold from mere survival to failure, but there is little indication that linkages contributed much to success.

The structural model has stressed the benefits of large size. The data on architectural firms indicate this is the case for some but not for all outcome criteria. Specifically, large size is beneficial for high-quality work, yet it is detrimental for profits. It seems to have contradictory effects on productivity, with small size maximizing simultaneously the likelihood of failure and of very high productivity. Similarly, although having complex goals is often considered optimal (see Wilson, 1966), a measure of this characteristic—diverse projects or little specialization—has opposite effects on quality and growth; specifically, designing diverse projects promotes the likelihood of winning awards (table 9.4), while specializing in a few project types increases firm growth (table 9.5). Advanced technology does influence dimensions of effectiveness, although in unanticipated ways. On the one hand, computer technology characterizes declining firms in the productivity analysis (table 9.2), but on the other, firms that succeed on the quality dimension also have computers (table 9.4). This suggests that an advanced technology benefits professional organizations in ways quite different from industrial or bureaucratic organizations; apparently, for example, unless members of the professional staff use computers for their own purposes, computers entail administrative rigidities. This inference is supported by the finding that routinization by formal rules is also associated with decline (table 9.2).

Earlier assumptions about the dual meaning of a large architectural component are borne out in the analysis. First, it appears to represent high overhead costs, for firms with a large component are unlikely to experience profit increases (table 9.3). It was also assumed that firms with a disproportionate number of architects have a more professional orientation than do others; such firms were more likely to expand in size, but only, apparently, if they could offset the high overhead that architects entail (table 9.5).

Theories about population ecology attribute to age protective benefits as the result of retention mechanisms (Aldrich, 1979: 45–51). The results here indicate that the most productive firms are older, on the average, but also that older firms were most likely to go out of business (table 9.2). Moreover, youthfulness is an asset for quality (table 9.4), probably because award committees tend to favor projects that are relatively avant-garde, which young firms are most likely to produce. Independent variables tapping the extent to which firms secured unique niches in 1974 include the types of clients they had. Corporate clients are critical in the analysis of size change: reliance on them is found either to destroy the firm or to result in substantial growth (table 9.5).

In sum, the results indicate that none of the models are sufficient for explaining failure and effectiveness. In two senses we have subjected these models to a severe test. First, the economic environment was chaotic from 1974 through 1978, and most models posit either variation or stability, not chaos. Second, these are professional offices, which, though they must sustain some profit to stay in business, pursue other goals as well, and most models deal with either business establishments for which the profit goal is central, or with government agencies, which are more likely to be transformed than to disappear.

### *Implications*

This research raises general issues that are briefly addressed. It is quite clear that there are not only multiple dimensions of effectiveness but also striking differences among the sets of predictors. In some instances, the prior characteristic that is positively associated with a given dimension is inversely associated with another. This suggests that each of the models reviewed is incomplete as each tends to focus on a single dimension of effectiveness and a limited array of independent variables. Further, the results indicate that those who work in organizations face a serious dilemma: what is a rational strategy with respect to one goal may maximize failure with respect to another. If, indeed, rational strategies are pursued, as Child (1972) proposes, organizational change can only be dialectical, since response or choice in one situation or at a given time must be renounced in another situation or at a later time.

Notwithstanding the complexity of the results, the dimensions of quality and profits help to simplify the overall conclusions because they highlight that very dilemma. Both dimensions are simply structured — group means are transitive with respect to the function — and this indicates that the effects of the antecedents on each of these dimensions are uniform. Yet the objective of maximizing profitability, as revealed in the analysis, impairs design quality. Although quality versus profits constitutes a special dilemma for architectural firms, owing to the artistic standards of architects, other types of organizations probably face similar dilemmas.

The nontransitivity of category centroids in the analysis of productivity and size reveals that factors that maximize effectiveness on either dimension also increase the likelihood of failure on the same dimension. These factors produce fulcrum effects that are critical becausae they generate conditions for tipping. The factors themselves can be described as high-risk investments, which can either be capitalized upon through flexible strategies and innovation (for example, by incurring cost to capture new markets) but which also increase the stakes and thus the danger of utter failure. It is assumed that the fulcrum effects of high-risk conditions will be more intense during periods of uncertainty and change, and when there is intense competition among organizations of the same type for scarce resources. Such fulcrum effects may be observed in other social systems. For example, economic uncertainty quite often creates political polarization. Similarly, in highly competitive occupations, both success and failure are often attributed to personal luck, owing to the striking similarities in the talent and ambition of those who fail and those who succeed. Indeed, the principle of the fulcrum effect is not new: it is clearly expressed in the old Yiddish proverb, "Az es vert nit besser, vert mimeyle erger,' ("If things don't get better, they can only get worse.").

## APPENDIX

*Independent Variables Defined (Grouped by Theoretical Model), Means, and N's*

| VARIABLES | $\bar{X}$ | N |
|---|---|---|
| *Entrepreneurship* | | |
| Size (log): Number of full-time equivalent staff as of April 1, 1974. | | |
| Logarithmic transformation to base 10. | .88 | 152 |

## APPENDIX

*Independent Variables Defined (Grouped by Theoretical Model), Means, and N's*

| VARIABLES | $\bar{X}$ | N |
|---|---|---|
| *Entrepreneurship (continued)* | | |
| Staff Fluctuation: Ratio of Maximum full-time staff in 1973 minus minimum full-time staff in 1973 to maximum 1973. | .25 | 146 |
| Complex Ownership: Five category scale coded sole proprietor (1), partnership (2), corporation (3), holding company (4), conglomerate (5). | 1.99 | 151 |
| Sole Ownership: Owned by single architect or not (dummy). | .40 | 151 |
| Centralization: Principal alone has the authority to manage project (dummy). | .33 | 145 |
| *Bankruptcy* | | |
| Productivity: Number of projects completed during 1973. | 12.6 | 151 |
| Profits: Percentage of projects commissioned from January 1969 through 1973 for which construction costs were at least one million dollars. | 41.9 | 149 |
| *Open System* | | |
| Joint Venture: Firm engaged in at least one joint venture in 1973 with another professional office (dummy). | .40 | 149 |
| Use of Consultants: Percentage of 1973 projects for which engineering consultants were contracted. | 63.80 | 141 |
| Affiliate: Legal affiliation with another organization (dummy). | .23 | 150 |
| N.Y.C. Projects: Percentage of 1973 projects located in the N.Y.C. metropolitan area. | .54 | 141 |
| *Structural* | | |
| Diverse Services: Number of design and production services out of fourteen provided by the office. (These are designated "comprehensive services" by the American Institute of Architects.) | 7.70 | 149 |
| Project Specialization: Lieberson's (1969) index of diversity, which measures degree of diversity or specialization with respect to nine project types. High value indicates specialization. | .55 | 145 |
| Computer: Whether or not staff have access to a computer (dummy). | .18 | 152 |
| Personnel Rules: Whether or not there are written procedures for personnel decisions (dummy). | .47 | 150 |
| Operating Rules: Number out of seven work procedures that are covered by written rules. | 2.00 | 146 |
| Percent Technicians: Ratio of full-time equivalent technical specialists to full-time equivalent staff (April 1, 1974). | .14 | 152 |
| Percentage of Architects: Ratio of full-time equivalent registered architects to full-time equivalent staff (April 1, 1974). | .45 | 152 |
| *Population Ecology* | | |
| Age: Years since established. | 17.6 | 152 |
| Private Clients: Percentage of 1973 projects commissioned by private individuals. | 19.6 | 149 |
| Corporate Clients: Percentage of 1973 projects commissioned by corporate and conglomerate clients. | 29.9 | 148 |
| Average Rating: Mean score on design quality as rated by 120 faculty members teaching at local architectural schools. (Separate survey carried out in 1975.) | .87 | 146 |

APPENDIX

*Independent Variables Defined (Grouped by Theoretical Model), Means, and N's*

| VARIABLES | X̄ | N |
|---|---|---|
| *Population Ecology (continued)* | | |
| Outstanding Ratings: Proportion of all ratings in the highest category of a five-point scale (see above). | .12 | 146 |

# NOTES

1. Reflected, for example, in unemployment figures for the metropolitan area. The unemployment rate for the New York City SMSA rose only slightly from 6.1 in 1972 to 6.9 in 1974, which was lower than that for most large SMSA's, but this rate reached 10.4 in 1976, well above the overall rate of 7.9 for all large SMSA's combined (U.S. Bureau of Labor Statistics, 1973; ;1975; 1977). Also see Weinstein (1977) for a discussion of the impact of the fiscal crisis on the urban economy.

2. National data for architects indicate some decline during this period in all regions of the country. There was a 12 percent decline in employment between 1973 and 1976 (Amercian Institute of Architects, 1977), with more than half of this decline occurring during late 1974 and early 1975 (American Institute of Architects, 1975). Comparable information for New York City is not available, although the American Institute of Architects' city chapter reported in May, 1975, a 50 percent drop in annual authorized project volume (New York City American Institute of Architects, 1975). Information on construction employment and firms provides the best overall indication on building activity. From 1974 to 1977, there was a 33 percent drop in Manhattan in employment and a 14 percent decline in the number of construction establishments; in contrast, for the nation as a whole, during this period there was a 10 percent employment drop but an increase of almost 20 percent in the number of establishments (U.S. Bureau of the Census, 1974; 1976; 1977).

3. One exception is Caudill, Rowlett and Scott; it rejoined its larger Texas affiliate. It is the only example of successful relocation we discovered in our interviews with architects.

4. Decentralization of project management has positive correlations with winning design awards (.19) and project productivity (.35); decentralization of client relations has positive correlations with winning awards (.18) and profits (.37).

5. Construction costs provide the best proxy for actual profits because the fee assessed the client for project design and other architectural services is a fixed percentage of these costs.

6. The technique of discriminant function analysis is based on solving the general eigenvector problem, $WA = \lambda Ba$, in order to derive the reduced space model with orthogonal dimensions (for the specific solution see Cooley and Lohnes [1971] and Tatsuoka [1970]). The maximum number of functions is one less than the number of groups $(g - 1)$ or the number of independent variables $(Z_p)$, whichever is smaller. Thus, in these analyses two functions are possible,

given three categories of the dependent variable. However, in the preliminary analyses no second function was found to be significant after derivation of the first, and for the results reported here, each solution is constrained to a single function.

7. The percentage of correct classification, an indicator of the predictive power for the function, is 44 percent over-all, but higher for the low and middle groups, for which it is 55 percent combined.

8. Classification results yield 37 percent accurate prediction, though elimination of the middle category improves this to 49 percent.

9. Over-all, the percentage of correct classification is 49 percent, and highest for the low and high categories, 55 percent and 68 percent, respectively.

10. The likelihood of identifying correct group membershp on the basis of the values of the function is 41 percent, and this likelihood is the highest, 68 percent, for the middle category.

# REFERENCES

Aiken, M. and J. Hage
 1968 "Organizational interdependence and interorganizational structure." American Sociological Review 33: 921–30.

Aldrich, H. E.
 1979 Organizations and Environments. Englewood Cliffs: Prentice-Hall.

American Institute of Architects
 1975 "Survey of firms charts decline in employment." Journal of The American Institute of Architects. 64: 41–42.

 1977 "Survey finds architectural employment at a standstill." Journal of the American Institute of Architects 66: 20; 24.

Barnard, C.
 1938 The Function of the Executive. Cambridge, Mass.: Harvard University Press.

Ben-David, J.
 1972 American Higher Education. McGraw-Hill.

Beyer, J. M.
 1981 "Ideologies, values, and decision making in organizations." Pp. 225–49 in P. C. Nystrom and W. H. Starbuck (eds.), Handbook of Organizational Design, vol. 2. Oxford: Oxford University Press.

Blau, J. R.
 1976 "Scientific recognition: academic context and professional role." Social Studies of Science 6: 533–45.

 1980 "A framework of meaning in architecture." Pp. 333–68 in G. Broadbent et al. (eds.), Signs, Symbols and Architecture. New York: John Wiley.

Blau, J. R. and W. McKinley
 1979 "Ideas, complexity, and innovation." Administrative Science Quarterly 24: 200–19.

Blau, P. M.
1968   "The hierarchy of authority in organizations." American Journal of Sociology 73: 453–67.

Blau, P. M. and R. A. Schoenherr
1971   The Structure of Organizations. New York: Basic Books.

Braybrooke, D.
1963/64   "The mystery of executive success re-examined." Administrative Science Quarterly 8: 533–60.

Campbell, D.
1969   "Variation and selective retention in socio-cultural evolution." General Systems 16: 69–85.

Caplow, T.
1964   Principles of Organization. New York: Harcourt, Brace and World.

Child, J.
1972   "Organization structure, environment, and performance – the role of strategic choice." Sociology 6: 1–22.

Cooley, W. W. and P. R. Lohnes
1971   Multivariate Data Analysis. New York: John Wiley.

Davis, J. A.
1961   Great Books and Small Groups. Glencoe, Ill.: The Free Press.

Deeks, J.
1976   The Small Firm Owner-Manager. New York: Praeger.

Evan, W. M.
1971   "The organization-set: toward a theory of interorganizational relations." Pp. 33–45 in J. G. Maurer (ed.), Readings in Organization Theory: Open System Approaches. New York: Random House.

Foster, G.
1978   Financial Statement Analysis. Englewood Cliffs: Prentice-Hall.

Goldberger, P.
1975   "For the architect, New York is home." New York Times, April 16, 1975.

Hage, J. and M. Aiken
1970   Social Change in Complex Organizations. New York: Random House.

Hall, R. H.
1968   Professionalization and bureaucratization. American Sociological Review 33: 92–104.

Hannan, M. T. and J. Freeman
1977a   "Obstacles to comparative studies." Pp. 106–131 in P. S. Goodman, J. M. Pennings (eds.) New Perspectives on Organizational Effectiveness. San Francisco: Jossey-Bass.

1977b   "The population ecology of organizations." American Journal of Sociology 82: 929–64.

Hazel, A. C. and A. S. Reed
1973   Managing the Survival of Smaller Companies. London: Business Books.

Hirsch, P. M.
1975 "Organizational effectiveness and the institutional environment." Administrative Science Quarterly 20: 327–44.

Hodgkinson, C.
1978 Towards a Philosophy of Administration. Oxford: Basil Blackwell.

Katz, D. and R. L. Kahn
1966 The Social Psychology of Organizations. New York: John Wiley.

Kaufman, H.
1976 Are Government Organizations Immortal? Washington, D. C.: The Brookings Instituteion.

Lawrence, P. R. and J. W. Lorsch
1967 Organization and Environment. Cambridge, Mass.: Harvard University Press.

McGuire, J. W.
1964 Theories of Business Behavior. Englewood Cliffs: Prentice-Hall.

Mahoney, Thomas A. et al.
1972 "The conditioning influence of organization size upon managerial practice." Organizational Behavior and Human Performance 8: 230–41.

Mayer, K. B. and S. Goldstein
1961 The First Two Years: Problems of Small Administration.

Meyer, M.
1979 Change in Public Bureaucracies. London: Cambridge University Press.

Miles, R. H.
1980 "Findings and implications of organizational life cycle research." Pp. 430–51 in J. R. Kimberly and R. H. Miles (eds.), The Organization Life Cycle. San Francisco: Jossey-Bass.

Miller, D. C.
1965 "Supervisors: evolution of an organizational role." Pp. 104–32 in R. Dubin et al.(eds.), Leadership in Productivity. San Francisco: Chandler.

Morrison, D. G.
1974 "Discriminant analysis." Pp. 442–456 in Robert Ferber (ed.), Handbook of Marketing Research. New York: McGraw-Hill.

New York City American Institute of Architects
1975 "Survey shows 1974 office activity in worsening slump." Oculus (May): 1.

Nie, N. et al.
1975 Statistical Package for the Social Sciences. New York: McGraw-Hill.

Osborn, R. N. and J. G. Hunt
1974 "Environment and organizational effectiveness." Administrative Science Quarterly 19: 231–46.

Paulson, S. K.
1974 "Causal analysis of interorganizational relations: an axiomatic theory revised." Administrative Science Quarterly 19: 319–37.

Pennings, J. M.
1980    "Organizational birth frequencies." Unpublished paper.

Pennings, J. M. and P. S. Goodman
1977    "Toward a workable framework." Pp. 146–84 in P. S. Goodman and J. M. Pennings (eds.), New Perspectives on Organizational Effectiveness. San Francisco: Jossey-Bass.

Perrow, C.
1961    "Goals in complex organizations." American Sociological Review 26: 854–65.

1972    Complex Organizations. Glenview, Ill.: Scott, Foresman.

1977    "Three types of effectiveness studies." Pp. 96–105 in P. S. Goodman, J. M. Pennings (eds.), New Perspectives on Organizational Effectiveness. San Francisco: Jossey-Bass.

Peterson, R. A. and D. G. Berger
1971    "Entrepreneurship in organizations: evidence from the popular music industry." Administrative Science Quarterly 16: 97–107.

Pfeffer, J.
1972    "Merger as a response to organizational interdependence." Administrative Science Quarterly 17: 382–94.

Pfeffer, J. and P. Nowak
1976    "Joint ventures and interorganizational interdependence." Administrative Science Quarterly 21: 398–419.

Pickle, H. B.
1964    Personality and Success: An Evaluation of Personal Characteristics of Successful Small Business Managers. Washington, D.C.: Small Business Administration.

Price, James L.
1968    Organizational Effectiveness. Homewood, Ill.: Irwin.

Ranson, S. et al.
1980    "The structuring of organizational structures." Administrative Science Quarterly 25: 1–17.

Satow, R. L.
1975    "Value-rational authority and professional organizations." Administrative Science Quarterly 20: 526–31.

Schon, D. A.
1971    Beyond the Stable State. London: Temple Smith.

Scott, J.
1979    "A theoretical critique of empirical models of bankruptcy prediction." Unpublished paper.

Simon, H. A.
1957    Administrative Behavior, 2nd ed. New York: Macmillan.

Starbuck, W. H.
1965    "Organizational growth and development." Pp. 451–533 in J. G. March (ed.), Handbook of Organizations. Chicago: Rand McNally.

Stinchcombe, A.
1965    "Social structure and organizations." Pp. 142–93 in J. G. March

*Blau and Lieben*

(ed.), Handbook of Organizations. Chicago: Rand McNally.

Tatsuoka, M. M.
1970    Discriminant Analysis: The Study of Group Difference. Champaign,
        Ill.: Institute for Personality and Ability Testing.

Thompson, J. D.
1967    Organizations in Action. New York: McGraw-Hill.

U.S. Bureau of Labor Statistics
1973    Geographic Profile of Employment and Unemployment. Washing-
1975    ton, D.C.: U.S. Government Printing Office.
1977

U.S. Bureau of the Census
1974    County Business Patterns. Washington, D.C.: U.S. Government
1976    Office.
1977

Weinstein, B. L.
1977    "The demographics and politics of economic decline in New York City."
        Annals of Regional Science 11: 65–73.

Whetten, D. A.
1980    "Sources, responses, and effects of organizational decline." Pp.
        342–74 in J. Kimberly, R. H. Miles (eds.) The Organizational Life
        Cycle. San Francisco: Jossey-Bass.

Wilson, J. Q.
1966    "Innovation in organizations." Pp. 193–218 in J. D. Thompson
        (ed.), Approaches to Organizational Design. Pittsburgh: University
        of Pittsburgh Press.

Yuchtman, E. and S. Seashore
1967    "A system resource approach to organizational effectiveness."
        American Sociological Review 32: 891–903.

Zaltman, G. et al.
1973    Innovation and Organizations. New York: John Wiley.

# 10 The Professional Supply of Design: A Descriptive Study of Architectural Firms

MAGALI SARFATTI LARSON,
GEORGE LEON, and JAY BOLICK

From Durkheim to Parsons and his followers, a long sociological tradition has viewed professions as occupational communities. Communal identity is rooted in the special bodies of theoretical and technical knowledge that only the duly initiated can legitimately claim to possess. Prolonged and systematic training thus constitutes the basis of common socialization into a profession; presumably, the effects of this socialization survive the dissolvent impact of different and heterogeneous conditions of practice. It is also on the grounds of their special knowledge and, therefore, of their special training, that professionals claim the right to self-selection and self-control. Corporate bodies of professional experts receive from the larger society the mandate and the authority to exercise this right in the spheres of both training and practice. Their autonomous, though delegated, functions of gate keeping and policing distinguish professions from other economic actors. Born of the expansion and diversification of market relations, the older professions may nevertheless be seen as special instances of *nonmarket* allocation of choices and risks, operating in special markets of services or labor (Arrow, 1976; Larson, 1977).

In recent years, the power of the professions has been denounced politically, from the right by defenders of free-market principles (Friedman, 1962) and from the left by movements of clients or consumers,

Funds for the preparation of the data were provided by a grant of the National Science Foundation to the Research Corporation of the American Institute of Architects, allocated to the senior author; computer assistance was generously provided by Temple University. Deborah Francis and Carolyn Frankel were responsible for the coding. The senior author is grateful to the Design Arts Program of the National Endowment of the Arts for a research fellowship (Grant N. 11-4213-093) and to Temple University for partial release time, which allowed for a part of this research.

*251*

often allied with professional dissidents (Ehrenreich, 1979; Gross and Osterman, 1972). The traditional sociological perspective, partly as a consequence of the latter movements, has come under increasing attack for both its empirical and theoretical shortcomings (see Ehrenreich, 1979, 1981; Larson, 1977, 1979). A descriptive study based on limited, though comprehensive, data cannot properly address either the political issues or the sociological controversies. It may, however, help to reformulate some of the questions raised by providing information on a very special profession. As is argued elsewhere in this volume, architecture occupies a special place among the older professions for reasons related to its position in the social division of labor, to the nature of its product, and to its history in different national contexts.

Throughout the history of the architectural profession, the distinction — or the opposition — between "mere building" and architecture reappears in different theoretical or ideological guises. Underlying the intellectual arguments are real conflicts between "professional" architects and building crafts or, in modern times, between architects and building trade unions, between architects and builders or real estate developers, and, last but not least, between architects and the rival professions, notably engineers, who also stake claims to expertise in designing the man-made environment. Unlike other established professions, architecture has not succeeded in establishing itself as a gatekeeper to the market for design services, of which it controls only a minor part.[1] The corollary of this lack of market power is both a great vulnerability to demand — marked by the sharp fluctuations of the building industry — and a close subordination of professional practice to the nature of the market. As in other professions, vulnerability and subordination express themselves in marked internal cleavages. The fact that the products of architectural design are always, to some extent, *public goods* makes the stratification of architectural practice more apparent to the public than is such stratification in professions that provide personal services.

In comparison with other established professions, architecture counts relatively few practitioners: self-declared *male* architects (the overwhelming majority in a traditionally male-dominated profession) numbered 37,000 in the 1960 Census, compared with 157,000 men who were civil engineers, 211,000 lawyers and judges, and 217,000 male physicians and surgeons. It was, however, a fast-growing profession: in the 1970 Census, male architects numbered 55,000, and their rate of growth (48.6% in the intercensal period) had been far higher than that of the other professional groups.[2] (We cannot assume, though, that the upward trend continued into the 1970s, marked as this decade was by an economic recession that had devastating effects on domestic building and, presumably, on related design activities as well.)

Probably to a greater degree than are the other established professions, architecture is still organized in a predominantly entrepreneurial mode around small, proprietor firms. Like other professions, it is sharply stratified: a small minority of large and often corporate firms that tend to offer both architectural and engineering services design most large-scale projects. They capture, therefore, the largest share of the fees paid for architectural services. Smaller firms, on the other hand, appear to be quite different in their organization, in their profitability, and in the recognition they receive for their work. It is tempting to assume that the differences among the smaller firms also correspond (as do differences between them and the large firms) to qualitative differences among the segments of the market they tend to serve.

Although all firms (and even the largest ones, at one or another time) engage in small-scale, or partial, types of practices, such as the design of private residences or — especially in hard times — remodeling, restoration, and interior design, a few firms of small to medium size have internal characteristics that would normally be associated with the bureaucratization common to large size. Thus, in her 1974 study of 152 architectural firms in Manhattan, Blau (1976) found that the few *small* firms offering diverse services, having differentiated internal structures (specialized subdivisions), and using written personnel regulations tended to win awards far more frequently than the more typical firms lacking such features. It appears from Blau's study that the smaller firms that win more than their share of awards may be a special kind of elite firm distinguished not by size, but by atypical bureaucratic features and, presumably, efficiency of organization. These firms centralize design activities under the relatively autocratic direction of a principal or principals, and the latter, one may assume, are exceptionally talented designers.[3]

The complex interdependence between types of firm and their markets is, again, indirectly confirmed by Blau's follow-up study of 1979 (Blau and Lieben, chapter 9, this volume). Our analysis, based on less information for each firm, cannot directly test the conclusions reached by Blau's Manhattan-based studies. However, some of her findings may be compared with the general trends that appear in a nationwide sample.

The following descriptive analysis is based on two main bodies of data. The first is a sample of architectural firms, larger than 8.5% of the total, drawn from a comprehensive survey of firms listed by the American Institute of Architects as members in 1977. The survey was conducted nationwide by Archimedia, Inc., for the AIA and published in 1978 as the

*Profile of Architectural Firms* (American Institute of Architects, 1978). Its purpose was to create a link, until then unavailable, between architects and their potential clients or other interested sectors of the public, by providing up-to-date, easily accessible, and easily retrievable information on AIA firms. The intention of publicizing architectural providers constituted an obvious incentive for responding to the mail questionnaire. The rate of response (after up to two requests for information and follow-up letters or calls) was 90%, which is exceptionally high for mail questionnaires.[4] Only those architectural firms were included that offered their services on a permanent basis and also had at least one registered architect on their staff and at least one principal who was an AIA member. While this last criterion excluded registered architects who were not members of the official professional association and an undetermined number of large architectural or engineering-architectural firms that do not join the AIA, it also assured us that the data represented a numerous and typical segment of the profession, namely, those architectural firms in which at least one principal valued AIA affiliation enough to pay the supplemental dues asked of members who are total or partial owners of their firms.[5] The data analyzed are therefore characteristic of firms in which at least one of the principals had both certifiable training and a traditional understanding of recognized professional standing.

To obtain the sample from the survey, we drew every tenth firm, after a random first selection, from the complete listing in the AIA *Profile*, excluding only the two firms located in Europe. We originally intended to draw a 10% sample, but inappropriate or incomplete reporting by the firms reduced it to 8.5%.

The second body of data consists of general demographic and economic data for each of the fifty states, to which we added data specific to architecture and construction.[6] The analysis of these data allows us to locate architectural firms within a matrix of general context variables.

We first present the geographical distribution of the firms in our sample. Second, shifting to our file of state variables, we examine characteristics associated with the volume and availability of architectural services at the level of the fifty states. Third, we return to our sample to discuss internal characteristics of the AIA firms, relating these to the quality of their work as judged by juries of their peers. In the final section, we examine structural characteristics that differentiate the firms which have won AIA awards from those which have not.

## GEOGRAPHICAL DISTRIBUTION
## AND ECOLOGICAL ANALYSIS

As could be expected, our sample of AIA firms is quite unevenly distributed among the nation's subregions and states (table 10.1 and 10.2). Six states contain, in the aggregate, 41% of the firms in the sample: California has 13%, Texas 8%, New York 7%, Illinois 5%, Florida and Pennsylvania 4% each; all the other states have less than 4% each, and 29 have 1% or less. At the subregional level, the 1977 distribution of AIA firms conforms very closely to the distribution of population (the Spearman rank correlation coefficient between firms and 1970 population is .84, significant at .01). The number of firms is less strongly associated with the population changes experienced by regions between 1960 and 1970 (Spearman $r = .70$, significant at .05). Not unexpectedly, subregions are far too large to reflect short-term changes.

As could be expected, the overwhelming majority of firms in our sample is located within large agglomerations (Standard Metropolitan Statistical Areas); only 11.7% of the AIA firms are active in small localities that are separate from larger urban areas; and the majority (52.5%) are concentrated in cities with a million or more inhabitants (table 10.3).

The location of economic agents obeys complex and changing economic factors, many of which are specific to each activity.[7] While proximity to resources and markets plays a role for all producers, the effect is different for differing activities, since the markets and the resources needed are also different. While the providers of professional services tend to concentrate where wealthy or so-called interesting clienteles can be found, research-oriented professions go where there are both research facilities and concentrations of brain power. Location is a factor of stratification among providers of professional services. Architecture is auxiliary to building, and building can go up anywhere, though not all types of building are located in every area. For instance, monumental buildings tend to be situated in important or capital cities, and so-called high-class residences are located in exclusive neighborhoods or vacation resorts. Architectural design can be sought from outside the locality where a project is to be situated — and it is, in fact, solicited nationwide or even internationally for important competitions. The smaller firms, however, cannot easily sustain the costs involved in entering unpaid competitions, nor can they easily afford the costs of prospecting relatively distant markets. Unless they are already well known and chosen from afar because of their prestige, they will tend to be restricted to their local markets. That there is such a large proportion

TABLE 10.1

*Number and Percentage of Firms in Subregions*

| SUBREGIONS (STATES INCLUDED IN EACH) | N OF FIRMS | % OF TOTAL |
|---|---|---|
| Northeast | | |
| (Me., N.H., Mass., R.I., Vt., Conn.) | 24 | 4.1 |
| Middle Atlantic | | |
| (N.Y., N.J., Pa.) | 85 | 14.6 |
| East North Central | | |
| (Ohio, Ind., Ill., Mich., Wis.) | 79 | 13.5 |
| West North Central | | |
| (Minn., Iowa, Mo., N.D., S.D., Neb., Ka.) | 45 | 7.7 |
| South Atlantic | | |
| (Geo., Fla., S.C., Del., Md., Wash. D.C., Va., W.V., N.C.) | 100 | 17.1 |
| East South Central | | |
| (Ky., Tenn., Ala., Miss.) | 25 | 4.3 |
| West South Central | | |
| (Ark., La., Ok., Tx.) | 69 | 11.8 |
| Mountain | | |
| (Mont., Ida., Wyo., Col., N.M., Arix., Ut., Nev.) | 40 | 6.8 |
| Paficif | | |
| (Wash., Ore., Cal., Ak., Ha.) | 113 | 19.4 |
| Other | | |
| (Puerto Rico, Virgin Islands) | 3 | 0.5 |
| | 383 | 99.8* |

*Percentages do not add to 100.00 due to rounding.

of small entrepreneurial firms in architecture suggests, therefore, a typically local pattern of activity. Moreover, the relatively young age of architectural firms (in our sample, half were less than thirteen years old), together with the predominance of single-principal proprietorships, that architectural entrepreneurs predictably seize opportunities when they are available. This explains the strong correlations observed, at the level of each state between the number of architectural firms or the number of architects employed and the volume of construction or the number of construction establishments. To these ecological correlations we now turn.

Our analysis of the state data confirms the predictable association between general variables, such as demographic growth and volume of construction (themselves strongly correlated), and variables directly relevant to architectural practice (table 10.4). Somewhat less predictable are the very strong correlations between various characteristics of architectural practice. For instance, because there are few architectural offices with more than 500 employees (and only one in our sample), a single large of-

TABLE 10.2

*States and Territories Ranked by Number of Firms*

| RANK | N OF FIRMS | RANK | N OF FIRMS |
|---|---|---|---|
| 1. California | 74 | 26. Hawaii | 8 |
| 2. Texas | 46 | Kansas | |
| 3. New York | 40 | 28. Alabama | 7 |
| 4. Illinois | 29 | Wash., D.C. | |
| 5. Pennsylvania | 26 | 30. Connecticut | 6 |
| 6. Florida | 24 | Iowa | |
| 7. Ohio | 20 | Kentucky | |
| 8. New Jersey | 19 | Wisconsin | |
| 9. Washington State | 17 | 34. New Mexico | 5 |
| No. Carolina | | 35. Montana | 4 |
| 11. Georgia | 16 | Nebraska | |
| 12. Michigan | 15 | Arkansas | |
| 13. Virginia | 14 | Idaho | |
| 14. Missouri | 13 | 39. New Hampshire | 3 |
| 15. Oregon | 12 | North Dakota | |
| 16. Colorado | 11 | Utah | |
| | | West Virginia | |
| 17. Louisiana | 10 | 43. Alaska | 2 |
| Massachusetts | | Maine | |
| Tennessee | | Mississippi | |
| 20. Oklahoma | 9 | Nevada | |
| Arizona | | Rhode Island | |
| Indiana | | South Dakota | |
| Maryland | | 49. Delaware | 1 |
| Minnesota | | Puerto Rico | |
| South Carolina | | Vermont | |
| | | Virgin Islands | |

fice may account for as much growth in the number of architects employed as could many small firms.[8] However, the strong correlation between number of architectural firms and number of employed architects at the level of each state (.95) indicates that a majority of the latter depend on the smaller firms for employment.

The predominance of small firms also underlies the very strong correlation (.99) between registered and employed architects: it cannot be interpreted to mean that most employed architects obtain their registration, for there are indications that only a relative minority of architectural graduates do so.[9] Owners of architectural firms, on the other hand, are almost always registered architects, or must have on staff a registered architect who can sign projects. What the correlation between the number of firms and the number of registered architects per state (.96) indicates is that firms tend to be founded by *local* architects and to recruit their most qualified personnel locally. For architects actually do obtain their registration in the states where they practice and can only

TABLE 10.3

*Number of Firms per City Size*

| POPULATION IN THOUSANDS | N OF FIRMS | % OF TOTAL |
|---|---|---|
| Not in SMSA | 68 | 11.7 |
| 1–199 | 43 | 7.4 |
| 200–499 | 93 | 16.0 |
| 500–999 | 73 | 12.5 |
| 1,000 + | 306 | 52.5 |
| Total | 583 | 100.1 |

transfer that registration to other states through relatively complex and nonstandardized reciprocal agreements, or by seeking certification from the National Council of Architectural Boards.[10] The correlations between the number of architectural schools in each state and the other variables related to architectural practice (number of architectural firms, .82; number of architectural employees, .79; number of registered architects, .83; number of construction establishments, .85) sustain the notion that architectural manpower tends to be produced and recruited within each state. However, the correlations between the number of architectural schools and the other variables lose statistical significance when a state's population is controlled (see partial correlations, table 10.4). This is to say that, on the one hand, *population* explains the higher number of architectural schools in certain states and, on the other hand it *also* explains the higher number of architectural firms and employees in the most populous states.

The demographic dynamism reflected by population changes within the five-year period studied is highly correlated with the volume of construction and, as might be expected, more strongly correlated with residential than with nonresidential construction volume in 1976 (the correlations are, respectively, .77 and .72). The two large categories of construction are closely tied, however (with an *r* of .92), since nonresidential construction indicates either economic development trends that eventually attract population shifts between states, or current shifts in population that create new service demands.

The number of architectural firms shows a stronger correlation with demographic growth than does the number of construction establishments (.72 and .63, respectively). Underlying these findings is the dependence of architectural firms on residential and population-linked, nonresidential construction, a dependence far greater than that of construction establishments, which acquire their largest volume of contracts in the field of heavy con-

## TABLE 10.4

### Correlation Matrix for Construction Activity Variables and Location/Production of Architects

| Variables | 1 | 2 | 3 | 4 | 5 | 6 | 7 | 8 | 9 | 10 |
|---|---|---|---|---|---|---|---|---|---|---|
| 1. Population change 1970–1975 | | .72 (.64) | .63 (.36) | .59 (NS) | .60 (.28) | .54 (NS) | .36 (NS) | .64 (.58) | .72 (.62) | .77 (.65) |
| 2. N of architectural firms in 1972 | | | .90 (NS) | .95 (.53) | .96 (.65) | .82 (NS) | .68 (NS) | .94 (.31) | .94 (.56) | .92 (.71) |
| 3. N of construction establishments, 1972 | | | | .89 (−.27) | .92 (NS) | .85 (NS) | .76 (NS) | .95 (NS) | .92 (.30) | .79 (NS) |
| 4. Architectural employees 1972 | | | | | .99 (.91) | .79 (NS) | .66 (−.35) | .95 (NS) | .90 (NS) | .88 (.54) |
| 5. Registered architects 1972 | | | | | | .83 (NS) | .71 (NS) | .96 (NS) | .91 (NS) | .87 (.47) |
| 6. Architectural schools (ACSA) | | | | | | | .87 (.67) | .86 (.25) | .79 (NS) | .64 (−.24) |
| 7. Degrees conferred, 1976 | | | | | | | | .76 (NS) | .70 (NS) | .50 (−.37) |
| 8. Total construction value in $, 1970 | | | | | | | | | .92 (.27) | .84 (NS) |
| 9. Nonresidential construction value in $, $976 | | | | | | | | | | .92 (.73) |
| 10. Residential value in $, 1976 | | | | | | | | | | |

NOTE: The correlation coefficients are Pearson $r$ coefficients; they are all significant at least at the .005 level. The partial coefficients, controlling for population size, are in parentheses. "NS" indicates a partial coefficient nonsignificant at alpha = .005.

struction. Architects are infrequently called upon to design heavy construction projects (water use and control, transportation — with the exception of airports, which are designed by architects — and electricity, gas, and communications); if they do participate in such projects, it is for the smaller, public-oriented aspects (such as, for instance, subway stations) or as employees of the large construction establishments that provide comprehensive construction-design services. Moreover, when dealing with *numbers* of firms or establishments, one must take into account the fact that the initial capital investment in construction is much larger than that in architecture. Ultimately, all that is needed for small architectural projects is a well-lighted room, a telephone, drafting equipment, and eventually some secretarial help. Would-be architectural entrepreneurs can therefore respond far more readily than building contractors to the opportunities afforded by demographic growth. Latecomers in the construction field are also likely to find that new opportunities are rapidly tapped by existing establishments that mobilize their excess capacity in response to growing demand. This is, indeed, what may have been happening in 1972, a year in which construction prospects brightened considerably.[11]

These data also permit inferences about the effects on professional education of demographic changes and architectural activities. If we turn, now, to the degrees conferred by accredited architectural schools in 1976, we observe strong correlations with other variables in table 10.4. It is tempting to interpret the strong correlations between the number of construction establishments in 1972 (.76) with the number of architectural firms in that year (.68), and with the number of registered architects (.71) and of architectural employees (.66), as possible indications of the manner in which architectural students choose their career. The degrees conferred represent the outcome of a variety of accredited programs: the B.A.'s and B.Sc.'s in architecture normally vary from 4 to 5 years' minimum after the high school diploma, 5 being usual at the prestigious schools; the M.A. degree in architecture normally requires 2 years after a first professional degree (with a 1-year minimum after a 5-year B.Arch.), and 3 years for students whose first degree is not in architecture (Association of Collegiate Schools of Architecture, 1979). We may therefore assume that a large number of the students who graduated in 1976 started their programs in 1971 or 1972, followed by a smaller number who either started college in 1970 or decided to study architecture after a nonprofessional first degree in 1973. Although 1969 was a record year for the physical volume of construction contracts awarded, the panorama of the late sixties was depressed by high interest rates and escalating contruction costs; in 1971, however, the dollar volume of contracts was beginning to rise and was expected to continue its upward trend (*Engineering News Record*, 1972). We might infer, therefore, that students who began the study of architecture between 1971 and 1973 may have done so in part on the basis of a rational assessment of the prospects for construction and, in particular, for that construction (residential and related nonresidential services) in which architects participate most directly.

These are, however, admittedly speculative interpretations. If we control the influence of population, most correlations observed in table 10.4 between architectural schools or the degrees they confer and other variables become statistically insignificant, as shown by the partial correlations given in parentheses. In fact, the correlations of both schools and degrees with the dollar volume of residential construction in 1976 become negative when population is controlled (they are respectively $-.24$ and $-.37$). This suggests that the 1976 volume of residential construction, though related to the absolute level of population, was nevertheless largely taking place in states that had fewer architectural schools and, therefore, fewer architectural graduates. Furthermore, the partial correlation between residential construction in 1976 and the number of architectural employees in 1972 remains positive and significant (.54), which indicates that the distribution of construction activities across the states sustained itself over a four-year period. However, the number of architectural employees in 1972 becomes *negatively* correlated with the number of degrees conferred in 1976 ($-.35$), reinforcing our interpretation: for a given population size, the states with a high volume of residential construction in 1976 were *not* states in which architectural education tended to concentrate. This interpretation is consistent with the population shift from the older industrial states toward newer growth areas having less developed, or more recently established, institutions of higher education.

Our analysis confirms the strength of the ecological linkages between mutually supporting activities. Construction, architectural design, and professional education appear in a cluster in which domestic, in-state construction (as reflected in both the volume and the number of establishments) takes the lead, showing greater association with the number of architectural schools than do the directly architectural variables. However, as shown in table 10.4 by the partial correlations, population size in 1970 explains much of the covariation observed: population size is therefore largely responsible for these ecological linkages between the background variables of architectural practice; in particular, it influences to a high degree the presence and level of factors dependent on the development of education. Two important points should nevertheless be kept in mind when interpreting correlation matrices and partial correlations. First, many of the original correlations vanish when controlling for population size, but many others do not: the relationships of the number of architectural firms to the number of architectural employees and registered architects, and to the dollar value of construction, are diminished, but remain quite strong. All of these, and, in addition, the number of construction establishments, also remain strongly correlated to population change, supporting the notion that expanding markets generate related entrepreneurial activity. Population size, therefore, explains these relationships only to a certain degree, for they endure after the effect of population is removed.

The second point to be remembered is that the correlations which become insignificant when population is controlled do not indicate that the relationships initially observed are nonexistent. Rather, the statistical "disappearance" of the initial relationships indicates that they were intimately linked to a third variable, in this case population size. Thus, for instance, states that have a large number of architectural schools really do have more architectural firms.

By 1977, when the AIA survey was conducted, there were clear signs that the building markets were picking up again after two very depressed years: gains of 16.8% were expected in heavy construction, of 8.8% in nonresidential building, and of 30.2% in multiunit residential building (*Engineering News Report*, 1977). Major nonresidential building markets had shifted, however, following population movements, to the South, West and Southwest. So too had manufacturing plants moved, with new plants concentrated in Texas, New Mexico, and Louisiana, while California, Texas, and New York led in plans for new office buildings; California, Illinois, Florida, New York, and Ohio led in projected stores and shopping centers. It is interesting to note, in passing, that, with the exception of New Mexico and Louisiana, the other states rank high in terms of the AIA firms they contain: California ranks first, Texas second, New York third, Illinois fourth, Florida sixth, and Ohio seventh (Table 10.2).

We now turn to some structural characteristics of our sample of AIA firms, noting again that 1977 was a year of recovery in architectural activities, following two bad years that may have substantially affected many of the firms.

## JURIDICAL TYPE AND AGE OF AIA FIRMS

In her study of Manhattan firms, Blau (1978) found that a firm's juridical type has a significant influence on a number of its other features. Although most of this influence could be explained by the close association of type *with size*, the type itself, independently of size, accounts for substantial differences in the degree of bureaucratization of a firm's practice. Corporations, in Blau's sample, are likely to exhibit higher values than are sole proprietorships and partnerships with regard to the following factors: the comprehensiveness of services offered, the fact of having an affiliate, a photocopier in house, and personnel rules and regulations, as well as the number of rules governing work procedures.

While we cannot assess in such detail the effect of type on bureaucratization, the chi-square tests performed demonstrate the existence of significant relationships between juridical type and size (the total number of employees); between juridical type and the ratio of administrative employees to the total manpower of a firm (a gross indicator of bureaucratization); and between juridical type and the presence of landscape architects and interior designers (a gross indicator of diversification of services). In our sample, however, these relationships are likely to be mediated by size. Table 10.5 presents the distribution of firms per juridical type and the mean number of employees for each juridical category.

A few words of explanation are in order about the juridical types listed in the AIA survey. Proprietorships and partnerships are simple forms: in the one, the individual owner(s) assume(s) legal and financial responsibility; in the other, the partnership is an arrangement between private parties, to which the state adds no stipulations or regulations other than those governing contracts.[12] In professional corporations, all owners of stock must be licensed professionals, while in business corporations, anyone can own stock. In the former type, however, liability for matters related to professional practice is still imputable to individuals. In other words, the corporate form does not allow professionals to hide from individual professional responsibility. Professional associations are simply joint ventures in which associates maintain legal and financial responsibility as individuals; there are only 10 of them (or 1.7%) in our sample.

Proprietorship is the most frequently observed juridical form, followed by partnerships, professional corporations, and business corporations. The corporate form only began to be used in architecture in the last decade. Table 10.6 shows that only 6% of our firms are multiple ownerships with more than 4 principals. The predominance of proprietorships and single principal firms confirms, once more, the entrepreneurial and individualistic character of architectural practice. It may well be, however, a venture fraught with difficulties and discontinuities. The young age of most of the firms (41% founded in the last 10 years) in our sample is therefore entirely consistent with the large number of small proprietorships and the fluctuating nature of the market for architectural services. Not surprisingly, the mean age of proprietorships (13.1 years) is lower than that of the other types, and 3 years younger than the mean age for the total sample (see table 10.5).

**TABLE 10.5**

*Juridical Type of AIA Firms and Related Characteristics*

| | | | | | | % OF ACTIVITIES IN 1977 | | |
|---|---|---|---|---|---|---|---|---|
| TYPE | N | % | MEAN AGE | MEAN N OF EMPLOYEES | MEAN N OF PRINCIPALS | In Same State | Other State | Abroad |
| Proprietorship | 268 | 46.0 | 13.1 | 4.3 | 1.3 | 85.0 | 12.7 | .5 |
| Partnership | 129 | 22.1 | 21.0 | 20.0 | 2.8 | 86.0 | 11.0 | 2.2 |
| Professional Association | 10 | 1.7 | 24.5 | 12.0 | 2.3 | 88.5 | 6.0 | 5.5 |
| Professional Corporation | 107 | 18.4 | 16.3 | 9.8 | 2.5 | 87.7 | 11.7 | 0.4 |
| Business Corporation | 67 | 11.4 | 17.2 | 15.2 | 2.6 | 84.4 | 14.1 | 0.0 |
| No information | 2 | 0.3 | | | | | | |
| Total sample | 581 | 100.0 | 16.1 | 10.2 | 2.0 | 85.7 | 12.2 | 0.9 |

TABLE 10.6

*Number of Principals in AIA Firms*

| PRINCIPALS | % FIRMS |
|---|---|
| 1 | 50.4 |
| 2 | 24.5 |
| 3 | 14.4 |
| 4 | 4.7 |
| 5 | 1.9 |
| 6 | 1.9 |
| 7 or more | 2.2 |

If we assume that an architect is likely to graduate at around 23 years of age after 5 years of college and likely to work for others (and obtain his/her registration) for another 8 years or so, it follows that architectural firms are likely to be founded by men in their early thirties. Let us give them 30 years of active professional life and assume that a man in his sixties must be considering retirement, or his succession as the head of an entrepreneurial firm. For our 1977 data, this means that small proprietorships or partnerships founded in 1947 or before and still headed by their founders would be old indeed, and lucky to have survived the probable absence of a principal during the war years. Conversely, we should find that the oldest firms in our sample are likely to be larger and have multiple owners. That this is, in fact, the case can be seen in table 10.7: the 75 firms founded in 1947 or before have a mean size of 29.45, almost three times as large as the sample mean of 10.2, and have more principals, on the average, than any other group.

The older firms are, in fact, a particularly interesting group, for they should reveal some of the conditions of lasting success in architectural practice. At the time of the AIA survey, half of the older firms had been in business since 1936 or before (the median age for these 75 firms is, indeed, 41 years) and over 30% had been founded in or before 1927. As one might expect, fewer of them are proprietorships (28% compared to 46% in the total sample) and more are partnerships or professional associations (37 and 4%, respectively, for 22 and 1.7% in the sample as a whole). The proportion of the newer juridical forms—professional or business corporations—is identical, however, to that of the sample. So also is the percentage of older firms having one or more branch offices (7 out of 75, or 9%, compared to 8.9% for the whole sample). Indeed, the juridical forms that have one or more affiliates well above this 8.9% are the business corporations with 21% and the professional associations with 20%, and only the latter type appears with above average frequency among the old firms (3 out of 10 professional associations are in the older group).

TABLE 10.7

*Age Distribution of AIA Firms and Related Characteristics*

| YEAR FIRMS WERE FOUNDED | N | % | MEAN N OF EMPLOYEES | N OF PRINCIPALS | % OF 1977 ACTIVITIES | | |
|---|---|---|---|---|---|---|---|
| | | | | | Same state | Other U.S. | Inter-national |
| 1947 or before | 75 | 12.9 | 29.4 | 3.2 | 84.4 | 13.5 | 2.0 |
| 1948–52 | 36 | 6.2 | 8.6 | 2.2 | 85.9 | 12.7 | 1.4 |
| 1953–57 | 63 | 10.8 | 9.9 | 1.9 | 90.8 | 8.2 | 1.0 |
| 1958–62 | 87 | 14.9 | 9.3 | 2.1 | 85.2 | 12.8 | 0.9 |
| 1963–67 | 84 | 14.4 | 7.9 | 1.9 | 80.6 | 15.7 | 0.4 |
| 1968–72 | 114 | 19.6 | 6.8 | 1.8 | 85.9 | 12.9 | 0.4 |
| 1973 | 24 | 4.1 | 4.1 | 1.5 | 94.6 | 5.4 | 0.0 |
| 1974 | 33 | 5.7 | 6.8 | 1.6 | 86.2 | 13.1 | 0.8 |
| 1975 | 23 | 3.9 | 4.8 | 1.6 | 81.9 | 11.4 | 2.4 |
| 1976 | 28 | 4.8 | 3.1 | 1.4 | 87.5 | 9.0 | 0.0 |
| 1977 | 16 | 2.7 | 3.5 | 1.7 | 89.9 | 8.9 | 1.2 |
| Total sample | 583 | 100.0 | 10.2 | 2.0 | 85.7 | 12.2 | 0.9 |

The success of the older firms manifests not only in their permanence, but also in the size and complexity of their work force: they are larger, they support more principals (31% have 3 or more, as compared to the 10.7% who do so in the sample as a whole), and more of them have design specialists on staff than does the entire population of AIA firms: 39% have at least 1 engineer, as against 17.6% of the sample; 12% have 1 or more landscape architects (as against 4.9%); 31% have 1 or more interior designers (as against 15.1%) and 41% have "other technical personnel" as compared to 22.1% in the sample as a whole.[13] The attachment to the more traditional forms professional practice, as well as the long-standing affiliation with the AIA, suggests that the largest and most successful of these old firms were ready to seize market opportunities, to diversify and specialize their personnel without departing from established modes of professional practice. They are, one could think, classic models of professional success.

We may ask now if substantive aspects of their practice distinguish the 75 firms founded before 1948 from the sample average. In 1977, the older firms reported the following work distribution among the various categories of architectural projects cited in the survey (sample average for each project category is reported in parentheses): commercial, office, and retail, 23% (26%); housing, 17.9% (21.5%); industrial 9.4% (7%); educational, 17.5% (15.5%); medical 15% (8.5%); other institutional, 5.7% (7.8%); and prime engineering, 2% (1%). The older firms also reported a lower percentage for interior design and planning. Despite the possible skewness of average figures, this indicates that the older firms tend to work more for corporate than for private clients. Table 10.7 indicates that, with the exceptions of the firms founded in 1975 and the new-born firms of 1977, the firms 20 years old or older (founded, that is, before 1958) had more international work in 1977 than did the others, which fits with the notion that professional reputation and international contacts take time to establish, unless exceptional circumstances intervene.

Our data do not allow us to go further, although they do indicate the presence of dominant professional firms: older, well-established, larger, with more technical personnel, working on larger and technologically complex buildings (such as might be included in the "industrial" or "medical" categories) and enjoying a national and international reputation. Obviously, this type of firm can appear at any time, provided circumstances are favorable. Among such favorable circumstances are wealthy clients and the willingness of the principals to adopt a corporate business form.

# SIZE AS ASSOCIATED WITH PROFESSIONAL PRACTICE

We turn now to an examination of the variation and influence of the firms' size, measured by the total number of employees of each firm. In her Manhattan study, Judith Blau reports that "size has pronounced and consistent influence with respect to overall project activity, organizational complexity, measures of staff composition and project quality" (Blau, 1978: 6). Despite the limitations of our data, we can explore similar relationships between size, composition of the work force, and other characteristics of the AIA firms' practice. While some correlations may be interpreted as *effects* of size, it should be noted that size itself is a dependent variable, determined by the productivity and profitability of a firm and conditioned, therefore, by the firm's age and reputation, by the nature of its clients, and by the scale and complexity of the projects it has and can continue to secure. We summarize in table 10.8 the correlations between the size of the firm and other aspects of practice that are found to be statistically significant; correlations between other characteristics of the labor force than sheer size and some dimensions of architectural practice are discussed further on.

As the table reveals, there are significant, although weak, correlations between size and the location of our firms' practice, as measured by the percentages of practice in the same state, out of state, and international. It is quite logical to find that larger firms are more likely to work nationwide and abroad; we can not tell, however, whether they simply add on international and out-of-state work to their local activities, which then tend to take second or third place in the firms' allocation of time and effort, or whether large firms tend to abandon the local market for projects of wider scope that are also, presumably, of greater scale, complexity, and profitability. It should be noted at this point that only a small

TABLE 10.8

*Significant Correlations Between Size of Labor Force
and Aspects of Architectural Practice*

| PERCENTAGE OF WORK | PEARSON $r$ | LEVEL OF SIGNIFICANCE |
|---|---|---|
| In the same state | −.22 | .00 |
| In other states | .16 | .00 |
| Internationally | .44 | .00 |
| In housing | −.10 | .01 |
| In medical projects | .09 | .01 |
| In prime engineering | .15 | .00 |
| In planning | .09 | .01 |

percentage of the firms in our sample (6.2%) do any international work at all. While all firms do at least some local work, 47% work *only* in the same state; of the 53% that do work in other states, 25.5% do less than 10% of all their work out of state while 27.5% perform more than 10% of all their work out of state.

The predominance of local practice fits with the large part played by housing in the activities of the AIA firms in our sample: it takes second rank to "commercial, office, and retail" and represents 21.5% of the average practice (see table 10.9). Housing is negatively associated, though weakly, with firm size (see table 10.8, col. 4) and with the presence of engineers on the staff ($r = -.14$), and it also shows a negative correlation with a gross indicator of bureaucratization, given by the ratio of administrative employees to the total work force ($r = -.09$, significant .10).

As shown in table 10.8, size is associated with the percentage of prime engineering conducted by the firms, with the percentage of planning in the practice, and with the number of medical projects undertaken, as a proportion of the total practice. It can be said, in sum, that the larger a firm is the more likely it is to design international projects and/or projects with a high technical component, as is true of the oldest large firms. Accordingly, the larger firms tend to do less housing and less "commercial, office, and retail work," as can be inferred from the negative association of the latter with the presence of engineers ($r = -.07$, significant at .04) and of other technicians ($r = -.10$, significant at .01).

The presence of design specialists other than architects—landscape architects and interior designers—is similarly associated with the kind of practice characteristic of larger firms: the diversity of design personnel is

TABLE 10.9

*Types of Building as Mean Percentages of the
1977 Practice of AIA Firms*

| BUILDING TYPES | MEAN PERCENTAGE OF PRACTICE |
| --- | --- |
| Commercial, office, retail | 26.3% |
| Housing | 21.5 |
| Industrial | 7.0 |
| Educational | 15.5 |
| Medical | 8.5 |
| Other institutional | 7.8 |
| Interior Design | 3.3 |
| Planning | 3.1 |
| Prime engineering | 1.0 |
| Other | 4.7 |

positively associated with out-of-state activities ($r$ = .12, significant at .00) and negatively with percentage of activities in the same state ($r$ = −.10, significant at .01); it is also related to the percentage of the firms' projects that involves planning ($r$ = .34, significant at .00).

We may consider now the effects this situation has on the quality of design as it can be assessed through the number of AIA awards reported by the firms in our sample.

## TYPE OF FIRM, TYPE OF PRACTICE, AND AWARDS

Our intention is to search for indications about the characteristics of the firms and their projects that tend to be associated with the achievement of professional recognition. The limitations of the data reported by the *Profile of Architectural Firms* (American Institute of Architects, 1978) are quite real. First of all, it is possible that the kinds of projects in which our firms were engaged in 1977 were anomalous with respect to their prior practice, for which almost a fifth of them had received AIA awards. Second, we only have information on AIA awards at the chapter, state, and national levels, and there are other types of awards for which we have no data. However, we can assume that awards granted by the official professional association are particularly meaningful for professionals who must submit their own work to be judged, and who thereby show that they care for the symbolic awards distributed by the AIA. Third, award juries pay little if any attention to what clients or users have to say about a building, or about how the building *performs* or whether it improves with use or not. Not surprisingly, we know of no study that has linked the winning of awards to an effective measure of client satisfaction, such as would be their repeated choice of the same firm for different purposes.

In sum, the AIA describes its honors program as intending to "bring attention to the achievements of individual architects" as well as promote public understanding "of the meaning and contextual responsibility of design excellence," but its awards are above all an official mark of esteem given by professionals to other professionals: as such, they constitute an implicit definition, for internal more than external use, of what architecture ought to be. Let us see now what portrait we can sketch of the kind of firm that tends to be given a leading role in this tacit definition of good architecture.

Table 10.10 presents the distribution of awards per region and the mean number of awards per firm in each region. As may readily be seen, the higher means are to be found both in the older regions (Middle Atlan-

TABLE 10.10
*Awards Won by AIA Sample Firms per Subregion*

| SUBREGION | N OF AWARDS | MEAN (AWARDS PER N OF FIRMS) |
|---|---|---|
| North East | 7 | 0.29 |
| Middle Atlantic | 57 | 0.67 |
| East North Central | 69 | 0.87 |
| West North Central | 24 | 0.53 |
| South Atlantic | 47 | 0.47 |
| East South Central | 20 | 0.80 |
| West South Central | 52 | 0.75 |
| Mountain | 10 | 0.25 |
| Pacific | 61 | 0.53 |
| Total | 347 | 0.60 |

tic and East North Central) and in growth areas such as the Eastern and Western South Central states.

Considering the relatively small proportion of sample firms that had won any AIA awards during their professional life (114, or about 20%), we decided to forego the analysis of multiple award winners and to dichotomize the variable, comparing the characteristics of the firms that had received one or more awards with those of the firms that had not won any. Table 10.11 lists the results of the difference of means tests performed. While differences were computed for 27 variables related to the work force and to the firms' practice, only 16 tests are significant. The Eta$^2$ values indicate what proportion of variance in each of the characteristics listed is explained by a firm's membership in either the awards or the no-awards categories. As is logical, the leading relationship is that between the winning of awards and the firm's orientation to design, reflected in the number of architects it employs. It is the latter's presence which accounts for the relationship with the next most important variable (in terms of Eta$^2$), the number of design professionals, composed of arthitects and landscape and interior designers. The two last specialties of design distinguish the most sharply between award-winning and nonaward-winning firms (the ratios between their respective means are the highest in table 10.11), but the very small number of landscape and interior designers employed by *either* category of firms suggests that their mere presence, while it makes a difference, is itself an effect of the total size of the professional staff, in which the number of architectural employees is more significantly associated with differences in design quality than are the (small) numbers of other design specialists. The same reasoning applies the the presence of engineering employees, which also clearly separates award-winning firms from the others; it is through their

*271*

TABLE 10.11

*Difference of Means Test*
*Award winners and Non winners*

| VARIABLES | FIRMS WITH NO AWARDS | FIRMS WITH ONE OR MORE AWARDS | RATIO | SIGNIFI-CANCE | ETA$^2$ |
|---|---|---|---|---|---|
| Mean $N$ of Architectural Employees | 4.17 | 14.45 | 3.47 | .00 | 5.27 |
| Mean $N$ of design professionals* | 4.40 | 15.64 | 3.55 | .00 | 5.13 |
| Mean $N$ of administrative employees | 1.05 | 4.42 | 4.21 | .00 | 3.78 |
| Total $N$ employees | 6.83 | 24.21 | 3.54 | .00 | 3.64 |
| Mean $N$ of landscape architects | .04 | .25 | 6.25 | .00 | 3.25 |
| Mean $N$ of interior designers | .19 | .94 | 4.95 | .00 | 2.49 |
| Mean % of activity international | .52 | 2.41 | 4.63 | .00 | 2.45 |
| % of firms that are corporations | 26.55 | 43.86 | 1.65 | .00 | 2.25 |
| Mean % of business devoted to planning | 2.75 | 4.66 | 1.69 | .00 | 1.61 |
| Mean % of business devoted to medical | 7.78 | 11.59 | 1.49 | .01 | 1.09 |
| Mean age (years) | 15.35 | 19.18 | 1.25 | .01 | 1.00 |
| Mean % of business devoted to educational | 14.47 | 19.55 | 5.08 | .02 | .93 |
| Mean $N$ of engineering employees | .71 | 2.99 | 4.21 | .02 | .91 |
| Mean % of business devoted to housing | 22.54 | 17.18 | .76 | .03 | .75 |
| Mean % of business devoted to commercial, office, retail | 27.25 | 22.62 | .83 | .05 | .63 |

NOTE: The variables are ranked in terms of the values of Eta$^2$ ,which indicates the proportion of their variance explained by the fact that the firms have won awards or not, expressed also in percentages in the first two columns of the table. The relationships are therefore ranked in decreasing order of strength.

*Design professionals include architectural employees, landscape architects, and interior designers.

dependence on the total size of the staff that their influence is felt, and the low Eta$^2$ value would suggest that the technological complexity of a project that demands engineering is to some extent dissociated from its aesthetic value. This inference becomes more plausible if we consider that neither the percentage of industrial projects in a firm's business, nor the percentage of prime engineering it does is significantly related to the achievement of awards.

In sum, because the number of specialists of any kind is contingent upon the total number of employees, we can interpret the winning of design awards as a variable that is multiply and most clearly linked to *size*, and to various components or determinants of size. Such characteristics as the percentage of international business conducted in 1977 and the age of a firm would therefore be related to the winning of awards through their association with size: indeed, international projects were not listed among the AIA national awards for 1958–1976 and would obviously not appear among local or state awards. Moreover, the top award winners in our sample, according to juridical form, are the business corporations, with a mean of 1.06, and these firms have 15.2 employees on average (mean), second only to partnerships (mean = 20.0). (see tables 10.12 and 10.5); in 1977, the business corporations reported no international activity at all.

We may, in conclusion, trace a tentative portrait of the firm that tends to win awards in our sample, based on the data summarized in Tables 10.10, 10.11, and 10.12. It is either located in one of the two traditional centers of architectural design, the Eastern Seaboard or the northern Midwest, or in one of the Southern or Western growth areas; it tends to adopt the new corporate business form and is, presumably, more highly capitalized and more bureaucratic in organization than the other types of firm; when it is not a business corporation, it engages in more international activity than other firms; on the whole, it is somewhat older; it devotes less of its time and efforts to the traditional small-scale activities (housing and commercial); and more of its work is in medical, educational, or planning projects. In any case, the award-winning firm is larger and it employs more administrators and professionals than the less rewarded firms; among its professionals, designers and architects, in particular, logically play an important role. It is, we could say, a successful *professional* firm, contrasting with the smaller, business-oriented and

TABLE 10.12

*Awards Won by AIA Sample Firms per Juridical Type*

| TYPE | N OF FIRMS | % WINNING AWARDS | MEAN % AWARDS |
|---|---|---|---|
| Proprietor | 268 | 9.3 | .27 |
| Partner | 129 | 21.7 | .93 |
| Professional association | 10 | 20.0 | .40 |
| Professional corporation | 107 | 28.0 | .73 |
| Business corporation | 67 | 29.8 | 1.06 |
| No information | 2 | – | – |
| Total | 583 | 19.5 | 0.60 |

marginal entrepreneurial firm that constitutes the majority in our sample and in the profession. It may also represent a type different from the large firm that emphasizes technological excellence and economic efficiency.

As Judith Blau discovered in her Manhattan study, the old distinction architects make in jest between clients "who want it good" and clients "who want it Wednesday" translates itself into the emphasis that the principals of large firms tended to place on economic criteria of cost, profits, and efficiency, over the criteria of user satisfaction and long-lasting aesthetic value, favored instead by the heads of small firms. Blau found, however, that "if small firms abandon this approach, they win more awards; and if large firms adopt [it], they win more awards" (Blau, 1976: 127). Her study suggests that the principals' ideas seem to have the most impact in the larger and more complex firms, while structural diversity and organizational efficiency are what help the smaller firms the most, if and when they manage to achieve them, which is not likely. Without minimizing the complex and largely undetermined nature of the design process, these findings create the impression that awards tend to go to balanced products that express both the constraints and the creative freedom of architectural work. Awards, we might say, seek to define that combination of "firmness, comfort and delight" which, since Vitruvius, has constituted the elusive essence of good architecture.

As in every professional field, only a few are called to this official task of "definition." First of all, the awarding juries choose projects that fit a pre-established idea of what architecture ought to be, or agree on what kinds of experiments and innovations ought to be encouraged. Since their notions are not made out of thin air, the choices tend to reinforce, within the profession, images consistent with the varieties of practice and the ideas of visible and influential elites. These images are diffused through publication, through the voice of official spokesmen, and, most importantly, through education, which is normally controlled by professional elites. In the second place, unlike other established professions, architects capture only a small and fluctuating segment of the market for design services (two-fifths, it is said without real basis, and one-fifth in home building); it follows that not too many of them have *both* sufficient control over the design process *and* a volume of work sufficient to allow concentration on the design of some projects, or to support innovative or architecturally ambitious work with proceeds from their bread-and-butter practice. This obviously works in favor of the large firms with multiple projects and a solid market position. In the third place, there has been, traditionally, a tendency (only partially corrected or reversed) to reward "perfect" buildings that tend to be of certain types – the monument, or the single house. While the latter tends to single out the exclusive dwellings of the rich, the monuments of our time are large-scale, institutional buildings commissioned by private or public corporate clients. This tendency also favors the large firm, which has the resources in personnel, equipment, and specialized human capital that large-scale design requires. However, overspecialization in high-technology projects (for instance, hospitals or factories), does not seem to favor the kind of design excellence that is officially rewarded in the profession. While it is conceivable that highly specialized firms may devote their technical specialists to a variety of projects, or hire for themselves the best design talent on the market, it is rather more likely that they would not: as in other professions, some segments go commercial or follow market trends, which is a very poor way of saying that they choose to seek material rewards *without* the mediation of professional authority—that combination of real and symbolic power which gives its holders the right to speak for the professional and to define its field. The largest providers of architectural design—most of those who make the list of 300 leading design firms—appear simply to have broken loose from professional control and the symbolic rewards it dispenses.

We are left, therefore, with two segments of the architectural profession which do not quite fit the *professional* image of authoritative success: one—the economic leader—is likely to be extremely under-represented in the AIA survey; the other—the struggling entrepreneurial firm, with one principal, few, if any, employees, and mostly small-scale projects that are seldom noticed by the profession—appears to constitute the bulk of our sample. We would like to argue that these diametrically opposed professional "marginals" design most of what architects design: the former in physical and economic volume, the latter in number of projects. Both are adapted to their markets and both are vulnerable to market fluctuations, although the entrepreneurial architect seems better able to adapt his small-scale, low capital practice to changing social needs and to people's wants. If our hypothesis is correct, it would suggest the need for a revision of what architectural education has been and continues to be—a revision that would take into account the uneven and segmented development of the design market, of which development our descriptive study offers indirect, albeit ubiquitous, evidence.

Furthermore, if it were true that the oldest design profession defines good architectural practice in terms that tend to exclude both the most numerous and the most powerful providers, the finding would confirm general trends observed in the law, for instance, and even in medicine. These trends ultimately suggest that the professional model organized around market control, autonomy, and peer review is itself becoming marginal in the evolving organization of highly skilled services.

# NOTES

1. Variable (and unreliable) estimates of the share of architect-designed buildings in annual building output in the U.S. range from 5% to 20%.

2. Selected groups of *male* professionals (figures in thousands) and percentage of growth in the 1960-70 period:

|  | 1960 | 1960 | % Growth |
|---|---|---|---|
| Total professional, technical, and kindred | 4,366 | 6,917 | 58.4* |
| Architects | 37 | 55 | 48.6 |
| Engineers (all specialties) | 864 | 1,210 | 40.0 |
| Civil engineers | 157 | 173 | 10.2 |
| Lawyers and judges | 211 | 260 | 23.2 |
| Physicians and surgeons | 217 | 256 | 18.0 |

SOURCE: U.S. Bureau of the Census, Statistical Abstracts of the U.S., 1977.
*Much of this growth in the total was contributed by teachers (82.8%) and accountants (27.19).

3. In contrast, for large firms, the advantage that size, resources, and number of projects confer for the winning of awards is offset, to some extent, by bureaucratic characteristics. Problems of communication and coordination appear to be generated by specialization and the existence of subdivisions; the presence of personnel rules and formal regulations governing work have a negative effect on the winning of awards, as does the lack of personnel participation in design decisions. In large firms only, the over-riding concern of the principals with economic and efficiency criteria, to the detriment of a concern for the needs and satisfaction of *users* (which are different from the requirements of *clients*) has a negative effect on the winning of awards (Blau, 1976).

4. The 1977 survey includes 6,845 cases in the United States. The estimated 90% rate of response yields an approximate total of 7,605 member firms. According to the special census study of 1972, architectural firms numbered 10,076 in that year; while this figure cannot be used as a firm base for estimating the percentage of architectural firms that are included in the AIA listings, we may use it as an indication, since the years 1972 through 1977 were marked by pronounced recession in the building sector and could not have exhibited much growth in the architectural sector. Taken indicatively, the AIA firms in the survey represent at most 67% of the total.

5. The AIA dues structure is double: members pay a flat rate, depending on the level of their association (members, associates, or fellows). Moreover, owners of firms pay supplemental dues (in addition to the regular dues), which are a percentage of their FICA payments. Interviews conducted among principals of very large firms in 1978 suggested that some of them considered themselves penalized by this dues structure and were, furthermore, in disagreement with certain AIA policies, which in their eyes were of exclusive benefit to small proprietor firms. These were reasons adduced for leaving the AIA. As a consequence of the crisis in construction, particularly acute in the Northeast, membership since 1977 has diminished in this region, though it has increased nationwide. We thank Pro-

fesor Peter Arfaa of the School of Architecture, Drexel University, for this information.

6. The following were used as sources for the state data file: Association of Collegiate Schools of Architecture (1979); U.S. Bureau of the Census (1970, 1977); Census of Selected Service Industries (1972).

7. While heavy manufacturing, for instance, tends to locate along resource and market-oriented transportation routes, industries that depend on "external economies" and a high degree of face-to-face interaction tend to cluster in central locations. For a more complete discussion of economic location factors, see Duncan et al. (1960); Hoover (1948); Perloff et al. (1960); and Vernon (1957).

8. In our sample, the modal category is 1 (who might be the actual principal), while the mean is 6 employed architects.

9. A study of graduates of 34 architectural schools found that the average proportion of those who obtained their registration (among various cohorts of graduates) was 34.8%. Despite the serious flaws of the study, the figure can be considered an indication of how many architectural graduates do not go on to obtain a license (Gutman and Westergard, 1978: 6).

10. A survey of the members of the AIA prepared by Case and Co., Inc. (1974), found that only 48% had NCARB certification.

11. The dollar volume of contracts grew by 19% from 1971 to 1972, in both total heavy construction and large-scale residential building, but only by 7% in total nonresidential construction (*Engineering News Record*, 1972: 39).

12. It is legally possible for partners in architecture to incorporate segments of their firm (for instance, their drafting services) while remaining a partnership, in which the principals bill each other on paper for service rendered or for using the incorporated parts. This kind of arrangement explains the greater flexibility of the partnership as a juridical form and its variability as a type of firm. We are indebted to Mr. Leon Ruderman, Certified Public Accountant, for this and other information on the juridical types of architectural firms.

13. "Type" is not equally significant for all the categories of design specialists. Considering only the most recent types, associated with bureaucratization and complexity, the percentages of firms that have one or more of the following are shown in the table below:

| Sample | | Professional Corporations | Business Corporations |
|---|---|---|---|
| Engineers | 18 | 19 | 40 |
| Landscape architects | 5 | 8 | 12 |
| Interior designers | 15 | 17 | 34 |
| Other technicians | 22 | 24 | 42 |
| Administration employees | 66 | 76 | 88 |
| Total *N* | 583 | 107 | 67 |

## REFERENCES

American Institute of Architects
  1978    Profile of Architectural Firms. Philadelphia: Archmedia, Inc.

Association of Collegiate Schools of Architecture.
  1979    Architecture Schools of North America. Washington, D. C.:
          Association of Collegiate Schools of Architects.

Arrow, K.
  1976    Essays in the Theory of Risk Bearing. New York: Elsevier.

Blau, J.
  1976    "Beautiful buildings and breaching the laws." International Journal
          of Sociology 12: 110–128.

  1978    Organization of Architectural Practice, Washington, D.C.: Associa-
          tion of Collegiate Schools of Architects.

Breckenfeld, G.
  1971    "The architects want a voice in redesigning America," Fortune
          Magazine 84: 144–155.

Case & Co., Inc.
  1974    AIA: Survey of the Membership. Washington, D.C.: American In-
          stitute of Architects.

Duncan, O. D. et al.
  1960    Metropolis and Region. Baltimore: Johns Hopkins University Press.

Ehrenreich, J. and B. Ehrenreich
  1979    "The professional managerial class." In P. Walker (ed.), Between
          Labor and Capital. Boston: South End Press.

Ehrenreich J.
  1981    "Class and Professionalism: Some Comments on the Sociology of
          the Professions," Unpublished paper. State University of New York
          at Old Westbury.

Engineering News Record
  1972    97th Annual Report and Forecast, Jan. 20.

Friedman, M.
  1962    Capitalism and Freedom. Chicago: University of Chicago Press.

Gross, R. and P. Osterman, eds.
  1972    The New Professionals. New York: Simon and Schuster.

Gutman, R. and B. Westergard
  1978    "What Architecture Schools Know About Their Graduates." Journal
          of Architectural Education 31: 2–11.

Hoover, E. M.
  1948    The Location of Economic Activity. New York: McGraw-Hill.

Larson, M. S.
  1977    The Rise of Professionalism; A Sociological Analysis. Berkeley:
          University of California Press.

  1979    "Professionalism: Rise and Fall." International Journal of Health
          Services 9:4.

Perloff, H. S. et al.
  1960    Regions, Resources and Economic Growth. Baltimore: Johns Hopkins University Press.

U.S. Bureau of the Census
  1970    Statistical Abstracts of the U.S.

  1972    Census of Selected Service Industries.

  1977    Statistical Abstracts of the U.S.

Vernon, Raymond
  1957    "Production and Distribution in the Large Metropolis, Annals of the American Academy of Political and Social Science, 114.

# 11 Structural Aspects of the Architectural Profession

JOHN CULLEN

## THE THEORETICAL PROBLEM

Social scientists and many different groups of occupational practitioners have had difficulty dealing with the structural or occupation-level components of professionalism. A trained incapacity to view occupational professionalism in anything other than definitional terms has developed. In the sociological literature on the professions the authors are continually plagued by the question of what occupational characteristics make a "true" profession. Similarly, the journals published by professional associations often contain articles asking: "Does our occupation have the characteristics of a 'true' profession?" This paper argues that there is no "true" definition of professionalism and that the quest for such a definition has little theoretical utility for social scientists and little practical utility for occupational groups. It suggests instead that, by looking at relationships among occupational characteristics and thus laying the groundwork for specifying the conditions that lead to the development of specific professional attributes, one can make useful theoretical statements to aid occupational groups in understanding their relative position in the system of professionalism. The profession of architecture illustrates these points.

Three major topics are dealt with. First, the theoretical drawbacks associated with searching for the "true" dimensions of professionalism are reviewed. Second, the distribution of selected dimensions of professionalism in the American occupational structure is examined empirically. Third, the professional status of architecture is viewed from the

This article is reprinted with the permission of the Association of Collegiate Schools of Architecture. It appeared in the *Journal of Architectural Education* vol. 31, No. 2, 1978.

perspective of a multidimensional view of professionalism. Architecture is then compared with other highly professionalized occupations.

In their classic study of the professions, Carr-Saunders and Wilson (1933: 284) analyzed nearly thirty occupations. They concluded that while it is impossible to distinguish professions from nonprofessions absolutely, "nevertheless the term profession clearly stands for something. That something is a complex of characteristics. The acknowledged professions exhibit all or most of these features . . . and all around them on all sides are grouped vocations exhibiting some but not all of these features." Statements such as this naturally beg the question of what these distiguishing features are. Not surprisingly, the vast majority of workers who have attempted to make general assertions about the nature of professionalism have begun (and also usually ended) by proposing some answer to the defintional question (Cogan, 1953).

The definitional approaches to professionalism fall into two categories. The first is a historical typology whereby specific occupational attributes are defined as professional and the process of becoming a profession is seen as the sequential development of the identified professional attributes (Wilensky, 1964). The second form of definitional typology is a dimensional approach (Elliot, 1972). In the dimensional approach, professions are considered as distinct from other occupations — either dichotomously or along continua — because of their supposedly qualitative differences on the elements or dimensions of professionalism. However, because occupations can be considered to vary from totally lacking to highly developed on a professional dimension, the majority of recent writings have subsumed the historical developmental approach under a broader application of the dimensional perspective. The professionalization of an occupation is then seen as the simultaneous movement along the various dimensional continua, with the occupations that are further developed on many dimensions being considered the more professionalized.

Perhaps the major deficiency in the definitional search for the intrinsic nature of professionalism is methodological. Many studies exhibit the tendency to adopt what Karl Popper has called "methodological essentialism. Methodological essentialism takes the stance that the aim of science is to arrive at the true nature of things primarily through an intuitive comprehension of their essences. From this viewpoint, the scientific understanding of phenomena is expressed through definitions.

Opposed to methodological essentialism is the position of "methodological nominalism." As Popper has noted:

Instead of aiming at finding its true nature, methodological nominalism aims at describing how a thing behaves in various circumstances, and especially, whether there are any regularities in its behavior. . . . The methodological nominalist will never think that a question like "What is energy?" or "What is movement?" or "What is an atom?" is an important question for physics; but he will attach importance to a question like: . . . "Under what condition does an atom radiate light?" (1962: 32).

Because their lists of the essential components of professionalism were derived not so much from pure intuition as from observation, some of the definitional typologies of professionalism are not completely in the methodological essentialists' camp. However, the preoccupation with "What is?" in nearly all typologies of professionalism has almost precluded the study of the nominalist question: "Under what conditions does an occupation develop a code of ethics?"

The predominance of the definitional search for the "true" characteristics of professionalism is linked to the objectives of many previous empirical investigations of professionalism. Two types of empirical approaches can be distinguished. The first is the simple case study of a single occupation, and the second is the comparative study of several occupations. Case studies have usually accepted some ideal-typical definition as given and compared the characteristics of the occupation in question with the definition. Comparative studies for the most part have taken a somewhat different approach: they have accepted certain occupations as "true" professions and then compared other occupations to the a priori accepted "true" professions. However, even with their relatively empirical as opposed to intuitive base, most empirical studies of professionalism have failed to go beyond the essentialist's question of "What is professionalism?"

The shortcomings of the case study approach suggest that a comparative study of a representative sample of occupations (both accepted professions and nonprofessions) might be the better method for achieving a general consideration of the sociological processes associated with occupations developing the dimensions of professionalism. To quote Blau:

> The comparative method, in the broadest sense of the term, underlies all scientific and scholarly theorizing. If we mean by theory a set of generalizations that explains courses of events or situations on the basis of the conditions and processes that produce them, every theory must rest on comparisons of contrasting cases; for to explain a state of affairs requires that the differences between it and some other state of affairs be accounted for (1965).

Comparative studies of occupations that have attempted to deal more comprehensively with professionalism have not been completely lacking in the literature of the sociology of occupations. Unfortunately, Blau's advice about the nature of comparative research has not been heeded. Perhaps most disturbing is the paucity of quantitative studies that attempt to examine the relationships among the dimensions of professionalism. As a result, we have little knowledge, for example, of what professional or other occupational characteristics are related to the fact that some occupational groups require lengthy periods of university-based training.

Hickson and Thomas are perhaps one notable exception. They (1969) have reported findings showing that an overall scale of professionalism was moderately related to the age of the major "qualifying" association ($r = .41$) and slightly related to the number of members in the association ($r = .15$). However, for the most part, they did not attempt to specify the relationships among professionalism's variables but, rather, they attempted to develop an overall scale of professionalism using Guttman Scaling Techniques. The Hickson and Thomas study notwithstanding, the sequential description of occupations as to their location on various professional dimensions unfortunately remains in vogue as the primary analytical technique for the comparative study of occupational professionalism.[2]

## USES AND ABUSES OF DEFINITIONS

Since it has been argued that encompassing definitions of professionalism have little theoretical or practical utility, one may then ask how professionalism should be conceptualized. Professionalism is perhaps best thought of as a broad "sensitizing concept" which tells us something about the occupational characteristics on which occupations are stratified (Blumer, 1954). However, any particular definition's list of characteristics is arbitrary, and even if a definition is accepted as specifying *the* elements of professionalism, it is a pre-emptory act to draw a boundary between professions and nonprofessions. Thus, for social science researchers, it is argued that the ideal types serve only as an aid in specifying *some* of the conditions that *might* give rise to the fact that different occupational groups have different prestige, income, and power.

For occupational groups such as architects, the inherent weaknesses of definitions of professionalism have two important implications. First, self-analyses that ask, "Are we a 'true' profession?" are probably meaningless. Architects worried about competitors from other occupations might find it more useful to ask the methodological nominalist's question: "What characteristics of our occupation probably lead to our present level of prestige, income, and power?" Second, even though it is argued that definitional questions associated with professionalism are theoretically meaningless, architects should realize that once a definition is accepted (especially by society's elite), the definition's impact on the social and economic well-being of the occupational group is often quite real.

Many occupational groups vie to be known as a profession or perhaps simply as more professionalized than some other occupational group(s). Moreover, some scholars argue that this process takes place through convincing society's members or agencies that the group is a "true" profession (Ritzer, 1975). For example, many occupational groups try to convince state governments that their occupation is sufficiently professionalized so that the state's protection through licensure can eliminate the "unqualified" from both practicing the occupation's tasks and judging the occupation's performance. Architecture went through this phase around 1900. Similarly, universities are often told that a particular occupation possesses techniques that should be learned only at a university. Recent empirical evidence has shown that, regardless of the intrinsic nature of an occupation's tasks, success at achieving licensure and education (beyond that seemingly required by the occupation's tasks) increases income and prestige at least slightly (Cullen, 1978). Such findings imply that the process of occupational professionalization is partly political. Freidson, one of the proponents of such a view, has written: "A profession attains and maintains its position by virtue of the protection and patronage of some elite segment of society which has been persuaded that there is some special value in its work" (1970: 72).

## AN EMPIRICAL DESCRIPTION

Table 11.1 shows several of the more commonly cited features of professionalism mentioned in the sociological literature. With varying degrees of success, all the occupational characteristics listed in the table have been operationally measured by previous research.[2] In order to illustrate some structural characteristics of professionalism and, also, to discuss architecture's location on these selected characteristics, five (of the numerous possible) dimensions of professionalism are considered here. These dimensions are: complex relationships with people, degree of organization, length of training, licensure status, and high prestige.

*Empirical Indicators.* Although most characterizations of professionalism note only the extremes of professionalism's features (e.g., low or high prestige), the *variables* of professionalism's features must account for variation among all types of occupations ranging, for example, from the least educated to the most educated. Hence, five empirical indicators of the selected dimensions noted above were chosen so as to tap

TABLE 11.1

*Selected Dimensions of Professionalism by Citing Authors*

| Dimensions | Akers | Barber | Caplow | Carr-Saunders and Wilson | Cogan | Flexner | Foote | Goode | Greenwood | Gross | Lewis and Maude | Pavalko | Vollmer and Mills | Wilensky |
|---|---|---|---|---|---|---|---|---|---|---|---|---|---|---|
| Complex occupation | + | + | | + | + | + | + | + | + | + | | + | + | + |
| Self-employed | | | | + | | | | | | | | + | | |
| Complex relationships with people | | | | + | + | + | | + | | | | | | |
| Altruistic service | | | | | + | + | | + | | | | | | |
| Long training | + | + | | + | | | | + | + | | + | + | | + |
| Well organized | + | + | + | + | | + | + | + | + | + | + | + | + | + |
| Code of ethics | | + | + | + | | | | + | + | | + | + | | + |
| Competence tested | | | | + | | | | | | | | + | | |
| Licensed | + | + | | | | | | + | | | | | | + |
| High income | | | | + | | | | + | | | | | | |
| High prestige | | | + | | | | | + | | | | | | |

NOTE: Aspects of this table were taken from G. Millerson, *The Qualifying Associations: A Study in Professionalization* (London: Routledge and Kegan Paul, 1964), p. 5.

a range of occupational variation on each characteristic (see table 11.2).

For most of the variables, the correspondence with the dimensions of professionalism are fairly evident. However, *complex relations with people* needs further explanation. This measure was derived from the U.S. Department of Labor's *Dictionary of Occupational Titles* (1965; 1966). DOT contains numerous analytical data for classifying more than 20,000 jobs. One of the DOT's basic assumptions is that all jobs involve functional relationships, in varying degrees, with data, people, and things. Using a sophisticated observation schedule, trained job analysts estimate a job's involvement with the three functional areas (data, people, things). Jobs are then ranked hierarchically in each area from the most to the least complex (Fine, 1968). Because of the obvious relationship to common definitions of professionalism, we are concerned here only with occupations identified as having complex relationships to people.

For this study, data for all specialized jobs forming the more general occupational groups were averaged so as to arrive at one overall estimate of an occupation's functional complexity of working with people.

TABLE 11.2

*Selected Dimensions of Professionalism by Corresponding Empirical Indicators*

| THEORETICAL DIMENSIONS | EMPIRICAL INDICATORS |
|---|---|
| Complex relationships with people | Complexity w/people: An eight-point scale noting the involvement and complexity of an occupation's tasks as they are applied to people. SOURCE: U.S. Department of Labor, *Dictionary of Occupational Titles*, (3rd ed. (Washington, D.C.: U.S. Government Printing Office, 965). |
| Degree of organization | Membership completeness: The percentage of an occupational group that are members of the major national occupational association. SOURCES: Computed from U.S. Bureau of the Census, *Occupational Characteristics* Washington, D.C.: U.S. Government Printing Office, 1973); M. Fisk, ed, *Encyclopedia of Associations* (Detroit: Gale Research Company, 1974); U.S. Department of Labor, *Directory of National Unions and Employee Associations* (Washington D.C.: U.S. Government Printing Office, 1971; and various surveys of occupational associations. See J. B. Cullen, "The Structure of Professionalism," (Ph.D. dissertation, Columbia University, 1977). |
| Length of training | Median education: The median education achieved by the individuals in an occupation's experienced civilian labor force. SOURCE: U.S. Bureau of the Census, *Occupational Characteristics* (Washington, D.C.: U.S. Government Printing Office, 1973). |
| Licensure status | Licensure: The number of states in which an occupation is licensed, certified, or registered by the state government. SOURCES: Council of State Governments, *Occupations and Professions Licensed by the States, Puerto Rico and the Virgin Islands* (Chicago: Council of State Governments, 1968); U.S. Department of Labor, *Occupational Outlook Handbook* (Washington, D.C.: U.S. Government Printing Office, 1974). |
| Prestige | Prestige: An occupation's ranking on a recently developed occupational prestige scale. SOURCE: D. J. Treiman, "Problems of Concept and Measurement in the Comparative Study of Occupational Mobility," *Social Science Research* 4: 1975, 183–230. |

## Relationships among the Dimensions

Table 11.3 presents the matrix of zero-order correlations and descriptive statistics for the five empirical indicators of professionalism's dimensions. These correlations are based on data derived from a study of 267

TABLE 11.3

*Correlation Matrix and Descriptive Statistics for Selected Dimensions
of Professionalism Based on a Maximum of 267 Occupations*

|  | COMPLEXITY WITH PEOPLE | MEMBERSHIP COMPLETENESS | MEDIAM EDUCATION | LICENSURE | PRESTIGE |
|---|---|---|---|---|---|
| Membership completeness | .21 | | | | |
| Median education | .48 | .47 | | | |
| Licensure | .39 | .33 | .55 | | |
| Prestige | .31 | .41 | .82 | .48 | |
| Mean | 1.3 | 23.8 | 13.2 | 8.9 | 44.9 |
| SD | 2.0 | 29.0 | 2.7 | 19.1 | 15.0 |
| *n* | 267 | 155 | 267 | 235 | 237 |

nonfarm occupations representing approximately 55 percent of the *individuals* in the experienced labor force (U. S. Department of Labor, 1972: 649–50).

An examination of table 11.3 shows that, not unexpectedly, the dimensions of professionalism are positively interrelated. For example, occupational groups characterized by a lengthy education nearly always seem to have higher prestige but have a lesser likelihood of having complex relationships with people.

The lack of higher correlations among the dimensions suggests that these oft-cited elements of professionalism are not as concentrated in a few occupations as might have been expected. This interpretation is corroborated when these same dimensions of professionalism are examined for their distribution in what is probably the most used system of occupational classification—that employed by the U.S. Bureau of the Census.[3]

Table 11.4 is a summary of the Census Bureau's major occupational classifications, distributed in terms of the elements of professionalism examined in this study.

Most "professional, technical, and kindred workers" (hereafter called professional) fall above the mean on nearly all dimensions. Only on *complexity w/people* do fewer than 50 percent of the professional occupations rate higher than the mean. One feature revealed by this table is that the Census's professional occupations do not have an exclusive dominion over the selected professional elements. While it is true that no other occupational type has the professional classification's heavy concentration of occupations in the "high" (above the mean) category, all but the classification for manual labor have at least some "high" occupations.

Based on the theoretical arguments stated earlier, as well as the em-

TABLE 11.4

Proportion and Number of Occupations Above the Mean
on Selected Dimensions of Professionalism (Maximum of 267 Occupations)

| | OCCUPATIONAL CLASSIFICATIONS | | | | | | | | |
|---|---|---|---|---|---|---|---|---|---|
| DIMENSIONS | Professional, Technical, and Kindred Workers | Managers and Administrators, Except Farm | Sales Workers | Clerical and Kindred Workers | Craftsmen and Kindred Workers | Operatives, Except Transport | Transport Equipment Operatives | Laborers, Except Farm | Service Workers[a] |
| Complexity w/people | 44.9(40)[b] | 100.0(19) | 88.9(8) | 40.6(13) | 0.0(0) | 5.9(1) | 50.0(4) | 0.0(0) | 26.9(7) |
| Median education | 82.1(73) | 31.6(6) | 22.2(2) | 12.5(4) | 0.0(0) | 0.0(0) | 0.0(0) | 0.0(0) | 3.8(1) |
| Membership completeness | 67.8(46) | 20.0(3) | 28.6(2) | 12.5(3) | 41.1(7) | 16.7(7) | 0.0(0) | 0.0(0) | 30.0(6) |
| Licensure | 57.2(36) | 35.7(5) | 0.0(0) | 9.1(2) | 14.3(2) | 12.5(1) | 0.0(0) | 0.0(0) | 0.0(0) |
| Prestige | 95.2(80) | 64.7(11) | 11.1(1) | 43.3(13) | 6.1(4) | 0.0(0) | 0.0(0) | 0.0(0) | 17.4(4) |

NOTE: Data from the Census Bureau's major occupational classifications.
  Because of missing values, the same number of occupations do not equal the same percentages.
[a]This is a combination of two classifications: "Service Workers except Private Household Workers."
[b]Number of occupations in parenthesis.

pirical findings, this paper's major assertion concerning professionalism can now be summarized. Like individuals, each distinguishable occupation is unique. Selecting some arbitrary occupational characteristics (called, if one wishes, "elements of professionalism") allows one to examine relationships among the characteristics and to examine occupational similarity or dissimilarity. Moreover, giving equal or unequal weighting to the selected elements, it seems possible to rank occupations as to their overall (but definition-specific) degree of professional development. However, arbitrary distinctions between a priori designated "professional" or "nonprofessional" occupations seem useful only for classifications employed for the convenience of data storage (as with the Census Bureau's occupational statistics). Perhaps the most accurate statement about professionalism's singular nature is that one occupation is clearly distinguishable from any other on selected criteria. However, there is no group of occupations uniquely distinguishable as "professions"; rather, there exists a range of occupations, some of which are more "professionalized" on particular criteria than others.

Before examining the implications for architecture suggested by this study's view of professionalism, an additional point must be made. Because the dimensions of professionalism can be measured, it is possible to engage in a more sophisticated analysis (than simple correlations), specifying the presumably antecedent occupational characteristics than can account for variation on any selected dimension. While such an analysis is beyond the scope of this paper, previous research employing the data used here has developed regression models predicting the features of professionalism by variables indicating both the intrinsic qualities of occupational tasks *and* organization-based occupational power. The major theoretical conclusion from the research was that, although most of the variation in the elements of professionalism results from differences in the complexity of occupational tasks, the conscious efforts of occupational groups to increase their professional stature lead to marginal gains in developing more professionalized occupational characteristics (e.g., lengthier education, more occupational licensure and higher income and prestige).[4] Although the specific analyses comparing the effects of power and task-related criteria on professionalism's elements have not been discussed in this paper, inferences for architecture can be drawn from the earlier research.


## IMPLICATIONS FOR ARCHITECTURE

Data are now examined for seventeen occupations (including architecture) with university-based educational systems. We use this criterion as the initial basis for our analysis because most occupations regarded as "professional" (including architecture) depend upon higher education for entry to the occupation. The occupations are: architecture, business, dentistry, education, engineering, forestry, journalism, law, library science, medicine, music, nursing, optometry, pharmacy, social work, and veterinary medicine. Table 11.5 shows the zero-order correlations and related descriptive statistics for the selected features of professionalism.

As with the sample of occupations in general (table 11.3) these data show that the dimensions of professionalism are almost all positively—but not perfectly—interrelated. Thus, although the correlations are slightly stronger than for the sample of 267 occupations, the lack of perfect correlations shows that a certain "status inconsistency" exists at even the highest levels of professional status.[6] In other words, these 17 occupations are not equally professionalized on all the measured occupational characteristics. Hence, although high professionalization one dimension increases the likelihood of high professionalization on another, even at the highest levels of the occupational hierarchy most occupations have an unbalanced professional development. Table 11.6 shows architecture's ranking on the five dimensions of professionalism chosen for study. Like most other occupations, architecture is inconsistently developed in terms of professional attributes.

The characteristics of professionalism vary in the degree to which they can be consciously manipulated by occupational groups. Ethical codes,

TABLE 11.5

*Correlation Matrix and Descriptive Statistics for Selected Dimensions of Professionalism (Based on a Maximum of 17 Occupations with University-based Educational Systems)*

|  | COMPLEXITY WITH PEOPLE | MEMBERSHIP COMPLETENESS | MEDIAN EDUCATION | LICENSURE | PRESTIGE |
|---|---|---|---|---|---|
| Membership completeness | .33 |  |  |  |  |
| Median education | .41 | .68 |  |  |  |
| Licensure | − .09 | .49 | .47 |  |  |
| Prestige | .32 | .37 | .68 | .59 |  |
| Mean | 4.0 | 54.9 | 16.2 | 31.2 | 61.0 |
| SD | 3.4 | 36.9 | 2.0 | 21.7 | 8.5 |
| *n* | 17 | 14 | 17 | 16 | 17 |

NOTE: For computation of this correlation matrix, veterinary medicine was assigned a zero on the measure for complexity w/people. This differs from the U.S. Department of Labor's reported score where veterinary medicine is given a higher rank because of complex dealings with animals. See the U.S. Department of Labor's description of complexity w/people in the text.

TABLE 11.6

*Architecture's Position on Selected Dimensions of Professionalism*

| DIMENSIONS | RANK/NUMBER OF OCCUPATIONS RANKED |
|---|---|
| Complexity with people | 14/17 (four-way tie) |
| Membership completeness | 7/14 |
| Median education | 7/17 |
| Licensure | 1/16 (ten-way tie) |
| Prestige | 3/17 |

for example, are easily created by occupational associations (although often these associations are not vigorous in enforcing them). However, the basic tasks of an occupation seem more dependent on technological advances than on an occupational group's conscious efforts at change. In between lie characteristics like the degree of licensure. Such attributes of professionalism can be influenced by occupational groups, but the success of such efforts depends upon the agreement of state legislatures.

Of the five dimensions chosen for study, licensure, education, and membership completeness tend to be occupational features subject to manipulation by an occupational group. Primarily through their organizational activities, occupational groups can affect the number and content of their licensing laws, the length and content of their occupation-related education, and the degree to which the members of the occupational group join the national association. Alternatively, since prestige tends to be a static occupational characteristic over time and among countries, it is probably less susceptible to direct alteration by the occupational group. (Hodge, Siegel, and Rossi, 1966) Perhaps even more difficult to change is an occupation's involvement with people.

In obtaining licensure, the requirement of advanced education depends on convincing others (e.g., university administrators, state legislators) that an occupation is sufficiently professionalized (or sophisticated) to be granted a curriculum at the associate, baccalaureate, or doctoral level. Success at developing university-based curricula has not been uniform even for some of the accepted professions (Vesey, 1965).

Primarily because it has failed to make advanced professional training the *minimum* requirement for practice, architecture ranks only seventh among the seventeen university-based occupations. In fact, in 1973, the National Council of Architectural Registration Boards reported that it was still possible to achieve registration as a professional architect without graduation from an accredited school and, in some cases, without any formal academic training.

While there are probably unique historical reasons why architecture has remained comparatively less developed on the educational dimensions of professionalism, some power-related processes might be operating as well. The correlation between the number of states requiring licenses and the median years of education is fairly strong (.47 for the 267 occupations and .55 for the 17 occupations). This suggests that even though a well-developed educational system probably increases an occupation's chances of being licensed in the first place, once licensure is achieved, all practitioners must (typically) meet the specified educational standards if they hope to work in licensed states.

Since all fifty states have some form of licensing or registration statutes for architects, one might assume that architecture has a sufficient breadth of licensing coverage to easily affect the educational system and, in turn, the educational level of its practitioners. However, there seem to be two basic reasons why architecture lacks the strength (as compared to medicine, for example) to mandate a lengthy period of education for all its practitioners. First, some recent data show that only about 60 percent of architectural practitioners are registered (National Council of Architectural Registration Boards, 1973). In this respect, it can be argued that architecture is less professionalized (on this particular dimension) than occupations such as nursing where all active practitioners must have a current license. Looking at the historical vicissitudes of licensure for the medical profession, one may conclude that architecture has the potential for developing stronger laws mandating the registration of all practicing architects (Tabachnik, 1976). Moreover, a fully developed licensing system would also control the informal practice of architecture by related occupations.

The second factor has already been mentioned, namely, the absence of a statutory requirement that an occupational license be granted only to those graduating from approved or accredited schools (Grimm, 1972). This is a crucial point because, once individual licensure and educational accrediting are linked, the whole system of establishing credentials comes under the occupational group's direct and indirect influence. With both complete licensure and accreditation, the power to specify the length and content of education and, hence, the qualifications for occupational practice, is virtually secure from outside interference (Also see Finkin, 1973).

This interpretation can be substantiated by again looking at table 11.6. Not surprisingly, the proportion of the total number of schools that are accredited is positively related to the length of education (.42), and fairly strongly to the total number of states licensed (.79). However, architecture's seventh-place ranking among the seventeen occupations for the percentage of its schools that are accredited suggests (even with architecture's complete licensure) that an important link in the credential system has yet to be developed.[7]

A well-developed occupational organization is probably necessary if an occupational group is to realize its potential power. Previous research analyzing the data for the 267 occupations found that the degree to which members of the occupation were also members of an association was a good predictor of nearly all the elements of professionalism selected for examination (including several not discussed here.). Architecture's mid-level ranking on membership completeness implies that many architects have yet to see the benefits of a strong occupational organization. One can speculate that the artistic nature of the work may generate an individualistic attitude that inhibits intensive participation in an occupational association. However, considering that some are now arguing that architects will have to undertake a deliberate organized effort to maintain the market for their services, the future may see a relative increase in the completeness of membership in the American Institute of Architects (Gutman, 1977).

To convince state governments and universities that a particular occupation deserves special protection and consideration because its performance might affect human welfare is a basic component of the professionalization process. If an occupational group can present a credible argument along these lines, the development of such characteristics as licensure and lengthier schooling seems to follow. Medicine has been very successful in using this argument in the past because the physician works directly with people. Can architects, whose relationship to the public is filtered through client bureaucracies and the building industry, use the same argument in order to advance their professional status?

Architecture's number three ranking on the prestige scale shows that, regardless of its slightly lower rankings on other dimensions, society holds the job of an architect in high regard. However, in 1970, architecture ranked considerably lower in mean income (seventh).[8] The lack of a closer correspondence between income and prestige may simply result from the depression in the construction industry rather than from anything intrinsic to architecture itself. However, the argument can be made (and the data noted above seem to suggest) that architecture suffers economically because it is not better developed educationally (and, thus, produces a labor supply larger than the needs of the economy) and because the profession is not well organized (and, thus, the AIA is not sufficiently strong to promote more favorable legislation and publicity). At the present time, it seems that the major occupational reward for architects is a high social evaluation rather than a high economic status.

*John Cullen*

# CONCLUSION

The theoretical discussion and the generalizations derived from empirical data might seem to lead us to suggest that architects can and should make gains along the various professional continua. However, in many respects it may not be possible or even desirable for architecture to increase its relative professional stature. First, a deliberate effort aimed at increasing professional status would probably require a high degree of centralization for several functions now spread among several organizations—the American Institute of Architects, the Association of Collegiate Schools of Architecture, the National Architectural Accrediting Board, and the National Council of Architectural Registration Boards. The independence of these organizations is one factor limiting architecture's relative power to control access to the profession and, in turn, to increase occupational rewards, such as income. However, since these organizations are already separate entities, it may be politically impossible to centralize control sufficiently or, what would be even more powerful, to form a single organization incorporating all presently decentralized functions.

Second, there is a question whether attempts to increase architecture's professionalization are justifiable in terms of the nature of the field. Should a vocation such as architecture, which is both artistic and technical, define the explicit criteria for "qualified" schools, students, and practitioners? While to do so would undoubtedly increase architecture's general professional standing, to attempt to "objectify" all aspects of the qualifications for practice seems somewhat contrary to the intrinsically creative nature of high-quality architectural work. There is a dilemma regarding the compatibility of maximal professionalization in the structural sense (i.e., gains in all the commonly accepted dimensions of professionalism) and maximal professionalization in the sense of occupational performances that best serve the public interest (i.e., innovative, beautiful, and safe structures). Who should benefit from architecture's becoming more professionalized, the members of the occupational group or those who purchase and use architectural skills? It is unlikely that the needs of architects and the needs of the public can be served equally well.

# NOTES

1. Compare the approach of Carr-Saunders and Wilson (1933) with more recent works, such as Akers and Quinney (1968), Millerson (1964), Wilensky (1964).
2. These authors represent only a selection of those who have cited dimensions

of professionalism. Moreover, it should also be noted here that some might not agree with this author's classification of their dimensions. See, for example: Akers (1970), Barber (1963), Caplow (1954), Carr-Saunders and Wilson (1933), Cogan (1953), Foote (1953), Goode (1969), Greenwood (1957), Gross (1958), Pavalko (1971), Wilensky (1964).

3. Although the correlations are, of course, among the empirical indicators of the professional dimension, for brevity of presentation, the text often refers to correlations among dimensions. See Cullen (1978) for a complete description of the data and its sources.

4. For each of the dimensions of professionalism, the percentage of professional occupations falling one and two standard deviations above the mean are: 19.1/25.8 for complexity w/people; 37.3/30.5 for membership completeness; 28.6/28.6 for licensure; 27.0/55.1 for median education; and, 48.8/46.4 for prestige.

5. Data for the seventeen occupations were originally gathered for the Comparative Organization Research Program at Columbia University. The support of the National Science Foundation's grant SOC71–03617 is gratefully acknowledged.

6. Of course, the smaller sample size suggests that the correlations are less reliable, since even one or two abnormal cases might affect the relationship.

7. Source: National Commission on Accrediting (nd).

8. Source: U.S. Bureau of the Census (1973 — table 19).

# REFERENCES

Akers, R. L.
1970    "Framework for the comparative study of group cohesion." Pacific Sociological Review 13: 73–85.

Akers, R. L. and R. Quinney
1968    "Differential organization of health professions." American Sociological Review 33: 104–20.

Barber, B.
1963    "Some problems in the sociology of the professions." Daedalus 92: 669–88.

Blau, P. M.
1965    "The comparative study of organizations." Industrial and Labor Relations Review 18: 323–38.

Blumer, H.
1954    "What is wrong with social theory?" American Sociological Review 19: 3–10.

Caplow, T.
1954    The Sociology of Work. New York: McGraw-Hill.

Carr-Saunders, A. M.and P. A. Wilson
1933    The Professions. Oxford: Oxford University Press.

Cogan, M. L.
1953    "Towards a definition of a profession." Harvard Educational Review 23: 33–50.

Cullen, J. B.
  1978    The Structure of Professionalism. New York: Petrocelli.
Elliott, P.
  1972    The Sociology of the Professions. New York: Herder and Herder.
Fine, S. A.
  1968    "The use of the Dictionary of Occupational Titles as a source of educational and training requirements." Journal of Human Resources 3: 365–75.
Finkin, M. W.
  1973    "Federal reliance on voluntary accreditation." Journal of Law and Education 2: 339–75.
Foote, N. N.
  1953    "The professionalization of labor in Detroit." American Journal of Sociology 53: 371–80.
Freidson, E.
  1970    Professional Dominance. New York: Atherton.
Goode, W. J.
  1969    "The theoretical limits to professionalization." Pp. 266–313 in A. Etzioni (ed.), The Semi-professions and Their Organization. New York: Free Press.
Greenwood, E.
  1957    "Attributes of a profession." Social Work 2: 44–55.
Grimm, M. L.
  1972    "The relationship of accreditation to voluntary certification and state licensure." Pp. 1–42 in National Commission on Accrediting (ed.), part 2, Staff Working Papers, Accreditation of Health Education Programs. Washington, D.C.: NCA.
Gross, E.
  1958    Work and Society. New York: Crowell.
Gutman, R.
  1977    "Architecture: the entrepreneurial profession." Progressive Architecture 5: 54–8.
Hickson, D. J. and M. W. Thomas
  1969    "Professionalization in Britain." Sociology 3: 37–53.
Hodge, R. W. et al.
  1966    "Occupational prestige in the United States, 1925–1963." Pp. 322–34 in R. Bendix and S. M. Lipset (eds.), Class, Status, and Power. New York: Free Press.
Lewis, R. and A. Maude
  1953    Professional People in England. Cambridge: Harvard University Press.
Millerson, G.
  1964    The Qualifying Associations. New York: Humanities Press.
National Commission on Accrediting
  nd      Procedures of Accrediting in the Professions. Washington, D.C.: NCA.

National Council of Architectural Registration Boards
1973    "Regarding NCARB Organization, Services and Procedures, Records, Certifications, and Examinations." Circular of Information No. 1. Washington, D.C.: NCARB.

Pavalko, R. M.
1971    The Sociology of Occupations and Professions. Itasca, Ill.: Peacock.

Popper, K. R.
1962    The Open Society and Its Enemies. Princeton, N.J.: Princeton University Press.

Ritzer, G.
1975    "The emerging power approach to the study of the professions." Paper presented at the annual meeting of the American Sociological Association, San Francisco.

Tabachnik, L.
1976    "Licensing in the legal and medical professions, 1820–1860." Pp. 1–24 in J. Gerstl and G. Jacobs (eds.), Professions for the People. New York: Schenkman.

U.S. Bureau of the Census
1973    Census of the Population: 1970, Subject Reports, Final Report PC (2)–7A, Occupational Characteristics. Washington, D.C.: U.S. Government Printing Office.

U.S. Department of Labor
1965    Dictionary of Occupational Titles (3rd ed.), vols, 1, 2. Washington, D.C.: U.S. Government Printing Office.

1966    Dictionary of Occupational Titles, Supplement, Selected Characteristics of Occupations. Washington, D.C.: U.S. Government Printing Office.

1972    Handbook for Analyzing Jobs. Washington, D.C.: U.S. Government Printing Office.

1973    Occupational Handbook. Washington, D.C.: U.S. Government Printing Office.

Vesey, L. R.
1965    The Emergence of the American University. Chicago: University of Chicago Press.

Wilensky, H. L.
1964    "The professionalization of everyone?" American Journal of Sociology 70: 137–58.

# PART IV

# *Controversies in Practice*

## INTRODUCTION

> *The great majority of urban dwellings in this country have a safe water supply.*
>
> ————Kevin Lynch

In a period characterized by rampant urban growth and central city decline, the services of urban designers have become ever more critical for our social and economic survival. Like physicians during a period of war or pandemic, we might expect that planners and architects would be in great demand. These, however, are also times of great fiscal uncertainty, declining construction, and growing political and economic conservatism. The fiscal environment clearly poses challenges for the design professions. Conflicting views of their roles will inevitably multiply. It is a time for professional self-examination. Social science can provide both organizational and ecological theories to aid this process.

The articles in part 4 suggest alternative strategies for urban design. The proposals made here range from attempts at minor reform to radical revisionism. They are not intended to represent fully the vast spectrum of strategies proposed in the literature, but rather to suggest core issues in the provision of urban form at the megastructural and microstructural levels.

The dominant theme is accountability. That is, whose self-interests are being promoted in the acts and the products of architects and planners? Several specific problem areas are identified by the authors:

- The problem of defining the client group, particularly in public sector markets where both form and meaning (the so-called public good) are not easily defined;
- The problem of what Gans calls "professional imperialism" among practitioners of all types, but particularly common among those who provide services that have complex value or meaning (social and aesthetic);
- The corollary issue of communication flows between the actors involved in urban design;
- The problem of control over the product, again especially apparent in the differences between providers in the public and the private sectors.

Gans, Friedman, and Genovese argue quite forcefully that the provider-client role must be redefined. The client is not the sponsor of professional services, but the user. This conception of the role relationship suggests a more complex social dynamic—a multiplicity of forms and meanings. Gan's proposal for a "human architecture" and the various advocacy planning proposals discussed by Genovese both suggest that the audience for architects and planners ought to be the user—that diverse group of people of all classes, cultures, and ages which makes up the urban mosaic. Such a task is quite difficult, as Gans and Genovese acknowledge. Architects and planners are interpreters of form and meaning, but their views are colored by their status within the professional class. Their interpretations are governed by aesthetic and social norms that are not informed by the diverse meanings and behaviors of the heterogeneous urban class of users. Low-brow tastes are legitimate interpretations of form, and they make up the great bulk of urban user demands. Given this view, it is only natural for Friedman to take the client relationship further and suggest a program for "do it yourself" architecture. The major problem with Friedman's revisionist proposal is the implicit assumption that users' stated needs will be congruent with their behavioral requirements. As ethnomethodologists are quick to point out, behavior is founded on often unstated assumptions about the social context (background expectancies). Despite their nonconscious qualities, these background expectancies have a profound influence over our everyday actions.

The Friedman proposal, while flawed, is intrinsically appealing because it challenges the professional imperialism characteristic of the design occupations. All the articles in this section address this problem. Gans discusses the difficulties of interprofessional linkages in practice, yet suggests the necessity of establishing ties between the academic and the practitioner. It is implicit here that social scientists can help improve the knowledge base of the profession so that designers can become competent "change agents" rather than "philosopher-kings." The dangers of the latter approach are underscored by the experiences of advocacy practice. As Genovese indicates, many advocacy planners abandoned the traditional emphasis as providers of form to take a broader "generalist" role in the community. Ill-prepared and ill-credentialed for such a task, advocacy planning failed to gain user support and government sponsorship.

Professional imperalism, as identified in these chapters, involves "telling" and "giving" actions, rather than "listening" and "responding" actions. Thus a corollary observation made here is that the communication flows between professional, social scientist, and user are not structured for an efficient and rational distribution of services. It is therefore important to understand the nature and significance of social science-practitioner communication. Yet it is also important to point out that the approach to knowledge is quire different in the two professions: social scientists dissect their subject matter, whereas practitioners interpret it. In short, the modes of thought are different, and this leads to natural communication barriers. Although, as Gans implies, this obstacle is not insurmountable, it requires an understanding of the language barrier. But the language problem goes deeper.

In the article above, Miller suggests the multiparadigmatic character of the social sciences. The multiple paradigm has created difficulties for the practitioner. As Genovese argues here academic planning is highly influenced by structural functionalism, a theory that does not easily conform to the assumptions of advocate planners.

The problem of the advocate's role obviously runs deeper than the flow of communication between academics and practitioners. How can one determine the needs of the user client and then translate those needs into action? Both Gans and Genovese are optimistic, but the methodology for need assessment is not clear in these pages. Certainly social scientists must play a role in this process.

The most difficult obstacle for all the proposals presented here, however, is neither imperialism nor the lack of communication, but rather the simple fact that planning and architecture are political. Much is done within the public sector under the watchful eyes of government officials. Thus, the ultimate product of practice is controlled by nonpractitioners. Under such conditions the provision of form is, at best, likely to reform rather than revise. Advocates have made serious errors in the past, but their failure was not simply a result of a poorly thought-out scheme for practice.

The papers in this volume underscore the difficulties of providing urban form. Planning and architecture are dominated by a multitude of paradigms, and they practice under organizational constraints. Understanding these paradigms and constraints is essential to successful, progressive urban design. The articles here provide analyses relevant for that understanding. Knowledge of the orgnizational and political context of practice underscores not only the limits of action but the possibilities of it as well.

# 12 Toward a Human Architecture: A Sociologist's View of the Profession

## HERBERT J. GANS

In recent years, architecture's main problem has been unemployment, but if and when the American economy returns to good health, architects will have to deal with some of the profession's other problems. My observations on these problems stem in part from having worked with and for architects for over thirty years, but also from architecture's similarity to other professions, including my own disciplines of sociology and planning. Consequently, I begin with a more general analysis of the professions today.

In my lifetime, at least, American professions have sought, among other things, to be of public service. They have wanted to serve by improving society through the application of their distinctive expertise—sometimes whether or not the improvements were actually wanted or needed by the society, and whether or not the expertise was actually relevant to these wants or needs. In other words, the professions have sought to do good as they defined good, in ways that also increased the power, status, and income of their members through a benevolent "professional imperialism" which has not always been benevolent for the ultimate recipients of professional services.

In addition, the professions have been largely peer-oriented. Practitioners have worked mainly for the approval and respect of their peers and colleagues; only secondarily have they been concerned with their clients' own wants or needs. Partly as a result, they have looked for clients who accepted peer values and practices, which meant, whenever possible, clients of similar socioeconomic status. Finally, in their educational programs, the professions have tried to train students to "advance"

Reprinted with some revisions by permission of the Association of Collegiate Schools of Architecture from: *Journal of Architectural Education*, vol. 31, no. 2, 1978.

the profession, that is, to be original, innovative, and prestigious (by peer standards), although in actual fact, many of the students have wound up in fairly prosaic jobs with little opportunity to be innovative.

During the 1960s, the traditional goals and structures of the professions came under strong criticism from students and young practitioners. Although they also wanted to improve society through the use of their professional expertise, they defined improvement as drastic if not revolutionary change—often toward a more egalitarian society—and they rejected the traditional professional alliance with the elite. In almost all professions, young people wanted to work less for peers and high-status clients and more for the poor. (In those professions that deal with individual clients on a case-by-case basis, they wanted to undertake class actions that would benefit large numbers of people at the same time.) In the process they also rejected traditional professional methods, so that, for example, sociologists gave up detached research, social workers moved from case work to community organization, and doctors and lawyers eschewed the commercial relationship with patients and clients. A few activists gave up professional methods altogether, resorting to various forms of political action that they hoped would produce a more democratic and egalitarian society.

## THE SITUATION IN ARCHITECTURE

Virtually all of these observations apply to architecture as well. Traditionally, architects have wanted to improve society through better building, whether or not this actually improved society in a way that society wanted to be improved. They have been peer-oriented and have pursued originality, so that too often architects cared more how a building would look in the architectural journals than how it would work in actual use; and they have gravitated to high-income clients because they were most likely to let architects do their own thing (Goodman, 1971; Brolin, 1976).

But architecture is also distinctive in at least two ways. First, professional imperialism has perhaps been greater, or at least more visible, in architecture than in other professions, partly because some architects felt that their role was to express the contemporary culture or the philosophy of their society through their buildings. Others saw themselves as social reconstructionists, who would build or rebuild social relationships—and thus, people's lives—through physically or otherside innovative plans and buildings. Indeed, some acted out what I call "the Fountainhead syndrome," the urge to remake society through building that obsessed the hero of the Ayn Rand novel.

Second, architecture's professional expertise involves taste and style, that is, aesthetics – and more so than most other professions. As a result, architecture has been caught up, if not always intentionally, in the long-standing debate over the merits of high culture and popular culture. The most innovative architects, and the architectural elite generally, are on the side of high culture, although they may not be aware of it, for they share its disdain for popular culture, and with it, for popular or vernacular building. Like other high-culture artists, they venerate folk art and folk building – as soon as the folk drop it – but they despise commercially produced products, whether television programs made in Hollywood or buildings designed by or for commercial builders. High culture is, however, a minority culture that attracts only a tiny – but affluent and well-educated – sector of society (Gans, 1974). As a result, architects play only a minor role in America's residential design, and most housing is designed by builders who respond to the aesthetics of the dominant popular cultures.

To be sure, other professions also supply only a minor portion of the product or service over which they claim expertise, and because of similar cultural conflicts. Medical aid is probably still administered more often by druggists and relatives than doctors, just as most counselling is done by ministers, relatives, and friends rather than by social workers or psychiatrists. Similarly, professional sociologists supply only a small amount of the total sociology produced in our society. Many Americans read popular sociologists such as Vance Packard, and far more resort to the vital but virtually invisible "lay" sociology that people develop on their own in order to deal with society. In all cases, there are some differences between the professional and nonprofessional service, but some of these are differences of style. Doctors often treat patients as collections of diseases rather than people; and, like sociologists and social workers, they supply their services in a technical language that puts off their patients and clients.

Of course, the minor role that architects play in American building is also a function of cost; few people can afford a custom-built house, or a Park Avenue specialist. Sometimes builders have rejected architects for the same reason; thus, when William Levitt made plans for his third Levittown in the mid-1950s, he called in two internationally famous architects to design new prototypes for him, only to find that their designs would cost around $100,000 to build. He was then selling houses at $11,500 to $14,500.

During the 1960s, young architects questioned the traditional ways of their profession in much the same way as young people in other professions. They rejected the elite architecture that built only for affluent clients and criticized the emphasis on aesthetics and social reconstruction through architectural methods. Some gave up the idea of designing and building altogether, becoming planners and political activists instead. Indeed, young architects seem to have played a proportionately larger role in the radical movements of the 1960s than young members of other professions, attesting perhaps to their own version of the Fountainhead syndrome.

Today, the ideas and plans of the 1960s are less visible, even if they have not entirely disappeared. However, with the coming of the economic crisis many architects, like other professionals, returned to their old ways, going back to work for their old clients.

## ARCHITECTURE IN THE 1980s

Many of the criticisms of architecture that emerged in the 1960s continue to be valid, in spirit if not always in letter. Still, times have changed again, and I want to consider what architecture should and can do in the years to come.

To begin with, it is wrong to think of architecture or any other profession in the singular, for no profession can or ought to be homogeneous. In a heterogeneous society, there should be many architectures, and sociologies. Even so, architects should concern themselves mainly with the design and construction of buildings, for that is their distinctive expertise. (This means they should not ordinarily try to be planners, a point to which I will return.) Also, architects should continue to be innovative whenever possible, but the greatest opportunity for innovation, as I will note in more detail below, is in designing buildings for the people who use them.

Furthermore, while some architects should continue to work for, and by, the standards of high culture, more architectural effort ought to be devoted to popular culture, because its aesthetic standards are as valid as those of high culture. As long as taste is determined largely by amount of education and income, different socioeconomic levels are entitled to have different standards of beauty and good design, and to have these standards put into practice. Until all Americans have an opportunity to obtain the education and income prerequisite to high culture, architects should be working for and in all cultures. This, as I understand Denise Scott Brown and Robert Venturi, is one of the points they want to make, although they are also engaged in using popular culture to develop their own high-culture form, much as high-culture composers incorporate jazz into their works.

Understanding and accepting the standards of popular culture may also be in the economic self-interest of architects, for it would enable them to play a larger role in commercial building: a rational strategy in an era when other clients are scarce. Competing with commercial builders is easier said than done, however, for, consciously or not, commercial builders have developed a much better sense of what rank-and-file clients, particularly home buyers, want than have architects. Whatever their other motives, builders do not look down their aesthetic noses at such clients. The varieties of neo-Colonial and neo-Spanish design that have dominated residential building for many years may not meet the standards of high culture but they have been popular for a long time, and their popularity cannot therefore be ascribed simply to the aesthetic ignorance or pathology of builders and home buyers.

To be sure, commercial builders will rarely employ the innovative designers who are held in highest regard by the profession, at least not until they can prove their willingness to work within popular styles. At the same time, the energy shortages of the future may provide a new opportunity for architects, for if energy becomes scarcer and more expensive, American building of all kinds will have to change, and designers who can come up with energy-saving solutions that are also popular in style will find themselves extremely busy. But such solutions cannot involve resettling people in a new version of the post-Miesian high-rise apartment building; instead, architects must find better ways of saving the single-family house, or of adapting the row house so that it can become a viable substitute for it.

A major distinguishing characteristic of high-culture architecture has been its self-conscious attempt to make philosophical and symbolic statements, but this is overdone. Buildings have many functions, utilitarian and others, and they can also serve as vehicles for statements, but not at the expense of their other functions. Architects are generally not accomplished philosophers in the first place; the statements they want to make are often half-baked or cliched even when the architecture itself is good. Moreover, it is plainly impossible to capture the ethos of a society or an era in a single statement. Modern societies are too diverse and eras of too short duration, but there are also better media for the pursuit of philosophy than buildings.

Much the same observation applies to the making of symbolic statements, except when a building's major function is to be symbolic. Symbols are perhaps easier to integrate into design without neglecting other functions than philosophical statements, but even so, their importance has been over-rated. In addition, the symbol makers tend to favor high-culture symbols and styles and to forget that the rest of the population may have different symbols. For example, many public buildings follow the dictates of high culture, even though most of the public, which pays for the buildings, does not share these dictates, expressing its feelings in the satirical names that are attached to such buildings. People might feel differently about architects if at least some public buildings expressed popular symbols and styles.

The Fountainhead syndrome has also been primarily associated with high-culture architecture, although even designers of otherwise conventional residential subdivisions have wanted to redo people's friendship choices, and to encourage their identification with the community through design and site planning. But whether the urge is to reconstruct the entire society or neighborhood sociability, architects cannot, and should not, try to play social engineer with architectural methods. In the last several decades many studies have been made on the impact of buildings, building types, and site plans on social relationships, other behavior patterns, and attitudes, and most of the research indicates that buildings and good design, however defined, have only a minimal effect on behavior and attitudes (Wilner et al., 1962; Gans, 1967). Moreover, even when effects have been observed, they have often differed from those intended by the architect (Cooper, 1975).

The Fountainhead syndrome is misplaced. Society cannot be remade through architecture, and architects cannot solve problems of poverty, mental illness, or marital discord through better design. Nor can they shape friendship choices, civic participation, community identity, and social cohesion through site planning. Their designs can make people's lives a little more comfortable or uncomfortable, but human behavior, and social as well as political relationships, are shaped by so many causal factors that rarely is any single factor of crucial importance. Even more rarely is architectural design or site planning that single factor. One so-called physical factor that may have some social and emotional effects is the amount of space, although recent studies of density suggest that high density does not by itself generate pathology. (Freedman, 1975; Baldassare, 1979). People who live in crowded conditions almost always suffer from other, more serious problems, notably poverty, and while lack of space may cause considerable discomfort, even architects cannot do much about it. Space is not a physical factor that architects can manipulate through design, but an economic factor which depends on the income of those purchasing or renting space.

Social reconstruction through design is also undemocratic, for architects are not political representatives, and are neither chosen by, nor accountable to, an electorate or other constituency. Thus, architects have no right to decide that people should be friendlier with their neighbors, that they ought to identify with their community — and that they should, therefore, use public open space rather than their own backyards.

Finally, architecture should de-emphasize aesthetics, or at least give less priority to the aesthetic functions of buildings, treating them less as works of art or pieces of sculpture. How buildings look from the outside and to the outsider is far less important than how they feel to their users. They ought to be beautiful, but their elevations, and their aesthetic functions generally, should not be the tails that wag the dogs.

## HUMAN ARCHITECTURE

Above all, architecture should be human. The term is merely a label, and one that has sometimes been used to indulge in polemics against tall buildings, but I mean by it that buildings should be designed for the people who will use them. Architecture should be user-oriented, to employ yet another label. Specifically, buildings should be humanly functional, comfortable, and beautiful—and when all three objectives cannot be met, they should be met in that order of priority. I use the term functional here in the literal sense: a building ought to perform the functions for which it is intended. A building should work as a mechanical system, of course, but more important, it ought to facilitate, or at least not get in the way of, the important and recurring tasks, and the social, political, and economic relationships that go on within it. By comfortable, I mean that a building ought to be convenient and pleasant for its occupants, although not all buildings can be comfortable. Some, I suppose, have to be awe-inspiring, and I doubt whether any designer can make a prison comfortable for its involuntary occupants, at least until penology is humanized. A beautiful building is one that satisfies the aesthetic standards of its users.

Functionality, as I conceive it, is particularly relevant to a human architecture, for it calls attention to the fact that the building ought to work for the often prosaic and mundane needs of people that are sometimes forgotten because the architect is emphasizing symbols or aesthetic goals. Above all, perhaps, functionality has to do with the allocation of the scarcest resource with which the architect works, space, so that major activities and relationships can be satisfied effectively. For example, in a house, functionality has to do with so locating the kitchen that mothers can watch their young children playing outside; in an apartment, providing play space for them when they cannot go outside but will not stay in their own rooms—as they rarely do. It means designing bedrooms for teen-agers so that they can entertain their friends with high-decibel records but without deafening their elders, and finding ways to give both age groups visual and aural privacy. In an office building, functionality means finding a design that will provide enough—and comfortable—space for both secretaries and executives. In short, human architecture is understanding how people actually use the buildings they live and work in, and then finding design solutions for these uses.

User-oriented architecture is simpler to propose than to design (Gutman and Westergaard, 1974: 320-30). For one thing, user orientation has implications for a building's functions, for the users should, in one way or another, have a role in determining the intended functions. Second, most buildings have diverse sets of users, and the issue of which users ought to determine the building's functions and its design, and in what order of priority, is a complex one. Occasionally, buildings can be designed to satisfy all users, but more often, they cannot, and then the priority issue becomes a political issue. Whether a house should be designed first and foremost for adults or children, or an office building for executives or for secretaries is at bottom a question of power, and normally adults and executives will end up with higher priorities. Architects cannot by themselves reallocate power, or even find solutions to power struggles. Ideally, they should be spokespersons for users in their discussions with clients, and make sure that those of lesser power do not automatically wind up with lower priority. More pragmatically, they should encourage discussions among clients and users as to how the building is to be designed, indicating that priority determinations are political ones. At the least, they should remind clients not to ignore users.

Clearly, buildings should not be designed simply for clients, and all other things being equal, first priority should be given to those users who make the most intensive or extensive use of a building. But all other things are not always equal; thus, a firm that can flourish only by attracting customers must obviously assign high priority to them. Building users who serve these customers would probably agree, since their pay checks depend on satisfying customers; even so, if these users are consulted, their wants will at least be put on the agenda. One complicating factor is that architects are usually hired and paid by clients, not by users, and must battle for the authority to consider the latter. In a competitive situation, those who do so may be at a disadvantage, for an architect who argues that office buildings should provide comfortable work space for secretaries as well as executives may obtain fewer commissions than one who pays maximum attention to executives. The experienced user-oriented architect can, however, argue that secretarial productivity and turnover are affected by pleasant working conditions and that these conditions can sometimes be made more pleasant through design. Admittedly, design has its limits; for no architect can design a building in which everyone, executives *and* secretaries, can have window offices. Nevertheless, addressing itself to users, and to the problems this raises, is what makes architecture human.

A second issue concerns the determination of user needs and wants. Need is an unfortunate concept, for too often it is projected onto users, and turns out to be what other people think users should need or want. I would emphasize user wants, and when not all wants are achievable, user choices among alternatives. Even wants are not easily determined, for while it may be simple to get people to say what they want, the user-oriented architect must also consider how people actually want to use, and do use, buildings, once they are inside them. Since no one can predict what people will do in a building they have not yet occupied, architects need to know, in considerable depth and detail, how people use different types of buildings—and building components—in the mechanical, social, and emotional senses of use. Architects should, in fact, be constant observers of how people use buildings; their own, those of other architects, and those of commercial builders. They should understand how use patterns are enhanced and hindered by various design solutions; and they should be talking with users to find out what they like and dislike about their present buildings and what should be changed in the future.

Observing use patterns and ascertaining user wants for the future is only part of the assignment, for architects must synthesize these two kinds of data, and this, too, is complicated. No synthesis can totally rely on use patterns, or else architects will only be perpetuating the status quo. On the other hand, the synthesis cannot rely too heavily on verbally expressed wants for the future, since even the most observant users cannot always express what they want, and even when they can, talk is cheap, and what people say they want may ultimately not be as important as how they have acted in the past. Finally, no synthesis is complete without the architectural input, combining the data with design ideas. One of the challenges of a human architecture is to develop and perfect this synthesis, through experience, research, and professional discussion and education.

## TALKING TO THE USERS: THE ROLE OF SOCIAL RESEARCH

When I suggest that architects must talk with users, I do not necessarily mean this literally, for in many cases the dialogue may be carried on by researchers, and besides, there is no single formula for everyone. Some architects are user-oriented by inclination; they have an intuitive sense of how people use buildings and an almost inborn ability to observe them, although even the most sensitive observer is most insightful about people like himself or herself in age, income, education, and interests. Other architects are most at home at the drawing board or with the calculator, and lack the skill and patience to talk with users.

Whatever the architect's own inclination, ideally, users should do their own talking, and should help to determine the program and design of their own buildings. One 1960s idea that has deservedly survived is user-participation in architectural and planning decisions. In a literal sense, such participation is often impractical, for even talking with the family of a client for a private house takes a good deal of time and energy; and no one can hold a dialogue with the eventual occupants of a subdivision or office building. Sometimes it is possible to talk with a sample of sur-rogates, people who are similar to eventual occupants, but often the dialogue will in fact have to be research: studies by social scientists, especially sociologists and psychologists, which provide architects with data on user behavior and user wants.

In recent years, there have been a number of attempts at team work between architects and social scientists, and some have been successful (Zeisel, 1975). I am also well aware, however, that often they have not worked out. Architects have claimed, and rightly so, that the social scientists have different interests, being more concerned with innovations in theory than with improved architecture; they have also complained, again correctly, that social scientists often lack the knowledge and the inclination to work with architects. Social scientists, they say, cannot adapt to architectural deadlines, and cannot communicate in jargon-free English. Most important, they are unable to come up with findings specific enough to be useful for design solutions, or are unwilling to make firm generalizations when their findings are ambiguous. Social scientists are equally unhappy with architects, charging—and often rightly so—that architects are unable or unwilling to use research findings. The complaints of both professions boil down to the charge that the other is unsuited to the teamwork task, suggesting that both must make changes in their methods of operation before effective teamwork can take place.

If social scientists are too often marching to theoretical rather than architectural drummers, architects are frequently at fault for asking the wrong questions. For one thing, some still want to be social reconstruc-tionists and reject social science findings which indicate that an architectural solution is irrelevant. Having once done a study of a low-income ethnic neighborhood, I am sometimes asked by architects how one designs buildings and neighborhoods that respond to the distinctive culture of low-income people or of an ethnic group, but this is a good example of the wrong question. The fundamental, or at least most urgent, user patterns do not vary by class or ethnicity; that is, different income and ethnic groups do not use dwelling units all that differently. They all need living rooms, bedrooms, kitchens, and so on, and they all put these rooms to roughly the same use. True, low-income people have traditionally socialized informally and in the kitchen, while high-income people entertain more formally and in the living room, but such class differences are few, and in most cases too insignificant to affect design.

The main distinction between the rich and the poor is in their ability to pay for space, and the main problem of the latter is to get enough space. Of course, poor people virtually never get new housing and they cannot hire architects, but when architects design projects for low-income people, they should worry less about designing for the distinctive characteristics of low-income social life and more about how to design functional, comfortable, and beautiful architecture when space is at a minimum. In addition, they should use their professional expertise and status to fight against low-income housing projects that try to cram their occupants into an unreasonably small amount of space. Together with researchers, they ought to determine the space requirements of low-income families, so they can develop proper space standards for the poor. I suspect that these standards will require as much space as for affluent families, thus casting doubt on the desirability of special (and, especially, small) housing units for the poor. Instead, housing will need to meet a universal threshold of space, with rent supplements for those too poor to afford the minimum.

As for use patterns in low-income or ethnic neighborhoods, these are not so rigid or permanent that they require special designs; in fact, such designs sometimes ask people to continue behavior patterns which they would just as soon give up. For example, among some low-income groups street life is not a choice but a necessity, born of lack of space in the dwelling; it would disappear if apartments were large enough. Among some ethnic groups, street life exists because of immigrants' cultural restrictions against inviting people other than relatives into the house, but these restrictions are not being maintained by today's third- and fourth-generation ethnics. More important, there are few people or cultural patterns that cannot—and do not—adapt themselves to available space and design. If one looks at first- and second-generation Italian neighborhoods in America, the social life is much the same whether people live in tenements, row houses, or single-family houses; whether in all-Italian or mixed neighborhoods; and whether the streets are wide or narrow, traffic-laden or empty.

The cooperation between architects and social scientists is just beginning, and early failures do not invalidate the possibility of a joint effort. Such an effort requires at least three separate tasks. One is the development of a basic research compendium of user behavior and wants for different types of buildings. Although considerable new research will be required to discover the fundamental generalizations about user behavior,

---

Herbert J. Gans

the task is not as huge as it might appear. There are many uniformities in the way people use houses, offices, factories, and the like, with relatively little variation either by demographic characteristics or region. Also, people's wants are more similar than commonly thought; what differs mainly is their ability to satisfy them.

The needed research compendium is already beginning to exist, thanks in part to the emergence of the sociology and psychology of design, sometimes called environmental sociology and psychology. To be sure, much of the research is still preliminary, of narrow scope, and overly concerned with theoretical, conceptual, and methodological issues. In part, architects, and architecture as a profession, have only themselves to blame, for they have so far remained quiet about their research needs and have left the agendas entirely to the social scientists. If architects would become interested in user research and exert some influence on those who fund such research, they might obtain more usable data.

But this also awaits a second task, the recruitment and training of architects who are sufficiently sympathetic to, and familiar with, the social sciences, and with the use of social science data in architecture to initiate research—at least to the extent of identifying architecturally inclined social scientists who will write the actual grant proposals and do the research. And this in turn must go hand in hand with a third task, the recruitment and training of social scientists who are interested in working with architects.

All three tasks require funds, people, and the development of new research organizations, teaching bodies, and curriculums in order to develop an effective interdisciplinary relationship, in which architects with some training in the social sciences, and social scientists with some training in architecture can develop a common language and research methods that contribute to the common objective. The overall effort will take time, which is why it should be initiated quickly, by academics in architecture and the social sciences, with practitioner support from relevant professional organizations to help obtain the necessary foundation and government funding.

The basic research compendium should consist of specific studies, the broader generalizations drawn from them, and translations, by architects, into broad and general user-oriented design guidelines (Cooper, 1975: chap. 10). These cannot always solve the specific design problems encountered by individual architects, however, and will have to be supplemented either by special studies or by social science consultants who can adapt compendium findings to specific design problems for architects who lack the time or money to do new research. It is to be hoped that the compendium can be updated and elaborated continuously with results of these studies or consultancies, and more important, by follow-

314

up studies of user behavior and user satisfactions once buildings have been occupied.

## ARCHITECTURE AND PLANNING

In the early 1950s, when I worked as a city planner in public and private planning agencies, most of my colleagues were architects, for in those days trained planners were few, and many architects thought that their professional training entitled them to be planners as well. Times have changed considerably since then, at least in America; architects can no longer become planners just by taking a few planning courses, any more than planners can also be architects by dipping into the architectural curriculum. Planning is rapidly shedding the remainder of its architectural origins and becoming an applied social science, although no one can now tell whether it will be an independent discipline, or one dominated by public administration, or by one of its equivalents in business or engineering.

At the same time, however, physical planning will continue to exist, because some of the issues with which planners deal, and some of the decisions on which they advise, have physical consequences and require design solutions. In fact, as some planning agencies and schools have de-emphasized physical planning, it seems to have taken on new life elsewhere, often under architectural auspices, and under the label of urban design. In some ways, urban design is closer to architecture than to planning, but even so, many of the issues with which urban designers must deal, especially in large cities, involve the same macroeconomic, social, and political questions with which planners also grapple, excluding the architect who is trained to work on smaller sites and with the standard design issues. In the long run, therefore, urban design must probably also split off from architecture, combining a small portion of its design expertise with a large portion of planning skills. As scarcities of energy and money increase, and as public expectations for the efficiency and effectiveness of public agencies rise, no one can be expert in both architecture and urban design, and the era in which the architect could function as a generalist who can also plan will finally end.

## ARCHITECTURE AND SOCIAL CHANGE

During the 1960s, some architects went into planning because they thought that the latter profession, having a larger scope, would be more able to bring about drastic social change. They were disappointed, for while architecture cannot do very much to change society, nor can planning, embedded as it is in business-dominated municipal politics. Indeed, it seems fair to say that most professions can do little to bring about social change, at least in a radical direction, for their employers or clients tend to represent the elite.

Radical social change comes about largely because of the interplay of macroeconomic and political forces over which no one group or stratum has very much control. More modest social change, on the other hand, is often the result of deliberate political activities, and architects, like all other professionals, can be politically active, either as professionals or as citizens. They can lobby, demonstrate, or run for elective office; they can also try to persuade their firms and professional organizations to lobby for changes they consider desirable.

As the 1960s activists discovered, however, there is not likely to be a revolution, especially one led by architects. Today, the opposition to social change, especially in an egalitarian direction, is once more apparent, and since few architects are politicians, and even those who are rarely have a sizable political base from which to operate, most architects will have to exert political influence through their expertise. As experts, they can play advocate and technical adviser roles in community organizations involved in building, or in fighting urban renewal or other programs to reduce the supply of inexpensive housing. They can also lobby for more research and action to reduce the cost of housing and housing maintenance.

Still, the main costs of housing are the price of land and money, which architects cannot affect, either as experts or as activists. If these prices are to be brought down, architects must join with other professionals and with citizen groups to undertake joint political action for the elimination of land speculation, and for the transformation of the housing industry into some form of public utility, so that all housing, except for the very rich, becomes a governmental responsibility, as it already is in many countries all over the world. But political action along these lines requires considerably more expertise in the economics and politics of housing, and of urban development and politics generally, than architects usually have.

## SOME EDUCATIONAL IMPLICATIONS

Most of the educational implications of my proposals for the future role of architecture are self-evident, and I shall only summarize them briefly. First, architectural schools should devote themselves to the training of architects, sending those students who want to be planners to planning schools, but they should also work with planning schools to develop urban design curriculums that properly train architects to deal with, or at least understand, those urban design decisions that cannot be based solely on architectural expertise.

In addition, schools should train students in what I called human architecture, encouraging in them an empathic understanding of—and curiosity about—how people use buildings, and teaching them how to apply a user-orientation to architectural programming and design. Architectural students ought to have sufficient training and practice in observational and interviewing techniques to develop the habit of and skills for informal observation of user behavior. Although architects need not do systematic social science research, they should know how to use it. Students of architecture ought to take courses in the various behavioral sciences so they can obtain at least a general grasp of what these sciences are about. More important, they will require courses within architecture that provide them with ideas and data on how people use buildings and how these findings can be applied. Such courses will have to be taught by social scientists who have themselves been taught to address architects, or by architects who have learned how to use design-relevant social research.

Furthermore, architectural schools should provide more courses on the economics and politics of building, housing, and related subjects. Architects must be knowledgeable not only in cost estimation, but also in the macroeconomics of housing (and other building), especially in an economy in which only a minuscule proportion of the population can now afford to buy a new house. Similarly, architects must understand the politics of housing and building so they can be familiar with the political context within which they work; and they ought to take a course on the political structure of their own profession, and on strategies of architectural and social change.

Finally, architects could also use more training in the aesthetics of culture so they can understand why so many Americans like neocolonial design and can create architecture that is beautiful by popular standards.

## CONCLUSION

My proposals probably sound revisionist to architectural activists who want to expand the horizons of their profession to encompass planning, and reactionary to those who want to transform architecture into a handmaiden for a future revolution. My proposals may also be unrealistic, for as sociological studies of the professions have shown, most professions are imperialistic and seek to enlarge their roles and increase their power to they can be the leader of the team — and of an ever larger team.

The human architecture I consider desirable is not new; essentially, what I am arguing for is only a variant of the now almost extinct idea that form should follow function, and buildings should be designed from the inside out, rather than from the outside in. In its brief life-span, the idea that form should follow function received more lip-service than drawing-board activity, however, and even when it was applied, it overemphasized a narrowly mechanistic conception of function. Human architecture must design for human functions; it has nothing to do with Bauhaus asceticism, letting the plumbing hang out, or the restoration of ornamentation. Rather, it requires attention to the users as social and psychological beings and to design solutions that allow them to live as they want to live — and in buildings they enjoy being in and consider beautiful. Human architecture may not be published in today's architectural journals, but it offers enough design and other challenges to involve several generations of practitioners, researchers, students, and teachers in an innovative, creative, and socially useful professional endeavor.

## REFERENCES

Baldassare, M.
 1979　Residential Crowding in Urban America. Berkeley: University of California Press.

Brolin, B. C.
 1976　The Failure of Modern Architecture. New York: Van Nostrand and Reinhold.

Cooper, C.
 1975　Easter Hill Village. New York: Free Press.

Freedman, J. L.
 1975　Crowding and Behavior. New York: Viking Press.

Gans, H. J.
 1967　The Levittowners. New York: Pantheon Books.

 1974　Popular Culture and High Culture. New York: Basic Books.

Goodman, R.
 1971　After the Planners. New York: Simon and Schuster.

Gutman, R., and B. Westergaard
 1974　"Building evaluation, user satisfaction and design." In J. Lang, et al. (eds.), Designing for Human Behavior. Stroudsberg, Pa: Dowden, Hutchinson and Ross.

Michelson, W.
    1970    Man and His Urban Environment. Reading, Mass.: Addison Wesley.

    1977    Environmental Choice, Human Behavior and Residential Satisfaction. New York: Oxford University Press.

Wilner, D. et al.
    1962    Housing Environment and Family Life. Baltimore: Johns Hopkins University Press.

Zeisel, J.
    1975    Sociology and Architectural Design. New York: Russell Sage Foundation.

# 13 Dilemmas in Introducing Activism and Advocacy into Urban Planning

## ROSALIE G. GENOVESE

### INTRODUCTION

Urban planning often seems to be an occupation in search of an identity and a mission, perhaps because its roots can be traced to several different traditions: the physical planning orientation of engineers, who were among the first planners; the architecture and urban design component, represented by the "City Beautiful" movement; and the concerns of urban reformers who sought to improve living conditions for the poor (Scott, 1969).

In seeking legitimacy from society at large and from governmental decision makers, planners in subsequent decades concentrated on developing their skills in physical planning as a way to gain acceptance. They also wanted to establish their identity as nonpolitical experts who advised politicians and officials. These choices made sense since occupations trying to become professionalized tend to use full professions like medicine or law as their models. Consequently, practitioners in new occupations seek to develop a body of theoretical knowledge and skills for its application, as well as a service orientation (Carr-Saunders and Wilson, 1964; Goode, 1957). Yet some planners always fought against the decision to turn away from the occupation's early social concerns and, in periods of social upheaval, the reform tendencies of planners have resurfaced.

Grateful acknowledgement is made to the Canada Council for its support during the research phase of this study. Special thanks go to the many planners who gave so freely of their time and their ideas. Sylvia Fava's helpful comments on an earlier version of this paper were much appreciated. Thanks, too, to Mark La Gory for his perceptive editorial comments.

320

Urban planning's latest period of social concern came in the 1960s. This paper presents an analysis of advocacy planning, an attempt by some practitioners to introduce a new direction in planning, one that would allow them to help eliminate the inequities of society. Many planners criticized the occupation's ideology and values, which were so at odds with their personal beliefs. They especially rejected planning's association with the power structure in cities and its failure to improve conditions for the disadvantaged. The destructive impact of urban renewal on many inner-city communities was especially regretted by these critics.

What follows is an analysis of why advocacy planning failed. It is written at a time when the need for advocacy in planning, as in law, social work, and other fields seems more essential than ever, given the proposed elimination or curtailment of so many social programs of the Kennedy and Johnson years.

## Advocacy Planning's Emergence

In the 1960s, advocacy planning became a way for practitioners to combine social action with planning practice. Paul Davidoff (1964; 1965) provided the rationale for this new form of planning by proposing that planners become advocates for what they deemed proper. He exhorted planners to express their values in their work, rather than to make dubious claims of "value-neutrality."

The crucial question was how this concept could be put into practice. What would be the settings for advocacy planning? Davidoff (1965: 334) suggested that planners could work for groups that had lacked a voice in past planning decisions. The objectives and values of these groups might coincide with the personal and professional values of advocate planners. Since he knew that few community organizations could afford to hire planners, he envisioned alternative organizational arrangements. For example, planners might work for pro- and anti-civil rights groups, labor organizations, political parties, real estate boards, and others interested in preparing their own plans. There would be pluralism in planning when the process involved many groups, not just those with power and influence.

When planners followed his advice to make their values known, they illustrated differing political philosophies and views of advocacy. Some traditional planners considered advocacy too radical a departure from accepted planning practice. They feared that advocates would work in areas for which they lacked special training, leading to "deprofessionalization" and loss of status for urban planning as a whole.[1] Yet many practitioners of medicine and law in the 1960s also questioned the tradition of professional neutrality and wanted to express their social and political values in their work (Gross and Osterman, 1972). Storefront law offices and community health clinics were results of these concerns.

At the other extreme were practitioners and ideologues who thought planners should play a far more active role in bringing about change. Their concept of advocacy planning signified a sharper break with past planning theory and practice.[2] Even supporters of advocacy criticized aspects of their views. Some thought it a mistake to mix two different concepts, pluralism and advocacy. Others thought that the legal model could not be transferred to planning, since the opposing parties in the adversary situation, for example, poor communities versus government agencies, were so unequal. There was also no independent tribunal comparable to judge or jury in law to render decisions in these contests.

The political philosophy on which advocacy rested was probably the major target of critics. Davidoff's model was based on the assumption that the American system was basically sound, but malfunctioning, and its deficiencies could be corrected. Such a position seems to favor reform and incremental change (Rein, 1971; Mazziotti, 1974). Others who favored basic changes in society thought advocacy planning might have the unwanted consequence of maintaining the system by promoting stability, by neutralizing dissent and protest, and by co-opting the poor (Kravitz, 1968; Funnyé, 1970; Piven, 1970). Numerous planners thought that advocacy planning needed a more radical analysis of inequality and other societal problems. (Grabow and Heskin, 1973; Kravitz, 1968).

Some characterized the planner's relationship with clients as elitist. Instead of speaking *for* their clients, as Davidoff suggested, they advised planners to serve clients by translating their needs and objectives into technical language, without making decisions for them.[3] By transferring their skills and knowledge to community residents, planners could also decrease their dependence on outside professionals and contribute to the community's increased self-sufficiency.

From the beginning, therefore, there were at least two different conceptions of advocacy planning: (1) the Davidoff model and (2) the concept of advocacy that begins to emerge from its critics. This second view sought a substitute for traditional planning theory, perhaps a socialist or Marxist orientation (Fainstein and Fainstein, 1971).

A basic difference in the two approaches concerned the role of technical skill in efforts for change. Those who identified strongly with urban planning wanted clients to have the planning expertise they lacked to gain more control over their neighborhoods. They undertook small-scale projects for community groups, like creating playgrounds or renovating buildings for community use. They also prepared critiques of plans proposed by government agencies and proposed alternatives. Those who saw themselves primarily as activists, however, often concluded that large-scale change was essential (Goodman, 1972). Consequently, they concentrated their efforts on building a movement for change.

## AN ANALYSIS OF THREE ADVOCATE PLANNING GROUPS

### *Initial Issues: Auspices and Structure*

One of the first tasks for practitioners who wanted to be advocates was to find auspices for their work. They needed some outside support, since even voluntary efforts entailed some expense. Planners who were part-time advocates while working at traditional jobs full-time found it difficult to sustain this arrangement indefinitely.

Consequently, practitioners knew they needed funding, but worried about the constraints attached to such support. Moreover, funding sources were limited. Some foundations provided seed money for innovative programs, but made no long-term commitments. Government agencies might attach many conditions to funds, perhaps curbing planners' freedom to work for change. Therefore, advocate planners were uneasy about possible compromises. Could they serve their clients effectively and still be accountable to their funding source? The alternative was some sort of informal advocacy work. These efforts were necessarily small in scope, but at least gave practitioners independence from outside control.

An organization's degree of formalization and scope was largely determined by its budget. At one extreme were groups with limited resources and largely volunteer staffs, usually students supervised by a full-time administrator. To survive, these groups usually had to find a regular basis for support. At the other extreme were organizations with budgets of at least $100,000 and staffs of eight or more architects, planners, and other professionals. Few groups attained this level of funding and formalization. In between, were groups with foundation or university funding, or perhaps a government contract. With a budget in the $30,000 to $60,000 range, such an organization might have a full-time staff of from three to six professionals (U.S. Office of Economic Opportunity, 1971: 23-24).

My analysis of advocacy planning is based on case studies of three groups in a Northeastern metropolitan area in the early 1970s.[4] Two fell into the first category, with little funding, a low degree of formalization, and reliance on volunteers. The groups I have called Community Services (CS) and Technical Assistance to Communities (TAC) were each affiliated with a major university in the area. The third group, Ideological Associates (IA), was one of the few advocacy planning organizations with a budget of over $100,000. After it received federal funding in 1969, the organization's staff often totaled twenty-five to thirty mostly full-time employees.

The auspices and settings for these advocacy planning groups influenced their philosophy, projects, and attempts to gain acceptance. CS had been started in the spring of 1968 as a graduate course in planning. When the research began, it was directed by its founder, a university professor who had also played a role in the formation of IA. Although started with a foundation grant, the group faced difficult times when this funding ended. The fact that it became more dependent on university support concerned both its first director and his successor. Although they would have preferred to have the program function independently of university auspices, such a move would have been difficult. For example, students might not be able to receive credit for their work.

The planning of advocacy activities using volunteers was complicated for CS administrators, since the number and scope of projects had to be decided before the number of students was known. Enrollments ranged from twenty to sixty students per term. The students were supervised by faculty members or by practitioners willing to devote time to community work.

Also started in 1968, TAC was headed by a faculty member. Fifteen to twenty architecture and planning students enrolled each term. It differed from CS in that it never deviated from its primary emphasis on technical assistance. It also received more support than did CS, perhaps because this university's planning and architecture faculty was more receptive to innovation. Nevertheless, both CS and TAC were short-lived experiments. They failed to become established entitites within their respective universities.

IA was only one of the three groups with the resources to develop a formal structure with full-time employees. It is also one of the few advocate planning groups to survive for more than ten years. However, during this period, its planning projects decreased as it undertook other kinds of advocacy work. The federal agency that funded the organization imposed few constraints on it, despite the changes that occurred in its work. As my research was ending, however, the organization was to come under closer scrutiny because jurisdiction over it was being transferred from Washington to the agency's regional office.

## Advocacy Planning in Practice

The history of these three groups demonstrates the difficulties advocacy planning had to surmount if it was to become a recognized direction within urban planning. It also illustrates its weaknesses as a form of practice. The experiences of IA and CS provide insights into different aspects of advocacy planning's problems.

IA grew out of the efforts of several planners who did "counter planning" even before Davidoff's advocacy planning articles appeared. Their actions represented their response to the deficiencies they found in much government planning, especially in transportation. They deplored a physical planning emphasis that failed to consider how plans would affect people. Several members of this informal group worked in city agencies, but obtained permission to prepare alternative plans as long as they avoided conflicts of interest. Other members, social scientists from area universities, were interested in community issues.

By 1966, a small grant had enabled the group to become officially established and to adopt a more formal mode of operation. A full-time director, who had a technical but not a planning background, and a secretary were hired. At this point, some members had begun to work more closely with neighborhood groups on housing, urban renewal, and transportation projects. They eventually won acceptance from many government officials who learned to respect the quality of their work.

Up to this point, IA provided technical assistance along the lines proposed by Davidoff. However, when IA received its first sizable federal grant, in 1969, its direction began to change. At that time, a large staff was hired and the group's founders became board members. An unsettled period ensued for the organization as one staff faction pressed for greater emphasis on organizing and social change, while another faction remained committed to the organization's original aims. IA's emphasis on community organizing increased when it began to work in neighborhoods outside the central city, a condition of its grant. Since the new clients lacked the experience and political sophistication of their inner-city clients, staff had to strengthen these community organizations before providing technical assistance.

The backgrounds and experience of staff also played a role in this shift in philosophy and work. New employees often had training and experience in fields other than planning. For example, the new director had labor organizing experience and an economics background. These staff members lacked the skills to provide technical assistance to clients, even had they wanted to do so.

The conflict within the organization was largely resolved when turnover resulted in greater consensus among the staff about its mission and work. Political education and radical politics became central interests and the goal of changing urban planning practice lost its salience. Board members who disagreed with IA's changed mission resigned. After its second director left, an interim director served until a successor was found. He, too, was not a planner.

IA's changed mission was reflected in the organization's structure. It had become a social movement group, or what Zald and Ash (1970) called a "searching sect." Consequently, it did not follow the more frequent organizational progression from a small, radical voluntary group to a more conservative formal organization. IA had a director and an administrative assistant, but no other hierarchical distinctions among staff members. Work was organized along functional lines with housing, transportation, research, and other groups. Each small group was responsible for its own hiring and firing. Salaries were uniformly low and based on need. Those with children, for example, earned more.

Urban planning practice and social change objectives were not successfully combined in this organization. As we have seen, social change and political action concerns overpowered its planning goals and activities as it moved in new directions.

University auspices would have seemed ideal for new approaches to planning education and practice, since so much innovation goes on within this setting. However, faculty members who identify strongly with their occupation or profession often are strongly committed to advancing its status, especially if it has not achieved recognition as a profession. Therefore, new approaches that depart from the occupation's established knowledge base or practice may be opposed by them. Advocacy planning was seen by many planners as a backward step for the semiprofession. They thought that practitioners should not engage in social action and political organizing, activities not part of the planner's traditional training or work.

Since occupations become professionalized by convincing the public that only those with specialized training are competent to perform certain work, practitioners emphasize the esoteric character of their occupation's knowledge and skills. Consequently, strains develop between traditional practitioners, who consider mystification the way to maintain or increase their profession's position, and their colleagues, who want to demystify the profession and narrow the distance between themselves and their clients or the public.[5]

Opposition to CS was based on its potential to harm urban planning's professionalization drive. Its approach to planning education also disturbed some faculty members. CS administrators favored giving students the opportunity to work on real problems faced by communities, rather than doing hypothetical projects in what they saw as the ivory tower atmosphere of the university. Some faculty members questioned whether these assignments constituted the rigorous professional training students should be getting, especially since students might spend part of their time organizing, mailing fliers, or doing other tasks that were priorities for the community organization. When student projects were juried, evaluators often failed to consider that real-life projects did not fit neatly into the period of a semester and penalized students for incomplete assignments.

CS lacked powerful supporters to counter the opposition, which was concentrated largely among senior, tenured faculty members. Some administrators also objected to the program because its founder had opposed university expansion into the surrounding community. Its strongest supporters were students and some younger faculty members. As soon as activism began to wane on campus, the university withdrew its support for the program.

# WHY ADVOCACY PLANNING FAILED

## *Advocacy as a "Segment" in Urban Planning*

The sociological literature on occupations and professions, especially the process approach proposed by Bucher and Strauss (1961), provides a useful framework for analysis of the failure of advocacy planning. This model, with its emphasis on change and conflicting interests, views professions as loosely organized sets of groups, each pursuing its own interests. This is a departure from the traditional view of professions as stable, cohesive entities (Carr-Saunders and Wilson, 1964). A nascent group, called a segment, may at first be small and outside the mainstream of an occupation, but may eventually become a major form of practice. To be successful, however, the segment must accomplish the following tasks: (1) establish its claim to an area of work by demonstrating its competence and by gaining acceptance from significant others; (2) proclaim its mission; and (3) institutionalize its activities. In addition, practitioners ι ually form associations to advance their interests. Bucher (1962) draws parallels between new segments and social moments, since they use similar strategies and tactics to gain acceptance. This comparison is especially appropriate for advocacy planning, which grew out of the larger social change movements of the 1960s (Ross, 1976).

Neither the planning groups studied, nor advocacy in general, completed the steps to become an established segment, although advocate planners won numerous victories for clients and had an impact on planning practice.

The task of establishing jurisdiction over a work area was difficult because advocate planners disagreed over their mission and how to translate it into concrete goals. The groups studied illustrate that advocacy could evolve in at least two directions — technical assistance and social action. IA members in the early years used their expertise as a basis for establishing legitimacy for technical assistance activities.[6] One founder noted that they were especially careful to do high-quality work that was noticeably better than the official plans they criticized.

However, since clients often equated expertise with elitism, "service" provided an alternative basis for claiming legitimacy with them. This option was stressed by university groups, since students could not claim to be experts. University groups often developed a trade-off strategy with their clients (Spiegel and Alicea, 1969). Students were to obtain field work experience in exchange for providing technical assistance to communities. But they had difficulty in convincing colleagues, university administrators, and even clients of their legitimacy. Clients were ambivalent at times about their assistance, questioning the competence and commitment of some students. When projects did not work out well, further questions about the programs arose. Yet some students were so committed to community groups that they worked with them for years and eventually became staff or board members.

When IA played down technical assistance, it faced difficulties in establishing jurisdiction over social action as its new area of work. Planners had no special claims to competence in organizing or political action. Community organizers, political scientists, social workers and others had equal or better claims to competence in this area. Planners were not trained to build movements for change.

Moreover, clients did not necessarily want the political education that IA offered. Community group members saw IA as too involved in its own internal struggles to give them the necessary technical support. Divisions within IA became apparent to them when IA staff members publicly disagreed about the course of action a community group should take. Independent observers confirmed that IA staff members sometimes advocated their political views too strongly, alienating clients, who turned elsewhere for technical help without a political message. These community group reactions to political education efforts were not unique. In her study of grass-roots organizations, Perlman (1976: 7) found that the radical rhetoric of the 1960s was "toned down" and "deintellectualized" in the 1970s when many groups became "anti-ideological."

IA's rejection of its technical assistance functions occurred at a time when some community groups had been awarded project development funds. Since they then had the resources to hire planners, it is significant that several retained established consulting firms, not advocate planning groups. In some neighborhoods, community-based technical firms or community development corporations were popular alternatives to working with outside professionals.

The experiences of these three groups reflect the difficulties faced by advocate planners in establishing their claims to legitimacy with officials, clients, and colleagues. The foregoing discussion also makes it clear that no overall mission was accepted by the spectrum of practitioners and ideologues in this nascent segment. The two major "wings" of advocacy defined their purpose differently. Groups that initially provided technical assistance found that, while they could help communities with small-scale projects, they had little impact on problems rooted in inequities of the larger society. This realization was handled in different ways. Some groups, like IA, became increasingly committed to political education and mobilization. In so doing, they broke away from the movement to change urban planning as an occupation.

Other groups accepted the limitations on what they could hope to accomplish, settling for improving conditions in the neighborhoods where they worked. For example, the Community Development Corporation (CDC) in San Francisco, funded by the same agency as IA, continued to provide technical assistance during the 1970s. When its planners and architects faced political and economic issues that they could not affect, their response was to continue to define their work as technical and to maintain their architectural emphasis. As Heskin (1980) notes, advocacy planning taught many planners and architects about the limits of their professional competence, since they were no more able than their clients to change society. The Pratt Institute Center for Community and Environmental Development, in New York, also displayed a consistent technical emphasis during the 1970s. Its projects included the construction of new housing, rehabilitation of several buildings, and planning a twelve block site for a community development corporation (*Planning*, 1977).

Planners who chose to help build a grass-roots political movement for change could not accept the more limited aims of their technically oriented colleagues. For their part, the advocates of technical assistance thought that the goals of the political activists were unrealistic and questioned whether communities were any better off after their intervention. There were no real attempts at rapprochement between these and other factions within advocacy.

Moreover, as already indicated, there was resistance to advocacy within urban planning as a whole. Some advocate planners became active in Planners for Equal Opportunity (PEO), which served as an alternative to the American Institute of Planners (now the American Planning Assocation). PEO, which often criticized the programs and policies of the larger association, was considered more relevant to the work of many advocate planners who maintained their professional identification.

As this brief discussion indicates, advocate planners did not successfully complete the first two steps in establishing a new segment. Their acceptance by clients and officials, as well as within planning itself, was mixed. Their mission remained a matter of controversy, and the translation of this mission into concrete activities was problematic. Consequently, institutionalization, often the most difficult step for an emerging segment, did not occur. Advocacy planning remained in a state of arrested development, and it resembled a failed social movement.[7] Of the three groups studied, only IA survived through the 1970s, but its focus had changed and many of its projects had little to do with urban planning. Its changed mission also created problems with its funding agency, which questioned some of its activities.

Despite the fact that a few advocate planning groups still exist, no permanent organizational arrangement for advocacy was established — either within government, within the university, or as an independent form of practice. As national priorities changed, and as activism decreased, even short-term grants were scarce. Even if advocate planners had developed one overarching mission and had been clear about how they could use their skills for change, they still would have faced this seemingly insoluble problem: Who would pay advocate planners for working with clients who were for the most part poor and powerless? The obvious answers were government or private foundations, but neither was committed to assuming this financial responsibility on a long-term basis.

Paul and Linda Davidoff (1978) discussed the funding issue, using Suburban Action Institute, an advocate organization they founded in 1969, to illustrate the difficulties. Its mission is to open up housing in the suburbs to working-class and minority families excluded from living in areas where new jobs are increasingly located (Davidoff and Davidoff, 1978; Davidoff, et al., 1970). The Davidoffs consider survival in the changed economic and social climate of the 1970s to be one of the organization's major accomplishments. Considerable staff time was devoted to obtaining the foundation grants and research contracts which kept the organization going. But such support also had costs. They argue that when advocacy planning relies almost totally on either public funds or private foundation support, it is difficult to insure that clients truly control the advocacy process. What is needed is "an independent base of financial and organizational support" (Davidoff and Davidoff, 1978: 118). The unanswered question is how this goal can be accomplished.

One conclusion to be drawn from this study of attempts to combine activism with professional practice is that social action segments need strong backing from powerful groups in the larger society, support which advocacy planning lacked. Such a segment's chances for institutionalization seem best when linked to a successful large-scale movement for change. Without such basic and widespread societal change, social action segments will have an extremely precarious existence.

## Legal Services:
### A Successful Social Action Segment?

Is advocacy planning's failure the common fate of most nascent segments in occupations and professions? A comparison of nascent segments in several occupations and professions suggests that success or failure is related to two factors: (a) whether the segment occurs in a full profession or a semiprofession and (b) whether it developed as a result of new knowledge and techniques or emerged from practitioners' beliefs and values.

Segments based on new technology often succeed, with clinical pathology, clinical psychology, and anesthesiology providing good examples (Bucher, 1962; Goode, 1960; and Lortie, 1958). If proponents can convince colleagues that the new segment will make their work easier or advance the occupation's status, the likelihood of success is improved. Public acceptance may not be crucial; although in the case of clinical psychology, opposition from psychologists and psychiatrists was offset by strong support from clients and the public (Goode, 1960).

Segments that arise from practitioners' values, especially about social change, must struggle for recognition and acceptance. However, social action segments in full professions start out with advantages over those in semiprofessions like urban planning and social work.[8] First, a full profession has a more highly developed abstract body of knowledge and techniques for its application. Semiprofessions rely more heavily on knowledge from other disciplines.

Practitioners in full professions also undergo a more rigorous period of training and socialization, usually emerging with a stronger professional identification than semiprofessionals possess. They have also tended to establish independent practices, although today they increasingly work in large organizational settings. In this respect, they have become more like semiprofessionals. Finally, professionals are accorded high status and have their expertise challenged less frequently than do semiprofessionals (although some change occurred in the 1960s with what Haug and Sussman [1969] termed "the revolt of the client").

Since medicine and law are the benchmarks against which professionalizing occupations are so often measured, legal services is a good example of a social action segment in a full profession that can be compared with advocacy planning. In this new form of practice, lawyers use

*331*

their skills and knowledge on behalf of the un-represented or the under-represented (Wexler, 1970; *Harvard Law Review*, 1967). In public interest law, a related form of practice, practitioners work to change existing laws or to enact new legislation.

In these forms of practice, lawyers function *as lawyers*, using their skills and training to assist clients. They differ from other lawyers not in the work they do, but in the clients they assist. In this connection, the ability of legal services to build on the profession's tradition of *pro bono* work was another point in its favor. Moreover, legal services lawyers play their role in an established forum, the courts, where judge or jury has the authority to render decisions in the adversary proceedings before them. This was the model Davidoff used for advocacy planning, but many of these elements are missing in the planning process.

It is still too soon to conclude that legal services have been fully institutionalized. When the Legal Services Corporation was established, in 1974, its future looked reasonably secure. Today, its existence is shaky, given President Reagan's proposed budget cuts.[9] Unlike advocacy planning, it may have been too successful. By representing welfare recipients, by assisting tenants with grievances, and by winning class-action suits, legal services lawyers have managed to acquire some powerful opponents who consider them troublemakers. Their experiences suggest that a social action segment may be in trouble if it is too effective in pursuing its goals for social justice. However, in the struggle to determine its future, the Legal Services Coproration will have powerful allies within the profession, including the American Bar Association and many state and local bar associations. Support will also come from clients and from other groups who support its mission and accomplishments.

Nevertheless, it still may take large-scale social change to ensure the fate of this segment. Like advocacy planning, it is dependent on outside funding for its survival and its fate may be similar, despite its greater progress toward institutionalization.

## FUTURE DIRECTIONS TOWARD ACTIVISM

### *Postadvocacy Careers*

With the failure of advocacy planning, practitioners had to find other ways to combine activism with planning practice. The careers of planners who left the three groups indicate some of these alternatives. Their choices depended largely on whether their orientation was primarily to planning or to activism and whether or not they wanted to work directly with community clients.

A few planners and architects were able to establish community-based careers and continued to function largely in the advocacy tradition. They developed housing or renewal projects for community groups. A recent *Wall Street Journal* article (1981) reports on a group of store-front architects in Chicago who advise families and community groups on renovating buildings. Arc Rehab Corporation is a nonprofit organization that charges clients for its services. Perhaps more firms like this will be formed.

Some planners believed that they could be "inside" advocates, taking jobs with departments that seemed responsive to community needs. Planners who took jobs with agencies or consulting firms often did voluntary advocacy work. This arrangement eliminated the problem of making a living through advocacy work, but it did not permit the planner to turn activism into a career, as many wished to do.

Various members of all three groups, and especially IA's founders, concentrated on their academic careers, which had continued uninterrupted. Several wrote books and articles about their advocacy experiences. One was appointed to a high public office and became its policy maker after spending years as an outside critic. However, he too returned to academic life when the administration changed. In a few cases, disillusioned planners decided that they would have a better chance to work for change by pursuing a law degree.

The dearth of opportunities for advocacy and activism in planning makes it evident that only small numbers of individuals will be willing to grapple with the difficult and uncertain careers faced by those who deviate from the accepted theories and practice of their occupation. The few who work as fulltime advocates are likely to be regarded as marginal practitioners and find many options closed to them.

## Lessons Learned and Unresolved Issues

Advocacy planning's demise highlights issues that must be resolved before future efforts to introduce activism into planning are likely to succeed. Two central issues confronting planners are: (1) With regard to knowledge, how can they build a cohesive theoretical base for a new form of practice; and (2) With regard to their role in initiating change, how can they best use their knowledge and skills? Advocacy planning's mission of providing direct technical assistance to under-represented groups may not be the most effective use of planners' knowledge and skills. On the other hand, planners are not using their skills if they engage in organizing or radical politics.

Warren's (1971) analysis of why antipoverty organizations could not develop innovative ways to eliminate poverty helps explain advocacy planning's difficulties. He started with the premise that there are two frameworks for analyzing the problems of inner cities. The first, Paradigm I, accepts the individual deficiency explanation of poverty. the other, Paradigm II, uses the "dysfunctional social structure explanation" (Warren, 1971: 272-73). The solutions they call for are quite different; either individuals or the system have to be changed. Paradigm I calls for reform, based on the belief that our society is sound, although its malfunctioning sometimes causes problems. Proponents of this paradigm favor such strategies as greater emphasis on democratic pluralism to alleviate these difficulties, believing that incremental change is sufficient.

No articulated belief system supports Paradigm II. Those who accept the dysfunctional social system explanation disagree about needed changes, just as advocate planners did. Moreover, Warren does not think that the technologies developed within the framework of Paradigm I are effective for Paradigm II. When community groups gained the power to develop their own programs, they ended up using existing technologies, i.e., those appropriate to Paradigm I. Their programs were not radically different from conventional ones.

In his view, city planners and social workers are unable to accomplish change because their skills are only appropriate to Paradigm I. Activists trying to develop advocacy in social work had problems similar to those of planners. A vicious cycle therefore exists, since Paradigm I will continue to be the dominant belief system as long as alternative technologies do not exist.

The lack of a comprehensive theoretical framework was an evident weakness of advocacy. "Doing good" and having the "right" values are not a sufficient basis for legitimizing a new form of practice. This theory-building effort would be helped by a deeper understanding of how planning's ideology and practice reflect the society's dominant economic and political theories and values (Fainstein and Fainstein, 1971; Goodman, 1972; Kravitz, 1970). Extensive analysis of the urban crisis will undoubtedly suggest planning's role in perpetuating and even intensifying inequities in society. If a conflict perspective seems to offer the best alternative for a new belief system, then more work could be done on strengthening this theoretical approach to urban planning.

This task need not be a solitary one for American urban planners. They would do well to collaborate with activists, practitioners, and academics in other disciplines and in other countries. For example, numerous radical geographers and social scientists have analyzed urban problems using a conflict perspective (Castells [1976]; Harvey [1973]; Mollenkopf [1977]; and Peet [1977]). Not only could urban theory and policy emerge from this cooperative approach, but a coalition of like-minded activists in a variety of settings could be formed to campaign for acceptance of their point of view. This theoretical framework could provide the foundation on which planners would develop their unique mission and technologies. Advocacy planning could not have gained acceptance as a new segment so long as practitioners did work (a) for which they were not trained or (b) for which a planning background was not requisite.

Even with a coherent theoretical framework and the development of new technologies, planners still face the difficult problem of gaining acceptance for a new form of practice, one not based on the traditional belief system of government and the majority of the population. This problem seems insoluble without large-scale societal change, since segments oriented to social action are far more dependent on public approval than are segments that arise to improve professional techniques or services.

What can activist planners do in the meantime? Their options are fairly limited. They can continue to work in universities to broaden planning education by providing alternatives to traditional theories and urban analysis. They can also raise important public policy issues. Those who do not find it against their principles can work for change from within. Admittedly change occurs slowly, or even in the opposite direction from that desired, but agency planners who attended graduate school in the late 1960s and 1970s are now attaining decision-making positions. Their exposure to the social movements and activism of that period may make them more receptive to the goals of activists.

These career directions seem poor substitutes for the activism that planners envisioned in the 1960s, but a widespread movement for change is unlikely now when conservatism and self-interest seem dominant concerns. The Reagan administration, claiming a popular mandate, is slashing funds for social programs. The Director of the Office of Budget and Management has even challenged the concept of entitlement developed over recent decades. So far, neither the disadvantaged nor their advocates have mobilized to protest these trends. Moreover, the cities are in more trouble than ever. Some urban analysts seem to favor revitalizing areas that seem salvageable while writing off the inner cities and their residents (Kasarda, 1980: 393–7). If conditions worsen, activism may re-emerge as inequities grow, so planners would do well to have in hand their proposals and plans for action.

*335*

*Rosalie G. Genovese*

# NOTES

1. For some views on the limitations of advocacy planning, see Keyes and Teit-cher, 1970; and Starr, 1967.

2. Among the many articles and books on advocacy planning, the following sampling demonstrates the diverse definitions and views of it as a form of prac-tice: Blecher, 1971; Hartman, 1970; Peattie, 1968; Piven, 1970 and Kravitz, 1968.

3. For a discussion of new types of relationships between planners or architects and their clients, see Harms (1972: 192-8).

4. See Genovese (1976) for an in-depth study of these groups. Social policy im-plications of advocacy planning's failure are discussed by Genovese (1979).

5. Tension was evident in many occupations and professions during this period. For a discussion of mystification and demystification with regard to medicine in France, see Jamous and Peloille (1970). Specht (1972) illustrates the fear of deprofessionalization in social work. Such concerns were far stronger among practitioners in occupations trying to gain professional status than among those in full professions.

6. Rein (1969) discusses various bases of legitimacy for social planning.

7. Articles in Rush and Denisoff (1971) describe the varying fates that social movements face. For an analysis of the stages in a social movement, see King (1966).

8. Etzioni (1969) contains articles that discuss the characteristics of semi-professions and the reasons why they have not achieved professional status.

9. There is still the possibility that President Reagen will veto the bill to con-tinue even this reduced funding for legal services.

# REFERENCES

Blecher, E. M.
    1971    Advocacy Planning for Urban Development: With Analysis of Six Demonstration Programs. New York: Praeger.

Bucher, R.
    1962    "Pathology: a study of social movements within a profession." Social Problems 10: 40-51.

Bucher, R. and A. Strauss
    1961    "Professions in process." American Journal of Sociology 66: 325-34.

Carr-Saunders, A. M. and P. A. Wilson
    1964    The Professions. 2d ed. London: Frank Cass.

Castells, M.
    1976    "The wild city." Kapitalistate 4-5: 2-20.

Davidoff, P.
    1964    "Role of the city planner in social planning." Proceedings of the 1964 Annual Conference of the American Institute of Planners: 125-131.

    1965    "Advocacy and pluralism in planning." Journal of the American In-stitute of Planners 31: 331-7.

Davidoff, R. and L. Davidoff
1978 "Advocacy and urban planning." Pp. 99-120 in G. H. Weber and G. J. McCall (eds.), Social Scientists as Advocates: Views from the Applied Disciplines. Beverly Hills: Sage.

Davidoff, P. et al.
1970 "Suburban action: advocate planning for an open society." Journal of the American Institute of Planners 36: 12-16.

Etzioni, A., ed.
1969 The Semi-Professions and their Organizations: Teachers, Nurses and Social Workers. New York: Free Press.

Fainstein, S. S. and N. I. Fainstein
1971 "City planning and political values." Urban Affairs Quarterly 6: 341-62.

Funnyé, C.
1970 "The advocate planner as urban hustler." Social Policy 1: 35-37

Genovese, R. G.
1976 "Advocacy planning: an attempt to develop a social action segment in a semi-profession." Unpublished doctoral dissertation, New York University, Department of Sociology.

1979 "Issues in combining social action with planning: the case of advocacy planning." Social Problems and Public Policy, 1: 195-224.

Goode, W. J.
1957 "Community within a community: the professions." American Sociological Review 22: 194-208.

1960 "Encroachment, charlatanism, and the emerging profession: psychology, sociology, and medicine." American Sociological Review 25: 902-914.

Goodman, R.
1972 After the Planners: Toward Democratic City Design. Harmondsworth, England: Penguin.

Grabow, S. and A. Heskin
1973 "Foundations for a radical concept of planning." Journal of the American Institute of Planners 39: 106, 108-114.

Gross, R. and P. Osterman, eds.
1972 The New Professionals. New York: Simon and Shuster.

Harms, H.
1972 "User and community involvement in housing and its effect on professionalism." Pp. 176-98 in J. F. C. Turner and R. Fichter (eds), Freedom to Build: Dweller Control of the Housing Process. New York: Macmillan.

Hartman, C.
1970 "The advocate planner: from 'hired gun' to politician partisan." Social Policy 1: 37-38.

Harvard Law Review
1967 "Neighborhood law offices: the new wave in legal services for the poor" 80: 805-850.

Harvey, D.
1973   Social Justice and the City. Baltimore: Johns Hopkins University Press.

Haug, M. R. and M. B. Sussman
1969   "Professional autonomy and the revolt of the client." Social Problems 17: 153–61.

Heskin, Al.
1980   "Crisis and response: a historical perspective on advocacy planning." Journal of the American Planning Association 46: 50–63.

Jamous, H. and B. Peloille
1970   "The French university-hospital system." Pp. 111–52 in J. A. Jackson (ed.), Professions and Professionalization. London: Cambridge University.

Kasarda, J. D.
1980   "The implications of contemporary redistribution trends for national urban policy." Social Science Quarterly 61: 373–400.

Keyes, L. C., Jr., and E. Teitcher.
1970   "Limitations of advocacy planning: a view from the establishment." Journal of the American Institute of Planners 36: 225–6.

King. W.
1966   "Career patterns of social movements." Pp. 13–17 in W. A. Glaser and D. L. Sills (eds.), The Government of Associations. Totowa: Bedminster.

Kravitz, A. S.
1968   "Advocacy and beyond." Pp. 38–46 in Planning 1968. Chicago: American Society of Planning Officials.

1970   "Mandarinism: planning as handmaiden to conservative politics." Pp. 240–67 in T. L. Beyle and G. Lathrop (eds.), Planning and Politics: Uneasy Partnership. Indianapolis: Bobbs-Merrill.

Lortie, D.
1958   "Anaesthesia: from nurses' work to medical specialty." Pp. 405–412 in E. G. Jaco (ed.), Patients, Physicians and Illness. Glencoe: Free Press.

Mazziotti, D.
1974   "The underlying assumptions of advocacy planning: pluralism and reform." Journal of the American Institute of Planners 40: 38, 40–47.

Mollenkopf, J. H.
1977   "The post-war politics of urban development." Pp 549–579 in J. Walton and D. E. Carns (eds.), Cities in Change: Studies in the Urban Condition. 2d ed. Boston: Allyn and Bacon.

Peattie, L. R.
1968   "Reflections on advocacy planning." Journal of the American Institute of Planners 34: 80–88.

Peet, R.
1977   Radical Geography: Alternative Viewpoints on Contemporary Issues. Chicago: Maaroufa.

338

Perlman, J. E.
  1976    "Grassrooting the system." Social Policy 7: 4–20.

Piven, F. F.
  1970    "Whom does the advocate planner serve?" Social Policy 1: 32–37.

  1975    "Planning and class interests." Journal of the American Institute of Planners 41: 308–10.

Planning
  1977    "Advocacy planning is alive and well in Brooklyn." January: 20–22.

Rein, M.
  1969    "Social planning: the search for legitimacy." Journal of the American Institute of Planners 35: 233–44.

  1971    "Social policy analysis as the interpretation of beliefs." Journal of the American Institute of Planners 37: 297–310.

Ross, R.
  1976    "The impact of social movements on a profession in process: advocacy in planning." Sociology of Work and Occupations 3: 429–454.

Rush, G. B. and S. R. Denisoff, eds.
  1971    Social and Political Movements. New York: Appleton-Century-Crofts.

Scott, M.
  1969    American City Planning Since 1890: A History Commemorating the Fiftieth Anniversary of the American Institute of Planners. Berkeley: University of California.

Specht, H.
  1972    "The deprofessionalization of social work." Social Work 17: 3–15.

Spiegel, H. B. C. and V. Alicea
  1969    "The trade-off strategy in community research." Social Science Quarterly 50: 598–603.

Starr, R.
  1967    "Advocators or planners?" American Society of Planning Officials Newsletter 33: 1–2.

U. S. Ofice of Economic Opportunity
  1971    "CDC's: What we have learned." Washington, D.C.: U.S. Government Printing Office.

Wall Street Journal
  1981    "Store-front architects for the poor." March 25.

Warren, R. L.
  1971    "The sociology of knowledge and the problem of inner cities." Social Science Quarterly 52: 469–491.

Wexler, S.
  1970    "Practicing law for poor people." Yale Law Journal 79: 1049–1067.

Zald, M. N. and R. Ash
  1970    "Social movement organizations: growth, decay and change." Pp. 517–37 in J. R. Gusfield (ed.), Protest, Reform and Revolt: A Reader in Social Movements. New York: John Wiley.

# 14 *Architecture by Yourself*

## YONA FRIEDMAN

The need for democratization in architecture is clearly evident from the present paradoxical situation in which users who have no right of choice must bear the consequences of the bad decisions of architects. It is architects who make the decisions and users who take the risks. Elsewhere I (1975) have described the roles of the architect and the user in a more democratic arrangement than currently exists. In this paper I illustrate these ideas by elaborating on a program whereby architects and users can jointly participate in decisions and, in some situations, the user can in fact make the design decisions. Although my examples refer to architecture, there are clear implications for large-scale planning in which users would participate as equals, or "solo it."

The proposal, Architecture by Yourself, attempts to deal with the main problem in architecture—communication. It is my contention that existing difficulties exist between the architect and the user, and these can be resolved through a basic restructuring of the form of communication. This new form of communication provides the very basis whereby the user's real interests can be fully satisfied.

## THE NATURE OF THE CURRENT PROBLEM

Any planning process starts with a person who wants to improve the actual spatial and design features of a specified environment. (I use "person" and "environment" in the generic sense; person can be a group or a collectivity; environment may be a room, a house, a neighborhood, a city.) The first step in traditional architecture is the architect's develop-

I would like to acknowledge the suggestions of Judith Blau in the preparation of this paper.

ment of the image of a future situation that he or she considers to be an improvement over the existing one. The proposal offered here is similar, but it would be the user, rather than the architect, who would be responsible for that conceptual image. After all, it is the user who best knows the problems with the existing situation and who will bear the consequences of the decisions. Thus, I agree with conventional practice, that architecture signifies the search and implementation of the ways and means that conform to the initial image. But the conceptual image must be developed in large part, if not entirely, by the future user.

The second step in the process depends on good communication between the person who constructs the image and the person who is interested in the ways and means to achieve this image—say, an artisan-builder. In order to assure a successful design, two conditions must be achieved: (1) the image conceptualized by the future user must be congruent with the ways and means established to achieve this image; and (2) the proposed ways and means must not involve consequences that are unacceptable to the future user.

It is obvious that, if the user who seeks out an architect has only a vaguely defined goal or cannot explain a goal in a sufficiently explicit manner, there will be serious difficulties. It is less obvious that, if the user has not communicated a precise goal, the architect cannot predict the consequences of the planning decisions, and thus, the basic condition for good architecture—and for good planning—is clear communication. But the sad thing is very poor communication prevails at present between the user and the architect. And when adequate communication does occur—as it often does in the design of houses for the wealthy elite—it takes a very long time from initial concept to construction, and goals are so vaguely stated that errors and ommissions are inevitable. Of course, any errors and ommissions always involve the user, never the architect. In short, the future user takes all the risk.

Consideration of risks is not that esoteric. It involves, for example, the evaluation of the acceptability of alternatives and an evaluation of the fit between the conceptual image and the effective results of the plan. When systematized, they are relatively straightforward. Such risks would be clearly minimized if the future user and the architect were the same person. Indeed, communication between a person and himself or herself is generally better than communication between two different persons.

Planners and architects, unlike Robinson Crusoe, cannot pose and solve their problems in a vacuum. Generally speaking, there are other people around us. This fact provides the main justification for the traditional role of the professional planner or architect. Specifically, professionals are supposed to balance the interests of users and other people, to assure equitable trade-offs.

This short analysis can be characterized more precisely in three statements:

1. The first part of the design process involves developing the conceptual image, evaluating acceptable alternatives, and calculating risks.
2. The second part of the design process must ensure equitable trade-offs between the user and other people.
3. The use of an "interpersonal language" that is objective and explicit is inescapable; equitable trade-offs with others are impossible without it.

The premise here, however, is that the user can learn the skills of interpersonal language. Thus, Architecture by Yourself involves not only a dialogue between the user and himself or herself (intrapersonal language), but also learning an interpersonal language to handle the trade-offs with other people.

The foundations for Architecture by Yourself are simple enough. They involve: a convenient notation for both intrapersonal language and interpersonal language, and a tool simple enough to implement both.

## THE LANGUAGE OF SELF-ARCHITECTURE

In order to define an appropriate language for self-architecture, it is first necessary to identify a three-stage procedure:

1. Designate one or more portions of existing physical space.
2. Establish the direct or indirect accessibility of all such designated space portions.
3. Establish appropriate qualifications for each designated space portion.

We can easily find some simple mapping rules that are consistent with this procedure. They are:

1. A designated space portion is represented by a vertex.
2. Direct access between two vertices is represented by an edge.
3. The qualification of a designated vertex is represented by a label.

Using this procedure and the corresponding mapping rules, any physical plan that belongs to the domain of architecture will correspond to a connected, labeled graph. This graph will usually be planar, at least for two-dimensional floor plans. The graph, then is the linkage between a physical plan and the language in terms of which the image is expressed. As such, it is a vehicle for intrapersonal and interpersonal communication.

This representation of a plan by a connected, labeled graph has several interesting characteristics. Formal features of the graph are amenable to interpersonal communication, whereas the labels are set by intrapersonal considerations. Furthermore, the graphs indicate a number of important planning constraints, which are implied by the choice of a particular linkage scheme. Such constraints include the following: whether or not the plan can be made without one or more corridors or staircases; whether each room can have a window to the outside; and, how many rooms can be large and how many have to be smaller. Also, mapping by labeled graphs facilitates qualitative judgements, economizes effort, and aids in the comparison of many alternative layouts.

The obvious advantage of the connected, labeled graph is that it is objective, explicit, and easily read. Admittedly this undermines the esoteric skills of the professional, but it allows the lay person to participate fully in the design process and to influence those decisions that affect his or her life. Another less obvious advantage of this technique is that it reveals the entire repertoire of plans on the basis of the mathematical solution.

### An Example

In the first step, the user translates a personal image into "linkage desiderata." For example, we specify here that we would like a home that contains a living room (L), a family room (F), a kitchen (K), a master bedroom (M), a nursery (N), and a utility room (U). We might consider all possible connections initially in terms of a saturated graph that is, the most connected planar n-graph (fig. 14.1).

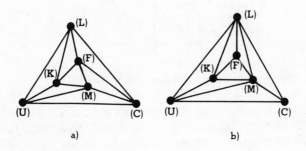

**Fig. 14.1.** The two saturated 6-graphs.

Second, on the basis of personal preferences we specify the spatial links we wish (fig. 14.2).

$$L \rightarrow K, F, U \quad (3)$$
$$F \rightarrow K, L, M, C \quad (4)$$
$$K \rightarrow L, F, U \quad (3)$$
$$M \rightarrow F \quad (1)$$
$$C \rightarrow F \quad (1)$$
$$U \rightarrow K, L \quad (2)$$
$$\overline{\text{Total } 14}$$

**Fig. 14.2.** The spatial links.

There is a total of 14 links in figure 14.2, but obviously half are redundant. Thus, we have a total of 7 links. This program can easily be resolved without a corridor or staircase. (In fact for 6 rooms there could be up to 12 links without any corridor or staircase, given that the number of links for a planar graph with 6 vertices is 3 [*n*–2], or 12).

Next, we label the graph corresponding to the program and we erase the unnecessary links (fig. 14.3).

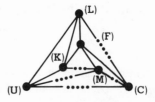

**Fig. 14.3.** Saturated graph A with desired correction pattern drawn on it.

We then redraw the graph we need in an appropriate form (fig. 14.4).

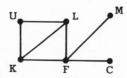

**Fig. 14.4.** The graph redrawn in an appropriate form.

This graph indicates that all rooms can have direct natural lighting, which we check by linking each vertex directly to another (additional) vertex, which represents the light source (fig. 14.5).

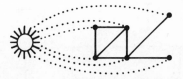

**Fig. 14.5** The graph with each vertex linked to a vertex representing the light source.

For the next step, we impose a bubble diagram on the original graph to check the alignment of rooms and to determine whether or not each bubble has the exposure we prefer (fig. 14.6).

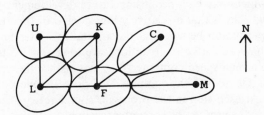

**Fig. 14.6.** A bubble diagram imposed on the original graph to check alignment and exposure.

For example, another alternative could be that shown in figure 14.7.

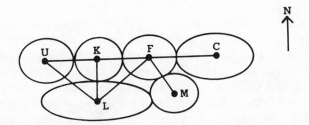

**Fig. 14.7.** An alternative bubble diagram.

Now, on the bubble diagram of figure 14.7 we draw the actual shape of each room, following our own preference. This leads to the sketch of the floor plan in figure 14.8.

This is merely a simple example to demonstrate the sequence of steps involved in self-architecture. More interesting architectural solutions can

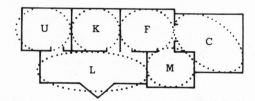

**Fig. 14.8.** The alternative bubble diagram with the shapes of the rooms added, giving a floor plan.

be derived from the same procedure though, of course, they involve more parameters, and thus more steps.

Much interest has been expressed in the computerization of this method, which may be a promising future development. However, one of its drawbacks is that a relatively long period of time is necessary for creative speculation between each step, and this interrupts the process. Because the speculative interruptions are long relative to implementation, even a high-speed computer does not reduce the time required by very much. Obviously, the computerized process follows the exact same sequence. At each step in the process a complete set of possibilities are presented to the user on the computer terminal, so the user is assured that there are no hidden alternatives. Properly programmed, the computer has this capability and may be superior in this regard to other methods.

## SUBJECTIVE ELEMENTS

Essential in the model used here is the separation between interpersonal and intrapersonal language. Thus far I have dealt exclusively with the interpersonal mode of communication which deals with elements of design that can be mapped by the topological properties of connected graphs. In this mode of communication, the foremost concerns are the constraints of design and other factors which must be considered when trade-offs involving other people are critical. Doors onto public thoroughfares, the use of utilities, and the situation of the house or the apartment are illustrations of constraints that involve neighbors. Constraints involving design include the necessity of the use of corridors, connections to the exterior, the possibility of opening windows or doors for assuring natural light, and the relative size of rooms. All elements belonging to these two categories — physical and social constraints — must be completely communicable. Anybody looking at the graph must be able to recognize them.

The situation is different with the intrapersonal elements, namely those subjective meanings attached by individuals to the spaces they use. Here I use the term "label" to show how subjective elements are worked into the design process. A label names some qualitative property of each room or space, and the meaning of the label will vary with the person who does the labeling. Therefore we can consider the labeling as a sort of shorthand in which the future user notes some desiderata with symbols that are meaningful only at the personal level.

If we consider the types of labels, we find they vary in the degree to which they are communicable. Let us imagine that a particular future user notes for a room of his or her apartment the following labels: round, large, and cosy.

Now the precision — the readability for other people — of these labels varies. "Round" is a tolerably well-defined term. "Large" is a relative term that can be understood only if we have some reference frame (for example, if we know the sizes of the other rooms of the same apartment). As for "cozy," the term is completely uncommunicable, as our future user may consider something cozy that I do not judge cozy, and vice versa.

If we consider these three sorts of labels — or the particular type of quality each of these labels denotes — from the point of view of their function in the graph, we find that they vary in terms of how dependent they are on the situation of a particular node in the graph. For example, the quality "large" can belong only to a room that is represented in the graph by a node situated on an exterior circuit, and "large," therefore, is completely dependent on the room's situation in the graph. Because such a label depends on the manner in which the node is linked to the other nodes in the graph, we shall term it "linkage dependent." On the other hand, the terms "round" and "cozy" are independent of the situation of the node in the graph (thus of the situation of the room in the plan) and will be called "linkage independent." We now depict the relationships between the three terms, "large," "round," and "cozy" and the qualities of "communicability," "noncommunicability," linkage dependence," and "linkage independence" in figure 14.9.

## OPERATION "LOOKING GLASS"

There is an interesting possible extension of the project Architecture by Yourself. As we have seen, there are three categories of labels:

1. Linkage dependent/communicable
2. Linkage independent/communicable
3. Linkage independent/noncommunicable

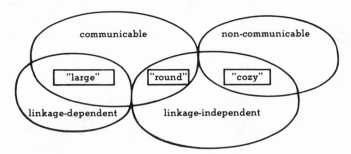

**Fig. 14.9.** Depiction of the relationship of labels and their qualities.

When one begins to use the method explained in this paper with the purpose of developing plans for a house, one starts by first selecting a preferred linkage scheme. Once this scheme is obtained, one continues to label its nodes—and perhaps the links—with labels indicating the qualities desired for each particular element of the house. Because each self-planner is different, the categories mentioned above will vary in importance from one self-planner to the next, so we see that, even when using a few parameters, there will be considerable variation in plans from one user to another.

When a computer is used, the self-planner's preferences and the consequences of these preferences are fed back to the planner. From the presentation of this image comes the expression "operation looking glass."

This is a simple example. The principle can be applied to an entire apartment, building, a neighborhood, and even, I believe, to the plan of a city. A basic underlying premise is that problems can be defined and solutions found only if we have adequate information that is explicit and systematically presented to the user-planner. Another premise is that each person must have the freedom to choose and transform the site for his or her own personal environment.

The system in its present state of development has two bottlenecks: one at the architect's end and the other at the point of actual construction. The first is so narrow that it restricts the arrival of information to the architect; the second hinders feedback about the building once it is under construction. It is possible instead to eliminate the architect and thus simultaneously eliminate both bottlenecks. If the future user is presented with a repertoire of all possible solutions—or better yet, an intellectual scheme with which to construct such a repertoire—the user can be informed, make decisions, and explain these decisions directly to the artisan-builder. For example, computer software provides an intellectual scheme with which the user can construct the repertoire.

In this way building is democratized by giving the power of choice to the future user. Any system that does not give the right of choice to those who must bear the consequences of a bad choice is an immoral system. But that is exactly the way in which architects and planners work. They make the decisions, and users take the risks. We must look for methods that will guarantee to the future user the power of choice.

## REFERENCE

Friedman, Yona
    1975    Toward a Scientific Architecture. Cynthia Lang (trans.) Cambridge: M.I.T. Press.

# Notes on Contributors

ROBERT A. BEAUREGARD is Associate Professor in the Department of Urban Planning and Policy Development at Rutgers University. He is co-author of *Revitalizing Cities* (1981), and writes on issues of planning theory, urban redevelopment, urban economic development, and social policy. For the past two years he has been involved in an evaluation of the Targeted Jobs Demonstration Program for the Department of Housing and Urban Development. He is a member of the Executive Committee of Planners Network, a national organization of progressive planners.

JAY BOLICK is finishing a BA in computer science and has a Master's degree in sociology from Temple University. He is interested in the sociology of the arts, particularly of popular music.

JUDITH R. BLAU is Associate Professor of Sociology at the State University of New York at Albany. Her published articles have centered on a variety of topics relating to the sociology of work, including the role of communication networks in scientific communities, the significance of organizational structure for quality care in hospitals, and power-sharing in professional organizations. A book on architects and their firms, currently in progress, will be published by MIT Press.

JOHN B. CULLEN is Associate Professor of Management and Sociology, University of Nebraska at Lincoln. His current research focuses on the nature of professionalism, technology and organizational structure, and the growth/ decline processes of organizations. Recent publications include *The Structure of Professionalism* (New York: Petrocelli Books, 1978) and, with Nancy Carter, *The Influence of Computers on the Structure of Newspaper Organizations* (Washington, D.C.: University Press of America, Forthcoming). Professor Cullen is also a Council Member in the American Sociological Association's Section on Organizations and Occupations.

JOHN FORESTER is Assistant Professor of City and Regional Planning, Cornell University. Interested in issues of power, organization, and politics in planning and policy analysis, he has published recently in the *Journal of Public Policy, Journal of the American Planning Association, Journal of Planning Education and Research Policy and Politics, New Political Science, Democracy,* and *Administration and Society.* He is co-editor of *Urban and Regional Planning in an Age of Austerity* (1980).

YONA FRIEDMAN is the author of books and articles on mobile architecture, energy alternatives, and self-planned architecture and communities. He resides in Paris but has taught at several American universities (MIT, Harvard, UCLA, and Princeton) as well as in Europe. He has received the Golden Lion Award of the Berlin Academy. He has consulted for various organizations, including UNESCO, and participated in the United Nations Conference on Habitat.

STEPHEN GALE is Associate Professor in the Regional Science Department at the University of Pennsylvania. His interests range from philosophical issues in geography to formal mathematical models of mobility. He is the author of articles in journals and books in the fields of statistics, geography, urban studies, and planning.

HERBERT J. GANS is Professor of Sociology at Columbia University. Trained both as a planner and sociologist, he now writes mainly on social policy, equality and the mass media, as well as urban topics. His most recent books are *The Urban Villagers: Updated and Expanded Edition* (Free Press 1982) and a reprint edition with a new introduction of *The Levittowners* (Columbia University Press 1982).

ROSALIE G. GENOVESE is a Research Associate with the Center for the Study of Women and Society, Graduate Center, City University of New York. She is the editor of *Families and Change: Social Needs and Public Policies* (in press) and has published articles on various aspects of planning, including Swedish suburbs and informal networks in American suburbs. Her current research interests include a study of dual-career families and she is the co-author of a forthcoming article on this topic.

ROBERT GUTMAN is Professor of Sociology at Rutgers University and Visiting Professor of Architecture at Princeton University. He specializes in the study of social and architectural theory as it relates to housing and urbanism. His most recent book is *People and Buildings* and he is currently working on a study of the home building industry. Professor Gutman is an honorary member of the American Institute of Architects.

RICHARD E. KOSTERMAN is an Assistant Professor with the Department of Urban and Regional Planning, Florida State University. He holds a Ph.D. in city and regional planning from Cornell University and is the author of several articles in the areas of planning theory and planning methods.

MARK LA GORY is Assistant Professor of Sociology and Urban Studies at the University of Alabama in Birmingham. He is co-author, with John Pipkin, of *Urban Social Space* (1981). His primary research interests include intermetropolitan differences in age and racial segregation, the ecology of aging, and the behavioral and social consequences of neighborhood environments.

MAGALI SARFATTI LARSON teaches sociology at Temple University in Philadelphia. She is interested in linking the evolution of art styles to changes in the social structure and in the organization of work. Her most recent book is *The Rise of Professionalism* (1977) and she has been working since on problems related to the education and employment of professionals and on a sociological analysis of architectural modernism.

GEORGE LEON is currently a Ph.D. candidate in the Sociology Department, Temple University, writing a dissertation on *The Historical Ecology of Housing Abandonment in Philadelphia.* Areas of current research and interest include Philadelphia's architectural history, neighborhood change and revitalization. He is also a member of the Housing Seminar of the Institute for Public Policy Studies, Temple University.

KATHARYN L. LIEBEN is a doctoral candidate in sociology at the State University of New York at Albany. Her interests are in the areas of complex organizations and occupations and professions.

PAUL MEADOWS, currently professor of sociology at SUNYA, has previously taught at Western Michigan University, Northwestern, Montana State University, University of Nebraska, and Syracuse University. He received his doctorate at Northwestern University in 1940. A contributor to *Fact and Value in Social Science; The New Sociology; Symposium on Sociological Theory; Among the People; Perspectives on the Human Community; Sourcebook on Immigration,* he is author of *The Culture of Industrial Man; John Wesley Powell: Frontiersman of Science; El procese social de la revolucion;* co-author of *Social Problems and Social Policy;* and co-editor of *Urbanism, Urbanization, and Social Change.*

DAVID K. MILLER is a private consultant specializing in social impact assessment, community involvement in planning and sociological data analysis. He has been director of Project IMPRESS at Dartmouth College and research director of the Small Schools Project funded by NIE. He has published several articles on simulation in the social sciences.

JOHN S. PIPKIN is Associate Professor of Geography in the State University of New York at Albany. His interests lie in urban and behavioral geography. He has written on models of spatial choice, travel behavior and urban retail structure, and has recently become concerned with broader, structural explanations of urban processes.

# Name Index

# Name Index

# Name Index

# Name Index

360

# Subject Index